Scenes and Apparitions

DIARIES
1988–2003

WEIDENFELD & NICOLSON

First published in Great Britain in 2016
by Weidenfeld & Nicolson
This paperback first published in 2017

1 3 5 7 9 10 8 6 4 2

A CIP catalogue record for this book
is available from the British Library.

PB ISBN 978 1 4746 0390 4

Typeset by Input Data Services Ltd, Somerset

Printed and bound by CPI Group (UK) Ltd, Croydon, CRO 4YY

Weidenfeld & Nicolson

The Orion Publishing Group Ltd
Carmelite House
50 Victoria Embankment
London, EC4Y 0DZ
An Hachette UK Company

www.orionbooks.co.uk

FOR

SARAH

True friend

CONTENTS

PREFACE

Diaries have a life of their own. Somehow the impulse to keep one comes and goes and it went after I resigned the V&A. However, it is significant that I began again in 1993, the year that I ceased to be a consultant for the Canary Wharf Development. Henceforth I would have to push my pen in order to make a living. In that context I recall James Lees-Milne writing that he kept a diary to keep his hand in with the pen.

It was obvious, when I began again, that it would be a different kind of Diary from that I had kept up to 1987 which had had two major institutions as a backcloth. Instead it would in a sense be a truer diary, one of a man making a living as a writer of books on history and garden design amongst other things. To that one could add occasional forays into radio and television. So the background to this volume is no longer London but the rural county of Herefordshire with, at its heart, The Laskett, where I still live, and its burgeoning gardens.

I have been a lucky man in having had a succession of great editors. Johanna Stephenson is one of those. To her I must add in the case of this book others: my literary agent Felicity Bryan and Alan Samson and his team at Weidenfeld & Nicolson. A book after all is a corporate effort with the text as its point of departure.

It is always important to remind any reader of a diary that it is a record of how the writer observed people and occasions at a particular time. How I would view both now might often be very different.

ROY STRONG

FRAGMENTS

1988 *to* 1992

After leaving the Victoria and Albert Museum at the close of 1987 I ceased to be at the centre of the arts world and there seemed little point in diary writing, so for a period of five years there are only occasional forays prompted by an awareness that I ought to write about this or that. This was a transitional period in my life during which I was a consultant to property developers Olympia & York for the public spaces in Canary Wharf. The company needed someone who was recognised as caring for the country's history and heritage. This was a hugely important project, endowed with all the excitement of the future, and I was able, for example, to take members of their talented staff down to the Crafts Council to encourage them to commission pieces by those involved in what was a renaissance in metalwork. My role within the company ceased with the financial crash of 1992.

At the same time I was involved in the media, first in a Channel 4 television series entitled *The Ancient Art of Cookery*, written and produced by an old friend of mine, Marc Miller, in which I was the presenter. I was 'discovered' by Anne Sloman, head of Radio 4 Features, and that led to an extraordinarily interesting period doing first of all programmes on Westminster Abbey and the National

Trust in her *Pillars of Society* series, leading on to series including one on the arts and government in the post-war period and another on historic towns. In these I had the creative stimulation of working with young people and learning the whole technique of radio.

Shedding the V&A was like an intellectual rebirth and I never regretted the decision. Much of my time was subsequently spent at our country home in Herefordshire at The Laskett, where the garden was beginning to come to maturity. Also, for the first time, Julia and I were able to travel together and, indeed, be together after periods when work on both sides had kept us apart.

What follows are a number of pieces written between 1988 and 1990, prompted by my awareness that some of the events in which I was involved needed to be chronicled, particularly those about the Canary Wharf Development, the proposed move of the National Portrait Gallery there and the debacle at the V&A.

1988

The Prince of Wales and the Canary Wharf development

Today the Canary Wharf scheme was launched. It was staged in that awful building, the Queen Elizabeth II Conference Centre. That was very handy for me only living at the other end of Victoria Street. The day before I was on tap, in particular in the evening, when some members of the Royal Fine Art Commission came: James Sutherland, Philip Powell and Sherban Cantacuzino with an assistant. It went well. There is something marvellous about this scheme, a grandeur, a sense of spectacle and theatre aligned with quality. The poor Canadians and Americans are completely mystified about the British and their reactions. A splendid person called Pip Errington organised the launch, tough and direct but a woman of high intelligence and integrity. So, mercifully, American pizzazz went and it was all very English and underplayed. About eighty press turned up and the project was, I believe, reasonably warmly received. There was a note of surprise in the air because they hadn't quite expected this and, yes, it might be good, at least in parts.

The evening exercise was more curious. After a lot of coming and going via Jules Lubbock and Colin Amery, the Prince of Wales decided to appear. It turned out that he was appearing in an architectural film for the BBC. So Paul Reichmann, César Pelli and I showed him around. Paul Reichmann is an interesting man, a dignified, taciturn Jew with beautiful eyes and a sweet smile. César Pelli is tall with a Latin twinkle and exceptionally articulate about buildings. So the Prince arrived and we trundled him around. He is awfully thin and wore a Prince of Wales check suit with a blue spotted tie and pocket handkerchief. He is not handsome but there is lively animation about his eyes, which are alternately puzzled, sad, smiling and, suddenly, wildly alert with a boyish swoop of his body. He inevitably had to set the pace and we accorded him an authority that he failed to exert, so that it all became a bit disparate. I felt that there was a strong streak of the young fogey in him but why not, because, like me, he loves decoration and fun in buildings. He was obviously pleasantly surprised by the grandeur of the concept and its sense of spectacle and style.

When eventually the television programme was screened I became overnight a hero of the architectural profession. The Prince had gestured to Pelli's tower, saying, 'Can't it be made a little shorter?' to which I replied: 'With all due respect, sir, if that argument had pertained in the Middle Ages we wouldn't have got the spire of Salisbury Cathedral.'

20 MAY

Farewell to Lord Kenyon

Two evenings ago Hugh Leggatt gave a farewell dinner at White's for Lloyd Kenyon, who had been Chairman of the Board of Trustees of the National Portrait Gallery for more years than anyone cared to remember. It was held in the room in which the Prince of Wales had given his stag party, a cream-painted classical job with portraits of glossy Regency gentlemen. I didn't recognise Lloyd to begin with, as the ice-cube glasses had been abandoned and he now wore contact lenses to aid his deteriorating sight (glaucoma). That made me sad and also regret being rather beastly about him. Hugh put me on his right and we really had quite an agreeable conversation. In his speech he paid me a sweet tribute, saying that life with me was 'like being attached to the tail of Halley's comet' and his memories were of those incredible days.

It was an odd *galère*. There was Kenneth Rose with the usual odd royal anecdote. I said that I thought that Princess Alexandra had been unhelpful over Beaton's photographs [that are among his archive of royal portraits donated to the V&A] and he said that she didn't want any family biographies, although one on James and Marina is due. There was Owen Chadwick, the new Chairman, distinguished, but I wonder how he will raise ten million for a new building. Alan Bowness, David Wilson and Peter Wakefield were there as wallpaper, together with the Leggatt boys and Gallery staff. Some of the latter, as the meal ended, really let their hair down on their frustrations with John Hayes, who just wrote catalogues for foreign museums and offloaded everything onto them, and they're unhappy also that he was trying to stay on until he's sixty-five. John Hayes is really very silly to do this, as Alan Bowness and myself agreed walking away afterwards.

John Hayes got his way. The Chairman extended his term of office by five years without referring it to the Trustees, some of whom were far from pleased.

MAY

The National Trust anatomised

I am having an enormously enjoyable time doing a programme for Radio 4 on the National Trust in a series called *Pillars of Society* with a bright current affairs producer, John Forsyth. It is stimulating to be the interviewer rather than the interviewee. I think that we've canned some really good stuff. James Lees-Milne was vintage material in Beckford's library in Lansdown Crescent in Bath. He's a pretty good seventy-nine year-old and gave a great performance until he began to get tired. And I got out of him what I thought that we wouldn't, that he knew perfectly well that he was taking the Trust in a different direction with his scheme for rescuing beleaguered country houses, to which a lot of members of the Committee who remembered the aims and context of 1895 objected. That will go into the BBC archive.

It was fascinating to analyse a great charitable institution and I concluded that its rise, along with the cult of heritage, coincided with the decline of the place once occupied by the Church of England in the mental mythology of the middle classes. The worship of God has been replaced by one of heritage. The voluntary stewards, guides and housekeepers are like churchwardens, sidesmen and congregation ministering to a building, once the church and now the country house, as a shrine of lost national glory and repository of a lost golden life of refined cultured gentility. More serious, however, were the forward projections on membership. By the mid-1990s they would top two million but would need 200,000 new members a year to make up for losing 200,000 a year: that is, they would enter a plateau simultaneously with the agricultural crisis, falling income, a decline in interest in country houses and a huge backlog on maintenance (£12 million already).

On the whole the National Trust emerged out of it very well, in spite of its sanitised vision of England and a version of history in which all conflict is removed. I thought Jennifer Jenkins interviewed quite badly, although it could be argued that she was evading answering the questions, but it was striking to me that she was the only one who failed to explode with a love of the National Trust and what it had meant to her in life. I began in fact to wonder whether it had given her anything at all.

28 JUNE

The Thyssen Collection

I think I should write that last week Peter Stothard, Deputy Editor of *The Times*, rang and asked me to write a leader on the Thyssen collection, which was up for grabs. Canary Wharf was an adumbrated location and, indeed, full-scale plans and elevations were made. Obviously several people were asked and the result was a huge piece in Saturday's *Times*.

17 SEPTEMBER

Winslow Hall

We'd long ago fixed a date to go to lunch at Winslow Hall with Gill and Edward Tomkins. It was a very cross-country journey but we had always had an affection for them, ever since those days in the Paris Embassy in 1975. Earlier this year they'd come to lunch at The Laskett and we'd had a glorious time – time for friendship. Winslow is a spanking William and Mary house slap in the middle of the town, with a fair acreage behind but with its façade virtually on the road. After the usual crawling around the house trying to find the way in, we succeeded by hammering at a window when we saw a young man; he opened a door and let us in. Edward appeared. He'd in fact been in the middle of taking a group around. He's a lovely teddy bear of a man, very huggable and droll, with marvellous blue eyes. Eventually Jill arrived, having spent the morning opening something. She is the perfect ambassador's wife, bright and warm, quite fine of feature and with the most impassioned eyes.

It was a beautiful, comfortable house, totally untouched by interior decorators, full of very good furniture and pictures but with the sofas with worn and faded loose covers. Dogs were everywhere, above all H.E., who is worshipped. Over an indifferent lunch we learnt that they were just back from a week with the Queen Mother at Birkhall, which sounded like the Royal Lodge routine multiplied. HM only appears after lunch, although, of course, she's up and around as she can be glimpsed in her battered old coat and hood taking the corgis for a walk. The party would be whisked off for a picnic in the glens, game pie non-stop, to which they helped themselves. The evenings were re-runs of *Dad's Army* for everyone to gurgle over. There seemed to be about five in all staying and they went over to Balmoral twice, which, Edward said, surprised him. It was a friendly house, quite contrary to what he had expected, and the rooms were large, light and airy.

They'd got Princess Margaret coming for the weekend on 31 October. Would we come for lunch? I'm afraid that we dodged it. It is a heavy autumn and four hours of driving each way is too much. I must say that they are very loyal to her. She had rung up and altered the date. Each time there is the ghastly listing off of the people invited and the arrangements to HRH on the telephone and then waiting for her reaction: 'Oh, I like them', 'No, I don't think I want to do that' and 'Can't stand them'. Gill then gets stuck with ringing up and somehow eliminating those not in favour.

HRH requires Friday to Monday to be crammed with expeditions and people galore. Winslow is a modest house for a princess, I would have thought. Just about ten can be got into the dining room. With a maid and a detective to sleep, that leaves room for two other guests. A cook is hired for the weekend and dailies wait and do the rest. Jill is a saint but I really wondered whether it was all worth it.

After lunch we toured the grounds, once designed by the famous seventeenth-century gardeners George London and Henry Wise but now hemmed in by semi-detached houses. It was less garden than a huge lawn flanked by a planting of very good specimen trees, alas many of them too close together. At the far end was a surprise, a piece of land that had been made over to the town, labelled 'The Edward Tomkins Bowling Green'. It was a huge success. The Tomkins are generous-hearted old-fashioned people of public spiritedness in the best sense. Julia and I are so glad that they have re-entered our lives.

17 NOVEMBER

Queen Elizabeth entertains her friends

The Queen Mother is remarkably loyal to her friends, for that's what the lunch at Clarence House was all about. She waved one hand in the air in that characteristic gesture and said, 'This all began as something else'. We never learnt what. There was Irene Astor, recovered from cancer and now living in Kent again, busy making a potager; John and Liza Glendevon, briefly in London from Guernsey; Garrett Drogheda in such a sad state that it came as a shock, hobbling on a stick, pathetically emaciated and with his right eye slightly distorted; Peter and Carla Thorneycroft, contrary monuments, like our hostess, to bravura in old age. I suppose that there must have been about eighteen of us around the table, the chief guest being Alfonso XIII's daughter, the Infanta, who lives in Rome, granddaughter of Queen Ena, I assume. I sat next to Ruth Fermoy, who confirmed what a blow Fred Ashton's death had been. He once even arranged the Queen Mother's hat for her, which she adored, telling Ruth that all her hats were awful bar one and she should have it copied in different colours. Every year on Queen Elizabeth's birthday that group – Ruth, Hugh and Fortune Grafton (who were also at the lunch) and Fred – would take Queen Elizabeth to the theatre in the evening, although it was difficult to find anything for her to see for she disliked any improprieties or shocks on stage. This year they'd taken her to *The Admirable Crichton*, which was rather a disaster as Rex Harrison forgot most of his lines. Afterwards Ruth gave them a supper of lobster and mayonnaise, packaging the remainder up for Fred, who said that it would last him three days. That was the last time she saw him. He had always said that he was terrified of dropping dead in Harrods, to which Ruth replied that that would never happen as he never went there.

Queen Elizabeth looked younger than almost anyone else there, on her feet the whole time. She had obviously loved the Beaton book and said 'I've got so many questions that I want to ask you. I'll give you a ring.' I wonder whether she will. It would be such a surprise.

The Hereford Mappa Mundi

This saga began for me on 17 November, when Adrienne Corri rang and said that Hereford Cathedral had sent the Mappa Mundi to Sotheby's. I was astonished. All I could think of doing was resigning from the Cathedral's Appeal Committee, of which I had not been more than a passive member, so I rang Hugh Leggatt, who wasn't there but must have passed on my information to *The Times*. Later that day I told Hugh Grafton at Clarence House about it, who was furious, and I told him to resign from being a Patron of the Appeal. When we arrived home at about 6.30 p.m. *The Times* was on the phone and so I did my bit, with the result, much to my surprise, that it went straight onto the front page. Thereafter pandemonium reigned, with three television crews up the drive in three days and hordes of journalists on the phone and radio interviewers arriving from nowhere. The outrage locally knew no bounds: they all were up in arms at not having been told.

Grey Gowrie, Chairman of Sotheby's, then appeared in the press saying that for a year he had been trying to arrange a private sale with the government and that he had spoken to Lord Quinton, Martin Charteris and Richard Luce. Luce, whom I telephoned to express the local dismay, was vehement in saying that Grey had never approached him. So was Charteris. Quinton only publicly said that just the chained library had been floated. My old friend Michael Borrie, head man in the Manuscripts Department at the British Library, said that no one there knew anything.

What must have stunned both the Dean and Gowrie was the uproar engendered. It was pleasing always to put this crisis into a broader context: that Hereford was the first of our cathedrals to go broke. It was likely that more would follow, with more sales thanks to the anomaly of their exemption from the Ancient Monuments Act, which permitted their chapters to behave in such an arbitrary way.

On Wednesday last, 30 November, I went to the Conservative Arts and Heritage Group meeting, where we were told by Patrick Cormack that there had been a meeting that morning between the Dean, Charteris, Gowrie, Quinton and himself and that the sale had been postponed. This was under wraps but would be announced next week. Hugh Leggatt and I urged that a select committee be set up to examine the whole question of the sale of works of art from public institutions. Cormack blocked that. This group was set up to advise the Minister on arts matters but we have never been asked to do it and the meetings are a structureless shambles. As a result, everyone feels that we are being used by the Minister rather than being consulted by him.

Martin Charteris, Provost of Eton and the chairman of the Heritage Memorial Fund, wrote to me on the 26th: 'I was proud of you and to be your friend when you resigned over the Mappa Mundi issue: you were absolutely right to do so.' The controversy over it was to rage on all through 1989, raising a torrent of press on the possible dispersal of cathedral treasures. In the end it had a happy resolution, with lavish grants from the Heritage Fund and a handsome new building by William Whitfield to house the object. Martin asked me whether I wanted to be on the trustee board for it but I said 'no'. My committee era had mercifully passed.

29 NOVEMBER

Farewell to Fred Ashton

Fred Ashton's memorial service in Westminster Abbey was the sell-out of the season. As we walked towards the Abbey we bumped into Marie Sygne Northbourne beating a retreat as she had failed to apply for a ticket. The Abbey was already jammed at 11.30 a.m. and we were escorted down the nave through a packed congregation to the choir stalls, where we were *bien placé*. Opposite sat the Airlies, Alicia Markova, Anya Sainsbury, John Tooley, Aline Berlin et al., while behind us I glimpsed Hugh and Fortune Grafton and Robert and

Mollie Salisbury. On my right were Carl Toms and Pam Harlech, and on Julia's left Anthony Dowell and his partner, Jay Jolley.

Fred had apparently said 'The Abbey or nothing' and he got the works, a huge theatrical spectacle. By the time we were seated, the Royal Opera House orchestra was half-way through the 'Panorama' from *The Sleeping Beauty*, which was followed by pieces from two of Julia's ballets, the *pas de deux* from *Month in the Country* and 'Nimrod' from *Enigma*. One felt quite tearful.

Up in the Sanctuary sat Madam, gaunt, with her neck halter swathed in scarves and her head in a turban, wearing flat sensible shoes, a stick to hand, indomitable at ninety. Next to her sat Michael Somes, once married to Antoinette Sibley.

Extraordinarily, the Queen Mother came as well as Princess Margaret. I think this must have been the only occasion when Queen Elizabeth has ever been to a memorial service, apart from Patrick Plunket's, She looked marvellous in black velvet and diamonds and vaguely peered at the service sheet, which I'm not sure she could actually read!

The service began with two ballet school students bearing Fred's medals and honours arranged on velvet cushions to the Sacrarium and thence to the altar. There were two readings and two addresses. The first lesson, from Ecclesiastes, was read by John Tooley, badly, the second from Proust by Anthony Dowell rather well. Madam excelled herself. I gathered that she discarded her notes, made her way to the microphone and uttered only a few perfect sentences, concluding with these words: 'Who am I to praise him? . . . I am overcome today by the stillness of the Abbey. Listen to that stillness and be thankful to God for Frederick Ashton.' Margot Fonteyn's tribute, too, was perfection in its own way, interestingly singling out both *Month* and *Enigma* as virtually Fred's two greatest ballets, reflecting an inner vision about character that came in old age. She ended by saying how she saw Fred looking down and saying: 'Oh, that's good, a full house!' That produced a ripple of laughter, which was needed. The only off-moment in the whole event was the Vicar of Yaxley praying for his church appeal and our being assailed by collection plates for it on leaving.

1989

The National Portrait Gallery and Canary Wharf, and The Gift

This month has been punctuated by two events. The first was a definite movement towards the possibility of the National Portrait Gallery going to Canary Wharf. This went all the way back to the June of last year, when I made the first overtures. The project began to move in December, when a new package came through roughly along the lines that Olympia & York would give the land (£5 million) and the infrastructure (in the region of £15 million), leaving the NPG to appeal for about £20 million. It would end up with a totally identifiable new building about twice the size of the present one. John Hayes and Malcolm Rogers came to Olympia & York and, although lugubrious as always, were, in fact, over the moon about the idea. I couldn't get John Hayes off the phone he was in such a frenzy about it. The proposal was to get Richard Luce down to the site but, oh no, he wanted to see me alone.

I went on the afternoon of 19 January. The model of Canary Wharf had been sent on ahead and was placed on a low table around which we sat, Luce attended by two bright minions, one his personal assistant and the other his museums buff. I said to the latter, 'Oh, what a bore for you', at which he gurgled. It was a relief going to see Luce for the first time not in my old Museum Director role of suppliant, so I could be as direct as I liked. He opened by saying, 'Can this be paid for entirely by the surrounding offices?' I ticked him off. What kind of society are we becoming if our great national institutions don't have even a modicum of state support? As I said, 'Sainsbury's didn't build the Foreign Office'. I gather that when John Hayes and Owen Chadwick went to see him the reception was cool and Chadwick kept his reserve. However, when I pointed out the financial deal, the gains, the inner city regeneration aspect, there was a change of tune. A lot hung on the sale of the existing National Portrait Gallery building and the new site there had a time factor too. (The NPG had acquired the option on building opposite the gallery in Orange Street.) Mrs Thatcher was launching the appeal early in April, with Willie Whitelaw as its Chairman. I rang today (30 January) and gather that all is now lodged with the Treasury, so it is at least being seriously considered.

On 25 January Robin Gill came to see me. He had once been Lew Grade's right-hand man on ITV and was a businessman of some genius who has now opted out and seems to spend his time on good works. He seemed to know everyone who was anyone; my name had been suggested to him by Hugh Casson and Pat Gibson. It concerned something called 'The Gift'. Robin Gill had struck upon the idea that something should be done in tribute to Her Majesty in 1992, the fortieth anniversary of her accession. He knew Bill Heseltine and had made overtures. Robin Gill's concept was to build in facsimile a number of the state rooms in Buckingham Palace that the public can't see. This would form a building, The Gift, in which there would be space for events and an explanation of the role of the Crown. Would I, together with Casson, come in on taste and design? The response, under wraps from British industry, had already produced a pledge of £12 million on an initial ring-round. Others to be brought in would be Cliff Chetwood and Nigel Broackes on the buildings side and someone else on the money side.

It is an intriguing and bizarre scheme and I wish that I could remember Gill's sagas with the Palace. His most interesting one was that, having got Her Majesty's agreement to The Gift, he realised that she wouldn't really receive it, everyone else would. So he turned round and went back to Buckingham Palace and Bill Heseltine and asked what the Queen would personally like. The reply was interesting. She was aware that there was no royal twentieth-century art collection and she wanted that!

2 FEBRUARY

The National Portrait Gallery and Canary Wharf continued

John Hayes has got the Canary Wharf bit between his teeth and is stirring away like blazes. He decided to begin to draw in his Trustees and so we assembled at Olympia & York in George Street at 9.45 a.m. to actually go to the site. It was a grey, misty London day, just about the worst you could have to go downriver to sell Canary Wharf. The financial arrangements now remain locked between the Office of Arts and Libraries and the Treasury. The few assembled NPG Trustees all looked like bundles: Owen Chadwick, very spry, in a shapeless trench coat with a bag slung across it; Hugh Grafton, pained at having to come at all, let alone to look at what to him was an architectural affront; and Marcus Sieff, rather deaf, clutching a walking stick that folded out to make a seat. John Hayes was late, which made things awkward, although he was, as usual, oblivious to the fact. He flashed his teeth in his accustomed manner as though it would somehow dispel the frosty atmosphere.

John Hayes is now sixty. The suit he had on must have been at least twenty years old and was buttoned around him with difficulty. His overcoat, which was of the same date, was buttoned with even greater difficulty and I noticed that it had leather binding to cover up the frayed cuffs. There is an unreality to his political sense. People exist, he believes, who will just dollop out £20 million to him. We walked to the pier at Westminster. Our group included Robert Maguire and Ron Soskolne from Olympia & York, the latter a great asset with enormous considered intelligence and charm. We travelled down by the Canary Wharf launch, the whole exercise at first, I felt, rather edgy. As Chadwick and I got into the launch and were alone for a bit, he asked me directly if I were Director of the Gallery now, what would I do. I said that ultimately it was the Trustees' decision but for the first time the NPG would not be the back door to the National Gallery and would have a total identity of its own and double the space. But it needed vision to make the leap into a new city that was going up. The National Maritime Museum, which was not far away, was a more natural twin for the NPG than the National Gallery.

When we got there the atmosphere warmed up, a great deal of ground having been covered in the launch, in which we had the model. The Trustees were genuinely astounded by the scale of it and the speed by which it would become a reality. There was a sudden realisation that this was not a Director's joke. Hugh Grafton noticeably began to shift ground and Marcus Sieff was converted, although Chadwick remained just canny.

Back we went to 10 George Street, through the marketing suite and then to lunch. Tony Combes appeared and, at the end, Michael Dennis. All went well. The offer, after all, was a good one: the land, a great deal of infrastructure and 'help' with the building. They asked for a definition of 'help'. Ron said expertise and building materials, that is, cheaper materials and building techniques that they alone had developed. At the end, as they got up from the table, Chadwick asked John Hayes to write a memo and said that the inner group of Trustees should hold a meeting as soon as possible. Even if all this collapses, there is no doubt that we have now entered the serious phase of looking at Canary Wharf for the National Portrait Gallery. As I pointed out to them, it was Mrs Thatcher's flagship for Dockland's regeneration and if they went there, fundraising would be far easier.

10 FEBRUARY

The NPG Canary Wharf saga continues and the V&A implodes

This week went up and down in respect of the NPG Canary Wharf project. Chadwick emerged as definitely against it. The failure of Olympia & York to send the necessary letter triggered hysteria on the part of John Hayes. It went off eventually on the Friday but I doubt whether the terms will be good enough to induce them to change course, the Board being far too conservative. The best that could happen is that the negotiations could continue.

This morning, Saturday, Elizabeth Esteve-Coll rang to thank me for not becoming involved in the public bloodbath in the media over the V&A. I feel very mixed over this but I've kept out of it as far as the media is concerned, although I have been constantly rung by them. It is impressive that not one member of the staff has contacted me, an indication, Elizabeth said, that they knew my integrity would not be compromised. It is odd to have had two letters and a call from her in just over a week and I felt that they were more symptomatic of a gigantic loneliness. In the longest of her letters she had said that she was about to take 'the surgeon's scalpel' to the V&A. A scythe would have been a more accurate description. I respect and like her but her way of going about things is so very different. Knowing that museum, you have to go about changes in an evolutionary and pragmatic way. Apart from when I was forced by government to carry out massive cuts in 1976–7, I always worked in that manner. Elizabeth, in sharp contrast, seems to believe in total schemes and total revolution. When I replied to her letter I wrote *prenez garde*, for the V&A staff is dangerous to cross. Members are in and out of the best houses, know the media and the Lords and Commons and have a vast network of contacts. I told her that she would only achieve change through strong allies within or without (and by that I didn't mean the Office of Arts and Libraries). In my case I always had them without but only a sprinkling within.

When I left she had already had it set up, she said, to get rid of certain dead wood but it didn't happen. She could have got away with it then piecemeal. Now she has waited over a year, with endless committees and debate and no one agreeing. The master paper I have not seen but the general drift is to abolish the media departments, create a massive administrative and collections management department to look after the objects and another department for scholars. In other words, scholarship is to be separated from access to and custodianship of the objects. Of all the blue touchpapers to light, this one is dynamite. During thirty years in museums the one thing I did learn was that curators actually covet, almost 'own' their objects. At one fell swoop she was sweeping away a fundamental premise which reigns in all museum collections that I know. She told me that the Trustees were unanimous in supporting the scheme and that Robert Armstrong went round the table one by one making them declare for or against it. The two I've had contact with since have backtracked. Inevitably, Elizabeth has been mauled already by both the Keepers and the unions.

The real explosion, however, only came this week. The previous Friday she gave the offer of voluntary redundancy to nine or ten senior staff. These included the existing Keepers of Textiles, Metalwork, Ceramics and Furniture, plus the Deputy Director. Since that moment, civil war has broken out. The Keepers via the First Division Association have asked for the Director's resignation. The atmosphere in the place must be terrible. The newspapers are full of letters and articles: scholarship destroyed, unjust dismissals, etc. I really wonder whether the Board realised what they had done in sweeping away by one vote nearly a hundred years of the Museum's history. Whatever the outcome, Elizabeth's directorship can henceforth surely work from nothing but distrust. The letters in the papers have been good ones. If such a change is necessary, it is so fundamental that it deserves a commission by government. Whatever I thought of those departments, in the cuts in the Seventies I didn't touch them, preferring instead to close and amputate one department in order to preserve the scholarship of the others. The V&A is not a polytechnic.

I do feel there is a certain arrogance towards it all on the part of both Elizabeth and the Trustees. She has no museum track record, no great public pull and few powerful allies. The Board don't like trouble and she admits that she will only survive if they stand solid. Armstrong after Peter Wright and the 'being economical with the truth' affair seems a diminished figure and, although he knows a great deal about the musical scene, does not seem to know about the visual arts or museums. Also, the V&A network has only just started its campaign. *The Times*, one knows, is stuffed with letters on the subject. I understand that the Museums Commission spent half of last Friday discussing it. Even if Elizabeth does get it through, there will be years of dispiriting slog ahead, with poison and enmity on all sides.

14 FEBRUARY

The V&A saga continues

I was appalled to hear on the seven o'clock news that Robert Armstrong had seen the unions and the Director's scheme was to be adhered to. Christopher Frayling spoke: 'We've got a strong Board of Trustees who'll see it through.' I talked to Hugh Leggatt and we agreed that it would be prudent for me to write to the Minister. This is what I wrote:

Dear Richard,

As you will have observed I have correctly kept out of the V&A controversy. As you can imagine, although I have some sympathy with some of her aims, I have none with the overall revolutionary concept which will destroy a century or more of history and knowledge. I believed in evolution and not revolution and much happened (now forgotten) during those fourteen years.

What disturbs me is the insinuation that this had to be done because the previous regime was no good and a failure. I am a private person with no protection from these insidious smears which it will, of course, be convenient to the supporters of the scheme to propagate. I turn to you to kindly guarantee that protection. The last week has left me depressed and miserable to see all I fought for seemingly thrown to the winds. I have bitten my tongue for a year over other things, including the horrendous poster campaign and the admittance of Sotheby's into the place. I have tried to behave impeccably, although beleaguered, but I will come out of my corner if one major move against me is made – and what I can come out with would be

deeply embarrassing to everyone. If I can help in any way you
only have to signal.

The full horror of what was happening at the V&A hit me today,
leaving me physically and mentally exhausted. I was picked up at
8.30 a.m. and taken by car to the wrong place in Shepherd's Bush
to film an interview on the changing character of Trustees and Gov-
ernors. Everything went wrong. No one knew who Mr Lee was.
He wasn't there. The fire alarms went off and we were pushed out
onto the pavement in the cold while the fire engines reeled up. By
the time that that was over I was in a filthy temper, having been
waiting for three quarters of an hour. At last Tony Lee appeared and,
being in a flaming rage, I knew that I wouldn't do a good interview.
I was completely unnerved so we had to do it twice. And by now
the pieces on the V&A had got worse, with the staff voting that
they had no respect for Elizabeth and demanding her resignation.
With these terrible pieces in the papers I had somehow to avoid the
V&A, so my main thrust was the successive phases of Trustees, old
aristocracy and gentry and established learning of the Fifties, the
new socialist life peers and professors of the Sixties and the yuppie
shopkeepers of Thatcher's England. No, I didn't mind the appoint-
ments being political. They always had been, on and off. What I
did object to was when the prime ingredients for appointment were
money or influence at Number 10, with no knowledge or sympathy
for the institution or the art it embodied. There was a breakdown
in the trustee tradition. So many now were ill-educated and ignorant. They were arrogant and lacked humility. That is the shift. They
therefore wanted to be the executive.

I have been beleaguered by the press but have tried to keep out of
it, but I feel very worn down and exhausted by all of this. The approach of Elizabeth Esteve-Coll and the Board appals me. The staff
can sometimes seem a difficult and treacherous lot but they have

knowledge and as long as I was there I protected them. It appears now I've gone and the Trustees have got their admin 'yes' lady, they can do what they like. It is barbarous. You can't separate knowledge of the objects from the objects themselves. The cruel insult to those people who have given their lives to the V&A is surely unforgivable. If they go and the Trustees have their way, how can she direct a museum on this basis? How can her changes go through with such vitriolic opposition? I was glad to see that Julian Spalding came out with what had happened at those interviews for the directorship. They eliminated Alan Borg in round one along with Richard Marks. They were both front runners with huge museum experience. This saga promises to be a long one.

16 FEBRUARY

. . . and continues . . .

Today the lid was blown off the V&A saga by Pope-Hennessy's letter to the *Daily Telegraph*. I have never read such vitriol, such vicious sarcasm against 'the lady who enjoys the title of Director' and her 'asinine changes'. In it Carrington was savaged for going to Christie's and Armstrong called upon to talk. Hugh Leggatt rang at 8.20 a.m. The pressure on you, he said, will be terrific. I was worried and eventually got hold of Arnold Goodman. He told me to keep out of it. The amount of spite flying around was at fever pitch. If any attempt was made by the Board to use me as a scapegoat, others would write.

I think Robert Armstrong has handled the V&A like a government department. But worst of all, this week has passed with no utterance and his role surely is to do just that? The situation could have been saved on Monday or even, at a pinch, now by delaying these decisions and going out to public consultation.

I also spoke to John and Eileen Harris. They told me never to utter because some of the curators involved in the campaign were monuments to malice and would axe me. Much of this was revolving around Peter Thornton, formerly Keeper of Woodwork at the V&A and now Director of the Soane Museum. Eileen said that she would indicate to the curators that I was working behind the scenes in their interest. This is a wretched business and the damage done can never be undone. As it is, I learn that fundraising has been affected. No one wants to give to a public disaster. An advert in *The Times* asks for cheques for a 'Save the V&A Fund'.

16 FEBRUARY

The NPG Canary Wharf saga also continues

While all of that was going on I was faced with doing a performance for Olympia & York for a delegation of NPG Trustees at Great George Street. It was hardly the ideal time and I arrived a few minutes late, having run the length of Victoria Street. More turned up than I thought: Professor Margaret Gowers, Henry Anglesey, Eduardo Paolozzi and Roger de Grey. I was rather dreading this but it went off far better than I expected. Anglesey I don't think liked it, but Gowers, Paolozzi and de Grey saw the enormous advantages. There was some quite sharp talking. John Hayes asked whether the model could be taken to the NPG for the Trustees' Meeting that afternoon.

After a few minor dramas, Robert Maguire and I found ourselves setting it up in what had been my old office. Tony Combes also came. I must say that I found it very difficult doing it cold in this atmosphere but we did what we could in twenty minutes to about seven of them, who included Henry Keswick, George Weidenfeld and Brian Morris. Interestingly, Oliver Millar remained in the Trustees' Meeting and didn't bother to come even to look! George's eyes and intellect lit up at the sight of it, so there was an ally there.

17 FEBRUARY

. . . and continues . . .

Back at The Laskett the phone rang all day. There is no doubt that everything has just gone too far. The Office of Arts and Libraries, having stood back, now wants to seek a solution. Just after midday Richard Luce rang me, an indication, Hugh Leggatt said, that he was absolutely desperate. He had spoken to Carrington, who felt that there was nothing he could do. He was responding to my letter. He was appalled by the vicious personal turn of events and the assassination of Elizabeth Esteve-Coll. I'm afraid that I rather let loose, stating that she had been ill-advised and then left defenceless. Luce pointed out that I had thought her a good thing. I think that he wanted me to speak or write something vaguely supporting her. I said that I couldn't because I didn't approve of what she'd done. The only hope seems to be to delay the redundancies and avert a terrible saga of legal action.

I rang Christopher Frayling. He is still behind her. He said that Armstrong is very wary of the press and told Elizabeth to put her tin hat on and lock herself up. Christopher had rung Elizabeth at the weekend and offered, like a knight in shining armour, to speak for the Trustees; but he shouldn't. He is not the Chairman or Deputy Chairman. It was Christopher who told Elizabeth to ring me. He said that she had said that these people had to be purged. Christopher believed that once this lot had gone a new lot would come up who would be upright. I said, 'The place corrupts them, all. I've seen it.'

As one thing goes under another comes up. John Hayes rang me at 8.30 a.m. to say that the Trustees' Meeting had been the most significant and charged of his directorship and that by a narrow majority they had voted to take negotiations further with Olympia & York, but that they were after more inducements. He then told me that even before I had approached him in June 1988 Richard Wilding of the Office of Arts and Libraries had told him that if he went to Canary Wharf he would not lack for money. I was amazed and asked him whether he had this in writing. John had also spoken that week to Number 10, and was told that it was a great idea. The next move was to get Marcus Sieff to see Paul Reichmann. If we can land this one, a great cultural cornerstone will have been laid in the Docklands that could affect the whole enterprise.

18 FEBRUARY

Surrender at the V&A

The nine redundant V&A staff have virtually all given in, amidst vicious recriminations.

19 FEBRUARY

V&A finale

We've reached the end of the V&A saga in one sense and the beginning of another. As I reflect on it, no one emerges from any of this with credit. I believe the Chairman failed to defend the Director.

The Board seems ignorant and doesn't truly know what it has done. Elizabeth emerges as looking tough and insensitive, her opponents as embittered. All of it is horrible. The sadness is that the V&A as we knew it has gone and is, therefore, immeasurably lowered in international esteem. It will take a generation to recover and in some ways never will. I think she is left with some people worse than some of those she got rid of. Those who went were some of them bad, others just pathetic and well-meaning and one or two very good indeed. The place has spiralled downmarket and it is the end of all standards. Yes, I suppose I really resent this piece of Thatcherisation. The money changers are in the temple.

If I had to sum up the whole ghastly saga, it is the end of a certain type of knowledge. I had to learn it thirty years ago when I came into museums from the university, rather despising it. It was concerned with physical contact and knowledge about artefacts. It is knowledge gained through a daily tactile experience, by handling, by looking, by observing, by listening to older colleagues. It is totally different from the plains of academe. It is unashamedly elitist and I defend it and always will. It depends on a photographic memory, on having looked and touched hundreds of thousands of things. Quantifiable it is not. Within the tradition of learning it descended from the antiquary from the eighteenth century. Most of it was oral and never written down. It was transmitted on a day-to-day basis, from one generation to the next, by a certain sort of wayward mind. In Thatcher's Britain there is no room for that kind of mind, that kind of dottiness. Curiously enough, its home now is in the saleroom, for there they must know because there is money involved. All through the centuries there has always been room for the modest scholar shuffling around with his books, papers and artefacts. He was a harmless enough figure, whatever his fixations. His refuges were few: once it was the Church, then the country house library, then fellowships at the old universities and museums. Now there are none.

28 FEBRUARY

Lunch with an old friend

Lunch with Mary Giles at the Chesterfield Hotel, Charles Street, not the Mecca of the Museum world but full of businessmen in not very good suits munching away. Mary is an old friend, the side-kick of several Arts Ministers, and when one knows that she was trained for the theatre, it explains all. She has a high colour and a twinkle and knows the mercenary ways of government. As a V&A Trustee she had had a hideous week or two with the phone never ceasing to ring, so in the end she took the receiver off.

Mary knows the Museum well, one of the few Trustees who do, and she said that there would very likely be another flurry of further exits as the place went into meltdown. *Private Eye* summed it up this week with a wicked parody of the Saatchi V&A poster campaign ('an ace café with rather a nice museum attached') with a picture of Elizabeth and beneath: 'An ace museum with rather a useless woman attached'.

I MARCH

Farewell to William Rees-Mogg

This took place at the National Theatre and was quite a rallying of the troops: two Arts Ministers, Luce and Gowrie (who sidled up to me re the Mappa Mundi, just announced as having been saved, and said 'And there'll be a good dollop of cash with it'); current and ex-Arts Council members, together with heads and ex-heads of departments. Luke Rittner had asked me to give the speech giving the present to William, which was my idea, a view by Gerald Mynott of his office and through the window to the park. We all sat through the performance of a Boucicault play of seemingly drear quality. But halfway through the second act they decided to camp it up and from then on it was a riot moving between a Hammer horror film and the Keystone Kops. The supper and the presentation took place in the restaurant afterwards. The speech went well and I was taken aback to be effusively thanked by Alan Peacock, who had been so vile to me when I was on the Arts Council. I couldn't escape from the egregious James Cook but at least enjoyed seeing many old friends. Charles Henderson, the new Deputy Secretary at the Office of Arts and Libraries, introduced himself. I said, 'Why bother with me? I'm the past', to which he replied, 'Oh no, your name is forever coming up'. It was clear from this encounter that they had done little on the NPG Canary Wharf project and that they rather hoped that it would go away because of what to do about selling the existing NPG building. They were supposed to be investigating this weeks ago and, as I thought, nothing had been done. I told him that Elizabeth had mucked up the V&A. I couldn't resist saying to Richard Luce that I'd built a temple to the V&A in the garden and that Julia on the phone this morning had said that she'd had a great idea: 'We'll make it into a ruin.'

1990

Each year the Queen Mother held what may be described as an arts weekend, the culmination of which was a recital in the Large Drawing-Room made up of music and readings. This was the last such occasion.

3–4 MARCH

Queen Elizabeth the Queen Mother in her ninetieth year

I never thought that we would go again but here she is in her ninetieth year and behaving like a seventy-year-old. All Queen Elizabeth's powers are still there. I was left whacked on the Monday after thirty-six hours on the go at Royal Lodge. I never observed her flag once. The other guests were Hugh and Fortune Grafton, the Cassons, Ruth Fermoy (the permanent hard core), Grey and Neiti Gowrie, Ray Leppard, the Poet Laureate, Ted Hughes with Carol, and us. The Hugheses arrived bearing a book of poems and a huge plastic box of Devonshire clotted cream. Queen Elizabeth adores gifts. I was quite pushed this time to find something that she would like that I hadn't already given her but then I alighted upon an extra copy of Osbert Lancaster's *The Littlehampton Bequest* and soaked off one of my bookplates! She loved it.

Queen Elizabeth was quite extraordinary. She seemed to stand for hours on end, stockings rather wrinkled and legs not that good, her hair gathered into combs at the back but with all those wonderful gestures and sing-song voice the same as ever. The first evening she was in a scarlet and gold dress with superb diamonds and a necklace with rubies the size of gull's eggs. The night of the recital she wore pale turquoise cut like a cape above the waist, with a necklace of diamonds and pearls and a huge diamond spray brooch. I said to Fortune that I wanted to remark on it but hesitated, but she urged me to do it. The reaction was one of lovely old-fashioned flirtatiousness, as though I were a young man passing a compliment at a ball.

The structure of the weekend was unchanged, with bow-legged Martin Gilliatt administering as usual, but really looking too exhausted. By now he's become a caricature courtier so that all the ever-so-correct things he says really mean nothing any more. The routine is to arrive and chat, retreat, bathe and dress and then dinner and chat again afterwards. Sunday consists of breakfast for the men downstairs at 9 a.m., ladies having trays in their rooms, all assembling at 10.45 a.m., be-suited, for church at 11 a.m., the party being split into two between those in the Royal Pew and the rest sitting with the congregation, then back to Royal Lodge, drinks with the Queen, Prince Philip, the officials, etc.; lunch, an expedition (this time to The Valley and Savill Gardens), back, tea, then just forty minutes in which to bathe, and change, down at 6.45 p.m., with the Queen arriving for the concert at 7.30 p.m., dinner, more chat, bed.

It's a cracking pace for a ninety-year-old! I have never known the Queen so relaxed and so funny. She came on her own in the evening to what was a less than brilliant performance. John Gielgud was rather at sea with readings from Horace Walpole and some poems, while Ruth Fermoy and Ray Leppard played duets, including that dotty 'gallop' which pops up in the programme most years. Queen Elizabeth sparkled and loved it all, with the Queen glowering at the other end of the table at dinner, wanting to move but to no avail!

There is an endearing shabbiness in areas of Royal Lodge. The stair and corridor carpet is often threadbare and patched and much of the paintwork touched up. Carpets have stains from leaking radiators and ceilings are grubby. For most of the stay no cold water could be coaxed from the washbasin tap. The decoration is very 1930s, all cream and sweet pea colours. The bathrooms are old-fashioned with chrome and lino tiles, rather empty, with the odd print, at the most, on the walls. In our bedroom there was a lot of painted and braided white wood furniture. This time the room was hung with paintings by Edward Seago suspended by cat gut from the picture rail. But it all conspires to give enormous character to the place, a reflection of her modesty and sense of comfort together with a slightly wartime atmosphere.

There is an enormous amount of food and drink consumed, in a way that the younger generation has abandoned. Four courses at dinner, with no *nouvelle cuisine* here but 'franglais' fare: roasts, well-cooked vegetables, gratin dishes, cheese and an array of biscuits, bread and toast with just about a salad on the side. Add to that a serious pudding, dessert with white and red wine and port to follow. Martin Gilliatt has to orchestrate the *placement* at table. When the dining room is full then the table is turned diagonally and an extra one introduced for the overflow.

Both the Valley and the Savill Gardens looked sad on the Sunday afternoon. Queen Elizabeth retreated from the first. To me there were too many trees. The Savill Gardens also looked over the top and desperately needed updating. We stood *en tableau* before Patrick Plunket's pavilion for a group photograph, Queen Elizabeth rather abashed as she'd put on an old three-quarter-length blue mac, the sleeve cuffs of which were in tatters. With that she wore lovely sensible walking shoes and a crumpled hat. It was an extraordinary sight, her wandering with us, people all around walking their dogs and doing a double-take as they recognised her. She was utterly wonderful as she smiled and exchanged a word with them, in the main controlling her corgi, Ranger, who was off his lead in what was a Royal Garden. She told Julia how someone, not recognising her, told her to put her corgi on a lead, to which the reply came: 'It happens to be my garden.' As usual one observes her real love of animals, her hand dipping down during the concert to fondle Ranger.

The Queen arrived in the evening wearing glasses and virtually stuck to them. She was enormously animated: she didn't like the chairs placed so far back and then began to organise things with rather a schoolmistressy air. I helped by pushing them around. She wore little jewellery and the inevitable red dress. She forms an enormous contrast with her mother still flirting and playing the Marshalin, loving to dress up and wear her jewels, almost swaying in her dresses, with a curved movement of her body and arrangement of her arms, whereas, in sharp contrast, the Queen's movements are angular and sensible.

Prince Edward didn't turn up in the evening, which was silly as he won't hear Gielgud again. Poor boy, he's not yet thirty and nearly all his hair has gone. No sign of Philip.

6 MARCH

The death of my mother

I was rung at 7.30 a.m. by my brother Derek. Mother had been taken into hospital the previous evening. She had been ill for the previous fortnight with her usual stomach and reaching problems but had been very weak and confined to her bed. Derek had been over twice a day and now, he told me, the hospital had called and told him that it would not be long. I asked how long and he said that he would let me know. An hour later he rang to tell that it was imminent. I began at once to get ready to go but within minutes Grace [my sister-in-law] rang to tell me that she had died. Yes, I did cry, but not since; perhaps that is to come.

But then, as I began to think about it all, she had herself created a slow death in our relationship from the moment I married Julia, whom she rejected. I can remember then throwing myself on the bed, sobbing my heart out. That was the first withering. The second, of course, was Brian [my other brother], out to bleed us for anything that he could extract. That was a terrible time, with Mother put upon to lie to me in Brian's interest. It quite shattered me. That was truly the second withering.

As long as Brian remained in my parent's house I could never go there, for fear of a scene. As it was, I caught flashes of it when I rang her, swearing obscenities against me in the background. However, nearly all those calls to her were reasonably happy ones. It gives me grief never to have seen her for the last eight years of her life and now it was too late.

There is something awful about the Strong family. I gather from Derek that Brian and my mother together were a re-run of my parents' marriage, just nagging and slamming at each other day in and day out. She led such a circumscribed life as she made virtually no friends, really none at all. She read romantic fiction and watched television, had no apparent interest in anything but always expected other members of the family to entertain her by taking her somewhere. One great oddity was that she could never bring herself to say the words 'Thank you' if you gave her a gift. I never did discover what that was about. She was possessive of her children on a scale that, in the end, was self-defeating. That house was one of unhappiness, bitterness and resentment. I wish I could think of it in any other way, everyone turned in on themselves, snapping and sniping. There was no common ground between any of the five members of the family other than blood, all of them different in terms of temperament, intellect and emotional response. Life for her was a failure: she'd married the wrong man, she couldn't cook, had no real interests, no initiative or sense of inquiry or delight in things apart from her children. She had loved her father and learnt one thing from him: that education was what, in the case of her three boys, she must fight for. That she did and I owe her an enormous debt for that: what she did she did at a price, years of taking every and any kind of job, clerical, library assistant, shop assistant, anything to get those extra pounds, which meant that I at least could go on.

2 AUGUST

The Prince of Wales's concert for his grandmother

As I predicted, we were on the guest list for this assorted event in the Ballroom of Buckingham Palace. Any sense of style and much else besides seems to have left the place. The concert was at 8 p.m. and we were bidden at 6.15 for 6.30 p.m. We duly arrived on time, as did many others, and parked the car in the Palace courtyard. We then made our way to the Grand Entrance, which was already overflowing with guests, and we were marooned there for forty minutes or so. As Queen Elizabeth is to be ninety, most of her friends must have been moving towards that age and there was much decrepitude in evidence and ancient flesh gathered into gowns of varying vintage. The guest list (or the acceptances) was as notable for who wasn't there as for who was. Several people we had always seen at either

Clarence House or Royal Lodge were nowhere to be seen. As far as I can remember we saw or spoke to Billa Harrod, 'Duke' Hussey, the Norfolks, the Graftons, Natalie Brooke, Brinsley and Joanna Ford, the Thorneycrofts, the Northbournes, the Salisburys, Bill Heseltine, the De L'Isles, the Spencers, Ted Heath, Douglas Hurd, Oliver and Delia Millar and the Airlies.

At 7.30 p.m. the wearying throng was at last allowed to ascend the staircase to the Ballroom, which, when everyone was seated, was only half full. The programme included two new pieces by young composers commissioned by the Prince of Wales. Both were film music and of no distinction but, as the Prince explained in his somewhat breathless programme notes, 'Why can't we have tunes any more?'

At 8 p.m. on the dot the Royal Family came in from the right: the Queen, the Queen Mother, no Duke of Edinburgh, the Prince of Wales, the Princess of Wales, the Duchess of Kent (no Duke), Princess Alexandra and Angus, Princess Margaret, the King and Queen of Greece and no Michaels of Kent. The Queen was leaden. Not one of them as much as smiled in the direction of the by then rather tetchy assembly. The Queen had the Queen Mother on her right, and she in turn had the Prince of Wales on hers, sunburnt and with one arm in a sling.

The concert, which was conducted by Ray Leppard, got off to a sprightly start with a Strauss polka, which jollied everyone up a bit. There was one touching moment. When Elgar's *The Sanguine Fan* was played the Queen Mother leaned over towards her daughter, surely asking her whether she remembered the matinée at which this was played and to which she had taken her and her sister as children. The rest of it was no good. The new pieces were quite unmemorable and Eric Coates's *Elizabeth of Glamis* too overdone and Palm Court for this orchestra. One of the commissioned pieces, a series of somewhat drear songs about Mary Queen of Scots, brought the whole affair to an abrupt and somewhat charmless end. The Royal Family got up and swept out of the room without any attempt to thank the conductor and the orchestra and not even acknowledging that the audience existed. The event should have exuded some sort of festive spirit, I would have thought, but no way. Perhaps they'd all had a terrible row off-stage.

What happened after, too, was a disaster. The Royal Family had a private dinner, which meant that the whole time they were trying to get away. We never saw the Queen Mother, who vanished. We did talk to Princess Alexandra and to Angus, who had seen Highgrove and was astonished by what I had done to the garden – his, he said, was suburban. I had a brief word with the Prince of Wales, telling him that I would be coming to train the hedges again, but all we got was 'We have to go to a family dinner. We should have been there ages ago.' I would have thought that their time would have been far better spent working on this not undistinguished gathering. Two-tier entertaining is never a good idea and this was a clouded, ill-starred if well-meant affair. It was an evening on the cheap that fell down on all counts, although, as someone remarked, at least the Palace was being used as Queen Victoria had intended it to be for a change, instead of merely a series of bedrooms. It all lacked style, was mechanical and devoid of any sense of occasion or élan. The aura was that of an event that somehow had to be got through. The footmen's uniforms were rather grubby and the flowers barely adequate. But it was a delight to see these rooms again, including the Picture Gallery, where a light buffet was served and we all milled around.

At this point I stopped writing a proper Diary for over two years but returned with a vengeance in 1993.

1991 *and* 1992

There are no Diary entries for this period, apart from my Garden Diary. That I was conscious of falling short is reflected in my occasional photocopying of letters to friends abroad. Nonetheless, those to an old American academic friend, Stephen Orgel, of which I occasionally kept copies, etch in the scene for these two years. Extracts from them will enable the reader to capture the flavour of the period and what was going on. Over everything hung the financial slump, which ended with Olympia & York selling Canary Wharf (which they later bought back) and the end of my consultancy.

The first letter is dated 9 March 1991 and begins by explaining the alterations to both house and garden, including the impact of visiting Monet's Giverny, after which I rushed out to buy all the yellow late-flowering plants I could for the Flower Garden. I continue:

At the moment I am working on three books, three radio programmes and six television programmes simultaneously. Oh, *Lost Treasures of Britain* appeared and did very well. A book club took 45,000 copies and it sold well at Christmas and I was really very pleased with it as a popular book. The last chapter led directly on to the radio, asking the question where conservation and the idea of heritage have led us, have we nothing to show in the UK for this century beyond propping up the past? For the radio I'm working with a brilliant young woman [Jane Beresford] through April. I love working with bright young people who aren't overawed by me but instead we needle each other's minds. . .

At the beginning of December I delivered 853 pages of A4, the garden anthology, *Everything in the Garden* [which became *A Celebration of Gardens*], to which I've continued to add things. My editor is sweet, educated, but not in the land of the living at least as far as the present tough book market is concerned. They are, however, very pleased with it, in fact he said or rather wrote that 'if there were a Nobel Prize for anthologies' I'd get it, and he was quite over-whelmed by the breadth of it, from Pliny to Chips Channon. It was very hard work, particularly to find really witty and amusing pieces (Katherine White's *Onward and Upward in the Garden* is a treasure trove!) and then to arrange the pieces in sequence in terms of subject matter and contrast. He loved it, although we both agree that we need to re-order the end bit to give it a final bang. Julia is doing very pretty illustrations, a delight. At the moment he doesn't want to cut anything bar two pieces, which means that it will probably be 500 pages long. It'll be out in October.

I then foolishly agreed to write a piece for H.J. Holtgen's *Festschrift*. You will love it but it took me back into late Elizabethan England. I think that I've solved the 'Persian Virgin crowning a weeping stag' [a picture in the Royal Collection at Hampton Court]. It is so obvious. The picture has just been cleaned, ravishing, and I stood in front of it and in a flash Essex [Elizabeth I's favourite, Robert Devereux, 2nd Earl of] crossed my mind. The stag is Essex as the transmuted Actaeon, as in Jonson's *Cynthia's Revels*. And then everything I touched fell into place: the regal pansies, the walnut – a royal tree, the fact that the picture must connect with Essex's friend Sir Henry Lee, for whom Gheeraerts, the painter, did this kind of picture as a special line. Here we are looking at the weeping Essex still protesting his love and loyalty to the Queen.

I really shouldn't have done the *Festschrift* piece because I have to finish *Creating Small Period Gardens*, the next design book. That is formidable. It is not easy to produce twenty designs to scale with every period detail and planting correct for small spaces running from 1500 to 1939. I've done seventeen of them but must plough on and finish the rest by the end of March. And then there's the text and the captions. It is to be published in May 1992.

None of this would have been a problem if *Royal Gardens* hadn't started up. That is chaos, as television always is. Last week I visited the last of the royal gardens, Balmoral, a visit which should have taken a day but extended over two due to Scottish fog. It was awful. I can't tell you the complications of this series. The only thing to be said in its favour is that it will provide for our imminent old age! [It didn't.] It also has to have a package book written by the end of December.

So I am already jam-packed with work. If I can get rid of *Period Gardens* I will feel a little freed up from having too many subjects and index cards whirring around in my mind. Once the television scripts/treatments are approved, which will happen this week, that too will be a hurdle crossed.

But I'm already having to think into 1992 and 1993 and Channel 4 are interested in me, so I've put up ideas for a couple series, one a European one which I would really like to do on 'lost' European civilisations like Burgundy . . .

Something that has given me more pleasure is to be nominated for the Columnist of the Year Award for my *Country Life* diary pieces . . . So this long letter will tell what is going on. It is a good and creative period of life. We nearly came to Yale to give a lecture but the war [in the Balkans] broke out and we cancelled. The war and the recession are not nice. Now we only have the latter, which affects me due to the cut in TV budgets and publishing being in a very bad way . . .

30 DECEMBER

This year has been a killer, no, not because of the recession but because of too much very, very tiring work . . . The year has been mainly focused around the media. *Present Imperfect* was a series on our architectural environment and why we're in the mess we're in. I worked with a wonderful young producer called Jane Beresford. At any rate they want more and I suggested and am doing a six-part series on the arts and the state since 1945. That'll be interesting, lousy pay but very intellectually stimulating. So I'm still very much on the cultural map.

Royal Gardens has the makings of a fine series. Again I've learnt a lot. It's been a killer, up at 5.30 a.m. and filming at 6.30 a.m., sometimes standing for hours in the rain and so on. The post-filming days go on and on and on. But the programmes are off-beat, informative with an edge, and quirky and funny, I hope. I've done everything from emerging from a Regency firework display amidst the ruins of Leptis Magna in Windsor Great Park to clambering onto a gallery of the pagoda at Kew clutching a six-foot-long gilded dragon. We did the last day's filming at Sandringham just before Christmas, with me careering up the drive in a 1910 chauffeur-driven car, swathed in scarves . . .

I am longing for the next work phase and for *Royal Gardens* to end. Then Felicity [Bryan] says it's into memoirs for me. I'm not sure what kind but I don't want to write words of vitriol and about art-historical in-fighting like Pope-Hennessy. Who cares? No one really, so I have chapters like 'Remarkable Women', 'Sir Portrait', 'Exhibitionism', 'Grand Occasions', 'Cecil', etc. I don't see any point in writing retribution and I feel very much that I want to give delight.

One of the great treats of *la vita nuova* is learning again and expanding one's facility for scribbling into other fields. Everywhere I go they all seem to follow what I'm up to and I bless the day that I wrote the letter quitting the V&A.

Julia is very well. It is so wonderful that she has adapted to a new life. Not in the least upset not to be designing something but running her massive vegetable garden and happy here, with no sense of frustration. It is so important in life to recognise its phases and anticipate and accept them gracefully as a way of moving on to other things.

Looking back, these two years were my media apogee, for what that was worth. It is an area in which you come and go and very few stay the course as tastes change and fashions in both presenters and contributors shift. Having stormed the establishment, I had become in a way part of it; on the whole, by 2000 the last person the media would want was someone over sixty – worse, a knight of the realm with a vaguely upper-class voice. My appearances since have been almost exclusively confined to doing pieces to camera remembering this or that worthy who had passed to higher spheres.

I enjoyed hugely working on the two radio series, Present Imperfect, *dealing with the heritage obsession and how it had stifled new creativity, and* Ministering to the Arts, *a studied romp through the relationship of government and the arts since 1945. The critics either loved them or loathed them and reading through what they wrote I can't help being amused by one who slammed into my 'incredibly mannered delivery, full of pernickety refinements of pronunciation and petulant stresses' and another's more rapturous response that 'it was a joy to hear Sir Roy conducting proceedings in his fine soprano . . . what a delight to have someone whose voice rises and trills like a lark at the end each utterance'. You can't win.*

Neither can you with television. The Royal Gardens *series dominated both years. As anyone who has made even a modest series knows, the demands on time and adrenalin are huge. The idea of doing such a series now fills me with utter horror. But I did write down the history of this particular venture, which stretched as far back as 1986. In that year I presented but did not write for Harlech television a programme on the great Victorian photographer Henry Fox Talbot. The end result seemed to consist of me wandering around Lacock Abbey in a white suit and broad-brimmed panama hat with the smoke machine in permanent overdrive. The suit came from my new friend Gianni Versace and is now in the V&A fashion collection. Much to my surprise, the programme went on to earn a string of prizes and Harlech asked me for other ideas. By then it was 1987 and my garden career had taken off and it occurred to me that no one had made a series on the royal gardens, royal series being very much the fashion then. Knowing that it was no use planning such a project without the imprimatur of the Palace, I wrote to Bill Heseltine, the Queen's secretary, and much to my surprise was granted permission.*

The ways of television are labyrinthine: having got the go-ahead, Harlech promptly turned it down and three years passed, during which other companies also turned it down, until by chance I had a meeting with Alan Yentob, who was head of BBC2 arts commissioning. He didn't warm to the project either, but it so happened that he was about to go on sabbatical and it was his stand-in during that period, Dennis Marks, who gave it the go-ahead. After much squalid horse-trading, about which I knew little, the show got on the road under the joint aegis of the BBC and Antelope Films. Looking back, I now realise that financially I was taken to the dry cleaners. This was a low-budget series; in fact, it was made on 50 per cent of the norm. That all the gardens appear only in one season of the year reflected vividly the fact that there was no money for a return visit. It didn't matter either how awful the weather: we all had to plough on regardless. It rained for nine hours without ceasing at Hampton Court but somehow on screen it looked like a summer's day. Accommodation was the nearest bed and breakfast and lunch was a Mars bar or a packet of Marks & Spencer sandwiches if you were lucky.

The autumn and winter of 1991 into 1992 went on planning and writing the scripts, the shooting following in the spring of '92. When it came to the various royal households, the right hand never seemed to know what the left hand was doing. Everything to do with filming at Buckingham Palace was a complete fiasco. We wanted to film a Royal Garden Party but were told that this was never allowed. That didn't worry me, for what I thought would be far more interesting would be a glimpse behind the scenes, with tea urns and pieces of Swiss roll and cups and saucers flying in all directions. On the day the director, Roger Last, and the film crew arrived early to plan the shoot. They wandered around and then noticed a whole line of waitresses with someone in a headscarf working her way along them. Much to their horror, they realised it was the Queen. Nor did the shoot later that day go according to plan. When we arrived behind the scenes to film what we had permission to film, a household official stepped forward and stopped us, saying that it was forbidden, and pushed us through into the actual party, which was precisely what we had been told we could not film. After much telephoning, this was sorted out. Nor did the actual appearance of the Queen go according to plan. About that I insisted on being briefed in detail. Needless to say, what the official said would be the Queen's movements bore no relation whatsoever to the route she took, so that the camera crew ended up in a heap.

At Osborne we mocked up the tent in which Queen Victoria sat and worked on sunny days, but alas this one was not. In fact rain clouds gathered and there was a howling gale. As I uttered the lines 'Here on sunny days . . .' my hair was streaming horizontally in the wind, the tablecloth was about to levitate and three crew members were propping up the tent for dear life.

After those and more dramas followed by long days in the dark, editing and doing the voice-over. The series was scheduled to go out in the spring of 1992 but, as it was considered that there had been a glut of royal series, it was finally transmitted in October. Four million viewers apparently watched each episode and the critics loved it or loathed it, as is their wont.

Perhaps my most important paragraph of this time occurs in a letter dated 10 October 1992 to Stephen Orgel. It was a pointer to future, although as yet I did not know it:

. . . my agent wants me to write a children's history of Britain. It was her idea and I was very surprised but children here are practically not taught history any more, certainly nothing about kings and queens and dates. There is nothing in the shops for seven- to twelve-year-olds. What little there is seems to be about the Vikings or Romans. Felicity tells me that I have a clear narrative style and it could be important to do this book rather than wade back into all that old Elizabethan junk again.

What I did not perceive was that my career on radio and television, far from taking off, had in fact reached its end and that I was to depend henceforth on the power of my pen.

1993

1 JANUARY

This period of the year is always very quiet. Nothing but gloom in the predictions for 1993, with Eastern Europe, Russia and Africa all falling apart. This seems for me to be a heads-down year of writing.

12 FEBRUARY

Taxing the Queen

I got up at 6 a.m. to be collected for the *Today* programme, which had sent a car all the way from London to take me into Hereford, seven miles away! When we got to BBC Hereford & Worcester it was closed. They'd forgotten to open it and so we drove back to The Laskett, where I did the interview down the line on taxation and the Queen and the creation of a Royal Collection Charitable Trust. I did not kowtow. What did it mean? Was it a new label on an old bottle? Was there to be a split between the Royal Collection and what was their own personal property? There was to be greater accessibility, but how? I said that opening Buckingham Palace had now moved up the agenda.

22 FEBRUARY

Travails of writing

A grey, cold day, during which I read a very boring book by E.F. Jacob on Henry V, so boring in fact that I kept on falling asleep over it. In order to write my book [*The Story of Britain*] I have to read something well written and stimulating to get me going. So I moved on to [Christopher] Allmand's biography of the king, which was much better. That led me on to consider the whole medieval section, which was quite difficult. I realised that having started in the middle of the fourteenth century I now needed to go back to 1066 and work forwards.

24 FEBRUARY

Sitting for Snowdon

I was to be photographed by Tony Snowdon for the April issue of the Italian men's fashion magazine *Uomo* as one in a gallery of gardeners. Patrick Kinmonth was in attendance as the stylist and my Versace black leather blouson and corduroy trousers survived the re-dressing; otherwise I was put into a Ralph Lauren black suede shirt and poured into black leather riding boots. Then came the shoot with me posed between two topiary box trees with a scattering of cuttings on the floor around them, set against a plain backcloth. Tony tucked a pair of secateurs into the top of one boot, telling me that this was where Vita Sackville-West had put hers. 'Give me more cleavage!' Tony yelled, at which point Patrick yelled back 'You can't do that to Roy!' The result was a cross between Heathcliffe and a rent boy in old age but, as Tony said, 'there's the cover for your next book'.

26 FEBRUARY

Gloom

All through this period it has been very gloomy, with everyone in a depressed state. This year is the first time we've felt the financial crunch: it's agony to get paid and I'm owed several thousand pounds, which I can't get out of anybody. Worse, I am faced with paying the tax for a good year in what is now a very bad year.

3 MARCH

Farewell to Sir Hugh Wontner

The funeral took place at St Clement Danes of Sir Hugh Wontner, once owner of the Savoy. The congregation was packed with a lot of the waxworks in well-worn blacks. The service was superbly done, with the touching addition of the madrigal from *Ruddigore*, reminding us of his connexion with the Savoy and D'Oyly Carte. There was lunch at the Savoy afterwards, with, amongst others, Patrick Lichfield, looking very white, who had read a lesson at the service; Liz Anson in a blazer and smoking like blazes; Mary Roxburghe, a bit tottery; Elizabeth Maclean, blaming me for ruining Hampton Court; and Martin Gilliatt, now eighty but looking ninety and a bad one at that. I sent my humble duty to Queen Elizabeth, who, I gathered, loved all my royal gardens stuff. Sir Ralph Anstruther was also there and quite funny about her.

25 MARCH

Béjart and Versace

We drove up to London after lunch to go to the Maurice Béjart ballet at Sadler's Wells, with costumes by Versace. It's an awful journey to what is a scruffy and remote theatre. The audience was devoid of glamour and I found myself sitting next to David Shilling dressed *cap à pied* in Versace and, because it was pattern on pattern, looked all wrong. The first ballet, *Mr C* on Chaplin, was an hour and forty minutes' indulgence. Then came the short one, *Sissi*, with Sylvie Guillem as the Empress Elizabeth. It was notable only for one spectacular moment, the opening tableau, in which the ballerina stood wearing Gianni's version of one of those legendary dresses one sees in the Winterhalter portraits. Thereafter it was downhill all the way.

5 MARCH

A working day

I stayed in and worked on William I. I can really get going if a chapter can be inspired by a particular book. It is often counter-productive reading huge academic tomes on the Normans that give far too much detail and are a dull read. Maurice Ashley's short *Life and Times of William I*, on the other hand, is a marvellous synthesis, ideal for boiling down. A copy of the book on Highgrove arrived, with a letter from the Prince of Wales saying that he'd just been handed my *Royal Gardens* book.

I AND 2 APRIL

Leeds Castle

We drove to Leeds Castle, where we were given a large room with a four-poster bed and were coddled by a butler and a footman. The reason was the Waterstones Literary Dinner and a lot of pressure had been brought to bear upon me to do it. It was done jointly with another author, Richard Bisgrove, a pure red-brick type wearing a blue suit with brown shoes, as Julia remarked, and a dirty tie. Alan Giles, the very bright head of Waterstones, was there, at what was dinner for eighty in a medieval barn. I think it went very well and was worth doing for a Middle England audience. Twenty copies of *Royal Gardens* were sold and I signed twelve more.

15 APRIL

Garden panorama

A glorious spring day, with blue sky and sun and warmth too. The garden looked utterly extraordinary bathed in an early mist and an incipient golden glow. Mike Jones the painter came and we embarked on what we had been planning, painting some of the ornaments: the pedestals on either side of the Ashton Arbour, the panels of the pedestals in the Flower Garden and of the recumbent stage in the orchard. All of it looked marvellous, so we went on to apply the same treatment to the pedestals in Covent Garden, letting Mike take home the ball finials to paint gold.

Then we left on our garden expedition, first to Tintinhull and then to East Lambrook. At Tintinhull, which we found disappointing, we bumped into Andrew Lawson the photographer. The garden is on the flat, with marvellous enclosed areas but little thought given to the 'borrowed landscape', resulting in such disasters as a new vista which, when you looked up and beyond, led the eye to an electric junction box. Even the beautiful little White Pond Garden was marred by a huge electricity pole. The planting, however, was superb and the great borders in June I feel must be truly remarkable.

We went on to Margery Fish's famous garden at East Lambrook, which is in the process of being recovered. That and the lack of labour accounted for much untidiness but it is still such an exciting garden, with dramatic changes of level deployed to stunning effect, a cornucopia of plants, an extraordinary, winding, intimate quality like a child's picture-book magic garden. There were very few formal accents. As at Tintinhull, there was brilliant underplanting of the trees, which inspired me.

29 APRIL

Buckingham Palace opens its doors

I wrote the chapter on Edward I and finished it. It came together well, I thought. I was interrupted by the news that Buckingham Palace is to open to the public. I did an interview on this for LBC with Angela Rippon. Oddly enough, the royals came through with exactly what I had said they should: open Buckingham Palace, restore some of the rooms at Windsor and do the Chapel and St George's Hall in the best of contemporary design.

4 MAY

Affirming Catholicism

I went to have dinner with David Hutt at All Saints, Margaret Street. David was in tremendous form and we spent most of the evening lamenting that the Church of England had sunk so low and that no words came from the present Archbishop of Canterbury to lift us. The Bishop of Durham had written a terrific piece for Affirming Catholicism and it does seem that the ordination of women is turning into a make or break catalyst for the Church of England. Everything at the moment seems up for grabs. There was a deep resentment of Roman Catholic triumphalism, with batteries of media covering conversions to Rome, but, in fact, Rome and Cardinal Hume grant nothing. Yet they make the pace in the press. It is so saddening not to hear Anglican leaders stand up and be counted for our very real theological position: the Church of England always leaves doors open. It accepts that no debate is ever closed. It is always there to be reopened, with the flexibility to move on.

6 TO 11 MAY

Italian interlude

Dario, Gianni Versace's driver, was at the airport in Milan to collect us and we arrived at Via Gesu at about 3.30 p.m. That evening it was just dinner à quatre. Gianni seemed in an incredible state, exuding huge energy, drive and warmth. I have never seen him better, full of excitement about his *palazzo della fantasia* in Miami, where every room was to be different. It is thrilling to see his enormous success, with no sign of flagging. Antonio has come on a lot and, apart from looking luscious and being very, very sweet, now handles a chunk of the *prêt à porter* collection.

8 MAY

Dick Avedon arrived at the Villa Fontanelle, a small Jewish New Yorker with tiny hands. He remembered that we met twenty years ago at the National Portrait Gallery. After lunch he showed us the proofs of his huge autobiographical volume. It is his greatest and falls into three parts. Overall it is a huge statement on beauty and its loss, on life and death, on bloom and decay, said so often through photographs of his family, capturing his father from middle age to death and his sister, who went mad. This is a man with an extraordinary eye, brilliant at the observation of surfaces and any line which is the essence of fashion, at penetrating the veil or rather lifting it, recording how laughter can turn so quickly to a scream. I found it very moving.

In the afternoon we went into Como to pick up Gianni's friend Nene Bellotti and walked happily in the rain. There was dinner for seven, with everyone relaxed and happy and the conversation flowing, from the Nineties depression to the royals. Avedon recalled how at long last Nancy Reagan actually rang him. Her opening words had been 'Hello, Richard. Do you retouch?' And he gave a wonderful account of photographing the army's gays.

9 MAY

Today we went to the Villa d'Este for lunch and joined Gianni and others by the lake. It is clear that he and Avedon are plotting something. There seemed to be an idea that Avedon would photograph me in Gianni's clothes. 'I will do the styling,' Gianni said. [It never happened.] Avedon's young photographic assistant, Mark, turned up and we lunched inside on several varieties of pasta, meat and ice cream. The weather was a dream and I loved seeing the grotto again. There's always a fag end to this kind of weekend, which came in the evening in the form of rather desultory run-down snatches of conversation. After dinner at 9.30 p.m. they all went back to Milan. I'm glad I met Avedon again. He's extraordinarily lively at seventy, more like fifty.

Reflecting later, it was a magical weekend. Gianni was relaxed, very rarely tired, engaged with everything, his mind bowling along, very much in love with Antonio. Seeing the Avedon photograph of Allen Ginsberg and his lover clutching each other naked, he said: 'I want to be photographed like that with Antonio.' Antonio at that point put his hand over the lower section of the picture, covering their private parts, and said 'Only so much.' We all laughed. Gianni is at his peak. They adore the new Miami house. 'I bought the hotel next door and will demolish it so I can have a garden.' Every room is to be a fantasy: a gold room, a white room, a modern room.

17 MAY

Highgrove comes to The Laskett

James Aldridge and David Magson, the gardeners from Highgrove, came to the garden and we cheerfully walked around it for two hours in a deluge. They came bearing plants. They said that a lot had happened in the Highgrove garden since I was last there, and told me something that I didn't know: that Lanning Roper had been initially consulted by the Prince but was by then too ill to help him. James Aldridge said that the only good bit of the garden was the potager, the structural planting in the other areas having been done so badly. I told him that all my efforts had gone into trying to rectify and conceal that fact. I'm afraid that I went on to tell them how difficult I found Richard Aylard and the whole experience had been of doing both the *Royal Gardens* television series and the book.

21 MAY

Garden folk

Mary Christie and Camilla Whitworth-Jones came to lunch en route for Camilla's house in Clwyd on what was a beautiful day. We had lunch in the conservatory, the table pretty with white lace over a dark green tablecloth and rose-decked china. Afterwards, as we were walking past a clump of aquilegias close to the fountain, Camilla revealed that her grandmother was Norah Barlow, the originator of this species, 'Granny's Bonnet'. Mary is enormously strong-willed and energetic and is deeply involved with Mary Keen and Christopher Lloyd in redesigning and planting the garden around the new opera house at Glyndebourne. Touring the garden, she seemed oddly oblivious to the importance of the role of topiary and statuary in the garden.

In the evening we went to a *fête* given by George and Grizel Williams at their house at Crickhowell. There were drinks beneath the laburnum tunnel followed by a dinner for fifty in a marquee. The guests were a lot of well-suited, upper-class and often rather dull people, but not too much so. Both brio and the young were absent. I sat between the gold-bespangled wife of the Lord Lieutenant of Dyfed and Lady Lloyd George, who had been hit badly by Lloyds and left with no money with which to restore a sixty-room Nash mansion. I had my usual cut and thrust with Peter Rees, who really is terribly reactionary.

The garden here, however, is some achievement. It is a landscape, a valley through which runs a winding stream embroidered with walks, splendid specimen trees, a towering obelisk, two bridges, one Chinese Chippendale, a lake, a wooden banqueting house and a spectacular vista to a gazebo by Quinlan Terry sited on an eminence. I love the fact that our host, George Williams, did all this from scratch in his seventies. It was sad, therefore, that the evening turned out to be an overcast and chilly one.

So many of these people leave so little imprint on my memory, although most of them I'd met before doing something or other, but they are so conventional that they slip from my mind. It is really rather awful of me because they always remember me, which is embarrassing.

22 MAY

The Michaels of Kent at home

We went to lunch at Nether Lypiatt with Princess Michael. The other guests were Shirley Sherwood, Michael and Linda Suffolk and Brian and Merle Huntly. He ran the Cecil Rhodes garden in South Africa. The Suffolks were very late and I thought we would never eat.

The garden at Nether Lypiatt has been greatly elaborated since we were last there: a parterre on the back terrace of box and germander in-filled with santolina and other grey foliage plants, a vista cut into the distance and the odd ornament that I didn't recall. The room in which we had lunch was so hot and airless that I was on the verge of fainting. Thank God that I got the window open but it upset me and left me anxious.

Princess Michael talks the whole time, non-stop, but she has tremendous style, energy and is a very good and unstuffy hostess, so it's not the usual royal Never Never Land. Prince Michael looks tired and ageing but he's very sweet with his dog-like, faithful eyes, stiff upright gait and impeccable, old-fashioned way of dressing. The daughter, Ella, is charming but incredibly plain, with her father's gentle nature. After lunch we toured the garden and then drove to the Suffolks' garden at Charlton. There was no great feeling for design here but a very strong one for plants and Linda loves them. There was a beautiful border of various coloured alliums mixed with very dark purple irises set amidst grey and yellow foliage: a knock-out. I also noticed roses trained through laburnums, but it did all need pulling together. On looking her up on return, I found that Linda's grandmother was Syrie Maugham.

30 MAY

An old friend stays

Antonia Fraser came to stay. It was good to see her again after all these years. She has a wonderful intelligence and brightness, a life-enhancer. We talked about just about everything/everybody: agents, books, old friends, the lot.

31 MAY

We had long, lingering talks over breakfast. Antonia is really happy with Harold [Pinter]. His father is still alive and living in Hove. He has kept his working-class attitudes while his mother, who died last autumn, went middle-class. Harold, she said, was a genius out of nothing as there wasn't a book in the house. Julia thinks that her present life suits her and it's a marriage of minds as well, although they both seem to preserve their own separate spheres, Harold going off to cricket or on stage and she to films, researching and writing books, this time one on the Gunpowder Plot. All the time she dressed in a most extraordinary way for the country, in high-necked dresses with no waist and Peter Pan collars with elegant shoes, not altogether practical for clomping around Herefordshire. However, off we went to Bacton church (where Blanche Parry, who had seen the Virgin Queen's cradle rocked, lies buried) and Abbey Dore (the world of the poet George Herbert living on), both of which greatly moved Antonia. There was much conversation the whole time about everyone and groans about Elizabeth Longford's royal obsession, which was positively a disservice. I think that she enjoyed herself with us. She has such a star quality and I've always felt her friendship. I've never had anyone to stay so uncurious about how the house and its contents look, as though she didn't 'see' them.

2 JUNE

The garden

Heavy rain overnight. This has been an extraordinary year for growth and also for transplanting things. Along the pleached lime avenue, Elizabeth Tudor, the cow parsley is at its height, dappled with alliums in various shades of purple looking just like a painting by Pissarro. Robin has established paths and patterns in his cutting of the grass, which has given further articulation to the garden. We discussed changing the Yew Garden with paving around the edges and gravelling it at the centre. I then pushed it on the computer and walloped out the first draft of an article on the portraits of Elizabeth I for Franco Maria Ricci.

In the afternoon I went in my guise of patron to the launch of the appeal for All Saints Church in Hereford. Victor Stock gave an address, which was a *tour de force* and very funny. It was all done well, with good food and wine and a little band playing Django Rheinhardt. But it did go on a bit, from 2.30 p.m. to 9.30 p.m. The bishop spoke and I mingled. Victor gave an embarrassing eulogy of me from the pulpit but he would, wouldn't he?

4 TO 7 JUNE

An unexpected tour of Wales

We began with the long drive to Bodnant, during which the weather lifted and it became a stunning June day. *En route* we stopped at Llangollen, a very Welsh little town with idiosyncratic architecture. We walked up the hill and at long last actually visited Plas Newydd, the house of the so-called Ladies of Llangollen [Lady Eleanor Butler and Miss Sarah Ponsonby]. This is really quite bizarre, a *cottage orné* with bits of old carving that they must have bought up or salvaged and applied to the place, rather in the spirit of Horace Walpole. The result is utterly unique and strangely modern, as some of these bits and pieces formed abstract patterns. It was full of odd details like the doorway framed in stained glass. The scale is small and the overall effect is an odd fusion of the charming and the weird. Outside they should have restored the garden, which included a Celtic circle, topiary yews and an arbour tower.

Alas, at Bodnant the rhododendrons were over, but it was an amazing garden with a vast woodland area banked with them, together with azaleas and with rare trees giving bold structure. The formal gardens descending from the house were a triumph, the descent being by way of a curved Edwardian pergola dripping with roses. Below lay the famous canal and Pin House with a very good use of brick for the paths, so that lots of references were snapped.

After Bodnant we drove on to Conwy and put up at the Castle Arms. This is an enchanting little town, like something out of provincial France, still encircled by its medieval walls. Within there was a memorable Elizabethan town house. All of this came as a great surprise and gave us great pleasure and delight.

5 JUNE

On Saturday we began by looking at the castle, which was a palace, and it continued to haunt us all day as we glimpsed it across the landscape and estuary, where it kept popping up again and again from different angles. We went on to Bodelwyddan Castle, the National Portrait Gallery's outpost for its nineteenth-century collections, which was very well done. It was so nostalgic for me to see so many of the portraits with which I had passed my youth. There I was recognised by the Director. On we drove to the Marble Church built by Lady Willoughby de Broke in the 1860s in the decorated style, with lashings of marble and sentimental sculpture, amongst which there was a revolting font with two ghastly children supporting a shell.

Next came St Asaph's, where we had a quick sandwich, a tired, worn-out, rather sad route to Llandudno. The cathedral was a large parish church masquerading as one, rather dull, and the poverty all around was tangible. We then took a back way to Llandudno affording stupendous views of landscape and sea. We invaded Bodysgallen

Hall Hotel to see the garden, which in fact turned out to be not much good and where the porter was rude. Alas, by the time we reached Llandudno we could find nowhere to park, but we could see that it was a pretty town with bright seaside architecture, including delightful canopies over the shop fronts. We therefore had no alternative but to drive around Great Orme Point, the rocky promontory into the Irish Sea, and then on to our hotel, the Deganway Castle, a rather run-down, shabby place in which we were given an eyrie but with a magical view back to Conwy Castle.

6 JUNE

We drove to Beaumaris on Anglesey, an enchanting, minute watering place with a solitary grand terrace, Victoria Terrace, and a wealth of picturesque sorbet-coloured houses. The castle was a delight, delicate in scale, seemingly small from the outside but splendid within: once again I was bowled over by the Middle Ages. The drive to get there had been a long, winding, tree-lined panorama dappled with light, looking one way out to sea and the other inland.

We moved on to Plas Newydd, the Angleseys' house. The setting is paradise enhanced by a Repton landscape overlaid with rhododendrons and azaleas, the house looking over the Menai Strait and towards the Menai Bridge. It is provincial gothick from the 1780s and not, I thought, that good inside, with a mass of dull family portraits. Far more interesting was the imprint of country house comfort left by the 1920s and 1930s: an abundance of bathrooms with painted furniture, huge baths and marble washbasins on metal stands, the bedrooms with kidney-shaped dressing tables, comfortable sofas, piles of cushions and books and masses of *toile de Jouy*, all very Fowleresque.

There was a splendid display of Rex Whistler's work. I can't think how he would have developed, for although some of it was inspired there was much that was facile. His mural in the dining room, however, remains an experience. No great colourist, Whistler seemed to me to emerge as Thirties neo-romantic *pasticheur* more than anything else.

After lunch we moved on to Caernarvon. What a spectacle, the castle magnificent, the town around the castle a delight – although much else was tatty and run-down. Then came Criccieth, another sweet seaside town, and Portmeirion, Rex Whistler's Plas Newydd mural brought to life, a fantasy constructed from architectural salvage, concrete, *trompe l'œil*, fakery and fantasy in fondant colours. The hotel was good.

7 JUNE

We drove back along the coastal road with stunning scenery betwixt sea and mountain, passing fetching stone-built villages bright with flowers. Just before Aberystwyth we turned inland and went home via Llangurig, Rhayader and Builth Wells along the Wye Valley. It was a dream, a golden day of such beauty, the whole landscape sparkling. This was a glorious four days, better than Ischia! We had explored a chunk of the UK we had never seen before. As we drove back the weather became better and better, so that by the time that we reached The Laskett it was a blazing June day. Everything in the garden had shot, the roses were out on the Beaton Bridge, the *Crambe cordifolia* seven feet high and the poppies in the Flower Garden at their apogee.

8 JUNE

Susan Hill

At about half past five Susan Hill came with someone called Rory Stewart. She is making a garden. Susan is enormously intelligent and talks without end. But she looked good all in white with a straw hat, the brim of which was turned up and pinned at the front. It was odd taking her round the garden, for it was as though she didn't 'see' it. She said that her garden would be bigger than ours, although when we had seen hers there was only some desultory planting near the house and no sign of a bolder, more comprehensive design and planting scheme. That was odd, so I guessed that to her the garden was a dream with no roots in reality. We shall see. However, we learnt that Myfanwy Piper was OK, very frail and thin at eighty-three, and that John's funeral had been a joy, with what amounted to a party afterwards.

17 JUNE

Mirabel Osler

We went for lunch with Mirabel Osler in Ludlow. As is so often the case in Ludlow, a narrow street façade conceals behind it a size-able house and garden. Mirabel has wonderful taste in a rather Arts and Crafts way, with a penchant for folk pottery and weave. This is a smiling lady in her sixties with bright eyes, her hair dipped a vaguely donkey violet, wearing ethnic clothes with odd braids and trimmings. But she's a life-giver from a background that included the painter Stella Bowen, who was a friend of her mother's, and Ezra

Pound, so there are occasional, extraordinary pictures from that period on the walls.

In a year Mirabel has made a delightful town garden with so many areas in which to sit and drink in the cascades of blossom. It was quite lovely, with its pleached limes along one side, its phoney door at the far end suggesting more, and a pretty brick and cobble path. Mirabel shows great taste in contrasts of plants twining round each other. She has also discovered how to 'torture' things – so I encouraged her.

18 TO 20 JUNE

Mark and Arabella Lennox-Boyd at Gresgarth

We drove north to stay with Mark and Arabella Lennox-Boyd at Gresgarth Hall, not far from Kendal. It's in Mark's constituency and they moved there fourteen years ago, a manageable gothic pile of about 1820 which, when purchased, looked gaunt and bleak but which now arises above Arabella's lake and magical gardens like a tiny Strawberry Hill fairy palace. Arabella is a life-giver, fifty-five, rather a bundle but hugely engaging and enthusiastic, with wonderful taste in plants and a feeling for gardens. Aristocratic Italian by birth, she married a Frenchman and left him, came to England and gradually drifted into garden design, taking en route a five-year course at Hammersmith Polytechnic. It's an odd marriage in a way, for she's bohemian and loves creative people. He is tall and lanky in tweeds and is a junior government minister, not at all the type who would seem to want an unconventional wife. But there's another side to him, designing complex sundials and a hydraulic machine which hoots like an owl.

The house is a monument to Eighties country-house style, having been done over by John Stefanides, with every comfort to an extreme: no fewer than three large bars of Floris soap in the bathroom and bowls of fresh fruit in the bedroom. The housekeeper and domestics were forever tidying the rooms and laying out one's pyjamas. We arrived in the midst of an event to raise money for disabled riders, so it was an evening largely spent in retreat, hiding, apart from a foray for a fork supper. The other guest was June Ogilvy, the estranged wife of Jamie, a thin, gawky woman in her late fifties with a nose like an eagle's beak. Everyone was tired.

On Saturday we went on a huge garden tour, for it is an enormously elaborate garden with four gardeners. The planting is a miracle of taste: nodding blues into pinks and purples, lots of clipped box and standard trees and every kind of prettiness. There was a lunch party for twelve: Fortune Stanley in her late sixties, a bit of a *grande dame*; the Sharps, he the National Trust rep.; John Martin, one of the Young Fogeys but now middle aged, to whom nothing seems to be right any more; and James Miller of Sotheby's and his wife.

In the evening we went over to Hugh and Grania Cavendish at Holker Hall, a large, menacing pseudo-Elizabethan pile but with wonderful gardens and a new cascade, which was very beautiful. Hugh, dark-haired and saturnine, was a Commissioner of English Heritage. I asked him whether or not Jocelyn Stevens would survive there. Jocelyn was so tactless and the whole drive was to reform and cage in expense, to re-think conservation and preservation. He had got the job because everyone else had turned it down. They had had to extend Edward Montagu for six months because they couldn't get anybody. What a ghastly job!

We arrived back late and slept late. On Sunday it was *en famille* and quiet and we sauntered around the garden, noting details. This is a paradise of flowers and Arabella is giving us two hundred 'Princess Irene' orange tulips. This garden had a terrific impact on me. I felt that ours lacked blossom and roses and decided to change the Small

Orchard and to plant Arabella's tulips around the topiary, edge the path with box and enlarge the beds. We drove home after lunch and sat in the Temple with a glass and mused on our own creation, which is so very different. Gradually we got a balance. After all, we hadn't got a large chequebook or four gardeners.

25 JUNE

Exit the Queen Mother?

The *Daily Telegraph* rang and asked me to write on the Queen Mother and gardening. I said why this rush on her? I've had so many requests of this kind lately. Reply: medical opinion is that her months are numbered.

28 JUNE

Highrove revisited

We left at 4.30 p.m. and drove to Highgrove. This was an event for the NCCPG [National Council for the Conservation of Plants and Gardens, now called Plant Heritage], at which I'd agreed to give the speech. Drinks were served in the open outside the front door. It was a gathering less of gardeners than of money: the Bankses, Arabella Lennox-Boyd, the young Ashbrooks, Hornbys, Carnarvons, Comptons, Lane Foxes, etc. The garden, I thought, looked overgrown and the potager was so cluttered you couldn't see the structure. My hedges and topiary, however, were being well cut by the gardeners. It's a funny garden, the result of too many people being involved in it. There are still unresolved areas and it lacks a coherent statement.

6 JULY

A visit to the begetters of Hortus

We left at 10.45 a.m. for lunch at a hotel near Presteigne with David Wheeler, the founder and editor of the literary garden magazine *Hortus,* and Simon Dorrell. What were billed as the star guests turned out to be two American academics. She looked a bit like an old school-marm and from her conversation didn't seem to know about anything other than Gertrude Jekyll. He was a silent Arts and Crafts man. Mercifully, the occasion was enlivened by Mirabel Osler and another art-historical couple. David is a sweet, bright-eyed man, rather large in build, a somewhat old-fashioned type, gentle by nature and with a beguiling openness about him. Simon is in his early thirties, not devoid of talent as a painter and graphic artist but he hasn't found his direction yet. He is small, spare of build and tends to dress like a soldier on safari. Like David, he is pleasant of disposition.

How isolated this Arcadia seems in such a remote Welsh valley, the garden with its incipient box hedges and sprouting yew arranged in avenues, and *allées* with a great deal of ornament fudged up on the cheap out of drainpipes. The setting, however, was beatific against the hills of Wales.

Meanwhile, in London the Queen Mother Gates were unveiled in Hyde Park while a ton of rose petals descended from the skies. They look marvellous! I'm so glad that I suggested Giuseppe Lund to Prince Michael.

During the summer I was busy working on a radio series about what had happened to our historic towns and cities.

8 JULY

Recording Ludlow for Radio 4

We breakfasted at 7.30 a.m. and I did my first interview with the rector of the parish church at 8.15 a.m. Then followed a crammed morning with fixed or tucked-in interviews in a variety of locations: up to a medieval hall in a wool shop, down into a Tudor cellar in a bookshop, seeing the planning officer, discovering a priest's window in the Citizens' Advice Bureau, not to forget meeting the mayor. A lot of adrenalin had to flow. Martin Buckley's assistant, a nice girl called Morag, turned up. This was a really hard-working day and I felt flaked out when I got home. The star event was 40 Broad Street, a grand house with unbelievable layers back, eighteenth into seventeenth centuries and then back further to the Elizabethan period and the Middle Ages. The house had belonged to the Palmers' Guild and a dried palm turned up in the roof. Martin is droll and laid back, a very sweet-natured thirty-seven-year-old with a beguiling quality and a boyish face from which stare out blue-grey eyes. But he has real warmth and a delight in both people and things. He charmingly presented me with a book of A.E. Houseman poems.

Gianni had purchased a palazzo in Miami and turned to me once again for ideas for his garden.

16 JULY

Versace's Miami garden and the rural church crisis

I spent all day on the Versace Miami courtyard garden. It is difficult to do much more than mount up ideas for it, so I've suggested mosaics, statues, a grotto and a cascade. In the evening we went to dinner with Esmond and Susie Bulmer at Poston. The house was a hunting lodge by Sir William Chambers but transformed by them into a hilltop *trianon* with panoramic views over the Herefordshire landscape. I gave them advice as to where they should place statues in the garden. They're a bonus and we never stopped talking, just about everything. Edward had been offered English Heritage but turned it down. We seem to be of a mind on most things and he agreed with me that the real crisis on that agenda was rural churches and not houses any more. Houses had run their course. The Church of England is now institutionalising dissent in the form of 'flying bishops'.

19 JULY

The race for the National Portrait Gallery

Charles Saumarez Smith rang me about his application for the directorship of the National Portrait Gallery. His biggest disadvantage is not having handled pictures or portraits. He has much going for him in an otherwise very thin field. Was it ever anything else? If Nicholas Penny put in for it he'd probably get it, Giles Waterfield unlikely and Julius Bryant is happy where he is. Malcolm Rogers, the Deputy Director, is hungry for it but John Hayes doesn't like him and I feel very uncertain. No, Charles Saumarez Smith stands a good chance indeed and he'd do it splendidly.

22 JULY

The V&A en fête

We went to the V&A for the fortieth wedding anniversary of Hugh and Marion Sassoon. It was kind of them to ask us and I was touched that the Museum had put on display the wonderful Elizabethan miniatures that his mother had bequeathed. It was the V&A as I would like to remember it. What a stunning evening! The flowers alone must have cost £20,000. Beneath the great dome we were seemingly hedged in by box nine feet high, an explosion of flowers in the centre of each side. As we entered the Museum there was an urn sited between the two great pillars of flowers spiralling to the ceiling and, on what in daytime serves as the information desk, there was another enormous urn with flowers ascending heavenwards. The tables were covered with claret-coloured tablecloths, each named after a herb, with a little pot of whatever it was placed at the centre.

The event began with drinks in the Pirelli Garden quadrangle, a marvellous space: I groaned to think of the battles and defamation I had endured in order to achieve it. There were quite a lot of people we knew: Dominique de Borchgrave, Vanessa Bernstein (now broken up from Alex), the Oliver Millars, the Geoffrey de Bellaigues and Diane Lever. The dinner was superb. I was happily placed between Marion's sister and that ancient television announcer Mary Malcolm. The only thing I could have done without was the cabaret, which went on far too long and too late. I had Reresby Sitwell huffing and puffing behind me. We got away at midnight.

26 JULY TO 4 AUGUST

Czechoslovakia in the aftermath

We got to the airport and found Roger White, the lecturer for what was to be a tour of Bohemian and Moravian country houses. There were fourteen of us in all, forming what seemed to be a perfectly good *galère*: an Australian couple; two American ladies, one of whom was hooked on Czechoslovakia; a weedy man; and a sprinkling of merry widows. The Czech guide who met us had limited English. Off we set on a bus through the rolling countryside affording distant views, rather beautiful and wooded with birch, larch and fir trees. We headed towards Brno, then down and onwards in the direction of Vienna. As we were making good time, there was a detour to see a monastery by Santini at Zeliv, a gothic and baroque cake with an overlay of gilt and fantasy. The actual monastery is now a psychiatric hospital for children. Inside there was a remarkable baroque emblematic ceiling dated 1745, although its iconography could have been 1645, a *mélange* of biblical scenes connected with food and allegorical *imprese* more typical of the seventeenth than the eighteenth century. The re-Catholicisation of the country in the aftermath of the Thirty Years War had stopped the intellectual clock.

The hotel at Jaroměřice was pure 1950s, more like a barrack or a school. There was no bath mat or shower curtain and a loo which was flushed by means of pulling a chain from an ariel cistern. The shower was primitive and we had bunk beds. The food was awful, a meat course followed by a second meat course. This provoked a demonstration and, after a struggle, they produced rough red wine and some kiwi fruit. The waiters looked on, horrified.

27 JULY

We drove towards Vranov, struck by the revelation of seeing so many wild flowers as no chemical sprays were used. This was beautiful, undulating country until we stopped at the foot of the sharp ascent to Vranov, perched high on an outcrop of rock. This was the first of our country houses and had been subject to a 1970s restoration, which, I suppose, was better than letting the place fall down; but the cheap, unlined curtain made of poor fabric said it all. The great spectacle was the Fischer von Erlach Hall of Ancestors, a massive oval room frescoed and stuccoed with over-life-size statues of the family's ancestors, figures lifted from a costume book who seemed to either strut or loll. Although heavy beneath, there was a fairytale quality to this place. The rest of the castle was far less interesting, late eighteenth century and covered with somewhat hard and mechanical decorative painting.

A pretty drive to Telč followed, the town square of which can't have been touched since 1800, a mixture of renaissance, baroque and rococo façades in ice-cream colours: pink, pistachio, lemon, blue and ochre. There was a handsome arcade around it but there was nothing in the shops. Here again the castle was a revelation, being a monument to the reception of both the renaissance and mannerist styles, with grotesque work, arabesques and *sgraffito* decoration. Outside there were Serlian windows and a double-colonnaded loggia, while inside the rooms of parade were the quintessence of mannerist exoticism. One, depicting the Labours of Hercules, had a virtually three-dimensional stag pendant at the centre of the ceiling. On we went, through an enormous hall, the walls decorated with scenes from Petrarch's *Trionfi* and an astounding polychrome screen; then followed a large hall hung with full-lengths of the Knights of the Golden Fleece, with a compartmented ceiling in the Venetian manner in gold, silver and azure; and finally, beyond that, a room with the Four Elements as its theme.

That evening there was a slightly less gruesome dinner. Fish actually appeared and we achieved fruit for dessert.

28 JULY

Today there was a long drive to Bučovice near Brno, a small, tatty town which, however, contained one jewel within it: the castle, albeit also run down. The exterior was Serlian while the courtyard within had a triple arcade bestowing on it an unforgettable airiness at odds with the over-life-size fountain from the late 1630s in the middle. But the greatest revelation was the interior in the style of François Premier's Fontainebleau. That was unbelievable. There was nothing in the least provincial about these rooms, which were the height of international elegance and sophistication. What was called the Imperial Chamber had a frieze of three-dimensional figures, including Europa and the Emperor Charles V, all in gilded polychrome, the remainder of the surfaces being covered in grotesque work in grisaille. As a room it was so exquisite that it reminded me of the little *camera* by Correggio in the *convento* at Parma. Next came one with the ceiling decorated with hares having a banquet, hares hunting men, one as a judge, another as portrait painter! It was worth coming to Czechoslovakia just to see these two miraculous rooms.

We then drove to Austerlitz or Slavkov Castle, a gigantic crumbling late baroque pile whose exterior might look something if it was cleaned and painted. Here the interior was a dull and unending bore but the garden had good statuary and, restored, would be terrific.

Our last port of call was Náměšť nad Oslavou, another renaissance castle with a Bramante double staircase as an approach. In 1949 this had been turned into a tapestry museum, to which tapestries were brought from confiscated properties all over the country. A couple of recent large gaps on the walls were evidence of those that had been returned to their owners. There were some fine tapestries but the rooms were dull bar a final *coup de théâtre*, the Library, a beautiful, long, low room with a stuccoed and frescoed ceiling as fresh as the day it was painted. In the town there was a bridge with baroque saints across it, just like the one in Prague.

The group continues to be fine, agreeable in a very ordered and quiet way, pleasant to speak to, punctual and attentive.

29 JULY

Another day of marvels. We started by visiting the church at Jaroměřice, which was rather fine, and then the great house, a pile painted in white and terracotta to delineate all the pilasters and mouldings the owners couldn't afford. There was a new, nondescript garden incorporating old statues, and inside the place was filled with stuff removed from various other houses. There was the usual Hall of the Ancestors, this time with four spectacular chinoiserie stoves and an abundance of fine woodwork and full-length portraits. The house must have had musical connexions of some kind as someone suddenly struck up the harpsichord. Later came a ballroom, light as gossamer in shades of white, green and pink, and a *sala terreno*, a garden room painted in *trompe l'œil* with *treillage* intertwined with Morning Glory.

On we went to Dačice, a sweet property, much smaller in scale, Biedermeier in style and Viennese in feeling. It had a charm and a purity stemming from the abstract geometry that informed the house both within and without. Everywhere there was an appealing modesty: even the Ballroom was small, with mirror doors and a marquetry floor. All it lacked was the dancers.

On then to Jindřichův Hradec, a house that had only just opened. Here we witnessed the Renaissance in full flood in Central Europe. The architecture was again Serlian and the rooms reminded me of those at Sabbioneta with their compartmented painted ceilings. There was, in addition, a Biedermeier part, all muslin and simplicity, and a medieval one with a room with a complete mid-fourteenth-century cycle of the story of Saint George and then, as a finale, a renaissance rotunda in the middle of a garden with its arcades painted white and deep pink. The interior of the rotunda was white and gold: stunning but, I fear, all wrong. It had once been a music house, the musicians playing below and the music coming up through the floor to those above.

We then stopped at Třeboň, which was another jewel of a town, with a square in marshmallow colours, a church with pillars down the centre of the nave and a huge Serlian *Schloss* in which Dr John Dee had resided for some years. We arrived at České Budějovice, where the hotel was much better, having had another day of surprises.

30 JULY

We began with the castle of Čzeský Krumlov, which, although much had already been done to it, was still in restoration. This was another mass of *sgraffito* and sixteenth-century painted decoration but much of it quite crude. There were three hundred rooms in this castle and as the restoration was recent, it was far better done. We saw a mid-seventeenth-century Roman state coach, quite startling, some stunning mirrors and superb furniture. But overall it was rambling and of no great architectural merit. There was an extraordinary set of bridges leading over a ravine to the garden, a large, abandoned rectangular plot with fine urns, vases and figurative sculpture, along with a cascade which didn't work.

Lunch followed, after which we were left to wander in the town, which was also undergoing restoration. This was the San Gimignano of Bohemia in the making. It was absolutely delightful and the difference between the restored and unrestored houses was riveting. In a few years this place will be unrecognisable.

We went on to Kratochvíle, a restored summer villa, a *sgraffito* Serlian box standing on a rectangular island with a garden at the back surrounded by a moat. Inside there were crude frescoes from the 1580s, hunting scenes, virtues and vices and episodes from Roman history. The house seemed to owe much to French renaissance *châteaux* of the kind recorded by Du Cerceau. Here there was a brave attempt to put the garden back but it was all wrong. On the way home we stopped at Prachatice, which had the usual *sgraffito* decorated houses in the town square and a hall church with a ribbed roof. We arrived back by 6 p.m. after a long, good day, the party still holding up.

31 JULY

We set off early for Hluboká nad Vltavou and arrived too early for the promised fleet of taxis that would have wafted us up the hill, so we walked. This is Bohemia's answer to Ludwig of Bavaria, a monumental Sir Walter Scott-inspired gothic pile with deer's heads and antlers sprouting from the walls. Within, it was 'hey nonny no' time, the castle bustling with people in period costume, including our guide, who sported a velvet train. This was a Scharzenberg house and one of those repositories to which all the best furniture from the other confiscated *Schlösser* had been sent. As a consequence the furniture was really astonishing, but overall the house was sunk beneath its florid and, at times, gloomy, heavy, panelled interior. As we entered one room, boys in eighteenth-century hunting attire sounded horns, which, I confess, had a certain charm. The stars of this place were the gothic Winter Garden, together with the quite bizarre veranda and balconies at the rear of the house, all complex ironwork tracery in the gothic style. In the stables there was a good collection of Bohemian medieval art and a mediocre one of Dutch seventeenth-century painting.

Thence to Červená Lhota for a convivial early lunch, with the usual piles of potatoes with everything. Here we only glimpsed the outside of the house, small, pretty and pink set on an island in the middle of a lake. Swiftly we moved on to Prague, visiting the Hradčany Castle area. It was a bad idea to come here on a Saturday as there were mobs of people; but how it has all changed since when I was last here in 1966, when all was decay and the balconies were collapsing onto the street! Now restored and recently painted houses lifted the whole scene. Our Czech guide was charming and useless, taking us to the cathedral when it was shut. The great hall of the royal palace was magnificent and I found myself incredibly moved to be in the room in which the famous Defenestration of Prague had actually taken place, remembering the terrible consequences of that for the whole of Europe in the Thirty Years War.

In Prague the hotel, the Ambassador, spruced up with white paint, bore some resemblance to what would normally be expected in the West.

1 AUGUST

We left on foot to pick up the bus in the great square to take us to a country house by Santini called Karlova Korona, that is, Charles VI's crown, built in the 1720s. It consists of a rotunda with three projecting square wings. This house, along with fourteen others, had been handed back to Prince Kinsky. The inside had been gutted by fire in 1943 and restored as a picture gallery, but that had now been replaced by Kinsky portraits and *bric à brac* of no great moment.

On to Kačina for an omelette lunch, and then up the drive of yet another astounding house, this time *c.*1810–20, in the neoclassical style. Its scale was palatial, with a soaring portico, colonnades and pavilions, one of which housed the library, a circular room with vast columns supporting a gigantic dome, the books, this time, still there. But mice were scampering everywhere and birds fluttering around within, to which were added omnipresent damp and decay. This must once have been a neoclassical dream, the ceilings and walls of its huge rooms etched with garlands of flowers and superb marquetry floors everywhere. What a house! But, alas, it was now reduced to being an agricultural museum, its contents dispersed all over Czechoslovakia. As we left, I ran round to look at the back. Yes, there was evidence of restoration but great swathes of the building were on the point of collapsing, the plasterwork everywhere falling in heaps on the ground.

At Sedlec we failed to get in to the monastic church, which is now a tobacco factory, but we did see the repulsive Ossuary, a macabre Hammer film set with chandeliers, obelisks and coats of arms composed of human bones. Moving on to Kutná Hora, we saw the glorious cathedral with its unique gothic ribbing and unusual late mannerist altars and confessionals. Then followed a walk through the town, past the Jesuit college with its terrace of gesticulating saints and angels. Returning to Prague, we took in the Church of the Sacred Heart, 1920s, very fine and unusual; but by then a number of the group showed signs of flagging.

2 AUGUST

Suddenly an aura of disappointment set in. I've always thought that such tours work for seven or eight days but then people's failings open up a divide. However, off we set for Horin, where we expected Princess Lobkowicz to meet us; but there was no sign of her. This was the most ravishing house, baroque into rococo but now a wreck. There was a *cour d'honneur* with four pavilions around it but it was overgrown with weeds, grass and assorted undergrowth. The glass in the windows had been smashed, the plasterwork was flaking and rising damp was visible. The roof had been patched up with cheap asphalt tiles, the relics of a fleeting attempt to turn it into a hotel. There we stood for three quarters of an hour in the hot sun while frantic calls were made. Of course, the Princess had forgotten.

So we went to the top of the nearby hill to Mělník, another Lobkowicz house. Still no sign of her, so we had coffee and studied the shop, after which we walked through a series of upstairs rooms hideously painted and set-dressed in a manner that was nonsensical. Then, suddenly, she appeared, cursing the shop assistants, and so back to Horin we went.

This turned out to be the highlight of the day, for inside we found a great suite of rococo rooms of the highest quality, utterly ravishing. Somehow they had survived, just, their walls pale rose, blue and lemon and white cartouches framing *capricci* and swagged garlands of flowers. This was both a faery paradise and a tragedy. Beyond these marvels lay the library and the bedroom, but minus their floors, the doors ripped in half and dry rot everywhere, along with dust, dirt, damp and chaos. This place had been reduced to a ruin and the upstairs was the same. God knows how the Princess will ever put it back. But she's a tough Swiss banker, entirely devoid of charm.

We returned to Mělník for lunch, which was no good. Then the Princess explained what restitution involved. She said that she spent her time careering around state repositories identifying Lobkowicz pieces, a search in which she was aided by inventories and by carrying around a photocopier in the back of a van. What she reclaimed was then divided into three categories: items that were usable at once; those that could be quickly restored; and those which were major tasks, which went straight into store. It was difficult to see how this could ever work. But oh, those faery rooms, which, together with those at Bučovice, made up the summit of this tour! She said that she would do what she could for Horin and then leave it to the next generation.

We went on to Roudnice nad La, where another Lobkowicz was meant to greet us but never turned up, at which point tempers began to get frayed. This place was enormous, as big as Buckingham Palace or Blenheim; but unlike them, it was a baroque morgue, a never-ending, characterless barrack, now a school for military music. Inside, the rooms had been chopped up into cubicles. This was deeply depressing and I couldn't see the point of restoring it. However, an American lady then appeared and said that they were raising funds for it to be a centre for Central European Studies. I'll be amazed if they achieve it.

3 AUGUST

A cripplingly hot day, the temperature soaring into the nineties. Off we went to Veltrusy, which had somehow survived its treatment at the hands of the State and was in fact a magical place, comprising a large garden pavilion, a rotunda with wings. Inside there were delightful, tiny rococo rooms, including a chinoiserie one. The grounds were very extensive, with a scattering of buildings erected in the 1780s for an English-style park. There was a gothic temple dedicated to horticulturalists, which had been badly smashed up, a Doric Temple, an Egyptian bridge and a gothic mill in the manner of Batty Langley. We lunched here, which involved an interminable wait of three quarters of an hour for a plate of salami. At this point tempers again began to fray. Back we went, stopping at Troja, a horrendously restored house, really ghastly, the garden small with modern lighting (some like lamp-posts), dahlias and roses, all wrong. Within, what had once been a beautiful house with a fine ceiling had been ruined by restoration.

4 AUGUST

We left the hotel early on what was our last day. There was a very long drive to Krásný Dvůr, which seemed rather ridiculous on our last morning, but this was redeemed by what turned out to be an incredibly elegant house that had belonged to the Czernins. It was a summer villa, small in scale, painted a strange orange-ochre on the outside. Inside it was a suite of airy rooms with filmy voile curtains, scrubbed parquetry floors, each room painted in pale, pretty colours, the walls framed by floral borders. Light poured in through the windows onto the charming Empire furniture. It was surrounded by a large park in the English style with a pavilion to Goethe, a fantastic gothic cathedral, a Chinese kiosk and a gloriette. The water had vanished from a garden that they were trying to restore. We were nearly late for the plane and arrived back at The Laskett at about 8.30 p.m.

12 AUGUST

And so back to work

I typed, edited and posted two more chapters of *The Story of Britain*, which means that twenty-four in all have been written, covering the period to 1485. What a relief! But I have to forge on down to the present day feeling that I mustn't exceed more than six to eight chapters a century, which means that the book will be about 180,000 words long. In the afternoon I cut a large section of the Orchard hedge while Robin started on that around the Hilliard Garden. At last the garden begins to look like something again.

17 AUGUST

Into our Bohemian period

Inspired by our Bohemia tour, we arranged for Mike Jones to come and paint the urns in the Hilliard Garden white; he then went on to paint more and more parts of the reconstituted garden ornaments cinnamon. Somehow this had the effect of pulling the garden together, so we went on doing more and more: the Shakespeare Urn, the Beaton Bridge, the ER Column. We then decided to paint the west front of the house deep yellow and apply blue trellis to it.

22 AUGUST

Arnold Goodman is eighty

Now this was an event. There must have been three hundred guests in a huge white tent and a forest of round tables. What a tribute to him: people returning from abroad just to be there and lots more who'd travelled up from the country. It began with a reception in the hall of Lincoln's Inn, full of masses of people one knew, too many of them looking much older, including ourselves! Still, it was a great catch-up. Our table was near Arnold's and had an odd mixture: John and Valerie Profumo; Asa and Susan Briggs; Vanessa Bernstein; the Master of University College, Oxford, Arnold's successor (Julia couldn't stand him); and a businessman with his partner. The speeches were curiously lacklustre, Ted Heath claiming Arnold for the Tory Party. The best, if too long, was by his rabbi, and that was touching: it was good to see a man put his faith at the centre. However, it was a most loving evening for someone who has always been generous and big-hearted to us for so very long.

23 AUGUST

I am fifty-eight

I had a happy fifty-eighth birthday, with the usual bottle of champagne sitting in the Temple. I don't feel too much about age. Sometimes I look at photographs and think 'Gosh, I look like an old gent', and then in others I look forty-five. But there's no going back and here I am in very reasonable nick, still excited about new things, still learning, still refusing to be typecast. I don't want the intrigue, the push and hurly-burly of yore. This has been an odd year. There was a very good end to 1992 and then disasters: a virus, not being paid and worrying over work. But it all picked up and I'm on course again. I sometimes think that I could do one more big public thing and feel angry at the preferment of others but, *laus Deo*, it soon passes and I think how lucky I am, the tranquillity and beauty of so much of my life. Always hold that in mind, together with a joy in people and in things. God has been more than kind to me.

24 AUGUST

The return of the Church

David Hutt's birthday and another lovely day but with a nip in the air. These two birthdays, falling one after the other and so often passed together, signal autumn. The leaves are turning early this year, those on the beech and walnut trees are already crumpled. In the morning I wrote an article on Harvest Festivals for *Country Life*. This, I'm afraid, took me back to the state of the Church of England, which David and I spent our time discussing on a long country walk in the afternoon. I do hope that Affirming Catholicism continues to grow, and indeed takes off, and includes a real journal of debate and not an Anglo-Catholic *Daily Mail*. David has been such a good influence on me and I'm grateful to him for my 'return to the Church'. It has seen me through and given me reconciliation with God, people and myself, which, if I had not reached, would have led me towards becoming a joyless old gent. It has given me both a discipline and also a radiance towards which to strive. It has also placed things in a perspective. *Laus Deo.*

Grateful for any gainful employment that might come my way in the aftermath of Olympia & York having to sell off the Canary Wharf development, for which I had been the consultant, I was relieved when a request arrived asking whether I might organise a major exhibition in Memphis, Tennessee.

6 TO 10 SEPTEMBER

Memphis, Napoleon, Gloriana and Elvis

6 SEPTEMBER

Almost all day on a plane to Cincinnati, where we changed for Memphis. It was a comfortable flight, during which I worked on the chapter entitled 'Reformation' for *The Story of Britain*. We arrived at Memphis and were met by Glen Campbell, the logistical maestro of what was billed as 'Wonders'. He was a casually dressed, big-built man with thick glasses who's into horses. We fell into bed at 2.30 a.m. English time and slept eleven hours.

7 SEPTEMBER

We met Glen at 10 a.m. and went over to the Cook Convention Center, with an aircraft hangar of an exhibition hall. The exhibitions are targeted at a non-art-based public, the current one being on Napoleon. The space was terrific, oodles of room for a bistro, shop, cloakrooms and a concourse area outside the exhibition itself. Up the escalator we went, plugging ourselves in to the sound guide, which we followed the whole way round. It was good – very good, I thought, telling a vivid story and making you look at all the key exhibits. Where it failed was in making the visitor see beyond them. The quality and finish of the installation was high and some of it was brilliant, the two main galleries in particular. Other rooms were too much all the same size, with painted walls and no use of pattern or texture. And it also cried out for more exhibits, as there was far too much empty space. Whenever textiles appeared, the low light levels rendered the area dull. However, I could go along with this. It was professional and I noticed in particular that the clothes were exquisitely mounted.

We then went to lunch at the Dixon Gallery, where we were given an alfresco platter by John Buchanan and his wife, Lucy. This was a small gallery in a private house with a very good garden. Afterwards it was back to the Center, where we were filled in on the background to the exhibition, which involved a lot of city politics and pizzazz. I don't have any trouble with the theatricality, which stems from any exhibition having to be very audience- and public-oriented. It is their show, Glen said, and not an art historian's trip. However, I wouldn't want to get caught up in city politics. In the evening we were taken to a bistro for a rather indifferent dinner.

8 SEPTEMBER

I went to their think-tank meeting. Twyla, the marketing lady, expanded at length on the importance of women in the cultural decision-making process of the family. The plan had been to let her and Jack, the public relations man, have their run, but she went straight in to Elizabeth I. That was lucky because we did also kick around Royalty and Empire for a bit. Elizabeth, however, swept all before it, although I emphasised the problems involved resulting from panel paintings and the fact that they wanted to borrow items for a whole year, from March to March, during months when houses were open to the public. However some electricity was engendered.

I then went with Glen and Jack to the Brooks Museum, set in a beautiful park. The museum was dead and the Director failed to appear, which, as he'd been told I was coming, can only be described as rude. Back we went to the hotel, getting us off any evening commitment. We had a quiet dinner and went to bed early.

9 SEPTEMBER

Over to the Center again, this time to 'talk turkey'. What they initially offered was derisory, bearing in mind that it would be three years' work involving choosing the exhibits, negotiating the loans, writing the catalogue, editing the sound guide and assisting with the public relations and education programme. They then moved the amount offered dramatically upwards . . .

After lunch we went to Elvis Presley's Graceland, a quite weird experience. This is a really nice colonial-style mansion done over with a mind-blowing vulgarity, using a lot of mirror glass and gold paint. It was really tacky. The Meditation Garden outside, with wreath-bespattered tombs, was creepy. Opposite there was a large support area with car parks and souvenir shops, all of which I wouldn't have missed.

10 SEPTEMBER

Our twenty-second wedding anniversary, engendering thoughts of gratitude, love and delight flooding through every precious year we've had together. How lucky we are! Our hosts were sweet and presented us with Napoleon glasses, mugs and jackets. We then 'talked turkey' again . . . And that wrapped it up.

The idea of an exhibition on Elizabeth I was to ebb and flow in my life throughout the 1990s. This one never happened and, as the reader will discover, resurfaced with the National Maritime Museum, for which I did a comprehensive treatment. This died too, eventually coming to life under the aegis of Dr David Starkey in 2003, the four hundredth anniversary of her death.

20 SEPTEMBER

The National Portrait Gallery saga

Charles Saumarez Smith rang. It seems that there were only five candidates for the directorship, so I'm not surprised that it's a straight fight between him and Malcolm Rogers. Charles sensed that the Trustees were not wanting a John Hayes clone but a breath of fresh air. On 4 October he faces the whole Board. I would feel that minds were already made up. I do hope that it's him.

30 SEPTEMBER

The restoration of the Privy Garden at Hampton Court

Most of the day was spent at Hampton Court seeing the proposals to restore William III's Privy Garden. About thirty of us in all gathered in William III's Banqueting House, a mix of locals and garden historians, Mavis Batey, Ted Fawcett, Brian Dix, David Jacques, etc., together with the Palace gang. There was a beautiful, clear blue sky and sun when we went to look at what the archaeological excavation had revealed. This is a wonderful project. It was fascinating to see the plinths for the statues unearthed, still intact, as well as the original trenches preserving the pattern of the parterre. The foundations of the steps were uncovered too and, surprisingly, much more was revealed of both the Tudor and Caroline gardens than I thought possible. After lunch in the Banqueting House we went to a nursery in the Home Park, where box plants had been laid out in rows so that a decision could be reached as to which variety should be used. The decision was a variety called Old Dutch. A sixteenth of the parterre was planted here and it did, I confess, look dull; but what I couldn't get over was the fact that the containing parterre box edging was kept to only about 4 by 3 inches.

1 OCTOBER

What is Quality?

Clive Aslet, the editor of *Country Life*, gave a lunch at the Savoy to discuss Quality. Others gathered around the table were Lucy Lambton, Lucia van der Post, Alastair McAlpine and Melanie Cable-Alexander. This was a fast moving and muddled affair, Clive wishing us to focus on which luxury goods had held their own during the recession, citing panama hats. I said, 'Rubbish, that's fashion.' The batting was fast and furious but what everyone was interested in was Quality of Life: fresh food, fresh air, new technological advances like the fax machine, which made life easier. Quality also resided in materials like stone or linen. We all had to say what was the most covetable item we had bought of late. I said my Versace black leather blouson. Lucy Lambton is sometimes a bit of a nitwit, certainly wayward and eccentric. Alastair was extolling the virtues of a cold bath every morning on doctor's orders. I could see the logic of that as he certainly looked thinner and was less frantic in the eye.

3 OCTOBER

The National Portrait Gallery in retrospect

Patricia Wheatley came from the BBC to do an interview with me on the National Portrait Gallery. It took from 9 a.m. to 2 p.m. to do it all, including the tracking shots. I hope she got what she wanted. Turning over the pages from the scrapbooks from those years, with me in late Sixties mod-gear or fancy dress, I did seem a bit over the top. But it did all work at the time.

6 OCTOBER

A new Director for the NPG

Charles Saumarez Smith rang me early. He's been offered the NPG and I'm really delighted for him. He'll be terrific. Someone, however, has leaked this to the *Telegraph*, saying that it was a disgrace that after waiting nineteen years in the wings Malcolm Rogers didn't get it.

8 OCTOBER

David Linley marries

We walked to St Margaret's. The weather had held and there were batteries of people looking on, together with a small army of photographers opposite the west door standing on a forest of steps and boxes. The entrance was garlanded with autumn leaves and flowers. We were very well placed halfway down the south aisle. Over the way were Beatrix Miller, Diane Nutting and the Sainsburys, with Roddy Llewellyn behind them. There was quite a King's Road swing to it, not at all the embalmed court. The great thing was the hats, which were of two kinds, the first very broad-brimmed, with vast bows and feathers piled into shoulder-width brims, and the second were what Julia called '*directoire*', that is, like truncated stove pipes in black velvet with feather and ribbon trimmings. Both were very pre-1914 but the effect was top heavy, worn, as they mostly were, with tiny suits with very short skirts. The flowers in the church were unexceptional. A small chamber orchestra played Handel et al. but the music wasn't that good either. The Royal Family are so small that you couldn't see them when they entered and there were a great many notable absences: Prince Charles, the Duke of Edinburgh and the Yorks. Prince Edward read the lesson well, in the manner of *Hamlet*. The bride had been got at by the image-makers and what genuine freshness she had had been obliterated beneath layers of make-up, which made her look old. Her hair was piled up into a chignon held in by a tiara. It was a very simple dress with a veil but not worn covering the face. I could hardly hear what she said, which was at least demure, but David Linley spoke well and clearly.

I'd forgotten how short the wedding service was. It was over in a trice and we were out, strolling across St James's Park to the Palace, where there was the usual fracas alleviated by champagne and eats. It was such a struggle to get up the stairs that we thought it was the reception line holding us up: but no. It was just as much a fight all the way to the Throne Room and back, saying hello to those we could. We were very pleased to see the Queen Mother, now very old and slight, in a ghastly apricot outfit. She was so pleased to see us and this time almost kissed Julia, and remembered to a fault the 1969 Elizabethan exhibition at the Tate, the 1983 miniature exhibition at the V&A, etc. And she obviously loves peering at my books, although Alastair Aird said that her eyes weren't much good now. We said hello to William Tallon who props up the Clarence House household, once a young page but now a square middle-aged man. We didn't stay that long and were on the road by 6.30 p.m.

10 OCTOBER

Sour grapes

The *Sunday Times* carried a large piece on the National Portrait Gallery, with Oliver Millar breaking the Trustee ranks and saying that Charles Saumarez Smith was the wrong appointment. That was really awful, followed by more quotes from John Harris saying that if Charles had been a gentleman he'd have withdrawn! I rang Charles to cheer him up.

I'd been asked to give a garden lecture to the Garden Club of Munich.

11 TO 14 OCTOBER

Munich

The flight to Munich was straightforward and we made our way to the Hotel an der Oper, where we were picked up by Axel von Saldern and driven to their house at Socking, a commodious semi-detached in a 'White Heights' suburb. I didn't catch the names of any of the four guests at dinner that evening: the two other couples were East German aristocrats and belonged to the forty thousand people who hadn't had their confiscated property returned. Those who did were the ones whose property had been taken by the GDR, whereas theirs had been taken from them by the Russians in 1945. One of them described how his father had managed to get the Dutch paintings out of the East in time to Hamburg and how the rest of the contents of the castle had been piled up in the courtyard and burnt by the Russians, who said that people must not see how capitalists had lived. The other couple knew that their pictures, including the family portraits, were now in a gallery in Leipzig. They were cultured, interesting people and there was much talk of the Thurn and Taxis sale, which consisted, they said, of throw-outs from the guest bedrooms. They had a huge admiration of British interior decoration and despised above all the Biedermeier. These people were aristocratic and international, with family connexions stretching across Central Europe.

12 OCTOBER

In the morning we visited the Residenz. It was good to see the *Schatzkammer*, with old favourites like Anne of Bohemia's crown and the Garter jewels of Frederick, Elector Palatine. We ate *Apfelstrudel* in a café and were picked up by Axel at 1 p.m. Today was the lecture day so the Garden Club of Bavaria ladies arrived, all well dressed, educated and fluent in English. Maria was organised so it all went like clockwork. I talked from 3 to 4 p.m., then tea and cakes followed until about 5 p.m. I gave them my lecture on formal gardens, which, I think, was a great success. Someone remarked that if a German had given it there would have been no enthusiasm, no humour and no jokes. We were taken for an early dinner at a restaurant by the lake in which Ludwig II drowned himself. It is quite difficult to escape meat, dumplings and cream.

13 OCTOBER

It turned out to be a sunny autumn day with a golden light animating the ochres, yellows and reds of the trees. We took the underground to Starnberg, where Axel and Maria picked us up and, after some erratic map-reading, we reached Neuschwanstein. Below the castle the roads were jammed with buses and cars. There was a long queue to get tickets and then we had to queue again under 'language' to get in. But it was worth all of that, for this is a place of total fantasy that has survived untouched since Ludwig left it. How I'd love to see a Wagner opera done in this way! I can't say that I warmed to mid-nineteenth-century Romanesque with all mod cons, but it had a curious fascination.

We lunched en route to Linderhof, driving past lakes and mountains and arriving just in time. Now Linderhof was quite something: not the interior, which was of a mind-boggling vulgarity, but the setting of this small palace and garden into the landscape. With autumn colour, this was a place of rare perfection, a formal garden of great simplicity, its axis on one side running up a mountain to a *treillage* pavilion and, on the other, to Bramantesque flights of steps leading to a gloriette silhouetted against a magical backdrop. The contrast between art and untamed nature was bold, and especially so with all the golden and russet tints of the hornbeam catching the light.

It was so kind of Axel and Maria to take us. We hugged them goodbye and felt that they were real friends. We wished that we had known them earlier, but life has its patterns and I feel sure that this was meant to happen just now.

14 OCTOBER

A rainy day but nonetheless we took the subway to Rotkreuzplatz and then walked to Nymphenburg, a very long way in the rain. By the time we got there we were soaked. We went round the palace, which was really rather empty, although it had some striking view paintings, both of it and of other palace gardens. We lunched in the Palm House and then embarked on an enormous walk to the Hermitage, the Pagodenburg, the Cascade and the Badenburg, all of which were closed, and thence to the Amalienburg, mercifully open. Now I was really delighted to see this again. It is one of the great miracles of interior decoration. I know of nothing finer, a vision of shimmering silver, pale blue and yellow. Everything about it is perfect and we had it to ourselves so that we were able to linger and drink in every detail, from the tiles in the kitchen to the alcoves for the dogs. There was delight wherever the eye fell. The walk had been through the gardens as re-laid out by Joseph von Sockel in the early nineteenth century, very beautiful with autumn tints in gold, auburn and russet lit up whenever the sun appeared. We had a finale in the coach museum with its glorious array of sledges and a whole battery of mad Ludwig's transportation, quite OTT.

16 OCTOBER

The appointment of Charles Saumarez Smith was announced in *The Times*, which has given much pleasure. Charles will be splendid and I wish him luck.

27 OCTOBER

The little princes on the train

I took the train to London and sat reading horrendously badly edited proofs while two pale-faced little boys in jackets and pullovers trotted by with a courtier type behind them. They looked vaguely familiar. On getting off the train at Paddington and seeing the Princess of

Wales, I realised why! She had much make-up around the eyes, short hair and was wearing a rather 1940s-looking grey suit.

28 OCTOBER

Jean Muir

I took Jean Muir to dinner at the Garrick Club, which was jammed. She was very pleased with herself and rather vain, I thought! She's ambitious still but now off the V&A as a Trustee and was complaining about Robert Armstrong. She was also opining about the piece on Elizabeth Esteve-Coll in the *Daily Telegraph*, which I in fact had read very carefully and thought was a fair judgement: six years into the job and she's still not on top of it. Jean is now president of the Royal Designers for Industry award and wants to raise its profile: but the problem is how, because the members see it as an honour bestowed and certainly not as a commitment to doing anything. We thrashed around on the clouded greatness of Britain and its talent and we joined in a universal bashing of this awful government. Jean was, as always, in navy blue, dress, coat, scarf, the lot, a little elf really, with straight hair tucked behind her ears, her eyes circled with kohl and her lips outlined in brown. Her face is now quite lined. But she's an enthusiast and a giver. She did keep saying how wonderful the television films about her were (honestly, they really weren't). I told her that she should have had one that lasted fifty minutes, but I don't think that that went down very well. She tried to hijack me to a jazz club – but no way.

30 TO 31 OCTOBER

The restoration of Stowe

I took the 10.07 train from Marylebone to Aylesbury, where Edward Tompkins met me. In the afternoon we went to see Richard Broyd at Hartwell House, converted by him into a hotel. I was surprised to see that so much of the eighteenth-century garden, as recorded in the famous view paintings, had survived: the column, the Gibbs pavilion, statues and much else. The church had been drawn into the composition as a 'ruin'. It had all been done very well.

From time to time Edward would come out with extraordinary accounts of his past, of being captured by the Germans and riding round next to Rommel in a battle, and then his incredible escape through Italy. Gill is the more old-fashioned of the two, a Benson by birth with a consequent grand rather Edwardian upbringing with governesses. Girls were 'gels', as it were.

On Sunday afternoon we drove over to Stowe, where Edward is the chairman of the appeal to restore the famous gardens. What an astounding house, the work of Kent and Adam, ravishing and very grand, and what a tragedy that it all went! The house is Central European in scale and much else about it reminded me of that part of Europe, the crumbling stone along with the insensitive modern structures dotted pell-mell around it. The scale is simply overwhelming in the grounds too, the distances between one part and another huge. Where parts had been restored it was a great transformation, the removal of the undergrowth and the pruning of trees re-opening up vistas. The most complete work that had been done was around the Temple of British Worthies. Everywhere I was conscious of a great feeling of the control of the terrain as a series of composed 'pictures', evident even on this dull, grey day.

Ambling through the great rooms of the house, it was sad to see all the evidence of the school – notices, chairs stacked, etc. – but we had to admit that, on the whole, they had been respectful of the house. William Kent's dining room is a stunner.

3 NOVEMBER

The V&A returns to haunt me

I was sent a copy of Robert Armstrong's letter to the *Telegraph* in defence of Elizabeth Esteve-Coll, with its sentence that under her directorship the place had been livelier than it had been for years. I rang up the V&A in a rage and demanded a correction. Later Robert rang and he agreed that the sentence had been a mistake and that he would correct it. He was affable and so was I. I reminded him of what I told him about the place (when he lunched with me before my departure I told him that however wonderful it was, there was an inner ineradicable canker). He said but couldn't that be changed? I said no, it was the nature of the beast – and equally why it had magic. I told him that Elizabeth must have been mad to have let the journalist near her for the day.

7 TO 10 NOVEMBER

Istanbul

7 NOVEMBER

We had an early call at 5.15 a.m., breakfasting soon after and driving to Heathrow for a smooth flight to Istanbul. This was a four-day trip special offer in the *Independent*. The group seemed a bit decrepit but they'll be OK. We decided to take every tour that was going as the only way to do it.

The Pera Palace Hotel is a time capsule: 1890s Ottoman Edwardian, face-lifted in the 1930s with cream and mirror glass. It has the smell of a run-down railway hotel. There was a large, gloomy marble central hall with tables and Turkish and Chippendale-style chairs, all pure Visconti. Every room along our passage has on the door a nameplate of someone famous who had slept there. We're quite lowly, only a boring Turkish president, while opposite it was Josephine Baker. Tough.

Our minute Turkish guide took us for a walk along the equivalent of Oxford Street, which was deserted, for we had arrived on census day. Everyone had to stay in, so we were driven through empty streets to the hotel as though the city had been decimated by the plague. It's a dirty, fascinating, meandering place. Flashes of everywhere from Palermo to Moscow sprang to mind, but cluttered and run down.

8 NOVEMBER

Leaving the hotel at 8 a.m., we went by bus to the Topkapi. I enjoyed the harem most, an extraordinary labyrinth of courtyards, galleries, marble and tiled rooms – some three hundred, of which we saw only four. What struck me most was the eighteenth-century overlay of baroque on rococo gilt mirrors and decorative painting. But it gave one an enormous insight into a lost world far beyond the endless museum displays in the rest of the palace. The kitchens were the exception, one left semi-intact with huge wooden cupboards filled with copper pots, marble tables, huge cauldrons, etc. From here the food must have fanned out to feed thousands. Most of the things were displayed in bulk with a single label, like 'Daggers XVth to XIXth century'. So it was a fearful jumble, with a lot of glitz to discount. The Marble Terrace was quite lovely with its fountains and pool. We had lunch in the cafeteria but couldn't get into Haghia Eirene and so went back to the hotel and then out for a boat trip up the Bosphorus towards the Black Sea. It was dull and overcast and the shoreline was heavily built up the whole way, but it was worth it to see the gingerbread Turkish houses, the wooden 'classical' villas and the odd palace. We were bussed back to the Covered Bazaar, one huge kaleidoscopic tourist trap, glitter, glitter all the way.

9 NOVEMBER

We left at 8.30 a.m. and sat in a traffic jam until we eventually arrived at the Hippodrome. There's still a lingering magic to the bronze coiled serpents from Delphi, the huge obelisk once clad in gold and the Egyptian one with its bas reliefs of Theodosius and his family looking down on charioteers, dancers and suppliants and on the obelisk being set in its place.

Haghia Sophia retained its wondrous, faded magic too, vast, gloomy, desolate, holiness hiding somewhere in its shell. But the grime! Grime everywhere, caked on the marble walls, pillars, floors, obscuring a tonal miracle of puce, pink, pistachio, white, bronze and gold. The sense of imperial spectacle that it once had left one speechless, the huge imperial doors, the empress floating in a gallery on high like a goddess. All that's left is a skeleton, a shell to vanished glories. Then on to the Blue Mosque, shoes off and in we went. This was so much better kept, a miracle of space, light, myriad decoration, tiles, painting, glass, carpets; a courtyard the epitome of geometric content; perfect.

Lunch was at an adequate self-service café, then it was back to the hotel and off again to the Sultan's Summer Palace on the Bosphorus.

This was 1860s French and Ottoman with bits from Bohemia, Germany, Italy and England. Bizarre that it was closer to Ludwig of Bavaria than you'd think, with everything too much: too much gold, too many chandeliers, a surfeit of decoration and everything too big. And yet it was both fascinating and really rather awful.

10 NOVEMBER

Another long day, grey, chill and rainy. We set out again at 8.30 a.m. and stopped first at the Mosque of Suleiman the Magnificent, an A1 knock-out by the great Ottoman architect Sinan. Shoes off and in we went to this very restrained, classic and beautifully proportioned building. We see Sinan's mausoleum, a stunning *tempietto* with a painted dome studded with diamonds, lined with Iznik tiles and huge covered 'hearses' in the centre. We then rushed to see Sinan's tomb nearby . . .

We moved on to St Saviour in Chora and for the first time came up against guided groups in droves yelling in Italian, French and German; but that didn't deflect from the glittering splendour of it. I remember it as a magical place and it still is, with its powerful images of Christ and the Virgin and scenes from their lives, a compositional and technical miracle. We had coffee and then off again through the rain to a carpet place, groaning and swearing that the last thing we want is a carpet. After a persuasive 'carpet cabaret' we ended up buying two, spending £600. We were all given baps and a glass of apple tea and became a commercial knock-over.

Thence we went to the Egyptian Spice Bazaar. By this time the weather was chill, murky and mucky. We sauntered up and down, buying Turkish rocket seed and looking at the pell-mell of dried herbs, fruit, spices, sponges, Turkish delight, et al. Finally, exhausted, we headed back to the hotel.

16 NOVEMBER

The Omnibus *film on the National Portrait Gallery*

I looked at the *Omnibus* film on the NPG, which I really thought was the worst arts television film I'd ever seen. It was a structureless drift, a series of disconnected impressions with nothing pulling it together. Everyone looked senile, very senile, aberrations that only the UK can produce. It was full of every cliché in the book: little kiddies learning, someone being painted, some odd flashes as to what a portrait was, but virtually all of it bad, very bad. I wish that I hadn't seen it. It was embarrassing.

17 NOVEMBER

The opening of the National Portrait Gallery extension

The day of the opening of the NPG extension. About six hundred of us were jammed into the new Twentieth-Century Galleries, which were our old offices painted white but with the addition of a chequered marble floor. The sound-bounce off that hard surface was awful but all looked clean and sharp. God knows about the twentieth century. What a mixture! There were few masterpieces: it was rather like a Royal Academy Summer Exhibition, an attempt to be 'with it' but falling short. The occasion, however, was done well, very well, with drinks and eats and a noisy military band. Everything was more or less on time and the Queen really made quite a funny speech: 'I can speak with some authority about portraits . . .' and ending with the rival attraction at the bottom of the Mall. She was moved around on a set route, Tim Clifford placing himself so as not to be missed. But what impressed me most was the thoughtfulness of asking everyone, including staff and secretaries long since gone, former members of the Office of Arts and Libraries, even the men who had hung the pictures. And, of course, there was a torrent of people I knew. Charles Saumarez Smith was there and I managed to introduce him to David Eccles and Drue Heinz, she reminding me that it was I who had introduced her to the Gallery. I saw Joan Sutherland and reminded her that she had sung *Messiah* and helped secure the great Hudson portrait of Handel all those years ago.

The evening was a smaller re-run with food. The dinner was in the top galleries, a lovely setting, round tables, plum damask tablecloths with dark red roses like shot silk with apples at the centre and guttering electric candles beneath shades. There were two hundred and forty of us scattered through the galleries. I sat between Shirley Anglesey and a painter's wife (her husband, Howard Morgan, had painted Antoinette Sibley). I saw the Angleseys go into a huddle of shock at her *placement* (we'd had a *froideur* years back) but I was determined to be absolutely charming, and stuck to it. What's the point of grinding long-past axes anyway? Brian Lang was also there, with his late Sixties hairstyle worn like a wig, and Nicholas Serota, cool and clean-cut, bristling and almost metallic. There was no conversation of any moment and the dinner went on interminably. At last I got up and said 'Hello' to Derry Drogheda, Bryan Organ and Alan Yentob. So many people that I knew and such a genuine feeling of warmth towards me, which was very touching. I only wish that the diaries for that period had been fuller.

19 DECEMBER

Into the pulpit

I got to All Saints, Margaret Street, at 10.40 a.m. and sat in David Hutt's sitting room. I was led downstairs backstage where there was a bustle of clerics, acolytes, servers, a thurifer, a crucifer, et al. A server collected and led me to a pew in the Sanctuary, next to Bishop Ambrose Weekes. Looking west, I could see what is known in theatre as a 'good house'. It was a Palestrina Mass with the works. I managed to get into the pulpit without colliding with the censer and really felt quite comfortable delivering the sermon, which made them laugh. God knows whether it meant anything to them or not. Afterwards I mingled with the congregation in the courtyard but no one really came up to me and said 'Well done' or 'I don't agree with you' (the sermon had argued for the disestablishment of the Church of England, about which, in retrospect, I'm not sure!) but they may have been intimidated – or have gone to sleep. I felt a bit sad about that, but then I was taken to the bar for a welcome drink, where there was a whirling mass of acolytes and congregation. It was by no means a church only for the upper classes: there was the usual quota of earnest aesthetic young men and bundly old ladies. The lunch afterwards was fun. I don't know how David did it. In terms of longevity I beat all the other guests, having first gone to All Saints in 1954 as an undergraduate, when, on leaving High Mass, you were assailed by evangelical demonstrations against popery in the C of E. There were eight of us, a mixed lot including Charles Williams's sister, Grizelda; a doctor from Gloucester, whose memories also stretched back to Father Kenneth Ross; and two ordinands, both of whom had a quality, especially the one in jeans and black leather with an earring, a pigtail and Doc Martens. They both seemed to bode well for the future. But I don't really know any more about the liturgical pageantry of All Saints and feel that it needs to change, longing now for a Catholic simplicity.

22 DECEMBER

Rosemary Verey and camp followers

Rosemary Verey came to lunch with her gay American gardener, Phillip Watson, and his friend Martin Maes. She looked better than she has done for a long time: older, shorter and thinner but more pert, sparkling in fact, and she was off alcohol. We went around the garden together and she was amazed at all the new ideas and changes, which was cheering, only regretting that she had not brought a camera.

Rosemary is going to do *Desert Island Discs* and is off to the West Coast of America with Christopher Lloyd. Christmas was to be with these two 'boys' at Barnsley. She seemed full of spirit and go, which I so much admire. It was good to learn that she was writing the story of Barnsley. She quite floored me when she said that the book she most wanted for Christmas was my 'Countryman's Week' collection from *Country Life*.

25 DECEMBER

Christmas Day

A very quiet Christmas Day. The church was full, about sixty-ish, I would have thought. There was an uninspired sermon about those 'out there' and us 'in here'. But it was good to be quiet together and not to overeat. So I produced pumpkin soup, smoked salmon with dill sauce followed by Stilton cheese and salad for lunch, and only two courses for dinner: old-fashioned roast chicken with bread sauce, bacon rolls, mushrooms, sprouts and roast potatoes followed by crème caramel. And champagne. We opened our presents as usual after church, which was very happy, me having lots of good soap and some books I wanted. We spoke to family on the telephone and then I suddenly sat down and began to read *The Story of Britain* from the beginning. It was such a good read! I hope well for this book if I can keep it up. We were in bed by eleven.

NEW YEAR'S EVE

Reflection

This was not a very good year, certainly not the first half of it, when I was dogged by an immovable virus and by a litany of projects that never materialised, by people who frankly treated me badly and by those who failed to pay. But recriminations are a waste of time and the debts to me must be written off. I enjoyed working with Martin Buckley on the pilot programme and I hope that we do a town series together. Julia MacRae has been a benign figure all through the year. Somehow the rapport is just right. Every call from her spurs me on to write *The Story of Britain* and I find myself at home and writing in a way I've not done before and, in spite of the agony, loving it. In the garden there have been transformations: a cinnamon colour wash on the ornaments, the new J and R parterre and the monument to beloved Muff among them. And that reminds me that our two new Maine Coon cats, Larkin and Souci, have lightened our lives.

1994

10 JANUARY

The Nutcracker

We went to *Nutcracker* at Covent Garden, which looked even more lovely after a decade, but Stephen Jefferies did a walk-through as Drosselmeyer and the *corps de ballet* seem to have taken up clog dancing. Afterwards we took Peter and Sonya Wright to the Garrick and had a happy and hilarious dinner. It was sad to hear how Anthony Russell-Roberts had had to sell Fred Ashton's house in Eye in a hurry to pay the death duties. It had to be vacated in three weeks, hence the decanting of its contents into a provincial saleroom, which was a disaster. Peter is such an agreeable and funny man. He'd been to Billy Chappell's funeral, the real end of an era. Peter revealed that he had modelled hats when he was young.

13 JANUARY

The British Library

Took a taxi to the British Library and tried to find the entrance, joining Valerie Singleton trying to do exactly the same thing. What a mess! This was a PR lunch and tour for the Spanish cultural attaché, Christopher White, David Barrie of the National Art Collections Fund and one or two others, with the Library's Chairman, Brian Lang, Michael Borrie and a few more of the home team. It really is an awful place. I don't like it, with its ugly expanses of red brick and awkward shapes, in style early 1960s built in the 1990s. If the reading rooms work and are efficient, that's all one can hope for. But it is neither beautiful nor uplifting. And what a ghastly building saga – and they are still years off finishing it, blaming the Treasury for the endless stop-start. The way of building struck me as incredibly old-fashioned compared with Broadgate or Canary Wharf. The PR Unit was in a hut and the lunch was not far off it in status, no taste, no style, no attempt by the Chairman to orchestrate conversation and make a case. Michael Borrie is sadly now agonisingly deaf, having caught mumps from one of his children, and it is so difficult to speak to him.

22 JANUARY

Lunch in Ludlow

We went to lunch in Ludlow with Mirabel Osler on a stunning winter's day. Her guests were the painter John Napper and his wife, Pauline, and Kathy Swift, an expert on books. Napper was a good mid-seventies, a big-built, intelligent if rather old-fashioned figure in a way, his pictures rooted in the 1920s and 1930s, but we liked them – her in particular. Kathy Swift was garden mad and really very intense. She's planting a huge garden, too big for her alone, I should have thought. But the food was delicious as Mirabel is a whizz as a cook: pâté, really good bread, Dover sole, potatoes, salad, a wonderful chocolate cake and good coffee. She is working on a French food book. I love her sparkle and delight in everything.

25 JANUARY

Beatrix Miller

I took Beatrix Miller out to dinner at the Garrick and we had a very funny evening. She's as evanescent as ever, lapsing into a wonderful calculated naivety from time to time. Not all the news was good: Peter Wood and Pamela Harlech had broken up, she in floods of tears; Liz Tilberis has cancer, badly it seems, and that is tragic; the Fashion Council was useless; and Tony Snowdon was not, it seems, getting the work as in some people's views he was 'difficult'. The Garrick was liberating after the San Lorenzo with Mara presiding like the Witch of Endor. Anne Scott-James was there so I said 'Hello' – rather splendid in her mid-eighties, very thin, still elegant, although a bit dazed, I thought.

26 JANUARY

The Garrick and Princess Alexandra

To the Garrick again, for lunch with Keith Jeffery, who lives now it seems entirely for pleasure and parties. There was the usual Garrick gathering, all looking old and untidy: Bevis Hillier blown up like a balloon, Robin Day, Kingsley Amis, Andreas Whittam Smith still rescuing the *Independent*. The trouble there is that they need a new editor!

At 5.15 p.m. I met Clive Aslet in the London Library and we went to have a drink with Princess Alexandra and Angus in Martin Charteris's old flat, done over in bland Tricia Guild style, all with featureless, bleached colour. We thrashed around a great deal, as one has known her for so long – on *Country Life*, Patrick Plunket, et al. The Princess obviously loved our little book on the garden. She is always so charmingly diffident, recalling how she had spent Christmas at Windsor in bed with flu one year, looking down the length of the Long Walk. Angus recalled how cross the Queen had been over Mabell, Countess of Airlie's memoirs: 'It comes to something when your Lord Chamberlain's wife publishes.' All that happened at Sandringham and poor Angus was so terrified, almost too frightened to come down to breakfast.

7 FEBRUARY

The National Trust lecture

We left The Laskett at 11.30 a.m. for London for me to give the National Trust Lecture in the Purcell Room. We arrived and I went straight to the artists' entrance and rehearsed. It was a sell-out audience. Angus Stirling introduced me handsomely and I was touched and offered congratulations to him on his knighthood on behalf of the audience and myself. Julia said that I did the lecture on the garden better than ever.

Afterwards we had dinner at Warren Davis's house in the Lavender Hill area. It was a drear terrace of 1870s houses but his had been transformed within into Victorian splendour with borders, swags and tassels. The other guests were Clive and Naomi Aslet, Alice Boyd and the Stirlings. Angus seemed worried about his imminent retirement, with only fifteen years in post for pension. It sounds tough but I can't understand everything that has been showered upon him (nor could Clive Aslet). He looked rather old and was stooping but Morar was very bouncy. Naomi, who sat next to me and who does non-fiction for Cassells, was a bonus. But the real star of the evening was Astor, the short-haired English cat.

15 FEBRUARY

Another lecture on the garden

To the Linnaean Society to give a lecture on The Laskett garden to the Garden History Society as part of their public series. Roger White arrived late. He would. It was a jam-packed house and the audience seemed mesmerised by it all: and there was prolonged applause, which went on and on, and very sweet things were said afterwards.

Then there was a dinner for six of us: Ted Fawcett, Roger White, Carol Newman, David Jacques and a large, capable lady who did public relations for the Society. It was very jolly but I could not go up the academic alley as did Jacques, who is spiky and was slamming into the restoration of William and Mary's great garden in Holland at the palace of Het Loo. I couldn't help noting how ill-dressed they were. Ted Fawcett was OK but Roger was in cords and Jacques in a woolly. I would never dream of turning up other than correctly dressed, out respect for the lecturer.

21 TO 24 FEBRUARY

A trip to Paris and the horrors of populism

21 FEBRUARY

We boarded an eleven-ish flight to Paris and, as Julia was on one of her economy drives, took the train and Metro to the hotel, which was less difficult than I thought. It was in the rue de Rennes, which was really too far out but I suppose that as all of it only amounted to £250 for a three-day round trip, one should not complain. The hotel itself was fine. We walked down to the St Germain area and to the rue Jacob and La Maison Rustique, the garden bookshop, where I made several good purchases. I groaned when I saw the racks of books in German on garden history: I can't keep up with it, alas. We used our free meal voucher and had a seafood feast. A great surprise.

22 FEBRUARY

We took the train to Versailles. The palace was very full but the queue for the exhibition [*Les Tables Royales en Europe*] was short and we got in quite quickly. This exhibition alone was worth the journey. It was stunning and it was only afterwards, on reflection, that one realised how much was missing – in this instance the food, the napkins, the tablecloths – so one realised that it fell short. It opened with a huge reconstruction of a Louis XIV centrepiece, a column of candles with a fountain in the middle. There were dazzling services of porcelain and plate, complete even with the suede-lined trunks in which they were carried. There was also a clever use of mirrors to double tables and give the impression of their size when fully laid. The exhibition was packed. It should have stopped in 1789 and dealt with that period in greater detail but instead it traced the gradual decline down to the depressing Napoleon III plate. One of the problems with the exhibition was that everything was over-lit: the exhibits were never meant to be seen like that.

We then did the palace interior, the *grands appartements* of the king and queen. The king's suite had a very good sound guide and I hadn't seen Louis XIV's bedroom restored. The etiquette of the *levée* explained on site was well worth listening to and clearly visualised. The richness of the re-woven fabrics was a reminder of the glint and glitter. But it was a good day, if long and tiring. Useful books were bought. We got back about 6.15 p.m. and went out to dinner locally.

23 FEBRUARY

We spent the day in the Louvre or, rather, at the new Pavilion Richelieu. I felt glad that I was no longer the Director of the Victoria and Albert Museum. Untold millions had been poured into creating this vast arena, which houses an amalgam of the V&A, the National Gallery and the Tower of London. Whatever we thought of the display, at least the place will enter the twenty-first century structurally in good order. What a contrast to the crumbling museum edifices of the UK, where government has no commitment, no forward vision. I hadn't seen the Napoleon III rooms before, pure *Traviata*, opulence untold – what a set for Visconti! Also the *Saint-Esprit* tableau, with so many items connected with Henri III, which stirred old memories of Frances Yates, who wrote so much about Valois court culture. And then there was the Liotard pastel of a plain old lady, which alone was worth crossing the Channel to see. But so much! One was exhausted: a morning was spent on French painting, followed by a very good lunch in the restaurant in the Pavilion, after which we looked at *objets* and the paintings of the Northern School. Enough.

We walked back, finding that it had rained, and rested. Later we found a small fish restaurant with pleasant service, and that was it. But my main memory of the day is of mass culture, of sitting in a gallery beneath the glass pyramid watching, even in late February, the teeming thousands pouring in, vast queues – six of them – the escalators never empty, bearing the mob up to art. Everywhere was thronged. I suppose that this was what we had fought to achieve in the UK but there was something just dreadful about it.

25 FEBRUARY

An echo from the past

This was a cheap Channel 4 TV programme in which Jonathan Meades, Sarah Kent and I went around the Tate Picasso exhibition. Meades was a somewhat self-important Billy Bunter but I warmed to Sarah Kent. We started 'cold', which wasn't easy, but it was painless, just a walk through.

Now what was unexpected was the make-up girl, Hilary, who was married to Brenda Bridgewater's son. Brenda had lived six to eight doors up in Colne Road and we were friends from about the age of eight to ten. It all collapsed when the Bridgewaters decided that it should be ended, which upset me, but I suppose, looking back, she was about to enter womanhood. That was the first normal family I'd ever been exposed to. They did things like sit down and eat together, which never happened at home. It was my first realisation that life at home was far from the norm. I recall being struck how Mr and Mrs Bridgewater went out *together*, something unheard of in our house. However, the real point of this is to record a tragedy. Brenda had been given MS through an injection and her husband, who was the carer, contracted cancer and died. Really awful.

6 MARCH

A reunion

Peter and Sonya Wright came to The Laskett, Peter for a reunion with Mirabel Osler as they were in the same class at Bedales over fifty years ago. 'Oh, you were such a beautiful boy!' said Mirabel, who used to wander around with her knitting tucked into her gymslip. Peter was not looking forward to coming out of the Ballet. Why, he protested, shouldn't he go on? He is sixty-eight. I feel that it is very difficult and a bad sign for his next phase of life. Sonya is marvellous, taking him off on courses like etymology – anything to occupy his mind in another direction. He is marvellous with his hands, at knitting and embroidery, and we plan to go on a crochet course together!

10 MARCH

The Snowdon lunch in the Oliver Messel Suite

The day of the Snowdon lunch at the Dorchester in the suite designed by his uncle, Oliver Messel. There was an odd *galère* of guests, very different from the list sent. Where were the ones I was told were coming – Anthony Hopkins, Emma Thompson et al.? So one had to put up with Alan Bates, Peter Hall and Patrick Garland! In a way the Messel decoration now seems oppressive, much sprawling gilt and mirror glass, but it must have been odd even at the time, 1930s romance in 1950s G-plan Britain. Initially I sat between Patrick Garland and John Mortimer. Patrick wanted to ask me frankly about moving on. I told him that I didn't miss any of it. It was liberation. He's planning his exit from Chichester. For the last year he's been under the doctor: the strain of it all was telling. John Mortimer revealed that he had had Elizabeth Esteve-Coll as his *au pair*. He had very funny stories about Michael Codron's boyfriend, how an Arab offered him one then two camels for him in a souk in Morocco. Myfanwy Piper was very busy and brave. John Mortimer said that John Piper had in fact died to her several years before his actual death, due to Alzheimer's.

We then did musical chairs and I sat next to Eric Clapton who, like Sting, had been filling the Albert Hall. I found him refreshing. Marriage break-up and death of his son, really awful, but he was an engaging, rather ordinary, short man with bristling gingery hair, in a neat striped Armani suit. He found Gianni Versace's clothes were not for him as he wasn't six or more feet tall with dark hair. It's extraordinary how many houses pop stars have. Eric Clapton has three and is building a fourth on Antigua.

Afterwards Jean Muir collared me and we sat downstairs drinking her fuel – champagne – while she plotted her next design strategy. She is really after her DBE. But I love her energy and the disorganised intelligence.

I went on to have tea with Brian Allen at the Mellon Centre. It was an oddly consoling occasion for he was very perceptive about life's phases. No, he couldn't see me going back into archives. There is a period of life when you do this. How one remembers those days! Day in and day out to the British Museum or the Public Record Office, working through mountains. We had a good thrash around that score, which I now feel is gone. It seems to belong to the past.

In the evening I took John Hayes out to dinner at the Garrick. I hope that it works out but he seems to have left retirement so late, sixty-five, to start a new life and with only a Civil Service pension. It's amazing that he's never even learned to type. Here he stands, having to discover how to be self-sufficient at a very late age. For him leaving the National Portrait Gallery is not liberation but deprivation. It'll take a year for it all to sink in that he's yesterday's man and that he has to make his own life and fill the day, as it is no longer filled for him. He'll find it very hard.

8 TO 11 APRIL

The Pinter weekend

Antonia had made it clear that she longed for Harold to see The Laskett, so willy-nilly the invitation went but Mexico and New York intervened until finally 9 and 10 April were fixed. Somehow I knew that this would be a marathon. Antonia had long ago left the land of reality over matters domestic. At sixty-three she moves like some fragile Dresden figurine, beneath enveloping Jean Muir dresses. Harold is also very substantial, with a thick, short neck, balding curly hair, a rubicund face and a stocky frame. He moves as though it were an alien activity.

Up the drive they came in their monogrammed Mercedes. I carried their luggage upstairs, where it was really very comfortable. I couldn't cope with an elaborate lunch so it was pasta, salad and cheese. It was at that point that the wine consumption got under way, and much of the weekend was spent with me going down to the cellar to heave up yet another bottle.

At any rate, after lunch came the garden tour and they were duly astounded. For a country visit Antonia was in a Jean Muir dress and Chanel shoes with high heels and pointed toes. Next we went as planned to Whitfield, where we had intended to leave them so we could come back to prepare dinner. This proposal produced panic in Harold, who dreaded being left with Lady Mary Clive and absolutely depends on Antonia. So we got to Whitfield in time for tea, where two tables with all the china, silver and cakes were laid in front of the fire. There were gathered George Clive and Penny Graham, with Mary Clive presiding, elegantly dressed and looking younger than ever. Antonia firmly sat down next to Mary while Harold, a bit at sea, looked on.

George took us to see the garden. Would Harold come? No, but when would we be back? Between 5.15 and 5.30 p.m., I said. And we returned and I said: 'There you are, 5.25 p.m.' We drove back to The Laskett, where Harold and Antonia announced that they were ready for their sleep. Meanwhile, I got the dinner in the galley below but indicated that drink would be available from 7 p.m. on. Julia took George and Penny (who had come over) round the garden and the dinner went well. Then there was the aftermath, for they sat up and drank and then there was one long and interesting conversation between Harold and myself about how we both owed everything to a remarkable teacher. In his case it was his English teacher, a suppressed homosexual who, after retiring, fell in love with a German lesbian, life thus ending in joy. He had died in his sixties and when she had rung to tell Harold, he sat down and wrote a poem. Thus Day One.

Day Two began with me getting up at 7 a.m. in order to clear up and get the second dinner on its way. Breakfast was at nine. Antonia appeared in a floor-length organza dressing gown. Harold was in towelling. 'How did you sleep?' I asked. 'Fine until you turned on the radio,' was the pointed reply. 'Was there anything in the news?' Harold asked. We had been asked to lunch by the Bankses at Hergest Croft. Dot arrived at eleven, just before we left, to make their beds and tidy up and was horrified to find all the lights left on.

Into Julia's car we got and drove north, Harold commenting on the beauty of the landscape.

We got to Hergest Croft at 12.45. I rang the bell. No one. Terrible thoughts began to cross my mind. I looked through the window and saw that lunch was laid, so that cheered me. I made my way round to the domestic entrance and rang the bell. A lady appeared and suddenly everything began to be OK: the front door was opened and we were decanted into the drawing room. Unease followed, rescued by the arrival of Lawrence and Elizabeth Banks and Hélène and Patrice Fustier. Hopes of liquid refreshment revived, only to be dashed by the sight of two bowls of Japanese crackers. However, everything was saved again when Lawrence entered with a tray and a bottle of champagne. Suddenly there was a revival.

Harold looked stricken at being placed next to the French lady at lunch but then suddenly found out how marvellous she was. After lunch there was to be an expedition to see the rhododendron valley and the magnolias. No, Harold didn't want to go. Antonia, however, did, so out we trotted. She put on what she described as her Bond Street boots and Elizabeth gestured towards a typical clapped-out estate vehicle. Antonia awkwardly got in and was jolted up and down over the almost vertical mud tracks. Then, with a jerk, we stopped amidst the mud and everyone fell out, Antonia rather gingerly. Elizabeth led the walk. Then we all went back to the house, where Harold, thank heaven, was having a wonderful time with Lawrence and Patrice Fustier.

Thence home where I made tea. The dinner guests this time were Jackie Thompson and Peter Florence of the Hay Festival and again it all proceeded swimmingly, rather apposite in view of the river of wine which vanished. We got to bed at nearly midnight, Harold being very pleased with the guests.

Day Three. Breakfast at 8 a.m. and I daren't put the radio on. Down they came, as on Day Two, and off they went at 9.15. Outside the Mercedes was iced up so Julia went to the garage and brought back her plastic scraper. Harold stood and looked on as Julia cleaned the windows and then, when she'd finished, stepped forward and said: 'You've missed that bit.' Exit Pinters. At 4.15 p.m. that afternoon my head fell on to my work desk with exhaustion.

13 APRIL

Farewell dinner at Spencer House for Owen Chadwick, Chairman of the National Portrait Gallery's Trustees

This was done with great splendour, some sixty or eighty in all, Trustees past and present, benefactors, staff, etc. I found myself next to Susan Crosland: I thought that I wasn't going to like her but I warmed to her. She had got on the board via Jim Callaghan after her husband had died. She made her living as a profile journalist and novelist. At one time she was going to write a life of Anthony Blunt and had spent a long time with Brian Sewell, hours and hours of it, and he'd inducted her into the gay world. One thing that I did think extraordinary was that he'd mentioned that years ago he'd asked me to dinner and then realised that he'd misjudged me. How I remember that evening! Gert Schiff, the Fuseli scholar, was there and all I could think of was how to get out of the place. There was much general *mêlée* but nothing of great note in the way of information. But they were kind to have asked me.

16 TO 21 APRIL

In pursuit of Prince Albert

16 APRIL

We joined the Prince Albert tour put together by Valeria Coke, former chatelaine of Holkham, as a way of seeing things in East Germany. The tour was made up of about twenty of the professional classes, recently retired and still on the move. We landed and changed planes at Leipzig. It was very cold and damp, with floods everywhere and drear, dull, leaden skies. The coach was OK and we arrived, due to the plane's delay, an hour late at Wörlitz. The villa, which was opened for us, was Palladian of a kind but rather strange, a mixture of bits and bobs from England, Italy and France. The real thrill, however, was the landscape park, which took over two hours to walk around in grey, dull, bitter weather. But oh how extraordinary it was, with echoes of Stourhead, Kew, Painshill, et al! There were utterly weird gothic structures, underground grottoes and neoclassical temples, all with a meaning. This is one of the greatest surviving landscape gardens, with allusions to Italy and Coalbrookdale (an iron bridge), yet having a religious perspective. It was just amazing.

17 APRIL

Another day of really awful weather, with low, grey, skies and very cold. A long drive first to Bad Lauchstädt, a quite enchanting eighteenth-century spa town with a concert hall and assembly rooms redecorated by Schinkel, with two flanking pavilions and a wooden colonnade with painted columns, and before it a triple row of pleached trees. This was an absolute jewel. There was also a c.1800 theatre, with its original scenery still used by actors from Weimar. It was all so primitive and provincial and modest, when one thought of the opulence of Bath.

On we went with a surprise visit to Naumburg Cathedral, with its wonderful early thirteenth-century sculpture: the amazing screen, entering into the Sanctuary beneath the arms of the cross, then the standing figures and the further revelation of the two main couples in niches flanking the altar. They exceeded every reproduction: what a miraculous bonus!

We had doggy bags for lunch on the bus on the way to Weimar, where there was more rain and chill. But we covered most of the architecture: Goethe's house with its mass of plaster casts and domestic rooms; the wonderful church with its Cranach altarpiece, dolly mixture woodwork and huge late sixteenth-century tombs stretching from floor to ceiling. Then on again into the park and a walk to the Roman House and, finally, the drive to Gotha.

18 APRIL

We started touring Gotha at 9 a.m., first visiting the amazing *Schloss*, approaching it via a beautiful walk through the town squares offering a panorama of medieval and neoclassical architecture. This was the usual vast *Residenz* and we toured the baroque state rooms, some of them rather splendid, especially the *Festzaal* with its bold plasterwork. The c.1800 wing had had a really awful neoclassical face-lift, very badly done, with crude painted effects. The court theatre, however, was really worth seeing, with its original scenery on a raked stage, wings, borders and cloths.

We then drove to Reinhardsbruun, an amazing 1820s gothic hunting lodge belonging to the Coburgs. Here we had a buffet lunch in the one remaining unaltered room decorated with gothic diaper tracery in gold and ochre on a green ground, gothic windows on both sides and a stencilled ceiling with lunettes bearing ancestor portraits in grisaille.

Thence to Meiningen and Schloss Elisabethenberg, another huge *Residenz* in white and ox blood. There disaster struck and we were twenty minutes late, so instead of being able to see the pictures, we were dragged round an exhibition on an actor called von Bülow for an hour and three quarters. It was so cold and there was no heating. On and on and on it went, through ghastly heavy 1890s neo-renaissance gloomy rooms. It was awful.

The town was well worth seeing: very, very dilapidated but a stunning range of architecture, from timber-framed medieval through renaissance into baroque and neoclassical. Then to the Goldene Traube Hotel at Coburg. When I entered the bedroom I knew that I had got something. I drank the cognac we had and shivered. There was nothing to be done about it. Dinner was at 8.30 p.m. but it was dragged out and we were still sitting there at 10.30 p.m., at which point we left. I slept for nine and a half hours, exhausted.

19 APRIL

A beautiful, stunning spring day. We set off on foot at 9.30 a.m. with the local historian as our guide, who, although knowledgeable, was slow and fragmentary. Coburg is a delight, with a very handsome square with the expected statue of Prince Albert by Theed. Suddenly there was so much really handsome architecture again. We went into the Rathaus with its eighteenth-century rococo room and another huge late sixteenth-century one. We walked on to St Moritz church, ruined in the eighteenth century, but with a huge and remarkable late-sixteenth-century polychrome tomb.

Then to Schloss Ehrenberg, which was a very great surprise, first through the neoclassical part, which is now a library, and on into the vast post-1815 suite done over by the future King Leopold and his brother Ernest II, replete with superb French Empire furniture: torchères, clocks, etc. This was lavish, grand decoration reflecting the huge influx of cash after the poverty of the eighteenth century. Everything was of real quality, unlike so much German coarseness. Then came a second suite of rooms for Ernest's wife Princess Louise, a delightful, small, elegant, silvery Empire suite.

Then it was back to the hotel and then off to Schloss Rosenau. This had been an old people's home until 1972 and then restored with a vengeance, with the result that it is now neither a house nor a museum. But we were glad to have seen it. Rosenau is 1820s gothic, early for Germany, the interior all sugary dolly mixture gothick.

20 APRIL

Another glorious spring day. We began with a visit to the Veste, the Coburg fortress. This was a medieval ruin done up about 1910–20 in an historicist gothic style. The few rooms were kept as the dukes had had them – gloomy – some with good French furniture, porcelain, etc. (but mostly not). When the old Duke dies the contents will be removed by his hard-up family and the castle will become wholly state-owned. The remainder is now a very good museum and gallery, the stars of which include a stunning glass and print collection. The two wonders were coaches of c.1560 and 1586. I was amazed, the earlier one pure Elizabethan, like the one in which Elizabeth I had made her entry into London in 1559. We picnicked outside and walked down through the Hofgarten and then wandered into the shops. This was a sweet little town.

At 3 p.m. we set off for Tambach, a heavy but restrained baroque country house. We could only go in to the chapel, which was very pretty in white, green and gold, with the fluency of Bavarian Catholic rococo. The Count appeared, tall and in his fifties, with suede knee breeches and tweed coat, and addressed us. His father must have been liquidated by the Nazis: his mother saved it all. Then on to Sesslach, a small, perfect walled town, a kind of Bavarian Burford. The real climax was the pilgrimage church of the Fourteen Holy Helpers [Vierzenheiligen] by Neumann. One knew its great rococo interior from pictures: a symphony of ovals, raspberry ripple scagliola, white, pink and grey-blue. There is an extraordinary *baldacchino* shrine in the middle, with a grille through which one peered at a patch of earth where a shepherd saw his visions of the saints – who knows, perhaps he did. But it's a beautiful place, overall aesthetically the best of the whole trip, a real finale.

21 APRIL

On the last day we visited Pommersfelden, a simply amazing mid-seventeenth-century *Schloss* of gargantuan size built by an Elector who was bribed to tip the balance. The entrance hall alone was worth coming for, a huge baroque staircase suspended in a many-windowed container with wonderful plasterwork. There was an astounding grotto on the ground floor, replete with glass fish on wires, very damaged but basically all still there. Alas, no National Trust to restore it! Then followed a tour of the state rooms, a huge loop, all totally unchanged, furniture, pictures, everything. A vast picture gallery, a mixed bag but a lot very good all hung floor to ceiling, room after room, so God knows what's there! Thence to the airport and home.

4 MAY

Eastnor Castle

Off to Eastnor Castle for a bit on a programme on Augustus Pugin being done by Joe Mordaunt Crook along with Judith Bumpus. We had a good time. It's a grim, monolithic place, glowering close-to, with no redeeming articulation of the surfaces. We did our impressions of the castle on the outside and then went in. *Little Lord Fauntleroy* was being filmed there, with a child in knickerbockers and an awful blond wig. We kept clear of that and did our bit inside in the drawing room, and then we were stuck because Sarah Hervey-Bathurst had offered us lunch. She's a sweet young girl and it was really generous of her. What a struggle it must all be. However, they live comfortably in one part of the castle and that works well.

8 MAY

A female cleric

A glorious day. We went to Kay Garlick's first Eucharist at Much Birch, a hideous church. I have not found the idea of women priests a difficulty. I can't explain why. It just seemed a revelation for our age and very right. It was a terrific turn-out, jammed, and a very happy one. The service was a bit too evangelical for me, with hand-clapping by the end. Swingy hymns – but why not? It's one way to work it for today, and especially for family services. The waxwork High Mass is often very empty. It is so difficult to see the way things will go, so many problems for the poor Church of England: dwindling congregations, the burden of the buildings, rent with divisions and no money. But I think of women's ordination on a par with Methodism: the Church of England lost out in the eighteenth century by not keeping it in. How the Catholic wing will sort their side I don't know.

23 MAY

The Chelsea Flower Show

The weather cleared and at 11.45 a.m. we went to pick up Peter Marston and walked to the Show. It was really rather disappointing, with only two good Show Gardens, by Cartier and the *Daily Telegraph*. I was very touched by three designers paying me '*hommage*', including those who had designed these, one of whom was Dutch and had read my *The Renaissance Garden in England* eight times. The Show was full of people we knew: Arabella Lennox-Boyd, George Clive, George Carter, Penelope Hobhouse, Robin Compton, etc. Everything this year was purple but there was very little, if anything, new. Still, inside the tents there were wonderful displays of bulbs, alliums, ferns and hardy geraniums.

We left at 5.30 p.m. and went to the National Army Museum for the Rex Whistler exhibition. This was a delight but also fatal in a way, because we went on to the Goya at the Royal Academy. This sunk Rex Whistler to the level of a *petit maître* with an amazing skill to delight, but he never really developed. The Goya was quite astonishing, a brilliant show. We left that exhausted to see *Shadowlands*, from which, again, we emerged exhausted by what was a sad tale of human redemption. Anthony Hopkins is a great actor, a master of reticence; but how odd it all was, if true. A tear or two trickled down my cheeks. Thence, after, to Café Fish. What a perfect, lovely, happy day.

26 MAY

Worries of a freelancer

I find anything to do with radio or television now just dreadful: but what does one do? Jean Diamond was moaning and groaning about the chaos. I would so like something to take me from this killing write, write, write – but I don't think I have any choice. *The Story of Britain* is a huge gamble – just £5,000 for two years' work – if it doesn't come off . . . I don't like to think about it. Julia MacRae rang up, ecstatic about my last four chapters and, as far as I can judge my own writing, they were good. I'm now into those covering 1760 to 1815. As always, it isn't easy and I dread all those academics waiting to pounce on what is a narrative history for beginners.

28 MAY

What to do with the garden

Rodney and Jenny Stubblefield stayed the night to discuss the will and what we were to do about the garden. She turned out to be a delight and he was more interested in it than we expected. It really reverts back to us to make overtures as to whether anyone would be interested. Julia reckons that it needs another ten years to bring the garden to its apogee.

30 MAY

Lunch at Whitfield and Lady Mary Clive

Lunch at Whitfield on a perfect summer's day, with blue sky and verdant greens. We discovered Penny Graham and James Kirkman sketching beneath the fountain. Mary Clive seemed younger than ever and suddenly this turned into a glorious and hilarious few hours. Having gone reluctantly, I went into top gear. The longer I know Mary Clive, the more I like her. Now nearing ninety, she has lost none of her brio. She too thought the Betjeman letters no good and the annotations by the researcher were covered with mistakes. Also, she didn't think much of Candida's contribution either. But Mary and I always have absurd conversations about history. Afterwards we went to look at George's mecanopses in the really wonderful wild ruin garden he has built.

2 JUNE WEEKEND

La Mortella and Susannah Walton

We were asked as guests of the Walton Foundation to stay with Lady Walton to see the garden last year but it collapsed as British Airways went on strike. This time there was no such impediment. I confess to a certain curiosity as to why us? I had no notion about Susannah Walton, whose book on her husband I hadn't read. She gave it to us and I read it on the plane back. It's a fast read, for she wrote as she speaks and it contains much of what passed in conversation with us during those three days but which her lawyer had chopped out. Lots of nuggets.

Susannah met us at the airport. She's a rather badly worn sixty-seven, hunchbacked with flabby arms and hair dyed pied, black and white. There's an earthy energy to the woman and William Walton chose well if he had in mind someone who would be bent on his immortality. Her features were dominated by large, expressive eyes and a large mouth, generally open, which she always painted with lipstick before we went out. She dressed in deep colours, wines and reds, loose-fitting and comfortable garments. But there was a more splendid repertory for state occasions. Now that she performed *Façade*, she dressed up: she showed us a wonderful Fortuny dress of blue with a bead embroidered gauze tabard over it and a perfectly awful silver hat with a blue aigrette at the front, made by a man in Amsterdam who makes cakes. He should have stuck to those.

Life was not always easy as she was twenty-five years younger than William, who had little if any money until late in life. But by the late Fifties they were to begin La Mortella, which arose between 1961 and 1962. I hadn't expected the house and garden to be so totally hemmed in by other houses and I hated the lack of remoteness. The house scales the rock face. It's a good, comfortable house, well thought through and managed, decorated in that Thirties style used by Beaton at Ashcombe, old bits and pieces of furniture and carving cobbled into this and that, white walls not heavily hung with pictures. The bedrooms were downstairs and the living rooms up. The focus of the house was called 'Time Square', a sitting room which led directly onto the terrace with a stunning panorama of the garden below, with its noisy fountains mostly turned off for quiet. On the walls hung John Piper's design for the *Façade* frontcloth, which passed to William Walton as a result of his affair with Jane Clark. It was really K's [Kenneth Clark's]. Scattered around there were one or two Pipers, Rowlandsons (*Portsmouth Sound*) and a Liz Frink (who did William's head). Susannah is a superb needlewoman, making huge copies of a carpet from Hatfield: at the moment she's on the last lap of the Stoke Edith hangings.

Every day had the same momentum. We got up at about 9 a.m., breakfast at 10 a.m., lunch at 2 p.m., dinner at 9 p.m., usually out. 'Reale' and her extended family kept the whole show afloat. She told us that we were the only people who had ever given her ideas for the garden. I was amazed that it had never crossed someone's mind to erect the Piper *Façade bocca* in three dimensions in the garden. She was wild with excitement about it. Before we left, Julia photographed me standing where I hope that she erects it as the source for the cascades.

This is an excellent garden, hewn out of and wedded to the rock. Below is an oval pond with a vast jet, a number of smaller fountains and a charming rill. This architecture she owed to Russell Page. One criticism: although stone has been used, there are too many concrete paths. But trees are her real obsession and up they have soared to a great height, pines, ginkgos and jacarandas. One of the problems is that the garden is split into two, below and then above, a huge ascent on foot (there's a funicular from the back of the house) and so it lacks a middle layer. Above, there's 'William's Rock', in which his ashes rest with an inscription by her, badly executed. Higher up there are ponds and cascades surrounded by green foliage plants, and even beyond them a Thai house in wood that had been shipped from Bangkok.

She opens to the public three times a week, which really doesn't interfere a bit: the loos and the tea house are well done. We discussed with her the structure of the foundation, with the fate of The Laskett very much in mind. We learnt a lot from this. Apart from her excessive talking, the vice of the lonely, we were left to get on with it and I found the place highly conducive to work, producing, to my surprise, two chapters of *Story* – far more than I dared hope. There were expeditions, to Ischia for dinner in a fish restaurant on

Friday – no good really – also to see the quite extraordinary castle and view from Vittoria Colonna's tower, and also its rectangular renaissance garden enclosure below, jutting out into the sea; and finally to Sant'Angelo, a pretty, tiny resort, for a quite wonderful dinner.

Susannah was up and off, leaving for Boston at 5 a.m. on the Monday, via London to get her hair done! She's got her life sorted out on and off the road as the Widow Walton, presiding over her garden and three gardeners, her embroidery and running the annual music school directed by Colin Graham.

The weather varied, on the whole not that good, with a dead, dull light and wind. The garden really looked awful without sun. But it was magic with. It was so interesting to meet someone who'd made a garden at the same time as us – but one so very, very different.

I wish I could remember all her gossip, like Ninette de Valois having a fling with Constant Lambert and when war broke out the ballet being in Danzig and having to get out fast. Ninette flung open the door of Margot Fonteyn's bedroom to find Constant there! The Droghedas weren't forgiven much. Joan, before she married Garrett, had slept, Susannah said, with most of the orchestra. Marion Stein and George Harewood were both crazy about Benjamin Britten, a situation saved by them marrying each other. She also loathed Joan Plowright, so that Larry [Olivier] would come on his own. But Vivien [Leigh] was always the great divide. And it was amusing the way that she referred to the 'perfectly awful' libretto for *The Quest*. How vividly I remember Doris Langley Moore describing how she had concocted this patriotic ballet to get Fred [Ashton] out of the army!

11 AND 12 JUNE

The Bath Festival

Michael Milburn had been after me for the Bath Festival for years. This was a happy package, a nice hotel in Russell Street, Handel's *Belshazzar's Feast* in Bath Abbey and dinner in the Assembly Rooms. Bath looked a miracle. Michael had come into my life via Luke Rittner, when I was looking for someone to run the new V&A restaurant. He's what I would describe as a gentleman into catering, a really nice man, and his wife, Penny, is a delight. At the dinner I was placed between Mary Keen and Grizelda Grimond. Mary is amiable, shy and at first rather off-putting, and seems to have wandered into horticulture. On my other side was Grizelda, rather dark and formidable. She had worked for Jacob Rothschild and then Neil MacGregor at the National Gallery.

I felt the searchlight fall so I gave her her money's worth. It was interesting to learn that Neil is disorganised, doesn't answer letters for months and that she was obviously the mainstay. Socially he's a wow, like me when I was thirty-one, but he's exhausted. Don't I know! I wonder how he'll control it all. His partner hates social events, so Neil is off on his own. I do think that he's a brilliant Director but I always think that there comes a time when the knife goes in somewhere. But it all looks OK at the moment. It will be interesting to see if he stays the course. She said that Malcolm Rogers had got a job abroad, a good one, and why not? Michael Levey is being coaxed back into giving the Slade Lectures. With her there I decided that I'd better do a mega-statement performance and I did. I think that it rather stunned her: I didn't want her to tell Neil that I was a geriatric in a siding.

On Sunday morning we had a walk and tried to get into the

Georgian Garden (shut) but did get into the Museum of Building, which was very well done and full of information. Then we went to lunch with the Fraylings. I don't know why I felt aggrieved but I did. Friendship needs both sides – and after all, one had done a lot for him – but he never made contact for years, so I cut him out as my literary executor. Julia, however, is always a peacemaker, so I gave him a ring saying could we pop in for coffee: instead we were asked for lunch, which was hugely enjoyable. Helen seemed frustrated, fed up with Christopher carrying the College, the Arts Council and the V&A. He's been on them all for so long, the V&A back as far as the late 1970s, I think.

Afterwards we went on to the American Museum and saw the Kaffe Fassett show, which should have been better. Then home to an agonising message from Anne Murrell. Jim has terminal cancer. There's nothing to be done. I rang her and was given all the awful details, with tears and a flood of irrelevant things like what's going to happen to his files. Logic had gone but I coped and then put down the phone and braced myself to ring him in the Royal Marsden. 'Roy, I was just about to write – it's terminal. . . .' None of this was easy, such a brave and nice man just wanting to put things in order. We spoke and went round and round, said and unsaid, it was all there. I put the phone down and was convulsed with tears. I went out and cut a parterre, very shaken.

14 JUNE

Richmond, Yorkshire and the Bowes Museum

The hotel at Richmond turned out to be pretty awful, as was the food. We sent the decapitated skinned trout back, comforting our-selves with the thought that it was only for one night. But we got into the Georgian Theatre as it was about to close. It is minute and painted in shades of grey and green, the boxes labelled 'Dryden' et al. I was very pleased to see it. We walked around the town, which was also a delight, very 1780s in a way, with its theatre, its promenade around the castle, its picturesque views and assembly rooms, charming and winding in spite of the awful plastic supermarkets in the main square.

We got to the Bowes Museum on time. Ivan Day was there to meet us and eventually Howard Coutts came. The historic food exhibition was an utter delight and we were bowled over by the Jacobean banquet, the *c.*1700 'dessert' and the eighteenth-century one, as well as a re-creation of a Mary Ellen Best record of a dinner table in York. They had all the excitement and energy of something new opening up. How well the food linked in with the other decorative arts: even the tonality was the same.

16 JUNE

The Three Counties Show

On another of this long series of hot, brilliant summer days we went to the Three Counties Show at Malvern, Peter Walker having asked us to lunch. The Show was a glorious hurly-burly, with everything from champion cattle to cake decorations. All were in holiday mood and it was good to see Peter not looking tired and in good form. Trying to talk was hopeless, as there were ten around the table. The couple that flanked me were really sweet, in their late sixties or early seventies, old-fashioned props of the nation, do-gooders who made me wonder where their successors were, although their children sounded pretty decent.

That evening Anne Murrell rang me. Jim had died at home very peacefully. He just slipped away. They all knew that it was going to happen so the children were fetched and they were all quietly with him. He had some of the Brandenburg concertos played. Then a query arrived about Edward Norgate and he had a flash and remembered, so really the last words he uttered were about the technique of miniatures. The funeral is next Friday at Putney Vale. I must go. She wanted something read. I'll look.

24 JUNE

Jim's funeral

I went to 8 a.m. Mass at Westminster Abbey. It was really beautiful, a circle of chairs in the Chapel of St Edward. I felt that I'd found another holy place and couldn't understand why I hadn't been there before. Very powerful.

Lunch with Clive Aslet went wrong as there were two cafés called Joe's. I was in Sloane Square and he was in Draycott Avenue. I leaped into a taxi but lunch was truncated to three quarters of an hour before I picked up some flowers and met Susannah Edmunds and two others from the V&A and drove to the crematorium at Putney Vale. It was the hottest day of the year, which did give light and joy to Jim Murrell's exit. There were lots of people I knew and it went well, with New Orleans jazz, me reading a piece by Nicholas Hilliard and Anne contributing a prayer. But they weren't Christian, so it was all set within a framework that was unfamiliar to them. He was a darling man.

I JULY

Bury St Edmunds and Helmingham

In wonderful weather we set off to see Robin and Pat Scutt outside Bury St Edmunds. As we were early I walked Julia around Bury, which is so beautiful, a bit like Ludlow, bigger but with the same quality. We arrived at Abbey Cottage to see what are a great couple in every sense of the word, he tall, big built and a very good mid-seventies, she the size of a house but endowed with a mad originality of character. We duly admired their new conservatory, were 'done over' by her small army of little dogs and had lunch in the garden, dodging the sun.

Then on to Helmingham, where we had a bed for the night. Xa and Tim Tollemache were fine but they were up to their eyes with children and a mother-in-law in a wheelchair. It was the NACF evening and it had been a sell-out for months, black tie with all the usual old fogeys but very nice. I love Helmingham, with its moat and rose-red brick. And the gardens get better every time, really ravishing, and Xa ever more knowledgeable. It was the usual format: drinks, garden lecture by me in the hall with lots of laughs followed by a buffet supper. At £40 a head it would have produced a good dollop of cash for the Fund.

2 JULY

Lunch at Ascott

We arrived at Ascott for lunch on a wonderful day. Oddly enough, it all went well. The house is like a series of black and white cottages meandering on forever, even though Evelyn de Rothschild's father knocked half of it down. There they live, in rarefied splendour. Three manservants for a lunch for six slightly took my breath away. The table centrepiece was one of Marie Antoinette's watering cans – quite a throwaway. The rooms had been redecorated by Renzo Mongiardino, the walls painted to look like Dutch blue and white tiles, against which was hung the famous Dutch picture collection. Victoria is American, pale, very shy and rather inscrutable. I wondered what she was interested in. Evelyn's burly but I concluded that he'd enjoyed having us and showing it all off. The Macdonald Buchanans were shipped in to leaven the party. They arrived very buttoned-up and then he shed his jacket and tie.

But the great thrill was to see Arabella Lennox-Boyd's garden. The part around the house was quite something. The scale was just right, a succession of small gardens hugging the house, strong on structure and with cascades of bloom. But that was only the beginning, as we fanned out after lunch to view a stunning restored Victorian bedded-out garden, quite amazing, a vast parterre and two astrological gardens. Victoria de Rothschild did have a real feel for it, with odd touches like a brown-burgundy garden. Julia promised to send them our burgundy poppy seed – and indeed did so.

11 JULY

Julia's birthday

Reg Boulton came and we discussed the two birthday commissions, two plaques for the Ashton Arbour: 'Enigma' 1968 with golden leaves falling and 'Month' 1976 with a kite and Ashton's profile. There was also Shakespeare and the FVS fountain emblem and the date, 1980.

He was hugely enthusiastic. We feel so strongly now that we must push on and etch into the garden its 'iconography'. Who knows how long each of us has got? With luck twenty or twenty-five years but we need to do things now.

12 JULY

The launch of the American Friends of the National Portrait Gallery

We were in town for a dinner to launch the Friends of the National Portrait Gallery. This was a slightly doomed affair, as there was a dinner for the retiring US ambassador the same evening, so Drue Heinz and Fleur Cowles backed out. It was also marred by a lack of hosting and no presentation line. It began with drinks in the Tudor Gallery, followed by dinner in the Regency Room, all perfectly well done. I sat between Ann Tusa and Linda Colley, and Julia between Christopher Foley and John Tusa. On her table there was a fracas as Foley said that Charles Saumarez Smith should never have been made Director. John Tusa and Julia slapped him down. At my table the waters were calmer. The Cannadines are a real academic pair but I do admire their work. I warned him to be careful about writing a biography of Andrew Mellon, as it would look as though he'd been bought out. Linda was deep into Victorian women studies. I'd hate to be an exile from my native country, even with all that freedom and money.

16 JULY

Lunch at West Wycombe Park

The Dashwoods entertained with brio, having some forty for lunch. I don't think we met them all – but neither did anyone else. Francis Dashwood, pushing seventy, leans on a stick (gout, I wonder?) beaming benevolently with a caring eye and Marcella, no longer a young beauty, radiates bonhomie to her guests. It was an odd *mélange*. The Weinstocks arrived in what looked like a hearse. Arnold Weinstock then proceeded to ask me to fix a deal for him with the National Portrait Gallery, wanting their portrait of Handel in return for one he didn't want of Garrick! He'd picked the wrong man for this deal: I'd saved that portrait of Handel by public appeal as one of my first acts as Director of the Gallery. It's the presumption of the man which is so frightful.

But the Dashwoods always attract a sprinkling of the vulgar. The lunch was in honour of Lord and Lady Stevens, he a short, puffy, pale-faced man seemingly devoid of any charm. George Weidenfeld was there with his new wife (number four), benign and actually not looking over one's shoulder as much as usual. He was cursing Oliver Millar over his behaviour in respect of the National Portrait Gallery appointment [of Charles Saumarez Smith]. Oliver had even rung up Drue Heinz screaming that Malcolm Rogers should have got the job. In fact Oliver lost it for him.

Well, there we all were on the colonnaded terrace, the lawns sweeping down to the lake, the steps flanked by Scheemakers lions as though it was a scene from the eighteenth century. I told Lucinda Lambton how good I thought her Windsor programme was. She's a benign, reckless, unpredictable bundle, her hair badly dyed and her face ageing but she's animated and expressive. Perry Worsthorne is like the White Rabbit, pale with white hair and dressed as though out of *Zuleika Dobson* in straw hat, cream jacket and ice-cream-coloured accessories.

The table was laid out the length of the terrace. I sat between Princess Pignatelli and Lady Quinton and drew a deep breath. Lady Quinton's painted features were hidden behind gilt-edged sunglasses, with a huge sunhat on her head and wearing a multicoloured frock. But she was OK and in fact I rather warmed to her this time. She's married into that vanished mafia of Sixties intellectual life peers – Annan, Briggs, et al. There were pretty models of the follies and temples in the park scattered the length of the table, alternating with pots of 'Baby's Breath' with sprays of white roses on top. Roast beef was a bit odd in the midst of a heatwave and I avoided it but the gazpacho was good and so was the raspberry flan.

The Airlies were there: I love them. She's always a life-giver, looking more and more like her mother, who is now ninety-three and in a bad way. Ginnie's had a good innings but she's coming off the Tate and National boards; she's had it all, although six children never leave her without a problem. David was as elegant as ever, although his jacket was filthy. Now sixty-eight, he is on his way out of the Household, where he has stayed longer than any.

There we all were. It was England on a perfect summer's day, a party in a Palladian country house spilling out around its confines, a reminder of just how much still goes on.

13 AUGUST

The Canadian Strongs

Lawrie and Vivienne Strong came to see us, along with three second cousins, all daughters, one with a husband. I don't know why, or perhaps I do, but I dreaded their visit in a way. Just anything to do with the Strongs stirs traumatic memories. Only after both my parents were dead did I feel released from it – relieved – at last I was myself, without all the squalid baggage of the family past, the feuds, cruelty, bullying and the playing on emotions. I slept badly, going over it all, asking why it had all been so awful. Why had Brian gone to the dogs? Why was my father so unloving and uncaring? Why was my mother so possessive? You can't rewrite the past and I escaped, vowing never to enmesh anyone in the way that they did. But the scars are still there. I could have done without that torrent of tortured memory.

However, up the drive they came and, of course, we had a wonderful time. They were normal, the only part of the Strong family that is. His father and mother had taken themselves off and made a decent life and brought up a family devoid of the horrendous complications we endured. So the party took off. He's hugely successful, the chairman of Unilever in Canada, now aged fifty-five, white-haired, athletic and very intelligent – and also very nice. So was Vivienne. They were direct, honest people one could do business with. I think my honesty about what the family meant to me came as a terrible shock to them but I can't conceal it any more. I'm over it, and now it can all be said. But they were fun and lively and extrovert and we laughed a lot and had a wonderful garden tour. I hope I'll see them again. How lucky he was to have united and loving parents and a sister he gets on with and can share things with. All that I mostly look back on is warring factions and emotional blackmail. On the other hand, what a spur to get out of it . . .

23 AUGUST

I am fifty-nine at Portmeirion

My fifty-ninth birthday and I don't feel any different. I talked to Julia about people one admired who coped with age. Gielgud came tops for me, no *folie de grandeur*, prepared to do any job, grand roles or small character parts and to just plod on working. There was no sign of power lust or bitterness at not having this or that. Julia had the idea that we should go to Portmeirion for the night. It proved an enchanted day with an early autumn light on the garden and the Welsh landscape, just beautiful. We were in the Gate House, John Lewis taste and comfort: antiques and Indian bits and pieces, with crewelwork curtains. A perfect dinner rounded off a very happy day. No regrets but a firm resolution to go on and write and create and leave our garden as a legacy of two lives and happiness. Portmeirion was lit by an enchanted light, its Thirties pinks, blues, terracottas and whites full of ideas in the way of wit and fantasy for our own garden. Hydrangeas flourish here, the steep site setting them off to advantage, garlanding the hillside in shades of blue into pink. Clough Williams-Ellis must have been an early pioneer of architectural salvage, snapping up bits and pieces of buildings and sculpture, a *mélange* of countries and styles put together in the spirit of Thirties romanticism.

14 SEPTEMBER

Revolution at the BBC

To Christopher's, the restaurant, to meet Anne Sloman. She has visibly aged and is now number two in a BBC shake-up of a vast TV/

radio news/current affairs department. She looked tired, is unhappy with her new boss, but she needs five more years to see her sons through university and that's it. It was the *reality* of the change that threw me. Once there was time for contemplation and fantasy and time for reflection but now it's all here and now and at once. No wonder one gets so little joy out of the media. It was so good to see her. She's extremely special.

24 SEPTEMBER

The Stokesay Court sale

We left early to go to the Stokesay Court viewing. I'd never made it to the house, although Philip Magnus Allcroft had been a Trustee of the National Portrait Gallery and was always very nice to me. The skies were leaden. It was the usual Sotheby *fête* with a field turned into a car park and a small army of county folk advancing to the house. They all looked pre-1939 with a late Fifties overlay. Stokesay after 1945 had only partially been lived in and everything from the 1889 house had been wrapped and put into the attics. Money had been thrown at the house. The quality of the woodwork and plasterwork was superb. But the overall impact gave me the creeps as it exuded unhappiness. It also seemed dirty and depressing, although rooms like the boudoir upstairs gave flashes of a period. There were really terrible pictures of the worst kind, I suppose from the Royal Academy in the 1880s, along with religious ones of a variety to make me give up Christianity. This was an uncultured house – and what kind of people were these to pass a century without as much as buying a new lampshade? How fresh the hand of Colefax and Fowler seemed, and oh for those comforts and freshness! The house outside was like a reformatory but inside the rooms were rather stunning, with incredibly beautiful views. We bumped into Robert Holden, Grey Gowrie and his mother, and the Cormacks. I felt that it had been over-hyped – and how awful those Allcrofts must have been!

SEPTEMBER

Cornish progress

We set off on a grey day to Cornwall to raise money for the National Art Collections Fund, arriving at Penheale Barton near Launceston (incidentally, Launceston Church with its encrustations of granite was extraordinary). Diana Colville, our hostess, is a widow, still very pretty, a Legh of Lyme Park, her father having been Comptroller of the Household, and therefore she was brought up at St James's Palace and Windsor Castle during the war, with the two princesses. She's a perfect hostess with an elegant county style. The house, which is not the main one, is granite 1820s Tudor with a handsome drawing room and good English furniture, a piano, Old Master drawings and pictures by Guardi and Zoffany. We had a very comfortable room in the guest complex. David Treffry, a kindly individual, came to dinner as the 'extra man'. It was an evening with a quiet dinner for six, the other guests being Michael and Charmian Reeve, a merchant banker and wife, OK, but no mileage there.

The next morning we walked around the pretty garden and were then escorted over to the main house, the manor, newly restored thanks to having sold a Leonardo drawing to the Scottish National Gallery. Norman Colville, Diana's husband, had had to live in the south for health reasons after 1918. The manor had begun its life as a small 1920s granite manor house but he had brought in Lutyens, who added wings in the nearby Castle Drogo style. Inside there was a stunning Jacobean hall screen encrusted with carving like ginger-bread, and here again were a lot of the good things he had collected: stumpwork pictures, early English furniture, tapestries and Old Master drawings. The garden is on different levels all around the house. I thought there were too many roses and an absence of verti-cal accents, but there was a good box garden designed by Gertrude Jekyll in squares. But the real spectacle was the yew hedge compart-ments, rooms forming cross-axes with herbaceous borders. What's left of these is still splendid, although much needs to be done to tidy it up and pull the whole garden together.

It was then back to the house, where there was a fund-raising buffet lunch. It was well done and went very well. I worked hard and spoke to everyone and made a little speech and they sweetly presented me with two hundred bulbs for the garden. An aged lady appeared seemingly from nowhere and announced that she was one of Sir Charles Oman's godchildren. That was amazing. I am always bemused that people apparently read, listen and watch what I get up to.

Christian Lamb then appeared and we left at three-ish to go via her to A.L. Rowse. Now aged ninety, he's still larger than life and all there, although this time very deaf and therefore forever bending his ears forward with his hands. His suit was filthy and his chin covered with tufted stubble but none of that impeded the voice booming on and on about a whole litany of people: in praise of Sir Charles Oman; in awe of Lady Oman; how Arthur Bryant was a second-rate mind and an appeaser; how Trevor-Roper was two-faced and would write praising a book and then knife it in a paper; how the late Duke of Beaufort's lady-love was the Duchess of Norfolk; how Queen Mary made him give her up; how Queen Mary had taken over twenty-three rooms at Badminton. He sailed relentlessly on, sometimes repeating himself. The house was dirty, damp and untidy. A lady aged eighty-six hobbled around on a stick but neither of them was in a fit state to carry anything. The kitchen was un-speakable, the walls stripped on account of the damp, everything in it was archaic and decrepit except for a new electric cooker, which stood in solitary state in the middle. Rowse then wanted to know all about our cats, what words did they know, did they respond to 'beautiful' – his white cat Peter did. We sat there shouting at each other across the teacups, which were a ghastly, common 1940s green. The view from the windows swept down to the sea, flanked by banks of rhododendrons. The room itself was a clutter of books and paint-ings with some pictures leaning against the walls. But Rowse was thrilled to see us and we did a photo-call exit.

We drove on next to Place, as it is surprisingly called, at Fowey, a real crumbling gothick extravaganza sited on the estuary front, a kind of Thomas Love Peacock fantasy, a meandering and un-thought-through house in which marble halls suddenly led on to maids' passages. The hand of the decorator had not reached Place and David Treffry, its owner, is totally oblivious to such things anyway, the result being a mish-mash of styles, colours and fabrics, some superb, others cheap rubbish, all cheek by jowl. It is a most inconvenient house. We were put into a guest complex, which he must let out, and which had the atmosphere of a boarding school. The bedroom had two lumpy beds and five chests of drawers, with a single bulb in a pleated shade to light it. There was a dressing room of sorts and a 'new' bathroom, which was a real muddle of Victorian fittings and nasty modern tiles. It even had a kitchen but with only one teaspoon. But there, like it or not, we were.

David is a kindly, benign and amiable man who either knows or who has met everybody. Off we went again at 7.20-ish to the Pethericks (we were late) for a bring a dish meal, this time I thought for about forty. I did my usual task of going around everyone and made yet another speech. There was much talk about gardens and they all love my *Country Life* pieces.

Friday turned out to be a grey day. The bed at Place is the worst I have slept in for years, just springs sticking in me and lumps all over. David Treffry just doesn't notice. In short, the guest suite is so thoughtful and so awful. The bathroom turned out to be pretty bad too; but at least it's clean.

We set off for a tour of the house at about 10-ish the next morning. Place will be a nightmare for whoever is its next incumbent. It is a meandering, winding oddity of a house, devoid of any feeling of freshness. It was heavily done over in the 1890s, mainly, I felt with dark, oppressive rooms heavy with gothick carving and plasterwork, all of it simulating wood. The drawing room, however, had an early 1920s overlay of the eighteenth century but, taking into account the Cornish time lag, it had a pre-1914 mock Georgian feel. Then there were the abandoned servants' quarters, the servants' hall with its table now a dump, although it had been operating until 1945. Cobbled onto the house like a rabbit warren were maids' rooms, a scullery, a dairy, a larder replete with old kitchen equipment, including the wire-meshed cupboard for meat, another which would have been filled with ice for fish and an area in which to hang meat. The woman who looks after David still uses the original kitchen, oddly workable – but there was not a Magimix in sight. There was a butler's pantry with a safe and steps to the wine cellar, and an odd hatch. But overall, I just longed to purge this house, freshen it and make it work. I felt uncomfortable and oppressed.

At 10.45 a.m. we went to Heligan, which was an eye-opener, a vast garden being restored by private initiative. The leading light is Tim Smit, a large, very direct man in his forties, ex the Bowes Museum and the pop scene. The garden is so large that they say it can take a hundred thousand visitors and not notice. This is not a design garden but a plant one. The kitchen garden had been restored with its apple tunnel in the making, all of it enclosed with a hedge of laurel and *thuya*. Old Cornish apple varieties were being collected for the orchard. What I hadn't seen before was a melon ground operating, with manure generating the heat for the pineapples. Then there were the tool store and the potting shed, all again put back. On beyond that to where there had been a huge flower border, on again past ranks of niches for bee skeps, then through a rock garden and on yet again. I admired their energy and drive: they were violently anti the National Trust and English Heritage, all committees.

We then drove on to Tressilick, but there was no time to look at it, and then a long drive to Godolphin. This is a magic house, small, remote, the remains of a long-gone grandeur still traceable. There was an extraordinary double loggia on Tuscan columns from the 1630s supporting what had once been a new grand suite of rooms, like Ham House, with a king's and a queen's side. Long since compartmented up, they're thinking of putting them back. All of this was an echo of the court and Inigo Jones. On the king's side this led on to the bedroom, the closet and the great parlour, then out from that by way of a little door to a privy garden that was still there, an Elizabethan granite-walled enclosure.

But the real excitement was the garden proper, nine acres of it. They were beginning to clear it and make a land survey – but it was all there, compartmented and terraced, with two huge rectangular ponds on the upper level, with massive retaining walls that I would have thought were also 1630s, although with endless bits added later. The surrounding raised walks were still there. All of this was a great excitement, after which tea followed with the Schofields, who were sweet.

Then came a hectic drive to the Tate at St Ives, which was architecture on the cheap, a big show of wasted space with its huge amphitheatre approach but devoid of a welcoming concourse area. Then followed acres of staircase to get to the restaurant, the shop and the rest. All of it was badly planned. The restaurant was all white and hard surfaces – the noise! No lecture theatre, so I spent an hour setting up for my lecture in their biggest gallery. The acoustics! Still, I survived. It was a packed house and I met Damaris Tremayne, the surviving sister of the previous owner of Heligan, and learnt from her how odd it was to see it come back. I also told the councillor lady what I thought of this Tate outpost. We escaped at 9.30 p.m., drove back to Place and were in bed at 11.30 p.m., to another agonising night punctuated by springs.

22 OCTOBER

Collected Papers *and Westminster Abbey*

A really vile day, with rain in torrents and wind so I put my head down and pulled out the illustrations for volume two of the *Collected Papers*, a wearisome process pushing my way through boxes or old photographs and notes. Still, I emerged with 130 out of the 160 needed, so Richard Barber would have no cause to complain. I packaged them up to be sent. The papers in this volume are a funny mixture, good and indifferent, some with new stuff, others boildowns of other material. God knows who wants them but there it all is. I must do a preface or two as I go along, to get rid of it. Looking at the stuff on George Gower, for example, it is really remarkable how little has been discovered since 1969, how even those lost saleroom pictures reproduced in *The English Icon* have never resurfaced. I only had two pictures to add.

I rang David Hutt, now a canon of Westminster Abbey living in a seven-bedroom house by Pugin I think. This is a happy and well-earned end to his career.

23 OCTOBER

Autumn colour

Suddenly a stunning day during an autumn incandescent with yellows, ochres, tangerines, caramels, oranges, crimsons and golds. The medlars looked unreal, like torches aflame, and what quinces! The trees were laden: I had never seen so many. After church, with all its usual dreariness, I worked in the Rose Garden, clearing leaves and hoeing the beds. Then I staked out and discussed with Julia the proposed Michaelmas daisy border in front of the house. That could look glorious, south facing and with a yew hedge as a backdrop. I then wrote a lot of the chapter on Ireland.

24 OCTOBER

Alone

A day on my own, the first of a whole week: a good discipline, for who knows, one day it may be just like that. The cats were unbelievably affectionate. Normally they bed down with Julia but this time they were either curled up in a chair in my writing room or playing tea-cosy on my desk. I typed up the chapter on Ireland, hoping that it was OK. The problem with *Story* after 1900 is to get any kind of structure. The heavyweight textbooks on the period are so crammed with fact and detail that it is a nightmare finding the broad brush. I turned down reviewing a new biography for the *Guardian*, realising that I mustn't get sidetracked any more, but get on with it. The weather was beautiful. I got out for a run and was then able to take both cats out for a walk, when I could catch them.

1994

29 OCTOBER

Julia returns

Julia arrived back from Canada tired and bleary-eyed [the Royal Winnipeg Ballet had staged her and Ashton's *Month in the Country*] and went to bed. Everything in Canada had gone very well but they weren't at all welcoming, apart from an evening with cousin Lawrie, which she enjoyed. He seems to have been kept in blissful ignorance about the Strong family. In Julia's absence I was able to edit and type up two chapters, 'Pax Britannica' and 'Splendid Isolation and War', so I'm into the 1920s.

1 NOVEMBER

Project for an exhibition in Memphis

Up and to early Mass at All Saints, Margaret Street, for All Saints Day. Then on to Charing Cross to meet Glen Campbell from Memphis. We took the train to Greenwich for a meeting I had set up with Richard Ormond, the Director, Stephen Deuchar, et al. I knew they would get on and I was right. I also thought that they would be fascinated by Glen's beguiling commercialism, and again I was right: they were. We cooked up a British Empire exhibition focusing on three orbits, America, India and Africa, with two hundred and fifty to three hundred exhibits. I do believe that this could be very good and certainly not triumphalist, with an abundance of wonderful artefacts. It would be for 1994. Heavens, I shall be sixty-four! Doesn't bear thinking about. It was a stunning day with blue sky and sun and Greenwich was a spectacle. We went up to the Observatory, which I'd never seen before. It was not very well presented, with too many bad props and tableaux, although the public lapped it up.

I took Glen to dinner at the Garrick after I'd been to Lord Strabolgi's party at the Reform Club – oh God, I'm so tired of gatherings where everyone is so old and raddled. I saw Hugh Jenkins, Baroness Blatch, Zorica Glen, the Birdwoods and a few others, and got out.

26 NOVEMBER

Present-buying

Julia went off to work and, as usual, I kept my head down and read. In the morning I went up to the printseller Norman Blackburn to buy David Hutt a present to commemorate his becoming a canon of Westminster. I just felt that I wanted to give him something marvellous, a bit like a wedding present! I alighted upon a large engraving of the scene in the Abbey set for the coronation of James II, the atmosphere somewhat surreal, being devoid of people. I also spotted a little framed late-seventeenth-century mezzotint of a bunch of flowers, which was very unusual, so I bought the two for £250. I was so pleased that David was bowled over by his gift. I don't think anyone had given him something so lavish before. He propped it up on a chair and couldn't take his eyes off it, and then showed me the plans and photos of his massive house, three floors of Gilbert Scott gothic – and very grand. I took him to dinner at Christopher's. We had everything to celebrate and it was lovely to see him so happy.

30 NOVEMBER

Harold Pinter's Landscapes

Drove up to London with Julia and went to the Hayward Gallery to see the German Romantic exhibition, which was a terrible disappointment. It was so badly done and lacking cohesion, although there were glorious pictures by Caspar David Friedrich, Runge and Schwind. But the purpose of our foray was to see Harold Pinter's *Landscape*, a two-hander in the Cottesloe. The National Theatre really has become very shabby and I'm afraid once we were in and it was warm and dark I kept on slumping off. The play was, however, beautifully written, the usual saga of the separation of characters on stage, Ian Holm and Penelope Wilton sitting at either end of a kitchen table. As always, it was rather strange but her part was really lyrical, touching and sad. Afterwards, on to Campden Hill Square for a quick drink with Paul Mitchell and to meet his cats. It was too short, as we had to get to Harold and Antonia about 7.30-ish. I had wondered how that evening would be. Julia's opening comment to Harold was 'She should have been wearing lisle stockings', which rather floored him. The house was as I always remember it, although there were signs of damp, with cracks in the plaster tearing the wallpaper.

7 DECEMBER

Bristol

I finished the longest chapter, 'Consensus and the Mismanagement of Decline', and couldn't find a single thing to say in favour of those

1951 to 1979 governments. And all I've written is a synthesis of what the historians say. It was a terribly difficult and exhausting chapter to write. However, I was picked up at 5 p.m. to go to Blackwells in Bristol to speak and sign books. It was pouring with rain, with flashes of lightning. I dreaded the occasion in a way – what to say? However, they were very nice and about twenty-five people sat in a bunch opposite me: I just talked about what it was like to be a writer and what I had done since I left the V&A. I think it rather took them by surprise. I did it off the cuff and signed about fifty books afterwards, in the hope that they would sell them. Everyone, however, was interested in that one-volume history of Britain.

12 DECEMBER

Elizabeth Esteve-Coll makes her exit

I just got on with the book. I was up at 6.30 a.m., having an early breakfast and walking the cats. Then it was head down and I typed, printed off and posted the chapter 'Empire to Europe' and began work on Mrs Thatcher . . . Then, in the early evening, Elizabeth Esteve-Coll rang to tell me that she was leaving the V&A to become Vice-Chancellor of the University of East Anglia. Why not? She's had a horrible time at the V&A and the University would be more her scene. I don't know what I feel about it. All I know is that she survived and it's a reasonable exit from a no-win situation. Also the University would take her on until sixty. I don't think she ever understood that museum. Under her it became a sea of bureaucracy. The exhibitions were mostly disastrous, *Sovereign*, *Sporting Trophies* and *Street Style*, all really awful. One or two of the new galleries were OK but she was dominated by the Trustees and under her the directorship lost ground.

1995

21 JANUARY

Beatrix Miller

In really ghastly weather, gales and rain, we drove Wilsford to see the parents of our Maine Coon cats. The result of this was that we realised that ours were mini-coons. On then to Beatrix Miller at Donhead St Andrew, arriving, thanks to the weather, an hour late. Beatrix is unique. Now seventy-two, with tinted curly hair, her features spring to life as intelligent conversation develops, suddenly her antennae twitch, her eyes sparkle and she tosses her head back and throws her eyes upwards. She has been one of the great figures in my life since 1968. Enormously private and shy, hopeless and yet, at the same time, hugely worldly-wise, she's unique. It's her tolerance and understanding of people, together with the forgiving of human weakness, which endows her with a remarkable quality. She never groans or complains.

30 JANUARY

The Tate re-hung

At the viewing of the Tate re-hang there was the usual arts mafia, with Henry Keswick saying that Isaiah Berlin was screaming about Avedon's photograph of him. There was a dinner afterwards and I was at a rather dull table between Christina Gascoigne and Marcia Blakenham. It was interesting to gather that Bamber Gascoigne, now sixty, realises that time is finite and that being on all those boards, the National Gallery, the Tate, the National Trust and the Royal Opera House, doesn't take you anywhere creatively. The evening was pleasant but it lacked sparkle and glamour. Dennis Stevenson is a fine chairman and gave a good speech. It's the age of money and the heavy gang.

8 FEBRUARY

The Ideal Home Exhibition

The entire day was spent judging the innovative ideas for the Ideal Home Exhibition. Apparently I was so successful last year that I was asked back. God knows who the other people were but I enjoyed myself as each demonstration whirled in and out, showing us new ways of washing paint brushes (brilliant), beds which contorted, one that even descended from the ceiling while the table below concertinaed, a car with new child-proof seats, and so it went on. Mercifully there were no yogurt makers or tin-openers this year. What it highlighted was the huge comfort of life today for most of the population.

In the evening Stanley and Jacqueline Honeyman took us to Jonathan Miller's *Così fan Tutte* at Covent Garden. It was rather a Glyndebourne type of production, only one set, cheap and cream-washed, the stage jutting out over the orchestra pit and everyone in Armani beige and more cream. Miller's work never lacks intelligence but it began to falter towards the end.

9 FEBRUARY

A friend becomes a Canon of Westminster

To Westminster Abbey for David Hutt's 'enthronement', which took place during Evensong and friends were placed in the choir stalls. Everything happened like clockwork. Victor Stock was on my left, looking very ebullient and larger – visits to 10 Downing Street heralded gifts to come (he became Dean of Guildford). There was a *mélange* of bishops and clerics in bundly clothes, the clerical women just looking a muddle. A computer print-out of the order of service made an amusing read, with directions on how to stave off the uninvited from the party afterwards. Still, it was impressive, with all those processions and silver wands and crosses and robed clerics and choristers in surplices and red cassocks. David had to stand in the arch leading into the choir, sunk in gloom. He read his piece in Latin and was then led by the hand by the Dean to his stall. David looked very different in his Abbey kit, as there were no Anglo-Catholic birettas and maniples here. But it was all happy and there were drinks and snacks in the hall of Westminster School afterwards, where the Canons were lined up for a photograph. Michael Mayne made a charming speech of welcome to David and his cats. It was all as it should have been.

22 FEBRUARY

John Major

For some weird reason I'd been asked to a binge at 10 Downing Street. It poured with rain and I arrived late, by which time the receiving line had gone. No matter, there they all were, the arts mafia screaming at each other. I spotted Judi Dench. 'I haven't been here since Margaret Thatcher,' I said, to which the reply came: 'Darling, I haven't been since Harold Wilson.' I then crossed the middle of the room, which was empty, to find myself pursued by John Major. 'Hello, Roy,' he said, 'How did you slip in without my noticing?' Well, I thought that was pretty cool coming from someone I'd never met before. I rather fell for him and said, 'Congratulations on Ireland,' for that day the cessation of hostilities had begun. From that we moved swiftly on to the establishment of the National Lottery, I recalling that Mrs Thatcher would never let it happen as it was against her Methodist upbringing. Then, at a given moment, he gave a speech, which, much to my surprise, was a very good one, beguilingly funny, while the Heritage Secretary Stephen Dorrell, stood by looking like a clapped-out car salesman. One had to hand it to the Prime Minister: he did have charm.

During our annual springtime few days in Italy we went to Lucca to have lunch with two old friends.

2 MARCH

Hugh Honour and John Fleming

Hugh Honour and John Fleming are people you'd have to invent if they did not exist. Expats of some forty years standing, they're still in the Villa Marchiò at Tofori outside Lucca. It was an awful day, rain non-stop, so Julia and I couldn't walk around Lucca as we had planned but hid in a café guzzling coffee ice cream until Hugh picked us up at the station. They both looked physically better than I last remembered them, still very 1950s Austin Reed. Hugh, however, had abandoned his greasy slicked-down hair in favour of having it short and wispy, a great improvement. He was in corduroys and a tweed jacket. John is now quite rotund and was also in corduroy but with a nondescript pullover. Both were noticeably hard of hearing, John more so than Hugh.

The villa retains its magic, such a superb space for living and working, with gracious high-ceilinged communal rooms with smaller ones opening off. The drawing room, now a bit dusty, is painted yellow and filled with huge bookcases, comfortable easy chairs with pictures, prints and *objets* everywhere: comfort, clutter and style, with no pretence and no decorating hand. We lunched on the ground floor in that pretty room I remembered so well, lined with the shelves filled with blue-and-white china. Hugh cooks rather well and drives, shops and gardens too. I often wonder what John does . . .

They were both hungry for British gossip and we were hungry for theirs. Alas, their circle is now sadly diminished, with Harold Acton and John Pope-Hennessy gone. With Harold they didn't end up on good terms, but in the case of 'the Pope', as he was known, relations went on to the very end. He enjoyed ten years in a handsome apartment opposite the Pitti looked after by a 'student' in his late twenties, to whom he left the lot. A most extraordinary 'last attachment', but not, we were told, a physical one. They lived in some style but on what it was often speculated. After he hit eighty the lurch downhill for the Pope was fast, thanks to sclerosis of the liver. I'd never thought of Pope-Hennessy as a drinker but he belonged to that generation that had a dry martini before lunch and dinner every day and wine with the meals. He'd been warned of the eventual consequences but he took no notice and so the disintegration started. The last time they had seen him he was in a wheelchair and the 'student' had to feed him. By then his memory came and went and he'd suddenly believe that they were in Dublin and off to the National Gallery, and he would go on to describe all the pictures and query some attribution to Uccello. Tactfully his young friend let him believe it all. The final breakdown came in Monteux, to which he had gone in *grande luxe* to recall his mother, Dame Una; but on the second day he had to be got back. Hugh and John said that although he retained his spikiness, he was really much nicer in his last years. There is to be a requiem in Brompton Oratory but I haven't the hypocrisy go. All one can say is that he had a good innings and could have had a much worse exit.

Here John and Hugh live except for six weeks of the year in winter, when they go off to warmer climes and someone house-sits. Otherwise they stay put, except for occasional darts to London or Paris. We have always had a fondness for them but they never stop talking and never ask us whether we are alive or dead. For them the world is that of academic art history with its rippling circles of, in the main, gay friends. How wonderful, I thought, to be free of that world.

But the villa is very beautiful, with its pond and lilies, its box topiary and the presiding persimmon tree. So one owes a lot of inspiration to them, perceiving the house as a working environment and as a creative centre but divorced from an institution. It was hugely enjoyable to see them again. Hugh spontaneously tore up some pretty daffodil bulbs for us to plant at The Laskett. So with 'we said' and 'we thought' and 'we did' echoing in our ears, we left.

15 MARCH

Durham

At long last the radio series on how historic towns are faring is under way. Martin Buckley, aged thirty-eight, is the producer, an engaging youth with a beguiling, disorganised quality offset by a passion for things, and also an affection. So I do like him and find him mentally stimulating and *en rapport*. We met at King's Cross station for the 9.30 a.m. train to Durham and I found someone from my Arts Council past on the platform: Mike Sixsmith, once, in the early Eighties, young and boyish but now, suddenly, middle-aged and bearded.

When we got to Durham Martin suddenly discovered that he'd lost the address of where we were staying. I groaned but he managed in the end to find it and so off we went to something called The Georgian Town House. This turned out to be an amiable, spotlessly clean bed and breakfast place run by a lady who is into interior decoration on the cheap with a vengeance, so anything in sight that could be stencilled has been stencilled. But it's a nice place and we started immediately into interviews. The first was with a beguiling couple, the Wallaces, in a house with layers of building back to the fifteenth century, although Mrs Wallace stays firmly in the warm in the kitchen. Next we visited a video shop, above which we opened cupboards revealing bits of a fifteenth-century house.

That night we were frozen stiff with cold. Martin swigged back five or six brandies and then we had too much wine with a filthy meal at an eatery called Bella Pasta, where the waitresses were in watered-down fetishist gear, black with an orgy of straps. We both talked too much and let our hair down. Martin told me that by leaving the V&A I had lost my power base. Had I? I suppose that

I did but I can't see it that way. I just see it as liberation and the ability to create and do other things. Is he right? I wonder and feel depressed but I can't go back.

Next day we were off again, first to Roy Gazzard, an architect, then to the Hawkwoods, who have restored a manor house, and so on and so on. It all passed by me in a kaleidoscope but all I can think of Durham is that they've mucked the place up. It's a spineless, reactive place, a monument to damage limitation, and I was left feeling sad, very sad. I think that any hope for the place has gone, fled, vanished long ago. There'll be a bit in the middle somewhere which is marvellous but that's it. RIP Durham.

21 MARCH

Richard Avedon

The Avedon exhibition at the National Portrait Gallery left me feeling that somehow one had seen it all before. But he's a good photographer and those vast prints of his work are carted round the world like Rembrandts. The exhibition was not a cheap experience, for Avedon charges about £8,000 a day. The National Portrait Gallery was groaning about the cost of keeping him in the Connaught Hotel for a fortnight, not to mention his entourage. Mercifully we missed the early part of the proceedings, which, we gathered, had been a disaster area, the *beau monde* having been caged up with champagne while Charles Saumarez Smith and Dick Avedon took Princess Diana around. Then the caged ones were let out but this time found themselves kept behind ropes. The result of this was that Nicky Haslam and a few others among the glitterati stormed out in rage.

We were asked to what turned out to be a dull dinner afterwards.

This had been intended for the workers but they actually didn't want to go to it, so instead went out on the town. In order to beef up the number of diners, others had to be press-ganged in. Charles tends to be socially oblivious to what is actually going on around him, so people were not introduced or moved around so that the dinner was never-ending and lustreless. However, what I did conclude was that whatever Avedon lacked, humility would come pretty high up on my list. The exhibition made no concession whatever to either London or the British. It was somehow terribly 1960s. This was a one-statement man – but what a statement!

26 MAY

A new Director of the V&A

I have not kept this diary for a couple of months. God knows why. Pressure of work, really, but I can record that I am pleased that Alan Borg got the V&A, a safe appointment. He's fifty-two, my age when I resigned it. At least it kept out Timothy Clifford, who apparently shot himself in the foot in the final round of interviews.

28 MAY

Jean Muir

We arrived back from lunch at Wenlock Abbey with Louis and Gabrielle de Wet and, as usual, turned on the Ansaphone. There was a message from Beatrix Miller, someone who never leaves such messages. She apologised for being so abrupt: Jean Muir had died. I rang her back at once. I couldn't believe it. Beatrix had been rung up and told by Mary Henderson in floods of tears. Beatrix was also in tears. Jean had died of cancer. For two years she knew that she had got it but told no one. She had even had both breasts off but no one knew. I put the phone down and then it dawned on me that she had gone and I too was convulsed with grief. Both on the Sunday and on the Monday I did the ring-round. I'm glad that I caught Adrienne Corri, who was very close to Jean. She was pole-axed. Adrienne rang Jean's husband, Harry, but he couldn't even speak. Even the housekeeper in London never knew and kept lamenting 'terrible, terribile'.

Jean is a great loss in my life. I didn't know until the obits appeared that she was as much as sixty-six, but even then it was all so tragic and far too early. She was always on my list of originals, self-created from little, exacting in her standards, *au fond* a puritan who epitomised hard work, discipline and quality with no compromises. But we had always laughed together so much and were always *en rapport*. She seemed to make the news endlessly, more perhaps than she merited, but it reflected the impression she always made. She had such brio and enthusiasm that it seemed impossible that she had gone. Over the last year, however, megalomania had set in around her period presiding over the Royal Designers for Industry, perhaps prompted by her awareness of her imminent finality. However, I recall ringing her a fortnight ago saying that we must meet up before the sunset home. Alas, that will never happen. I shall miss going into old age minus someone so zany.

EARLY JUNE

A Versace weekend

Everything goes like clockwork with a Versace weekend. We emerge at the airport and there's Dario, a large man forever smiling. It was certainly *brutto tempo* as we drove into Milan to the Via Gesu. The normal *claire-voie* iron gate had fabric stretched behind it to screen out peering eyes from glimpsing the décor for the imminent men's show. In fact the palazzo courtyard now permanently houses an iron infrastructure in which to stage the fashion shows. The firm came out of the Via Gesu some years ago and the whole palazzo is given over to the 'Atelier Versace': offices, fitting rooms, library – it stretches on and on. Gianni's own apartment now seems almost incidental, so one can understand why he spends Thursday to Sunday at the villa on Como.

His personal assistant, Patrizia, welcomes us. Benevolent Gianni, Versace's manservant, swings open the door and we are 'at home'. We love him and his wife, Lucia. They love us and we muddle along in bits of Italian and French. The apartment hasn't changed that much. Like all of Gianni's houses, it has been in every magazine. I'd hate that but it's all part of the machine to remain on top, rich, glamorous, inaccessible, style-setting. Renzo Mongiardino, the decorator, is a genius, the interior subtle with beiges and greys deployed in an abundance of paint effects, stipple, marble and stencil. It is beautiful and the ideal vehicle for kleptomania, antique sculpture, neoclassical furniture and bibelots, a mania for flower pictures which cover the walls of the dining room followed by a run on garden pictures for a passage, thanks to me on my first visit. What have now been superimposed onto this symphony of subtlety are Gianni's fabrics in the form of sofas, armchairs and cushions upholstered in silk velvet in all the vibrancy that is so Versace. In a funny kind of way it's marvellous but it does have the drawback of making the antique fabrics and carpets look dowdy.

On Friday, after lunch with Franco Maria Ricci and Laura, Dario picks us up and we steam off to Como. I always think of it, since the first time I went there, as a magical place. The villa sits in a great slice of landscape sloping down to the lake, with the hills rising sharply behind. It is a large neoclassical villa, again seen in a million magazines, a yellowy buff colour with browny faun shutters framed by a handsome mid-nineteenth-century planting of trees – planes, pines and cedars – magnificent specimens with huge boles. In the case of the plane trees, their branches sweep down to the water in the most beautiful way. When I first came in 1986 there was no appreciation of this or any attention to the garden. We then sat amidst a faded parterre and dusty gravel paths. I remember scribbling on paper ideas for a garden, to include statues and urns. The next time I came with Julia, Gianni took us to our room, flung wide the shutters and said: 'Here is your garden!' And there it was, a vast army of statues and urns dotted across the landscape, with fountains playing and parterres planted. It was really very touching.

We were strolling in the grounds when Gianni appeared. We waved and he came down to us and we strolled on together. I always see him as vulnerable and alone, like Atlas bearing the world, in his case the world of his own commercial empire. As the weekend progressed, much emerged. At dinner that night we saw that he had aged (he will be forty-nine this year), his face tired and transparent. But then we learnt that he had a cancerous growth near a nerve near his left ear. All that had been traumatic enough without friends like Elton John ringing up in floods of tears. The cortisone treatment had been unpleasant but he's OK now; but it all took a toll and I could see that.

It is always touching seeing the frailty of a megastar but he remains immensely lovable. And Antonio is a real bonus: a great amiable bear. His life has not been easy either, with a beloved sister dropping dead suddenly at fourteen and a hypochondriac mother. But he's funny, quiet and calming and Gianni needs all of that. Miami, we learn, is a success and we look at the photos of the fantasy house, again projected through every magazine in a way that we would hate. And 'my' garden (I had sent designs) is, more or less, almost there. But why go there to be quiet and then invite Madonna and Sylvester Stallone, and then find the place besieged by the media?

There are contradictions. The eternal lure and the need for the mega-event, the Second Coming, as it were, with all the hype. But what he really needs is to protect himself. There's now a fourth house in New York. Once again, he's in love with it. And it will take more things. Every inch of Como is festooned, neoclassical lamps in the *salone*, antique plaques in the dining room, another room bedecked with children's portraits, my bathroom banked with putti pictures, our bedroom etched with Roman processions and games. It never ends. But there are paradoxes. The bathroom and our bedroom may be an art gallery but there's nowhere to hang anything. Paper handkerchiefs have appeared but not clean soap. These rooms are resolutely exhibits rather than thought-through as guest rooms. There's nowhere to sit, no writing paper, pens, bath essence . . . All that is so strange.

He was so tired that both of us were glad to enjoy his company, laugh and catch up and go to bed early, to sleep in the afternoons and to stroll. To be quiet with someone is real friendship. Nothing need be said. That is beautiful. I love coming here. There is nothing sleazy about it. There is no 'scene'. It is the private side – and makes me glad I escaped. Yes, I'd like a little more cash to scatter, but not much, just enough not to have to worry and to make The Laskett garden even more remarkable. But I'd never want what he has: I'd find it too much, one's life in every aspect a perpetual publicity machine. But how far Gianni has come in the eight or nine years since we met, now extending into licensing, into Versus, Home Signature, etc., with multi, multi millions. Underneath he loves our strange friendship, for we're totally uninterested in being part of that machine. It gives him joy to hear of my books, our garden and the house. I just hope that he is not killed off by his own creation.

9 JUNE

We open the garden for the first time

Enormous garden works have been completed in time for our first garden opening. Two groups from the Garden History Society came. After days of grey, cold and grim weather the sun favoured us. Few roses are out yet, everything being so late. Half the first group got lost, so the second group in the afternoon was twice the size. This meant that I ended up with no voice. Still, the garden looked terrific and Robin had done us proud.

Roger White, the GHS secretary, stayed the night and we learnt from him that Gervase Jackson-Stops and friend both have Aids, with Gervase in and out of the Brompton. What an appalling waste of someone with talent. *Gardens Illustrated* showed his Menagerie Garden, which is a real delight.

In the evening we rushed over to Cheltenham and I opened a retrospective exhibition of the work of Robert Welch at the Art Gallery and Museum. What a lovely man and what lovely pieces, with a very wide scope, from altar vessels to loo seats, from craft items to the mass produced, in style a mixture of modernism, Morris, baroque and Scandinavian post-war. There was the English love of pattern and of the Georgian et al. Afterwards the Director, George Breeze, and about twelve of us had dinner together. It was a very happy occasion with nice young people to talk to. It is always interesting to find out their attitudes and what they are up to.

13 JUNE

The BBC party

I arrived in London in time for Radio 4's so-called Summer Garden Party at the Chelsea Physic Garden. This has been the coldest June I can remember, with leaden skies and a deadening chill. But there was a desolate group huddled in the open there. God knows who most of them were but I talked to John Humphrys, James Naughtie, Prunella Scales, Timothy West and Rosie Atkins of *Gardens Illustrated*. Also to Michael Green, who loved my Ludlow programme, especially finding the palm [in the roof of a medieval house, a relic of a pilgrim]. But I was there to do my bit supporting the new programme on gardening in which I will be assigned a star spot. This is being made by Tern TV in Aberdeen, not the best base for it but that's what it's like these days. But the people are enthusiastic and bracing Scots, so that's a bonus.

14 JUNE

The Country Life *awards*

The day of the *Country Life* awards, another wheeze thought up by Clive Aslet. It took place at the Lanesborough, the old St George's Hospital on Hyde Park Corner, gutted and turned into a poor man's Carlton House with mock Regency plasterwork, drapes and furniture. The dining room where we met was raspberry ripple. It was an odd array of judges. There was Anne Heseltine in yellow, her hair deflated and her leg bandaged after an operation. We talked of an exchange of garden visits. Max Egremont, upon whom the hand of late middle age is now leaning heavily, so he's thickening and his face sagging; but he's a benign man. I rather took to Tracy Worcester, a bouncy new aristocrat well into anti-sexism, all things organic and the rest of it, but she was a real breath of fresh air. Add to them John Patten, who made a violent attack on the National Trust, and Hardy Amies, highly critical of *Country Life* for not using upper-class girls for their frontispiece. He shocked me when I said to him 'Wasn't it a shame about Jean Muir?' 'No,' he replied which was not nice. In the evening I took Beatrix Miller to dinner at The Garrick. She's always a life-giver.

15 JUNE

Hampton Court en fête

We'd been bidden to Hampton Court by Simon Thurley, the dapper young man responsible for transforming the place, to hear Caballé sing. It has been one of the joys of my life to see Hampton Court come back to life. And now it has a high glamour. He took us through to the King's Privy Chamber and threw open the window, and there it was, the Privy Garden, verdant green, a dignified swirl of grass, box and sand punctuated with cones of yew and standard plants interspersed with flowers. This is a great triumph but it will take time to convince the British. I first wrote about the possibility of restoring this in about 1978 and I am glad to have lived to see it.

Everything was done in the best style. There was a hive of corporate dinners scattered through the palace, a thousand in all being fed. The concert was in the courtyard, very well arranged, and we were in the front row. It was what I would call an entertaining romp: Act II of *Traviata*, Act IV of *Otello* and the triumph scene from *Aïda*.

Soldiers in the guise of hussars acting as trumpeters, mistaking their cue, took up their places on stage in the middle of the *Otello* death scene! But it was a delightful evening. David Mlinaric, Christopher Gibbs and the Harrises are among the friends I feel we've known forever. Christopher Gibbs used to be thin and decorative but his waistline has gone, everything on him is crumpled and frayed. And yet he has the hotline to Paul Getty, so he is courted by everyone and seen at everything. John Harris is going a little dotty, I fear. Flamboyant as ever and as enthusiastic, he is writing his memoirs. They will be very different from mine.

16 JUNE

The Praemium Imperiale fête

The occasion was the grand *fête* for the Praemium Imperiale, the great Japanese art prize. Most of us assembled at Westminster Pier in black tie and evening dress, a motley, elderly crew but full of friends. But off we went in a boat with balloons soaring upwards and champagne flowing. Judi Dench leaned against the bar looking exactly like the part she's playing at present. There was an exchange with Norman St John Stevas, who said that he had tried to get me to be a Commissioner, only to be told that at fifty-nine I was too old. But I was touched. All the way to Greenwich we sat with Jeremy and June Hutchinson, she a little scatty now but really sweet, he benign. Jeremy Isaacs sauntered over to tell Julia how her letter on the Opera House's workshops had created such an impression. Alan Yentob had pointed at my hair as being like his: to be honest, we're both awash with it.

As we swept by, so much looked marvellous, including Canary Wharf. At Greenwich we disembarked and thence by bus to the

Naval College. In the chapel, which is Wren done over by école de Adam, very itzy-bitzy, we watched Edward Heath conducting (mercifully only three items). Then to drinks and a mill around with Princess Alexandra, who was fine, but Angus looked very decrepit. We then moved into the Painted Hall for a never-ending dinner. There were speeches, the Japanese one weird, with recollections of a Crown Prince learning from George V about constitutional monarchy. We then reeled out for Beating the Retreat in perfect weather, a great spectacle. Then to the boat and back again. We went to bed at 1.45 a.m., zonked.

26 JUNE

The garden series

Life is full of surprises. A year ago I was rung up by Tern TV Productions from Aberdeen. Would I be interested in taking part in a gardening programme? Well, yes, why not? It seemed a good idea. Radio needs something outside the monotonous banality of *Gardener's Question Time*. I didn't give a thought to it until this year, when it suddenly took off. God knows how I crammed it all in. Up to Shetland, Dumfries, Brixton, Luton, Tredegar . . . But bit by bit the series has settled down and I think it's rather good. Hopefully it will go on.

They are an affable lot, fresh-faced, giving and enthusiastic and good to work with: Annie Malcolm, my producer, and David Strachan, the head of Tern. David, a Church of Scotland minister, is a touching man who sees his ministry fulfilled through this and not through the Church any more. Interesting in itself. The only jarring note is Edi Stark, whom Radio 4 wants in the chair most of the time. She's a hard-boiled, professional, *Reader's Digest*-type who seems to know nothing about gardening and slightly presses the wrong buttons. But one is stuck with whatever Auntie Beeb wants. It will be interesting to see how we end up.

It is rather a run-round, up and down to Aberdeen and endless one-night stays in the New Caledonian Hotel. This week I took a plane to Aberdeen, where the weather was positively tropical: it was like noonday at 4 a.m., when I almost leapt out of bed thinking that it was 8 a.m. My role is to push the gate open into six contrasting gardens over a period of six weeks, with studio bits in between. So far I've done the restored eighteenth-century parterre at Tredegar and the national collection of dianthus at Weston-under-Penyard. On this trip there's a tiny garden in the Shetlands, Ian Hamilton Finlay's new garden at Luton and Charles Jencks's cosmological fantasy on the Keswick estate outside Dumfries.

28 JUNE

Two great and contrasting gardens

I had always wanted to see Little Sparta as I thought that this was the most original of post-war gardens. Annie and I were given a 1.30 p.m. interview with its creator, Ian Hamilton Finlay, so we wandered around the garden first. I was quite unprepared for the scale, which is modest, a mosaic of small, contained areas and meandering paths with trees and shrubs and much low-maintenance planting. The garden comes as such a surprise, for the approach is up an ascent through three farmyard gates and along a rough track. There it sits at the far end on the hillside like some symbolic aberration. Ian Hamilton Finlay suffers from agoraphobia and never leaves the domain, learning about the world around him by means of books and photographs. Perhaps this accounts for the scale of the myriad sculptures and inscriptions peppered across the landscape. Everywhere one walks there are tiny columns or plaques, or strange gate piers like the ones bearing hand grenades. There's such a plenitude of them as one wanders up and down through this extraordinary fantasy world scattered around a large pond, a meandering stream and cascade as well as a small lake. It's like a contemporary Bomarzo: a huge gilded head of Apollo rises out of the ground, trees are planted into the sculpted bases of columns while dedications celebrate Dürer, St Just, Robespierre, Caspar David Friedrich and Laugier. There are buildings and monuments, all of them quite small, a pyramid, and a grotto celebrating Dido and Aeneas. The imagination roams round the classical world, with inscriptions from Ovid and others, and then swoops down the centuries to embrace the French revolutionary period and then the condition of our own time, with strange groupings in which *Et Ego in Arcadia* depicts shepherds discovering a tank with a skull and crossbones upon it. Great use is made of columns of all kinds, complete as well as broken, and also of their capitals. A crofter's cottage looking across a pond has incised onto it classical columns and an inscription which identifies it as The Temple of the Muses.

As we skirted the pond a small, elderly figure appeared waving a sheet of paper. It was Ian Hamilton Finlay, a kindly, almost avuncular figure with a soft Scottish accent and a lilting voice. The paper was a plan of the garden. Off we set again and then, on the dot of 1.30 p.m., we made our way to the modest house – more a cottage – and carried chairs out onto the terrace to do the interview. This was really about his latest garden at Luton, the principles of which are those of Little Sparta. Here is a man who left school at fourteen, who had surrounded himself with an imaginary landscape peopled with allusions which could only come from a deep knowledge of classical literature, the German Romantics and French Revolutionaries. He was tremendously fluent, lamenting the impoverishment of the garden in our own age, in which the focus is on the colour supplement and the television. In the past the garden was a point of departure and a setting for profound ideas, many of them esoteric, and he cursed those who had let education slide so that elementary allusions as, for example, the one to Apollo and Daphne, were no longer understood. But he had a benevolent view of things, for all he wanted from his visitors was that they should enjoy his garden. I asked did it matter that they did not understand it? No, there are many levels of understanding and none was to be despised. It was difficult to reconcile this kindly man with the image of him often projected outside as a crypto Nazi sympathiser who depicted Apollo holding a machine gun and not a lyre.

The garden made an enormous impression upon me. There are lessons here to be drawn for The Laskett. I admired the modesty of it. There was little money here and yet he had made something more significant in its way than Sissinghurst or Hidcote, a recovery of the great tradition stretching back through William Kent and others to Alberti.

This was a day for weird gardens. Next we tore along and up to Portrack House outside Dumfries to see Charles Jencks's new garden. The house is a small but handsome Georgian one, taller than it is wide and sited amidst rolling Lowland country. His mother-in-law had told him and Maggie to go ahead and do whatever they wanted to do to the garden. She's ninety and has just had open-heart surgery but is still plugging on. Maggie descended the stairs, her head wrapped in a turban, and it was clear that there was no hair beneath. I always associate turbans with loss of hair with chemo-therapy for cancer. I hope not. [She died of cancer a week later.] Maggie was much sweeter than I remember her, less assertive. Charles was a willowy delight, a kind of mad west coast of America profes-sor, this time gripped by proselytising a new architectural repertory based on post-Newtonian views of the cosmos and, above all, the chaos theory. That plus an obsession with soliton waves was grafted onto Maggie's Chinese geomancy and the result was in the process of being imposed onto the Keswick parkland. It was going to be huge, with lakes and meandering streams and man-made mountains evoking dragons and snakes and earth tremors. The effect so far was rather piecemeal and as yet needed to be drawn together, but it was certainly original, another kind of symbolic landscape embracing visions of both heaven and hell. The soliton wave was everywhere. Near the house there was a gravel and turf parterre base on it. At the back of the house there were two lakes, sharp-edged, with huge sculpted terracing around them rather like an amphitheatre, and a mount sixty feet high with a spiralling path to its summit. A vast potager with box-edged beds was in the making. There were soliton-wave iron entrance gates, the piers topped by post-Newtonian models of the universe, and equations on its creation were applied as a fret across the top of the greenhouse. Along one side ran a stone wall constructed with huge waves, arches and inscriptions. This must be the weirdest superimposition onto the Scottish landscape for centuries. It was less coherent than Little Sparta but it is too early to judge it.

I JULY

Sir Peter Wright retires

Peter Wright is one of those people who exudes good sense and affection. The ballet world has been lucky to have him and, I suppose, he it, but the idea of retiring from it did not please him. I remember him bursting out with 'Why *should* one retire?', which I thought boded ill for it is something to come to terms with before it happens. Shortly afterwards he was stricken with myasthenia gravis, a horrendous disease that affected his sight and, on steroids, he blew up. So the gala at Birmingham was in aid of that charity.

As galas go it was a beautiful evening, a balanced programme to show off the Birmingham Royal Ballet of his creation: Balanchine's *Serenade* and a *pas de deux* from *Romeo and Juliet*, along with funnies like a lot of old dancers donning their tights for *Façade* and sentimental touches like the Royal Ballet school children dressed as tiny sailors. As in the case of such evenings, all sorts of people swam into view to be greeted with a kiss, a smile, a nod, a wave. Where we sat there was Pamela Harlech, poor thing, having hurt her back, hobbling along on a stick, like Carabosse in black with a bit of gold glitter, while in front of me I contemplated what was left of Anthony Dowell's hair. The final parade was to the opening polonaise from the last act of *The Sleeping Beauty*. It went on and on until, at last, Peter and Sonya, amidst a snowstorm of gold dust, made their grand entry. Speeches followed. Jeremy Isaacs was rather mundane and much of it was lost as he didn't turn to face the audience. Anthony Dowell was brief. And then came Peter's, which did seem neverending. By then it was well past eleven. But Peter loves this kind of event and he clearly savoured every moment of it and forgot no one. He was then created Director Laureate and he beamed as a wreath of laurel resembling a horse harness was hung round his neck. Still, his achievement deserved it. He leaves a genuine legacy, a virtually new company and tradition in Birmingham. All the rituals were gone through and flowers rained down on the stage.

Princess Margaret, back from San Francisco, graced the occasion. No ripple of applause for her when she first entered. Afterwards we were bussed to the Convention Centre for a perfectly awful dinner and got to bed at 1.45 a.m.

3 JULY

Dutch visitors

We opened the garden to a group of Dutch garden owners. They came in two batches of fourteen. I worked like blazes on tweaking the garden up to being *à point*, including spending £48 on two standard white 'Kent' roses to fill ghastly blanks in the Flower Garden. It looked pretty good. I'd been asked what we charged and I said, oh forget it. Could they bring a plant? Well, I said, I love box. So up Laskett Lane marched this body of upper-class Dutch, each clasping a pot with a three-foot-high box tree. We had a wonderful time showing them the garden and didn't regret the decision. It is a tremendous pleasure to show to those that know and I learnt so much about box, how to cut it, how to take cuttings, how to prune it to encourage growth. Both lots stayed about two hours and we were left in a happy haze.

JULY

Drought

This summer we have begun to relive the drought horror of 1976. Week in and week out the sun has gone up like a golden disc into a bright blue sky. At first one was delighted but as the weeks passed, thoughts took another direction. Each day began at 6.45 a.m., when I stepped into the garden in my pyjamas to water part of the garden. That was before breakfast. Robin would then arrive and we'd move on to the Rose and Jubilee Gardens and the Fountain Court. Then, as everything got worse, we began to have to water the Yew Garden

Publicity shot for the first of the National Trust Lectures at the Purcell Room, 1988

The Canary Wharf Development is launched, March 1988: Paul Reichmann, me and Michael Dennis

Picnic at Powis Castle with Rosemary Verey and Julia, September 1989

With Jean Muir on the beach at Dunstanburgh, November 1989

Weekend party at Royal Lodge, March 1990: left to right, Ted Hughes, Neiti and Grey Gowrie, me, The Queen Mother, Hugh Casson, Fortune Grafton, Carol Hughes and Hugh Grafton

Placing the statues of the Four Seasons at Highgrove, April 1990, with glimpses of the yew hedges being cut into swags

In *Versace* scything in front of Kensington Palace, summer 1991,
for the television series *Royal Gardens*

Above left Turfing the Jubilee Garden at The Laskett, 1990

Left Pleaching the limes on Elizabeth Tudor Avenue at
The Laskett, autumn 1991

Breakfast at Versace's Villa Fontanelle on Como, May 1993:
left to right, Richard Avedon, Nene Bellotti, me, Gianni Versace and
Nicole Wisniak

Lunch party at Whitfield, May 1994: left to right, Clare and James Kirkman,
Mary Clive, me and Penny Graham

Coffee in Bordeaux, 1994

At La Mortella with Susana Walton, June 1994

Lunch with Hugh Honour and John Fleming at the Villa Marchiò, Lucca,
March 1995

and the knots. Add to that the cans and buckets to the clematis and roses in the Spring Garden. Slowly one became more and more manic, dreading the dawn of each day. The poplars have withdrawn, the silver birch tree leaves are yellow and the fruit trees in the orchard have begun to shed their fruit. If we don't have rain within the next ten days, I fear frightening casualties.

20 JULY

The Story of Britain

This still continues to be an extraordinary saga. Every time we open a newspaper or turn on the radio, history pops up again. The night before last I caught Conrad Russell eulogising C.V. Wedgwood, praising her narrative skill and her interpretation of the period. How ironic, praise from academe which killed her off, but now, alas, too late as she's got Alzheimer's. Typical.

There is something weird about *The Story of Britain*. It will either be my bestseller of all time or a total disaster. Who knows? But the vibes and ripples are good. Julia MacRae is simply incredible, like a galleon ploughing forward, undaunted. She tells me that I've written a masterpiece, which frightens me. Her standards are exact and exacting. She brushes the academics to one side: 'Your book will be read, theirs won't.'

We're at the stage of it being half-designed, with battles about the cover. The earlier image has already been discarded, lettering only was considered but felt to be too funerary and was dropped, so we're now back to pictures. Julia's Rowland Hilder has been replaced by my suggestion of Stubbs's *Threshers* in the Tate. I hope that works. Offers have already come from the United States and a printer has come forward and offered to do another blad for nothing. We don't even know how he knew the book existed but they are passionately keen to print it. Simon King of Hutchinson is roaming about and one television company, catching a glimpse of it on his desk, is already after it.

I can only describe all of this as bewildering. It has been a quite wonderful team with which to work, all with a sense of commitment and an enthusiasm I haven't experienced for a long time. But it is a long lead up to next May. It would be so marvellous if it did take off. I long for some financial security instead of always worrying a bit – but not too much. I'd like to feel that after seventy-five I wouldn't have to slave all day and every day until I drop.

20 SEPTEMBER

The sale of the Royal Naval College, Greenwich

I'd noticed this topic float into the public domain but it was Simon Jenkins's article in *The Times* on 9 September which made me MAD. I faxed a letter and it was printed on the Monday, the first on the subject. The *Independent* took it up with a vengeance. I was quoted, along with quite a *galère* of others, and there was a mugshot. On Thursday the *Evening Standard* asked me to write about the row concerning the felling and replanting of Queen Anne's ride at Windsor. On Friday they asked me to write on Greenwich. I polished off both, Greenwich in a frenzy, which was printed on Tuesday 19th. As a result I did two radio interviews on the 20th. I only hope that all this *Sturm und Drang* gets somewhere. It is utterly appalling to sell the lease on the Royal Naval College for a hundred and fifty years – Wren, Vanbrugh, Hawksmoor and Thornhill – here is a great lump of our heritage which cries out to kept together and not sold down the river by a government that pays lip-service to heritage and complains that children have no history. ITV news rang and I said that I'd go to London and do a news piece to camera.

21 SEPTEMBER

Shame on them

The ITN car collected me and took me down to the bank opposite Greenwich, which was lit by a glorious golden autumn light. This was for a piece to go out on Wednesday. I did a furious denunciation to camera, lifting up the Knight, Frank & Rutley glossy brochure and, unfolding, held up the page with the pictures of Michael Portillo and Virginia Bottomley and rained shame on them.

The car then took me to Heathrow for a trip round German gardens.

14 OCTOBER

My history teacher is eighty

Joan Henderson is eighty. A surprise party was laid on for her by Alasdair Hawkyard in his little house in Camden Town. It was very sweet as the stucco-fronted house with its door onto the street had its windows festooned with balloons. I was dragooned to open the front door when she was 'delivered' to what was a surprise of a kind that she would only take from me. So I swung wide the door and presented her with volume two of my *Collected Papers*. Really she cheerfully swam along on the tide, not looking much different from when she taught me forty-five years ago! A little limper, yes, but not that much. Her dipped brunette hair was, as usual, neatly in order, her face powdered, her rather owl-like glasses in place, and she was in a silk dress of a kind that only people of that age wear. So we sat and talked and reminisced, after which a gargantuan buffet lunch followed. I left at 4 p.m. and it was still going on.

That's a long and precious friendship. It's amazing that she still has so many young devotees who take her out. While she was there the phone rang from time to time, and it was invariably people who couldn't be there to wish her well. It was very touching that so much care and attention had gone into the occasion. I love the way she just plugs on, something from which to learn.

AUTUMN

The end of this year I'm slave-driving myself to finish the *Country Life* book. Day in and day out I sit, turning the pages of volume after volume until I become quite dizzy and practically fall off the chair. The last phase has developed into a drudge. These cover the grim post-war years, when the magazine is more and more out of tune with the new world of the Welfare State. It gets dull, a set formula which relentlessly goes on and on. In the drear Fifties and early Sixties it didn't somehow matter, but when things really began to change in the mid-Sixties, *Country Life* didn't. It just mummified.

I find it a struggle to keep going with this book: it's like reliving a chunk of one's own life, all those heritage crises. But there's no energy or excitement about it. God knows how one's going to pull the book together. I'm surprised how drear it all was. After all, we subscribed to *Country Life* all through those years, I suppose as a comfort factor in awful times. But looking at those 1970s issues I can't now imagine why we did.

4 DECEMBER

The historic towns series

Yesterday I travelled seven hours by train to Norwich via Birmingham and Ely, a depressing journey mainly in the dark and rain. On Ely station Martin Buckley and I sat like Romanian refugees. I was two nights in Norwich, one in the perfectly awful Maid's Head, a Moat House hotel, and the other in The Beeches on the outskirts, which was far more comfortable.

Martin is irascible and laid back, with middle age beckoning, but he's got an inquiring mind. He still lopes around like a student at thirty-eight. I think we get on fine but the making of the series has been so spread out that it is in danger of losing edge and direction, so now it's all hands on deck as we struggle to pull it together as the programmes are broadcast. Overall, from being reveries they've become indictments: they're tracts for the times on towns going under fast to the 'doughnut effect', a ring of suburbs and shopping malls with a hole in the middle. That's what gives the series its thrust and I haven't held back. Durham got the boot. But Norwich has always seduced me as there's still so much left and the Council's new uses for old buildings policy seems enlightened, with a 50% increase in those living in the inner city, a mix of young and old, richer and poorer, and freehold as well as rented.

It was bitterly cold in Norwich, with icy winds from Siberia. Some of the interviews went well, like the one with the city planner; others, like that with the cathedral surveyor, were dull and lifeless. Every old building was a palimpsest and we explored an arts centre that turned out to be a rich Tudor merchant's house with a compartmented 1520s ceiling and, upstairs, a handsome hall. The Dragon Hall, in the red light district, yielded two massive halls out of six tenements. Norwich emerged as a handsome and vibrant city with a spring in its step. Its residents like their 'island' status, although they deny it.

On the Monday evening we had dinner with Clive Scott and his wife. He'd rescued Martin from being flung out of the University of East Anglia. But he was a bright and indulgent academic in the best sense of the word and an FBA to boot, so he must be quite distinguished.

The Beeches hotel had an extraordinary garden from the 1860s attached to it, which was set within a small valley, with some weird built structures that made use of the throw-outs from the local brickworks – bits of gothicky strapwork et al. used to create ruins, a fountain and fantastic walls. The garden is run as a trust.

I arrived back in London and at last contacted Random House. *Story* is now to be published in September 1996 and not May, which threw me into a deep depression. I had finished it on Christmas Day 1994. It has just dragged on far too long and the thought of performing around it almost two years on is almost too much to bear.

END OF THE YEAR

So what kind of year has 1995 been? On the whole I think a good one but very hardworking, in a way too much so and I fell behind on the *Country Life* book. There's my old seven-year-cycle theory and I feel the truth of that, for I seem to be entering into a better or rather different phase. That rectangular, joyous lady, Julia MacRae, has really lifted me. Some people, I think are 'reserved' for you at different times of life. I'll be content if I can do the run with her of *Story*, the *Diaries* and the book on the nation's civilisation. I never feel alone when I'm working with her.

Radio ended on an up. Peter Everett, Martin Buckley's boss, thinks that I have so distinctive a voice that a series ought to be set around me and not me around it for 1997. If that flies it could go on for 1998 and 1999. I've made the decision to change performing agent. Jean Diamond of London Management is certainly larger than life and I love her but really I've got nowhere. So I'm seeing Sue Ayton of Knight-Ayton. Conran Octopus has pulled itself together and I really will enjoy trying to write a book on ornament. The *Diaries* also beckon. So 1996, give or take a bit, is all there.

I'm glad that Elizabeth Esteve-Coll has moved on. It feels to me like a huge cloud going from the V&A. I had lunch with Alan Borg before Christmas. He's fine but still rather in that 'Little Boy Blue' phase, although he's already beleaguered by cuts. That job is a no-win one like the Royal Opera House. But I'm glad to think that I can go back to the Museum and I salute him for making that contact. In 1997 I've agreed to open the new Silver Gallery, which seems apposite.

1995's greatest loss was Jean Muir. I really miss her, maddening and wilful though she was, but such an original, so passionate and so funny. Oh dear, what can I say? Losses like that will happen so much more now, and who knows when one's own span will be up? And I'll also miss Graham Rose, who commissioned my first garden piece for *The Sunday Times* in 1979. What a delightful man. But he smoked like a chimney and cancer took its toll, again too soon.

The summer and the drought wore me down, but what travel! Florence, Como, Holland, Germany, Vienna – all stimulating, punctuating the year with excitement and giving me new garden ideas . . .

1996

Writing projects reviewed

The opening weeks of this year have just been grind and influenza and very boring. This has been a wind-up period, the end, I feel, of a phase stretching back to 1988. All kinds of things have come to an end and others have started up. *The Story of Britain* has gone at last to be printed. Julia MacRae forever sings its praises. Who knows? Maybe it'll be the one book for which I will be remembered, an attempt to open the door into our past for everyone before it is shut. I feel this great passion to write broad introductory books. The need is there and, if I can, I'd enjoy writing its companion on the island's civilisation. *The English Arcadia* I feel mixed about. I hated the rush in which I had to write it. I loathed the physicality of handling and turning all the pages of those vast volumes of *Country Life*. But I learnt a lot about the 'mythology' of Britain as created and sustained in this century and it left me wondering where we go from here. It was a hieratic aristocratic vision, but it was also pastoral and benign. How is it to be taken into the twenty-first century, if indeed it is to be?

And now I'm into the *Diaries*. They have been an extremely interesting experience. I have found it quite difficult to begin. To be honest I didn't really learn to write until the mid-1970s, so some of the stuff from 1968 and on needed tidying up to make any sense of it at all. I feel that I ought to do the *Diaries* now because who knows when one will drop off the perch? Also, so many of the people I write about are no more, so that is an incentive to publish. In addition, one needs to print them before the people who know the frame of reference have also gone. Plus, I found, it was a great act of reconciliation. To face up to one's own past is quite a challenge for it is to come to terms with failure as well as triumph. The V&A had utterly traumatised me and I felt that I had been a failure. As I start typing up those V&A years in the light of what has happened since, I no longer get that sense of failure. All the time I feel how much was achieved, against tremendous odds. Also the *Diaries* are not just a saga of internal wrangles. I remember deciding that they should record a social panorama and they do. They're tremendously funny. Some of it, of course, I can't print. My only regret is that I wish that I'd written more. For the whole of 1974 and half of 1975 I stopped, and even earlier on it ebbs and flows; but thank God I wrote what I did, for it is fascinating. In a way, if I had written more it would have been boring and repetitious. As it was, I took up my pen when people and occasions struck me as extraordinary. And who wants to read about my office life anyway? My letters to Jan van Dorsten make up for a lot. I had no idea that they were so good: good because I was writing to a professional of the same age, good also because I was writing to someone abroad so that I needed to paint a picture of the situation here. I've printed off about two hundred and fifty pages so far – 1968 to 1976 – but the real bulk is yet to come. I must also think about how to begin and when. How lucky I am to have Julia MacRae watching over me and chortling. I would like to think that I'd written one of the diaries of the era. Probably not. Oh but how late it was that I learnt to write!! It took me until I was forty to write like Cecil Beaton was able to do in his late twenties. But then I had none of his advantages, none at all.

All three projects mean a staggering sequence of publications: 16 September *Story*, 16 October *Arcadia* and May 1997 the *Diaries*. They are so contrasted that it will be interesting to see how I emerge out of it all.

22 FEBRUARY

The garden in the winter of 1995–96

We have had three falls of snow and much ice and rain too, with both the Jubilee and the Kitchen Gardens like lakes. But each year now that we have Robin as a full-time gardener we make further inroads, tidying, reclaiming, giving point and shape where there was none before. There is still, however, much to be achieved. Reg Boulton's marble 50th Birthday Garden slabs erupted with the frost and all of that will have to be re-done when spring comes. I can't wait either for Mike Jones, the painter, to start painting the Temple and other built features, as we had seen done in Germany. Robin did a great deal to the shrubberies, clearing them and then lower-limbing some of the conifers backing the Flower Garden. This has brought a new spaciousness and the excitement of affording tantalising glimpses of things to come.

Around The Folly [our guest cottage] we've planted laurels facing the road, a medlar tunnel and yew hedging. We've not started on that tiny garden yet. We're all geared to pave the Yew Garden, however, and Julia has done a brilliant design to accommodate the box given us by good friends, making it into one large parterre.

Then I urged her to go on and design a layout around the knot in front of the house, which she has done. I feel that we must just bang on and do it, but we're driven mad by the lack of a reliable builder. Reg Boulton is doing the plaque for the entrance to the garden, inscribed with our initials and the word 'CIRCUM-SPICE', a crib from the inscription in St Paul's for Wren, and I'm still after a Latin inscription for the Temple. Stephen Orgel, when he came to stay, was such a self-indulgent misery that I got nowhere.

Working through the Diaries and the Van Dorsten letters, I was astonished to see how much there was about the garden. Its whole history, masses in fact, compared with so little on either Sissinghurst or Hidcote. But here is ours, recorded blow by blow, flower by flower, for over twenty years. This is another book . . .

28 FEBRUARY

Florence

We left for Florence on Monday to use up our Air Miles, or rather, Julia's. This is the third year we have done this. It came at the right moment. The *Country Life* book had exhausted me and, because it was written under such appalling pressure, it reactivated vertigo. Then followed 'flu, which knocked me out, together with coping with a new computer.

These have been beautiful days in Florence, a chill wind but bright blue sky and warm sun. The days have a momentum: breakfast at 8 to 8.30 a.m.; 9 to 9.30 a.m. off for stroll to look at something, lunch at 12.30 p.m. – pasta, salad, wine, water and coffee; back to the hotel for a two-hour rest, about 4-ish another stroll, back by 6 p.m., rest, bath, dinner, bed and sleep by 10.30 p.m. It has restored me and

I've learnt to dawdle. I feel no compulsion to rush or accumulate information for something, just to look and enjoy. We went around the Palazzo Signoria again, for me reliving scenes from a chapter in my book *Art and Power*. Even though we were early we had to queue for the Uffizi, where again it was a case of visiting old friends like the Piero della Francesca portrait of Federigo da Montefeltro and his wife, Bianca. Then there was the usual visit to the Medici tombs – every visit to that mausoleum is more extraordinary than the last. This time there are signs of them being cleaned, and how wonderful that would be! This morning we went to San Lorenzo first, Michael-angelo's architecture striking me as so odd and the famous staircase leading to the library so awkward. Then on to San Marco, which I first visited in 1955 when I was very *quattrocento*-struck, full of Berenson and Wölfflin and treasuring my little Skira book on Fra Angelico, one of the very early colour-plate books after the war. It's the frescoes in the cells that are so marvellous, the off-white dis-tempered interiors, each cell with its oval-topped door and window, each window with its shutter, the shutter itself with an inner shutter. Even the hordes of tourists couldn't defeat the utter calm of the place, which relates to atmosphere, the proportions, the timelessness and the sense of space yet enclosure, the simplicity of each monk having his fresco, some better than others, but the colours bleached and pale and the array within of fondant pinks, scarlets and golds familiar from the panel pictures. How I had longed to see these fifty years ago as I turned the pages of that Skira book, and there was always that experience of the shock of the original against the reproduction in the book, in terms of size and location. How sated we are today with so much. Do people still get that sense of the privilege and revelation of the actual object? I hope so.

13 MARCH

Fleur Cowles at home

Fleur Cowles still keeps open shop. We have gone there on and off over the decades. The format is always the same. The approach is through the gloomy staircase well of Albany with its uniformed porter and up past grim-faced doors. By the time one gets to hers the door is flung wide with two servants standing there, one being the butler with what remains of his hair dipped auburn and arranged *bouffant*. There are always two tables for dinner, one rectangular for twelve or fourteen and the other round and seating ten. The hall itself is poky but it prepares you for what follows, for Fleur's décor is original and that is part of its charm. It is all very New York, wholly inward-looking, claustrophobic, overheated and over-arranged. She uses the strong colour and pattern that Americans love, in Fleur's case veering towards the dolly mixture syndrome.

Through a small door you gain access to the first large room, a pre-1914 Arts and Crafts one if you look at it hard enough, for there is a vast inglenook fireplace along one side in the manner of Ashbee. But everything has been painted and overlaid with such a multicoloured cosmetic, much of it consisting of her own paintings, that what it began its life as could easily be missed. The dinners are always black tie and there is a permanent fixation with royalty, this time the dinner being for the Greeks. Everyone who comes through this small door is greeted by Fleur and then does the rounds.

Fleur must be nudging eighty, a short, squat woman, her rather weak eyes this evening exposed and not hidden behind dark glasses. She always dresses to effect, usually wearing something to exhibit this or that piece of jewellery that she has designed. Tonight is coral night. Two large explosions of it serve as earrings and there is an asymmetrical collar of it round her neck. Tom, her husband, is nothing other than warm and benign.

The line-up is made up of some her old favourites, like the representative of Monaco Barney Ivanovic, once the handsomest man in the room. Fleur loves ambassadors, names and the rich. Judi Dench and Michael Williams looked bewildered by the world into which they had stepped and we fell on each other with whoops of joy. Gayle Hunnicutt is well into middle age, her hair piled like a cushion on her head. Her husband, Simon Jenkins, a little portly now, is lined and greying. Sukie and John Hemming join them in being also dedicated to the 'scene'. Mark Birley and sundry others completed the picture, including the extraordinary Chinese author of *Wild Swans*. I never got to speak to her but she was magic.

Then we all processed into dinner through two small rooms, the first a dressing room with a day bed in exotic shades of orange and red, the room a monument to calculated clutter, with a table with two hundred little boxes arranged upon it. Then through the bedroom with, as usual, a couple of Fleur's latest pictures casually propped up against a chair so that we wouldn't miss them. Everything was bedizened and painted but always with a beguiling originality – and all inward-looking, like a cocoon.

Then on into the great room, a huge Adam-style cube, quite magnificent decorated in Wedgwood blue and white and again a kleptomaniac's dream. The large table is always in the window, the small, round one in the middle. Everything is designed by Fleur and you're told that just to drive the point home: candlesticks, ceramic pieces, the plates, the lot. The food is invariably filthy, tonight deep fried scampi with a sauce out of a bottle, a piece of chicken on a slice of toast spread with pâté, some vegetables and, finally, a killer of a pudding, a chocolate cake piled high with scoops of ice cream. I sat between Lady Renwick and the Queen of Greece. Lady Renwick is French, rather petite and hugely intelligent and teaches French at one of the international universities in London. She was fun. The Queen of Greece has a long Scandinavian face, fair hair, her features not intelligent ones, and wearing a black dress with lace furbelows. I was obviously placed next to her as being good at queens! In fact it was only me that made any conversation. She talked of the recent marriage of one of her children at Hampton Court Palace with all its logistics. The King was thrilled that day that the Greek courts had ruled that he could have a Greek passport and that his palaces and their contents were also his. He's now a rather florid kind of man, not, I thought, very fascinating but that may be because I have no interest in Greek politics.

The dinner over, the ladies went and the men were left in the English fashion. Then we got up and went and were offered glasses of water on returning. We mingled and I talked to Michael Williams; then we escaped. It's always the same. It's like a bower in which dwells this phenomenon called Fleur Cowles. She bestows on herself an importance that history will not accord her. She paints bad multicoloured pictures of animals and flowers and has designed a lot of rather nasty kitsch ceramics. There used to be a theory that the butler painted her pictures. No, I don't think so: they are not good enough. And of course there's the famous anecdote about the butler saying 'Miss Cowles, the King is on the phone', to which came the immortal reply: 'Which king?'

MID-MARCH

Lecturing to the Dutch

As in England, in March it was still freezing in the Netherlands, with leaden skies. I had been asked over at the behest of Margreet Diepeveen to give a star lecture at Zeist. For this we were popped into a converted mansion house hotel in the bridal suite, all pink and flowers but very comfortable. On the Saturday we went to the Vermeer exhibition in The Hague, for which the tents tacked on to the Mauritshuis were bigger than the house itself; one of these was a vast hall filled with desks and a cafeteria and another contained a large shop. The English edition of the catalogue was already sold out and, even though we had tickets, we still found ourselves queuing to go in. Once in, it was jammed and you had to be tall to see anything at all. But it was rather unforgettable, crammed with all the old favourites like the milkmaid and the view of Delft.

At noon we got to the church in which I was to lecture, where immediately disaster struck. Half of the windows were not blacked out and the slide projector and the screen both turned out to be virtually useless. I was traumatised and just sat immovable. Panic then set in. Eventually at 3 p.m. we got back to the hotel, ate and changed. On return we found that the audience was jammed. Again and again the projector broke down, so that the lecture lasted two hours, with me holding the audience by ad-libbing on practically everything and anything, which sucked my adrenalin dry. Then followed a book signing, after which came a party and then a dinner. By 8.30 p.m. I couldn't take any more, went to the hotel, ate with Julia and collapsed into bed.

However, in spite of some awful weather we saw some wonderful gardens, including Walenberg, past its prime but still marvellous. On the Sunday we saw an incredible small garden in a suburb somewhere, a box garden held in by a yew hedge and then the whole held together by beech. We went into Belgium for lunch with Patricia van Roosmalen in her Fowleresque house. A New Zealander by birth, she has an extraordinary quality, so that even in winter her garden is a miracle of concision and contrast. She owes much to the fact it was laid out by the man who did Walenberg.

24 MARCH

Madresfield

We went to lunch at Madresfield, Charles and Rosalind Morrison having entered our lives via George Clive. I had been there three or four times over the decades during the reign of old Mona Beauchamp. I really didn't like the house then. In a way it had closed in on itself and one couldn't look at anything properly. But Mona was rather splendid, a handsome, matronly dame who went around in a white Rolls-Royce. I long remember meeting her, seemingly bent beneath necklaces composed of gold ingots, at the opening of the *Age of Charles I* exhibition at the Tate Gallery.

The Morrisons, however, have humanised the place. At the entrance over the moat six dogs were jumping up and down everywhere. As we arrived we saw Martin and Gay Charteris slowly emerge from their vehicle. Both are now old, Martin with a hearing aid, although every so often as sharp as ever. After lunch I sat next to him and told him of my unhappy 'Royal Gardens' experiences with the Prince of Wales's office. Martin hadn't enough words of condemnation, although, he added, HRH was 'a nice boy'. They go up to London four days a week to make a living in the Lords, but Gay's at a loose end there really. But it was so good to see them both again.

Rosalind's daughter by her first marriage to Gerald Ward, Sarah, was there and reminded me that she been in HRH's office when I did the television series. I'd forgotten. The other guests were the Smiths, John and Christian. I'd never taken to him before. I always thought he disapproved of me but I might have been wrong. Today we shared mutual eulogies about the incredible Arts and Crafts decoration added to the house – the library and its carvings, the huge finger-plates and the tiny Anglo-Catholic chapel painted all over in a late Pre-Raphaelite style with angels and St George and the Virgin and the Lygon children floating amidst a flowery mead.

The food left a little to be desired. Roast beef in the aftermath of the BSE scare seemed inapposite, along with a heavy steamed pudding. I didn't know that the latter still existed. But Charlie and Rosalind are a benign couple and one could poke around and look at the incredible pile-up of stuff, really unbelievable. Alec Cobbe had re-hung the pictures, a huge improvement, but it's such a mish-mash of family portraits and French worthies. In fact the Beauchamps must have been shopaholics during the Revolutionary period, as there was masses of *boulle* along with portraits of French kings, aristocrats and their mistresses.

At the time I reminded myself that Madresfield was the original Brideshead. The house rambles round a courtyard, a series of rooms connected at odd angles mainly in rookery nook Elizabethan revival style but, beneath all that, genuine. But it was so good to see the cobwebs blown away.

20 MAY

Reflections at the Villa Fontanelle

I am writing this at the Villa Fontanelle, wonderful days of absolute quiet, our host, Gianni Versace, having had to go to open his shop in Venice. It is always wonderful staying here, even if, as it has been this weekend, on and off rainy and cloudy. There is tranquillity and quiet broken only by the lapping of the waters of Lake Como.

Looking back, I finished work on the *Diaries* three weeks ago. Typed up, they came in at about 550 pages of A4. Now that they are done I can't really 'see' them any more. I had to do them in a rush. I couldn't bear to spend the whole year wallowing in the past and parts of them were somewhat traumatic. I had always thought 1977 a bad year but 1985 and 1986 probably eclipsed it with the sense of having reached the end of something, not knowing how to get out, and the V&A seeming to go so fearfully wrong. I didn't write that much and what little that was there was agonising. It was extraordinary how the mood changed from the moment it was public that I was going. All the fun in life flooded back, along with the observation and interest in things.

Well, now it's all gone. Julia MacRae won't be editing the *Diaries* until June and intends to spend the summer on them. I suspect that a lot will have to come out. I wrote to Ion Trewin that we'd got the block of marble and now it had to be sculpted, although more that I put in brackets can probably stay in than I at first thought. I suppose that it will be a 350-page or so book. Somehow it was a relief to have done it, tidied it up and put it away, that part of one's life as though it were another world, distant like another era to which I no longer felt I belonged. It had come and gone. Somehow there was a restoration of faith.

I know that the National Portrait Gallery had been a landmark, that no one can deny, but I was struck by how enormously innovative the V&A period had been, in spite of my struggling against all the odds: government, staff and press. It was not an unimpressive achievement. Perhaps, in time, that will be recognised.

Beatrix Miller always says that my life goes in seven-year cycles and in a funny way she's right. Taking that as a starting point, 1995 was the start of a new cycle and, indeed, I think that it has been. I've deliberately changed course. Gardening will go on but the books to come will be very different. Will they be a success or not? Who knows? All I hope is that they produce enough income to sustain the direction in which I want to go. I have already just begun the companion volume to the history, one on the country's civilisation. I've started with the period 1066 to 1200, the Romanesque, just to see how it works. It is refreshing to have the excuse to read it all. Also, the Middle Ages seem so straightforward and coherent. This is a book that must let down a wider backcloth. It must be set into a European context and, like the history, it is a sorely needed volume.

18 JUNE

George Weidenfeld at the National Portrait Gallery

Yesterday evening we were bidden to the Portrait Gallery for the unveiling (*sic*) of a portrait of George Weidenfeld. It is strange but pleasurable going back there these days. The evening kicked off with drinks in the Twentieth-Century Gallery. George's portrait, a head and half shoulders, mercifully wasn't unveiled but was just hanging there. It was by Gerald Benney's son Paul, who appeared decoratively dressed in a Regency waistcoat of ivory silk with gunmetal buttons, striped, baggy oriental trousers with a belt loosely swagged across them, and a black jacket. He was rather envious of my voluminous Rhett Butler white frock coat. However, to return to the portrait, which was like but not that much – rather plasticised, in fact, and not catching the sharpness of the eyes, but rather recording a bored, reflective look.

This was a Weidenfeld-esque gathering: Nigel Nicolson (we both recalled our invasion of Sissinghurst with Pam Hartwell all those years ago) and Anthony Cheetham of the firm along with his sweet daughter, who had married the headmaster of Whitgift. Then there were the Wolfsons, Marcelle and Tony Quinton, the Chadwicks, benign, Peter and Iona Carrington, plus a further sprinkling of the rich being nobbled, along with the Chairman of the Board, Henry Keswick and Tessa. The Carringtons looked far from well, she thinner and lacking energy, having some blood complaint, and he with pancreas trouble and having had to give up drink, looked deflated. I told him that I had a chapter in the *Diaries* entitled 'Carry on Carrington' and we giggled over letting groups into our gardens and thus making an honest bob or two. He took me over to look at his own portrait, good across the eyes but the jawline was too heavy and wrong. Chrissie Gibbs brought Camilla Cazelet. He is so establishment these days, an *éminence grise* in his boring dinner jacket and short clipped hair, so very different from the caftans and beads of the past. Henry Keswick made a not very good speech, which mainly indicated that George's portrait ought to be in the National Portrait Gallery of Israel. George responded well, and clearly loved the Gallery, but all the time I was thinking how horrified one's predecessors as Director would have been to see a portrait of a Trustee hung and unveiled in his own lifetime.

Then we went to the top floor, where there was a perfectly pleasant dinner at half a dozen round tables. I sat between Marcelle Quinton in fuchsia and George's daughter, who remembered when she had first met me at Este during Diana Phipps's house party in 1971. Marcelle was off to excavate in Israel and on to other points, including a Greek island. Next to her, Leonard Wolfson sat huddled, pecking at a few crumbs. I avoided him as I never forget how perfectly awful he was over the V&A Primary Galleries. Thank heaven that I don't have to suck up any more.

THE SAME DAY

Elton John's garden

En route for London we went to Woodside, Old Windsor, to see how my Italian garden for Elton had turned out. The weather was Italianate, with a cloudless blue sky and hot sun. It could in fact have been Verona. Inevitably the house is a bit like getting into Fort Knox but once in the kitchen there was Elton in a suit by Richard James. He is the most affectionate man and today was in vibrant mood, spontaneously delighted to see us and thrilled with the garden. He's about fifty, slightly shorter than me, a little portly, something that must cause him show-business agonies, with a benign if undistinguished face but attractive in the way that an amiable teddy bear is.

In to the drawing room we went, which had all the French windows flung wide to what was a vision. I was really excited. The garden looked wonderful. There it was, glinting in the strong sunlight, the almost white balustrading and arcade softened with washes of ochre, the four beds edged with box with their four clipped yew cones and life-size statues of music-making satyrs underplanted with red geraniums. Where the arcade split in two it led on to a two-hundred-foot-long pleached lime avenue leading to a thirty-foot-high obelisk topped by a golden ball. I was entranced. I'd done the garden because of Gianni Versace and I'd got it right. How odd at sixty to find myself capable of doing such a thing and have the ability to write a six-hundred-page narrative history. I briefly bathed in my own capabilities, vowing always to keep going till I dropped.

We then strolled around the gardens, Elton wanting to pick my brains. Should he put a flower bed by the railway carriage? No, I said, it would look like Bournemouth. We told him to paint the fencing around the potager blue-green, picking the exact colour from his multicoloured shirt. And then he took me to another area by a lake with a view to Windsor Castle and asked me to do something with it. I said that I saw a kind of wilderness: rooms of hornbeam, beech and yew, cabinets filled with statuary, the hedges forming passages and from time to time 'windows' affording views onto the lake and also back to the Castle. 'No hurry,' he said, and I couldn't think about it anyway until the autumn.

Gianni and Antonio had come through the day before for lunch and that was good to hear. They had been over for the antique fair and I was glad that they had seen what I had done. Gianni and Elton are drawn to each other, both hugely creative people but also shy and lonely, released but also imprisoned by their stupendous creativity and also by all that money. But we really liked Elton. There were hugs, kisses and 'darlings' all round and off we went to London.

3–4 SEPTEMBER

The garden moves on

Patrick Bowe came to write up the garden for the centenary issue of *Country Life*. He's a large, benign, observant soul whose perceptions about the garden were refreshing. He made one look twice. I said apologetically that so much of it as a formal garden was mathematically out of true and he said that that was one of the things that added to it. All the Italian gardens, he said, were 'out'. They were planted, as The Laskett, by eye and that gave them their magic. German gardens were geometrically exact and hence lacked that quality. All sorts of things came up. The profusion of what he called 'ante-rooms' was one: Torte's Garden for the Yew Garden, the space around the Shakespeare Urn before the avenue, etc. He was fascinated by the fact that the two great avenues were not at right angles but pincered, not 'T' but 'V'. He especially admired our variety of levels.

This has been a year of huge activity, pressured by the sense that we are no longer young. The Yew Garden was paved and box trees from Monaughty planted. Julia's paving design using ochre, reddish and grey slabs worked enormously well. It will all call for much recutting of hedges. The new box I intend to cut abstract so that the old-fashioned parterres in the middle will be set within a modernist frame. Reg Boulton produced the slate inscription based on a line from Andrew Marvell, 'Green thoughts . . .'

In front of the house everything is in chaos and at a standstill in the making of a new garden. The mount still stands and Julia has bought an iron spiral staircase for it. I gave her a large cast-iron 'eighteenth-century' window, which will free-stand somewhere, and we are also going to investigate water, two fountains. There is a huge amount to do here when the builders return in October. It is all so unlike anything that we've done elsewhere.

Disaster, however, struck in the so-called Rose Garden. The major roses in the corner spandrels began to die, so they had to go. I purchased four Italianate baroque statues of the Seasons to replace them. They look marvellous but made the boy warriors look wrong, so they were moved to 'Covent Garden' and the obelisks from there to the Rose Garden. In other words, the usual musical chairs with the ornaments. Then the failing amelanchier out of the group of four at the centre had its death warrant sealed by a woodpecker. We've bucked at coping with the consequences of this for years but now we have to do it, cut down and uproot all four. This is a huge blow. We've consulted and they'll have to be replaced by four ten- to twelve-foot-high beech, whose roots go lateral, which we'll clip into standards and underplant with box. This means that in winter they'll keep their leaves and visually link with the beech hedging opposite. But all of this is quite a dramatic thing to have to do.

Meanwhile, Reg Boulton has done the inscription for the Temple in Greek: 'Memory Mother of the Muses', the key to the garden's iconography. It looks splendid. Then Sharon Powell of Crowthers rang me and said that she had seen two pieces of the fourteenth-century Palace of Westminster at a place at Stow-on-the-Wold. They seemed to be 'me', she said. They were. What a wonderful way in which to mark *Story*! One is seventy-three inches high, a huge coat of arms of Edward I, quite magnificent. The other is a large rose with a crown over it. They had come from the Bishop of Lincoln's palace, where they had formed part of the gate piers; they had originally made up the decorative parapet between the second and third floors of the Palace of Westminster's waterfront façade. For once I just blew £9,000 and didn't regret it. Indeed, I reckoned them to be a bargain, bearing in mind that an Italian reproduction baroque statue can cost £5,000 to £8,000. The plan is for the shield to replace the collapsing Gothick Arbour and the rose to go at the head of the Serpentine.

It's age and the acquisition of The Folly which have brought on such a ferment. The Folly, with its bright colour and its sense of fantasy, has triggered us over colour wash in the garden. We got the painter to paint the ground of the column at one end of Elizabeth Tudor Avenue blue and later applied the same treatment to the Shakespeare Urn at the opposite end. The garden as a result begins to look more and more unique.

20 SEPTEMBER

Beatrix Potter and Patrick Garland

Earlier this week we caught up with Julia's *Beatrix* at the theatre in Malvern. I had not seen it before and rather hesitated, but it's a perfect piece in its way. Patricia Routledge was superb as Beatrix Potter, able to shed the years with her face as though by magic. The set was High Top to a tee but the play was a strangely old-fashioned experience, a throwback to those 1960s one-handers that Julia did with Patrick Garland. Also, it lacked bite and too much about Beatrix Potter was elided. She was after all a tough sheep farmer who wrote books about fluffy animals. That never came out, nor how vile her childhood and her parents were. I'm afraid that the people who hold the copyright don't want to lose the softened image. At any rate we all trotted round after and told Patricia how marvellous she was and I signed copies of *Story* for her, for Patrick and for Judy Taylor.

On Friday Patrick came to stay the night. It was like coming home. He's in his early sixties now, still with that beautiful voice and actor's gestures and, now he's lost weight, some looks have returned. But at times, in repose, he looks sad, as though something in life had been lost, which in a way it has. He was at his apogee twenty years ago but then went off the tracks and spent all those years at Chichester, which was a waste. Who will ever remember them? They eroded him and took him away from writing. He was fascinated by everything, the garden, the house, how we lived, my workroom. He needs a new direction. Directing Shakespeare in Regent's Park is another waste of time, but there it is.

On the morning he left we sat and had coffee in the conservatory. Somehow I told him of the series I had put together for Diana Rigg kicking off as the wicked Frances Howard, Countess of Somerset. Patrick knew about her and then, suddenly, we all got excited. This was more where things were, he said, another *Royal Hunt of the Sun*, spectacle and blood on the stage, courtly etiquette and ritual and then the canker beneath. We started to visualise the tableaux with Chichester in 1998 in mind and Julia designing, Patrick writing the script and me producing the contemporary references. I rushed up to my library and brought down three books on the topic. Patrick took one with him. There was a sparkle in his eyes and his whole face and body were animated. Maybe he'll do it. He adored staying in The Folly, so perhaps our playwright will take up residence to put together *The Overbury Murder*. Who knows?

1996

3 OCTOBER

The Story of Britain

This has been a phenomenon. Publication day was 16 September, a Monday. Late on the 14th we arrived back from Italy, so there was a turn-round of little more than twelve hours before I went off to London in order to get up early to do the *Today* programme on Radio 4 at 7.50 a.m. That set the pace for a four-day media onslaught orchestrated by Colman Getty and the redoubtable Liz Sich. Already a month before there was a sense of excitement. The extraordinary piece by A.N. Wilson, 'Why we must all love Roy Strong', predicting that *Story* would join *The Story of Art* and *Civilisation* as an all-time bestseller, and the *Sunday Times* profile 'Precious Relic of the Sixties', with a cartoon of me looking like an 1890s aesthete, set the scene.

Then came the reviews: Tony Quinton and Robert Blake favourable but non-committal: I think that they were too old to 'see' what I was trying to do. Then followed Linda Colley in *The Times*, David Cannadine in the *Independent* on Sunday, Blair Worden in the *Spectator*, Richard Davenport-Hines in the *TLS* and Andrew Roberts in the *Mail on Sunday*. I have never had such reviews. Overwhelming, the *TLS* one so much so that I read it twice, thinking that it could only be a send-up! Only one filthy one later in the *Independent*, which was largely a personal diatribe, but that was offset by Charles Saumarez Smith's in the *Observer*, which combined a very favourable review of the book with a reappraisal of my period as Director of the V&A. It was very perceptive and it will be interesting to see what happens when the *Diaries* appear next year. All of this was accompanied by the bestseller lists. By 30 September *Story* had risen to number one in the *Evening Standard* non-fiction list and, I am told, will rise from number five to number three in the *Sunday Telegraph* listing on 6 October.

But to return to the media onslaught. What was striking about this was the fact that virtually everyone perceived the book as news, as a publication that was desperately needed. So the *Today* programme and *Sky News* and other interviews and discussions of all sorts honed in on identity, Europe and the lack of basic historical knowledge. It was a marathon with a finale on the Thursday at the National Portrait Gallery, a party with quite a turn-out, masses of old friends and glitterati. I gave, I am told, the right speech, wearing a Nicole Farhi frock coat. Afterwards there was a dinner at the Caprice for those who had worked on the book. What a team, which embraced my literary agent, Felicity Bryan, whose idea it was, Julia MacRae, my inspiring editor, Douglas Martin, the designer, Diana Phillip, the picture researcher and Keith Perry, former Head of History at St Paul's who kept me from making too many gaffes. I retreated, tired but happy, to the country.

The great bridge has been crossed, for I dreaded being hatcheted by the academics; but those I respected didn't do it. The aim of this book is a modest but necessary one and I made no claim as to originality. The response has been astonishing. Now I must now be out across country speaking and signing until Christmas: Canterbury, Oxford, Birmingham, Chester, Bath, Manchester . . . These days you have to market your own wares. Much will depend on the ability of Random House to get the books into the shops while the demand is there. It will be a relief when it's all over. It's already reprinting but I long to move on to the companion volume on the civilisation of Britain.

1996

The garden again

Our great plans for the garden this autumn at first seemed doomed to failure. The 1990s fantasy garden to be created in front of the house was to include a mount, found objects, the gravelling of the existing knot, and a couple of fountains. The builder started and then moved off in June, leaving a bomb-site. He said he would come back but hasn't, in spite of endless promises through the whole of the autumn. By this time he was supposed to have paved the Elizabeth Tudor Avenue and built the gate piers to the Orchard. The frustration was horrendous.

In the end I got things moving again. The great replanting of the Rose Garden went splendidly. A team headed by an engaging young tree man, Chris Mason, came on a brilliant winter's Saturday in November and achieved moving three out of the four of the amelanchiers; the fourth, which was too large to move, had to be dug out and sawn up. Two we planted near The Folly and, with luck, they'll prosper. Four beech were planted in their stead and I clipped them into standards. The following week some lovely glossy *Buxus sempervirens* came from Elizabeth Bainbridge go around their bases. So that was a triumph.

Through Sharon Powell we got on to Steve Tomlin of Reclamation Services at Painswick. Thanks to him, the installation of the masonry went like clockwork. Again on a sun-dappled day, two excellent masons came, who had been trained at Gloucester Cathedral, and the Orchard gate piers and finials went up in a morning. Alleluia! They look stunning. Suddenly that part of the garden's composition has come together and the 'proscenium' framing the vista to the reclining stag looks a knock-out.

Today, 16 December, I am writing this, for tomorrow the two Palace of Westminster pieces will be delivered. The Gothick Arbour, riddled with wet rot and disintegrating, has been moved to another Orchard alcove and a huge ironwork support has been anchored into the ground to take the grandest piece, Edward I's coat of arms. I wonder how it will look? Splendid, certainly, but there will be knock-ons as I don't know whether the planting already there and the blue wire obelisks will look 'right' with it. The rose and crown will go at the head of the Serpentine Walk, where there was an old exit from the Rose Garden.

Meanwhile I've also pressed on with Reg Boulton for plaques for the column at the head of Elizabeth Tudor Avenue. The column was one of Elizabeth I's emblems and I want plaques linking her and the present Queen. I'm hoping for two crowns and two ERs.

After Christmas, on 6 January, Steve Tomlin and his men return and promise to pave the avenue. I don't care any longer what it costs! I want it done and I won't be killed off by what I've labelled a 'Hereford syndrome' any more.

1997

EARLY 1997

The Galanthus Gala and the garden

January and February at the best are dead months and this period seems more than usual marked by an engulfing gloom. Only one day stood out for blue sky and brilliant sunshine and that was the occasion for the Galanthus Gala at the Royal Agricultural College at Cirencester, one Saturday, jam-packed with snowdrop fanatics and nurseries. 'I've got sixty varieties' seemed to be the triumphant norm, which made our thirty or so seem feeble, but Julia added half a dozen to her collection.

That was part of what has been months of frenzied building activity in the garden. The builder never returned, a well-meaning, hopeless Hereford man who couldn't read a plan, never came when he said he would and, in the end, drove us raving. Depression set in, but with it the will to get on and do things born of the realisation of advancing age. Whatever structurally has to be done to The Laskett garden has to be done now. At sixty-one and sixty-six we must press on, but how?

213

Steve Tomlin fell into our lap via Crowthers in December. Ex-LSE and Foreign Office, this is an engaging Mr Fixit who runs an architectural salvage yard to excite near Painswick, but who also has energy and excitement about our garden. So it was that he came to site the two pieces from the fourteenth-century Palace of Westminster, and through him came wonderful craftsmen like Richard, who built the gate piers in the Orchard, and Philip and John, who laid out the walk along Elizabeth Tudor according to Julia's design. The change to that is quite extraordinary, like a renaissance palazzo floor stretching into the distance. And then we had to do much fudging around the Shakespeare Urn because it was a bit 'off'. Steve produced piles of broken tiles, which were laid in a manner to deflect the eye from the asymmetry. The path has been lined with what will be a low yew hedge with hollies, which I intend to train as standards, arising from it.

But this did make the vista to the V&A Temple seem very dull. Julia revealed her great scheme that we should construct a ravine into which the visitor would descend, and then ascend from it to the Temple. But all of this will depend on *Story* and the *Diaries* engendering dollops of cash. But before even that happens, Steve's merry men must move to the front of the house and complete the garden there left like a bomb-site by Doug Stokes.

24 FEBRUARY

Enter A.N. Wilson

I gave a lecture for the National Trust in the Purcell Room on The Laskett garden. It was a sell-out. A.N. Wilson introduced me. He's an extraordinary man: I find him so difficult to place. There's so much to admire about him. The bravery to stand up and be counted, to differ, to be unashamedly elitist, all of it aligned to an appearance and manner which sometimes make me feel younger than he is. But he introduced me as though I was Queen Elizabeth's Lord Burleigh, a man of achievement turning from the dolours of public life to tend his garden and philosophise. I was touched and gave him a hug afterwards, which rather threw him. But what Julia MacRae told me afterwards was even more touching. The applause at the end was prolonged but she said that it was that at the beginning which was really significant: it was of a kind only accorded to those greatly beloved by the public. I wanted to shed a tear.

29 MARCH

Death of a heroine

It was sad to hear on the news that Veronica Wedgwood had died, in a way a merciful release after a decade of Alzheimer's. She was a large figure in my life, although after we moved to Herefordshire we lost touch. To me she was sacred. Joan Henderson had pressed her books into my hands as a schoolboy, *Velvet Studies* and *William the Silent*. How I adored them! I recall rushing home from school to catch her on the Third Programme, arguing with Hugh Trevor-Roper and another scholar about the causes of the Civil War. To her, human beings, their foibles and failings, always figured large. History to her was about humanity. Who could ever forget the panorama she painted in the opening chapter of *The King's Peace*, a vision which took the reader by the hand on a walk across country in Caroline England? Veronica was my heroine, so I was discomfited when I became an undergraduate that her work was so despised, always referred to in a patronising way. So began her long eclipse already by the middle of the 1950s.

How can I describe her? Inclining to short, with her hair tightly pulled back from the face into a bun at the back, a somewhat rubicund complexion, eyes that twinkled with intelligence and humour. In dress rather nondescript, shoes flat with no heels, and safe suits or skirts and blouses. But it was her voice that was so marvellous, so alert and endowed with an inner warmth. She always spoke about the past as though she were seeing it. Veronica was one of my referees for the National Portrait Gallery directorship and I'm proud to have contributed to her seventieth birthday *Festschrift*. By then she was in almost complete eclipse, marginalised by academe. They effectively broke her. So volume three of the Civil War trilogy never came. Worse, it was Jock Murray, I think, who got her off into writing a history of the world. Every time we met her, usually at the Opera House, I would ask her 'Where are you now?' 'China in the fifth century' would be the reply. This was a waste of vital years. Only in 1996, when she was beyond knowing, did I catch a Radio 3 talk by Conrad Russell, repenting and saying that she had been right all along. Those academics had treated her cruelly. She was a great historian, a great writer, a generous and gracious woman. I recall her writing in *The Author* an article saying how she came to do what she did, how after her degree she had to choose between close-focus academe and 'the great tradition', history as narrative and literature. She chose the latter. Jacqueline Hope-Wallace, her lifelong friend and companion, sweetly wrote to me that I had always been a 'true believer'. I always was. To me she was a sacred ideal.

MARCH

The comet

There seems so little of moment this year. The most exciting event was stepping out to view the great comet. The night sky was cloudless, star-dappled and, looking north, dominated by this quite extraordinary phenomenon with its great luminous tail. One can see how such a thing once presaged the death of princes.

Otherwise I read and write, pushing on with what is now called *The Spirit of Britain* [later reissued as *The Arts in Britain: A History*], having just reached the sixteenth century. It seems to be going well but it is daunting to think that I must finish it by September 1998. This a 'between year' and I must press on hard while there is quiet and space. I fear that the *Diaries* will disrupt me much.

6 APRIL

Elton John is fifty

When the invitation card framed in an abundance of gold arrived, I said to Julia, 'We must go. It'll be extraordinary.' And so it was. It was staged – the only word for it – on a Sunday night at the Hammersmith Palais. The invitation read: 'Dress: Costume/Fancy Dress'. Julia hates that kind of thing and went dressed in her usual way. I wore my black velvet frock coat and choirboy frilled shirt. When we stepped out of the taxi, one of the press photographers yelled out 'It's Roy as Einstein!' That must have been because my long white locks were by then standing up all over the place.

On we went past a phalanx of barriers and explosions of flowers in psychedelic colours so weird that under artificial light they looked precisely that, artificial. A girl dressed in a wig and eighteenth-century panniers ticked us off on a list and we filed in to find ourselves in a dance hall, a black hole lit by spots and complexes of lights. Along one side ran a stage, from which an orchestra and a singer belted out hits from the pre-pop Vera Lynn era. On the periphery of the dance floor were arranged tables covered with leopardskin-patterned cloths scattered with glitter foil confetti and sinking beneath explosions of roses in clashing shades of pink, orange and yellow that erupted from vases made of tangerines. There was a battery of wine glasses at each place, including one ruby glass. The whole effect was deliciously, deliriously over the top. The noise was deafening.

Ahead of us loomed an ever-growing assemblage of guests in fancy dress. It was incredibly difficult to work out the sex, let alone the identity, of virtually anyone. As so many recently released films had been set either in Restoration England or in that of Jane Austen, there was a superfluity of cavaliers and Charles IIs, Elizabeth Bennets and Mr Darcys. In addition, there was a gaggle of men in kimonos, extras from *Madame Butterfly*, and another group whose disguise came out of *A Hundred and One Dalmatians*. One woman arrived with her partner, attired as a Dalmatian, on a lead. There was also a fair amount of uniform, ranging in date from the Battle of Waterloo to the Second World War, and a couple of women with feathered headdresses at least four feet high who cut a swathe through the crowd.

There were the usual 'Oohs' and 'Aahs' as recognition gradually percolated through the throng. We spoke to David Linley, unrecognisable as a cat in a furry jumpsuit and feet like vast pedestals, his wife Serena somewhat unfortunately cast as Cruella de Vil. Dominic Lawson appeared as an extra from the Court of Charles II, a kit fixed up for him by his office, and Stephen Somerville as Sergeant Bilko. Heaven alone knows who all the rest were, but what was touching was that the media were kept firmly out. This was Elton's private party for his friends. And it really felt like that. This was a world of its own, with no sense of constructing a scene at all; he just threw everyone together, from his domestic staff to the celebs of the pop world, giving the occasion a curiously endearing quality.

At about 8.15 p.m. Elton entered, with David Furnish, to the sound of a fanfare. Both were in white and silver, *cap à pied*, Louis XIV-style with huge skirted coats, massive wigs, silver shoes and stockings, everything catching the light and shimmering. On entry I only caught Elton side-on and in this initial epiphany might just as well have been Marie Antoinette, for he wore a towering silver wig on top of which was perched a fully rigged ship. From his shoulders fell a train of silver spangled gauze borne up by two semi-naked blonde youths. He then promptly disappeared, no doubt to be photographed, reappearing minus the ship and train.

He's a lovable man and moved around from table to table greeting everyone. It was extraordinary coming face to face with what looked an overgrown schoolboy dressed as Prince Charming at the ball. I kissed him on both cheeks and said I looked forward to his hundredth. Then suddenly a huge swan sledge was propelled on to the stage as if it had escaped from *Lohengrin*. Elton and David then went on stage, Elton seizing a flashing, bejewelled sword and cutting his birthday cake. A team of formation dancers straight out of *Come Dancing*, all white tie and tails and furbelows a-flutter, appeared seemingly from nowhere and took the floor. Dazzling. Every kind of light went on and off. By then the atmosphere was already heady. The clubbing scene at full pelt took over, the crowds swaying this way and that to the music. This, I thought, would go on forever, but we left at 11 p.m. We had, however, enjoyed the party. What it never lacked was a feeling of real affection and that must go back to the man. He goes on my shortlist of originals.

21 MAY

The reception of the Diaries

The *Daily Mail* jumped the gun and started serialising the *Diaries* on 5 May, a week ahead of schedule. The reason was that the Election was so dull and the Tory cause a lost one, although no one had anticipated quite the landslide that followed on the Thursday. It is painful even to recall what the *Daily Mail* did to those *Diaries*. They began on the Saturday with an innocuous profile of me but what was filleted out during the week that followed was every bit of royal tittle-tattle they could extract. This flew in the face of the letter I had had from Paul Dacre, the Editor, saying that they would do one day on the Sixties social scene, another on the Thatcherisation of museums, etc. Instead it was relentless spreads of pictures of me with every member of the House of Windsor and contractions of the text that reduced everything to the status of soundbites. Paragraphs and sentences between sentences vanished. I had no control and somehow had to sit it out until the Friday.

Of course, they caused a sensation. The other newspapers, galled that they hadn't got the *Diaries* and hindered by an inability to get a copy until the legal ban was lifted, manufactured what they could. I said nothing. Terence Conran in the *Telegraph* let off his usual salvo about me being a disastrous Director of the V&A in his customary abusive style. Then, on Tuesday, the *Independent* had my picture on the cover of their supplement with above it 'Bitch of a Diary', with four columns within by Jonathan Glancey based on nothing because he hadn't read anything: the book was still embargoed. All of this left me somewhat shell-shocked, so I was not at my best on the *Today* programme. Never mind: I had succeeded in getting on to it for two books running. By then A.N. Wilson had written a page in *The Standard* giving thanks for Pepys, Alan Clark and me.

On Thursday the embargo was lifted and the books were delivered to the critics busily sharpening their axes. *The Times*, following exactly the sequence of the Alan Clark *Diaries*, purchased second serialisation rights, so on the week of 12 May, off we went again. I couldn't even bear to look at it. At a glance, however, it looked good pictorially and people tell me that it was well enough done; certainly also that it was funny and a good read.

By the following Tuesday I had got my second wind and did a first-rate interview with Paul Vaughan for *Kaleidoscope*. He hadn't read the serialisations but had read the actual book. For the first time there was a serious and pointed discussion instead of someone going on about what I had written sixteen years ago about the Princess of Wales's voice! Indeed, all that week the TV and radio were fine. Anyone young loved the book. For them it caught an incredible, vanished era. By the time I did Sheridan Morley for the Radio 2 arts programme I walked into the studio and he said 'This is a major diary on a level with Harold Nicolson and Chips Channon' and we moved off from there.

The printed reviews swung pendulum-wise from torrents of abuse to apotheosis. God knows the hidden agendas. A large number of the antis seem hardly to have actually read the book. For some it triggered an almost uncontrollable outpouring of venom on the far side of normality. In this Hugh Montgomery-Massingberd and Brian Sewell led the way. Robert Hewison twisted the knife in the wound in the *Sunday Times*, but then it suddenly all went into reverse. Selina Hastings loved it in the *Sunday Telegraph*, A.N. Wilson in the *Guardian* portrayed me as a poor Elizabethan coming up to the wicked city and hobnobbing with aristos bedizened with ruffles, making my statement and retreating to the country, while Richard Davenport-Hines beatified me in *The Times Literary Supplement*. Ion Trewin of Weidenfeld rightly remarked that Antony Thorncroft's review in the *Financial Times*, which cast me as Mr Pooter in Wonderland, was the first one to display any evidence that the man had actually read the book from cover to cover.

On 12 May the *Diaries* were number one on the London bestseller list and the following Sunday they entered the national list at number six. Meanwhile, I have embarked on what is a gruelling series of appearances reading them, doing on-stage dialogues and signing copies. I kicked off in Malvern, then Birmingham, Windsor and

Canterbury. This week Waterstones in Kensington, then Charleston and Hay-on-Wye literary festivals, followed by a merciful break aboard the QE2 and then back to a wearying list until October: Dartington, Salisbury, Cheltenham, Manchester and the V&A.

What really counts is the public. They're not fools and they see the agendas of the critics. I've been so touched by the strangers who just wander up and say how much they've enjoyed them. All the distortion by the media and the talk of revenge is really nonsense. I remain convinced that the time was right and that, although they're no masterpiece, they record a life and a period. My instincts tell me that they will grow as a point of reference. Inevitably some people are miffed – and I admit that they are waspish in places, but not malevolent. To me they record a world that I've left and to which I will not be returning. Some of it was fun, some of it untold misery. I'm glad I wrote it down, or at least my version of it. Of course people's versions of the same events will inevitably correct mine. But all the *Diaries* do is record what I observed and thought at the time. And I get very cross with people who talk to me as though I'd compiled them yesterday! It was all written so long ago, another age, another time.

I still treasure the assessment of Weidenfeld's chief reader, someone whose name I do not know and who knew nothing of the world about which I wrote: 'This is a wonderful book. Roy Strong is an extraordinarily vivid writer and his set pieces and character portraits are second to none. He emerges not only as admirable but lovable.' Only time will tell.

The Labour landslide has, I believe, also been conducive to the reception of the *Diaries*. They were seen to record not only one age which had gone, the Sixties, but also another, the Eighties. Periods never fall neatly. The Sixties lasted from about 1965 and ended abruptly with the oil crisis in 1974. The Eighties only got into full gear about 1983 and went into decline with the recession of the early

Nineties. Every Conservative I've talked to is so pleased at this clear-out of a tired, disunited, shop-soiled government, which lacked energy, drive and vision. The irony is that New Labour is really the old one-nation Toryism round again, or that is how I would view it in this immediate aftermath. What a relief to have a new cast of characters and a fresh start! But ever since 1988 I have always been on the periphery and happy to be so. The thought of doing all that pushing and shoving again appals me.

23 TO 25 MAY

Harold Pinter and Antonia Fraser stay

It was the Hay-on-Wye Literary Festival. We were all three perform-ing on the Saturday: Antonia at 12.10 p.m., Harold and myself both at 4.10 p.m. Earlier I'd learned that Antonia was coming so I wrote and offered a bed, although Julia rightly pointed out that by Friday I'd be knocked out what with the Chelsea Flower Show, the *Country Life* gardeners' dinner, a *Diaries* reading in Kensington and a dia-logue at Charleston. She was right. I was. I arrived back pop-eyed from Charleston at 12.45 p.m. on the Friday morning, exhausted. No matter, The Folly had to be put in order and a meal for six cooked. In for a penny, in for a pound.

Harold and Antonia arrived about 5.45-ish in the Weidenfeld car, both looking very out of place in the country. Antonia was in black court shoes and a shaggy coat with broad horizontal stripes in black and off-white and Harold in a raincoat, looking like a bank manager. They were both somewhat tottery, Antonia having had knee prob-lems and Harold with a slipped disc. Antonia's movements could be mistaken for being royal, Harold's uncertain and bewildered.

We'd asked the *Sunday Times* literary editor and wife, Geordie and

Kathryn Greig, to join us for the evening. They arrived early for a garden tour before dinner. The evening wound up at 12.45 a.m., one magnum and three bottles of champagne and one bottle of claret having been consumed. Julia didn't drink and Geordie stopped at ten as he was driving. Everything was fine until half-way through dinner, when Mrs Thatcher popped up. She produced tirades. How ashamed Harold was that he'd ever voted for her and then no words were strong enough to condemn her and all that she represented. As a consequence of her, we now lived in what was virtually a police state. I said that if he had had to deal with what I had in the way of unions in the late Seventies he'd be grateful for much that she did. That didn't go down well, and then Geordie fatally admitted that he'd been to Eton! But Antonia is always the saving grace, acting as a brake, answering back and temporising Harold's demagoguery.

The next day we went to Hay-on-Wye and I had a wonderful audience of about six hundred for the *Diaries*. We all had an agreement not to go to each other's but Harold was the star: £8 to see him and £6.50 for Antonia and myself, and then there was a huge book signing queue for him.

As they were leaving us on the Sunday, Harold said, 'You've created a paradise.' Apparently they'd strolled round the garden together. That was rather touching. There's affection in the man and he obviously likes coming to us, perhaps because we're a similar alliance: a nouveau married into one of the established classes.

3 JULY

Chris Smith and the New Statesman *lunch*

Lunch with the neighbours – or, rather, at Station House, Victoria, with the *New Statesman*. It felt like the old days going to one of these lunches, this one being, I discovered on arrival, for the new young Heritage minister, Chris Smith. The *New Statesman* staff, headed by their bright and welcoming Editor, Ian Hargreaves, were both youthful and charming. Other guests included Christopher Frayling, thinner again at last and dressing the part of Rector of the Royal College of Art; Stephen Daldry, Director of the Royal Court Theatre, pinch-faced and short-haired; a rather benign BBC man with brilliant Titian hair in a page boy cut, animated and to the point; the novelist Jonathan Coe, who turned out to be the man writing B.S. Johnson's biography, thoughtful, quiet and gentle; and Nicholas Snowman.

Chris Smith and his henchmen entered besuited and immediately took their jackets off and hung them over the chair backs, a real New Labour gesture. He opened the batting with a re-run of his Royal Academy speech: art for the people, access to art and education. Now in my sixty-second year, I have the wonderful advantage that, unlike everyone else round that table, I had nothing to suck up for. So, launching in, I said that ministers for the arts fell like confetti from the skies and that he said what every other minister had said since Jennie Lee. That upped the temperature. But I noticed that he avoided the ideological and general, in fact never replied to one of my theoretical challenges, but always went straight to the particular. He's not an impressive man but seems benign. I don't see him destined for any of the greater offices of state.

All round the table it fell to particulars as to who gets their hands on what. Smith did make the point that there would be less emphasis on marketing and product. But his tear-jerking story of a poor old lady who wept when she heard opera singers in person smacked of earlier Socialist Lady Bountiful-ism. When I threw the Millennium Dome exhibition at him, all he could say was that 'it was a window into the future'; but my statement that all such exhibitions had always been political went unanswered. Over museums, all he could do was talk about charges but side-stepped the concept of rationalisation and the problems of unending expansion. He's an improvement on the head girl prefect era of Mrs Bottomley but he's no charismatic genius with a vision, as far as I can see. Rather a teddy bear, I thought. At least he had some feeling for things cultural, which is a nice change. But perhaps this bear will learn to bite.

JULY

The garden

Nothing but rain this year. The growth in the garden is therefore quite extraordinary. We opened it three times, twice for Border Lines and once for the Somerset Gardens Trust, when, alas, it poured. Everyone who sees it is amazed but Julia and I still feel that there's so much still to do. At least there's not been the worry of drought. The great Elizabeth Tudor Avenue still takes my breath away, although there are a few losses of yew on the inner hedge. The other success has been the 'Sun Hit' standard roses in the Yew Garden, seemingly disease resistant, with dark green glossy leaves and an abundance of smallish yellow flowers.

Steve Tomlin and his gang at last are getting on with the garden in the front of the house. The knot is done, in-filled with gravel and with lapis and amethyst glass cullets. The fountains have begun to be lowered into place and the so-called 'howdah', a viewing platform made up of various architectural metalwork pieces, is to be seen by Julia next week at Painswick. It all begins to look extraordinary and everyone visiting the garden has been much excited by the project – and also admiring of our boldness at painting the house blue and yellow. Suddenly it can be seen for the first time and, as the colour scheme goes through the whole garden, both are seen as a unity.

We've also kept Reg Boulton going, now busy doing a plaque for the Oman pinnacle from All Souls College.

16 JULY

Versace is murdered

We learned yesterday afternoon that Gianni had been shot at the entrance to his Miami mansion. He was dead by the time they got him to the hospital, after which a mayhem of media was let loose. By now it seems that the FBI think it's the work of a gay serial killer. For me it is the loss of a precious and private friend.

We first met through Rosa Maria Letts, who approached me to ask whether I would let a Versace fashion show take place at the V&A. He flew in and from the moment he entered the room there was an instant rapport. He was not tall, indeed photographers had to find ways of overcoming this. His was an olive complexion of the south but the stubble, the cast of the head and jawline, the receding curly hair reminded me of the heads of Roman emperors. He had an expansive brow and hugely intelligent brown eyes.

This was a friendship that flowered. For over a decade we went and stayed with him in Milan and at his villa on Como, usually in the spring. In between there would be faxes or he would ask me to write a piece for one of his books or send him ideas for his garden. He was a man of quite exceptional energy and drive, with an untold ability to assimilate visual information. He devoured magazines, art books and catalogues. They would stand in huge piles everywhere, with pages flagged. He adored '*il mondo del pop*' and any kind of fantasy, for which, he said, there should always be time. His public image totally belied the reality of the man as we knew him. Publicly it was hype, glitz, extremes, the stars, over the top. My memory is of a quiet, shy, gentle man, generous and thoughtful, enshrined in his monochrome neoclassical palaces. There was never a raving 'scene' at Como. It was always tranquil – and indeed it was always for just such a weekend that we went. We met at meals and talked or sat in happy silence. He felt secure with us, knowing that we didn't need impressing, didn't need a 'scene', just the pleasure of being with him.

He always seemed so lonely to me. Antonio was usually around, lovable, laid back and funny. But he didn't live with him. Gianni had a prince-like quality; or perhaps he resembled more than anyone I have known what it must have been like to be in the orbit of a renaissance prince: the splendour of the interior decoration, the elegance of his table, the collections that spread everywhere – the utter madness of some of it. There was also, however, a restlessness about him, which accelerated through his forties and as houses multiplied, with new ones in New York, Miami and London. His designs for the theatre were followed by ones for home furnishings, including ceramics, and then there were his subsidiary clothes collections, Instante and Versus. The empire never ceased to expand. Then there were those extraordinary books, beautiful in a way but also rather awful. In one aspect he was intensely private, yet in another he apotheosised by himself in those huge volumes about himself, every room in every house and his fashion enmeshed in a phantasmagoria of rock, pop, homoerotic nudity and dreams of royalty and regality. Whatever did it all mean? I wonder.

Gianni had an enormous drive to create and to shock, and also an obsession with quality of workmanship. He had the ability to break boundaries in new techniques with fabrics and leather. I think he saw the whole world as the kingdom of Versace, with us all wearing his logo of the Medusa head.

He was never malevolent or unkind. Dismissive, of course: 'Armani make woman look like secretary. Woman beautiful, sexy.' His books brimmed with homoeroticism, but I can't say whether he was 'happy' about this. In the 1990s he became quite open about his homosexuality. It made him have no time for the Catholic Church, so a requiem in Milan Cathedral would have surprised him. I always remember his dislike of being touched by anyone. To me he always seemed alone but complete.

He described me once to his Milanese butler as '*un uomo molto fino*'. And he would ask my opinions about things. One felt a joy in his presence. He was one of those people who lifted everyone and everything around him. I shall miss him. A light has gone out.

I couldn't face going to Milan for the requiem mass in the Duomo attended by Sting and Elton John. Few, if any, knew of our friendship, and that's how we wanted it to be. Gianni's on my shortlist of originals I've known and someone I continue to miss.

17 AUGUST

A great garden disaster

The quiet of a hotel lobby in Bologna, a ghost town as it is *Ferragosto*, enables me to put down the full horror of what I can only describe as the Great Garden Massacre of 8 August. Robin was doing a splendid job cutting the Rose Garden hedge. The last piece to be cut was the culmination of the vista, which was to be trained as a yew arch leading down into the Scandinavian Grove. Something radical must have happened to my powers of observation because I thought I had described to him what had to be done but he must have misunderstood what I said. By chance, I walked into the garden later to check something for an article I was writing. I turned the corner to the great vista and then I was as one stricken. A great chunk of the hedge that I'd waited twenty-three years to train had gone, the vista completely wrecked. It was though I had seen a corpse. I was transfixed, horrified, stunned. I couldn't get over what had happened. It haunted me all day, all night. It was the most appalling blow. Five years at least would be needed for it to grow back again.

Robin came in on Saturday and we both tried to put it right by equalling the damage on both sides, so at least it looked symmetrical. I racked my brains as to how to solve the problem, the wiping out in twenty minutes of one of the garden's great set pieces. The one effect we had never included, I thought, was a garden gate, mainly because we couldn't afford it. Afford it we would now have to. In order to deflect the eye from the horror that had been perpetrated, we would have make one. I recalled ages ago a baroque doorway which Chilstone [manufacturers of reconstituted stone architecture and ornament] had in their architectural catalogue, so I rang them. It would have to be freestanding, I said. No one had thought of that, so at least it'll be original. Mercifully, from the point of view of putting it up, Steve Tomlin is virtually in residence. What was generally used as a 'front door' would be provided not with pilasters but with solid pillars. The architrave would have to be more substantial and steel rods would have to be run up through the pillars into it. So be it. It'll cost me Robin's wages for the year to put this disaster right. They have pledged to deliver everything by the end of September and the arch is to go up from 1 October. This is the biggest reversal yet: I could have done with none of this happening.

28 AUGUST

Death of a brother

Brian Strong died of a heart attack on 18 August; this is written ten days later. But what can I write? The news came to me when we were staying with Franco Maria Ricci at Masone, near Parma. Dot, our daily, came on the 'phone and gave me the news. It was like when my father died, only worse. It was as if a weight, a curse, a threat had at last been taken away from me. There was nothing I could do and I felt nothing, just that a chapter was finally closed that had already ended with me fifteen years ago. Why is it that virtually everything to do with the Strong family has always to be so utterly awful, so humiliating, so haunting? Why aren't there those normal family relationships of joy and love, turbulence and tranquillity? I can't answer that.

It had been worse for Derek [my elder brother]. He only found out when the Social Worker rang and said, *en passant*, 'Now that your brother has died . . .'. Derek didn't know and was upset. I heard the whole story, how Brian had tottered round for his £150 or whatever from Social Security and a bit of shopping, shuffled his way back to find that he'd left his front door key inside. He was so fat and in such a bad state that he could hardly walk a hundred yards without sitting down and puffing. He decided to go round to the back. The garden is a jungle. He forced his way through the back gate and then fell over and had a heart attack. He cried for help. Eventually someone came, the ambulance arrived and efforts were made to resuscitate him. But it was too late. He was dead. It was not a pleasant end.

I couldn't go to the funeral. I just couldn't. He never went to either of our parents' and my last memory of him was of virtually drawing a knife on me in the kitchen. Where oh where did it all go so wrong? There's a streak in the Strong family that I've always found disturbing. He was the only one out of the three of us for whom my father had any time. Brian was sporty, his hair tinged with red, but he was violent even as a child and never disciplined or controlled. He exerted power by brute force. He was secretive, too, and – even worse – a compulsive liar. But he was also bright. He needed a man to control him but my father opted out. And my mother always caved in to him. Over the years everything went to bail him out until the house was virtually emptied: he even took her engagement ring and obtained a second mortgage on the house. Everything for Brian was a quick fix, from car dealing to God knows what else. Much was concealed from me. He served at least two jail sentences and was extradited from the USA for attempting to smuggle drugs. His marriage was a disaster. And yet there was a good side. He taught maths and physics privately and was apparently a very good teacher. But oh, what a liar! He would lie that he was working when in fact he was a full-time student somewhere. He even once induced me into taking out a bank loan in order to bail him out yet again. And he was always right.

Early on I sensed that I had to draw back, but he persecuted me. I have some of his letters, written by someone mentally unbalanced, deranged. And then he started to ring me up, threatening – ring and ring and ring. It was terrible. Julia was shattered. We changed the telephone number. Eventually I learned that he took the allowance I made to my mother, so I redirected it via Derek.

Eventually he lost everything but, of course, it was never his fault. He declared that a family conference should be held to agree how to bail him out yet again. No way. And so he returned to live at Colne Road. As long as he was there I never went to my parent's house again. It was so terrible, so traumatic that I went to a priest, Gerard Irvine, and through him to a lawyer, John Underwood, to seek guidance. I was guilt-ridden. Gerard looked at me and said: 'You must never go there again.' So I never did see my mother again, for the last seven years of her life. That, too, haunts my inner recesses; but even she, in the end, was corrupted by him.

After she died Brian began to go downhill. Derek only let details slip from time to time: Brian had been on drugs since his twenties. He was diabetic and had failing eyesight, living in a ghastly state in one room – the upstairs bedroom – at the house in Colne Road, while the rest of the house fell apart, unpainted, the guttering falling off, the garden untouched for a decade. Derek, saintly as always, went to see this pathetic figure from time to time.

Even at my apogee there was always this dark figure hovering over my shoulder, waiting to pounce, grinding, relentless, bent. Looking back, the whole of my life has been fleeing that family, struggling to detach myself, to get far enough away to make a life and a home full of the old-fashioned virtues I was never surrounded with as a child. It is all so unnecessary and so very sad.

SEPTEMBER

Diana, Princess of Wales

We drove over to Hay for the day to gather copy for an article but oh, how poignant to see the humble town shops with pictures of Diana and the announcement that they would be closed on the day of the funeral. Around the war memorial were banked faded bouquets of flowers and messages. What an extraordinarily surreal week this has been. Heaven alone knows what it must have been like for those at the centre; it was exhausting enough for those, like me, caught up on the fringes of this tide of emotion.

That began last Sunday morning. I went downstairs, turned on the radio as usual and was astounded to be at the receiving end of pieces of information that made me realise that Diana was dead. My first thought was that she had committed suicide. No, it turned out that she had been in a car crash. It was all so unbelievable. By late afternoon I was rung by *The Times*. Would I write a piece for their Saturday supplement on Diana's image? 'Who else have you asked?' 'No one. You were the editor's first choice.' So I said 'Yes', knowing that I would have to write it in a trice to go to press on Monday. It teemed through my mind and I delivered it by midday.

The week was one long essay in shifting sands, so I was relieved that when the article appeared it read well and I wouldn't have re-written a word of it. It was another message to the Palace that won't be listened to. Oh, the potency of such an icon: a great beauty and a great humanitarian, someone who put her humanity first and not the fact that she was a princess. She looms as one of the great icons of our age. Moreover, she was not a contradiction but represented the possibilities of late-twentieth-century woman, to be able to wear a sexy dress by Versace and follow Mother Teresa.

The rest of the week was weird. We were in isolation here but the TV and media conveyed the unbelievable tide of emotion let loose. Julia MacRae, not a dyed-in-the-wool royalist, went to Buckingham Palace. As she approached, the perfume of the flowers was overpow-ering. She was utterly transfixed by what she saw. Not just the Palace but the entire Mall engulfed in flowers. It was overwhelming. But there was little or no reaction from those up in Balmoral.

On Wednesday I was rung by the *Today* programme to give my views on the implications of all this, together with William Rees-Mogg. By then it was clear that something serious needed to be said. It was a chaotic morning. For the second time BBC Hereford failed to open the studio and, after much panic, I returned home. *Today* had held the piece and I went on after the eight o'clock news 'down the line'. By then I had marshalled my views: firstly that the reaction was so extreme that it revealed an emotional vacuum within people which no one could fill. Secondly, never had the gap between the monarchy and the people been wider. Everyone was out on the streets, young and old, yuppie and punk, yet no one royal had ventured south. Not even was the flag at Buckingham Palace at half-mast. The lack of response was appalling. It revealed two things: that whoever was in the Palace had lost contact with the people and secondly, that reacting by the rule book doesn't work any more. Of course we need our sense of historic continuity, but we must move on.

The rest of the day I spent fending off the media wanting me to repeat myself. On the day of the funeral we watched the box. It was quite extraordinary. The previous day the Queen had come south. She and the Duke of Edinburgh met the crowds outside the Palace. No great welcome there. Prince Charles and the young princes had fared better at Kensington Palace. The Queen did her broadcast, quite cleverly with the view up the Mall behind her. The funeral was like nothing I'll ever see again. This was national catharsis. Crowds, tears and flowers. In the end the service was spot-on. Elton John didn't leave a dry eye in the house and Charles Spencer was a man of courage to speak as he did. But it was people power that showed. Elton had been greeted with applause outside the Abbey, as was Charles Spencer, and this time the tide rippled in through the west door and the congregation also began to clap. Charles Spencer's address was deeply touching but with a subtext that didn't flinch from laying much at the door of the Royal Family. The cameras must have been told to keep off them. In a way they might just as well not have been there. It was in effect a Spencer funeral.

The consequences of this fascinate me. The Queen Mother's funeral could never match it [it did]. Never have I seen such a panorama of ordinary people making clear what they wanted. They want a monarchy, yes, but they want it human and compassionate. The present cast suddenly looked past its sell-by date. No one can respond to this. All eyes now fall on that tall, blond fifteen-year-old, the image of his mother. Will he turn into a royal zombie or can he save the monarchy? It's a terrible, terrible burden to bear. In five years' time he will be twenty and all eyes will be upon him – but they love him already, for his mother's sake, which is a great head start.

5 OCTOBER

The triumphal arch

The weather has been thrice blessed, golden sunshine and the warmth of summer. Steve Tomlin saw to it that we had his best mason, Dave Russell, to put up the great arch. Steve had found in Bristol a stunning set of stones for the pavement on which it would stand. On Wednesday these were laid. On Thursday the two great pillars went up. They were left on Friday to consolidate, looking like the device of the Emperor Charles V. Already the eye was taken from the disaster behind. Saturday was the day when it finally went up. It looked terrific, huge, but, from a distance, taking up the lines of perspective as though we had always planned it to be like that.

Reg Boulton came and he is going to carve the Latin inscription for it, provided courtesy of Joe Trapp's son: '*Conditor horti felicitatis auctor*' ('They who plant a garden plant happiness'). At the time I was writing a chapter on the 1640s and 1650s and looking at pictures of the Double Cube Room at Wilton. The great door there has a cartouche between the pediment. I asked Reg whether he could do the Oman arms. Yes, he could. It would look marvellous. Perhaps I can now afford to adopt those arms and thus round off the story: when I was knighted I couldn't afford to. We have done so much but we mustn't stop. . .

The cartouche was never commissioned and I finally petitioned to adopt my wife's arms during the last weeks of her life, although Garter gave me ones somewhat different, including a crest of a blue cat's head with a golden helmet!

236

7 OCTOBER

A.L. Rowse

The papers are full of obits of Leslie Rowse. Ninety-three is a good innings and he'd been in hospital for the last few months – indeed, he was there when he got his CH. Raleigh Trevelyan acknowledged my congratulations to Leslie. I'd dedicated *The English Renaissance Miniature* to Rowse and he dedicated *Reflections on the Puritan Revolution* to me. I still haven't read the latter! I've flicked through it, yes, but everywhere my eye falls there are that bias and diatribe that were his undoing.

What an extraordinary man! He was as a god all those years ago when, as a humble grammar school boy, I read *The England of Elizabeth*. He fired me with a love of that age, and for that I'm eternally grateful. But where did it all go off the rails? When did that ego explode to become 'infallible' and 'absolute'?

My next memories are of him giving damning reviews of my early books. And then, after marrying Julia, I decided to ask him to give a grand lecture at the National Portrait Gallery. I can't think now what it was on, but Julia was the bridge, Oxford and the Omans. Sir Charles Oman used to ask Rowse to tea at Frewin Hall when he was a young, left-wing type. And he also admired Carola. So, suddenly, I was 'in' and there followed a regular flow of eulogies. He even asked us to the Encaenia luncheon at All Souls on a rain-sodden day. And then, if we voyaged to Cornwall, we went to see him.

In Cornwall there was a circle that was very loyal and loving to him. I think of Raleigh Trevelyan and David Treffry of Place. Rowse would sit in his rabbit warren of a house, the ceilings falling in, the walls damp and books in cascading heaps everywhere, the kitchen primitive. But his energy and intellect were always extraordinary. He was in many ways more like a politician. He needed an audience in front of which to perform. No question of 'How are you?' or 'What are you up to?' From the first moment of encounter the floodgates were opened – everyone, everything, every age – he knew it all. One didn't get a word in edgeways. And yet there was a twinkle there. Everyone was called 'dear' or 'sweetie', especially men.

He was an elitist, an arch High Tory. And yet he was really lovable. I think that he was aware, as he bashed hither and thither, that it was all a bit of lark really. That was what I liked about him. Otherwise he'd have been insufferable but, in fact, he wasn't. There was always a warmth that made up for that stupendous ego. He deserved to be honoured far earlier than he was. Opinionated, infuriating, inflated, most of it was the buzzing of a bluebottle in a jam jar. Underneath all the arrogance he loved his country, its history and traditions. Indeed, he felt deeply about them in the same way that Cecil Beaton did. God knows what out of that torrent of stuff he wrote will ever be of any use. Not much, I fear. His diaries are to come; I wonder what they will hold.

In many ways his life was a tragedy. People like him are needed to remind us of yesterday. The sadness is that his books on Shakespeare and the Dark Lady and his own vanity took him over the top and made him a figure of fun – derision, indeed. But for all his weaknesses, he made history news. He may have been wrong but that didn't matter. He was a great if maddening figure who caught the public imagination. There's no other historian like that.

Rowse's diaries were eventually published and I reviewed them in Country Life. *I wish they hadn't been, for they revealed and sadly confirmed the worst side of the man. They were also surprisingly insular and he was remarkably unobservant about the period through which he had lived.*

31 DECEMBER

New Year's Eve reflection

Goodbye 1997. People tell me it's been a good year for me. Who knows? But thank God we're over the *Diaries* and I'm down to 1750 with *The Spirit of Britain*. Let's hope that 1998 will be a quiet year, as this one has just been too active: it's no wonder people are 'Roy Strong-ed out'. So am I. But the end of the year for us has been drear, with a street robbery in Barcelona, Julia being laid low with 'flu again and Robin, the gardener, gone. In a wider perspective, I shall scream if I read one more article about 'Cool Britannia' or 'The People's' this, that or the other, or that we are witnessing a kind of 'New Dawn'. New Labour may be refreshing but they're not the Second Coming. All we've seen is a cosmetic barrage of spin-doctor speak. Nothing much has changed. How could it in seven months? I hate New Labour's denial of our past, not that I want to wallow in heritage any more. But we're stuck with a government that thinks that food is the equivalent of a work of art like a painting or a sculpture. Are they mad? Devolution also depresses me. Will we see the fragmentation of the country? It has taken centuries to create a coherent culture and tradition. Is it to be thrown away in the interests of political correctness and multiculturalism? It is so easy to destroy things but so very difficult ever to put them back.

1998

As Susan Hill says, these are the weeks to put one's head down and write. With age, the weeks after Christmas become more difficult to cope with, seemingly nothing but unending gloom and bad weather. Outside, the rain fell until late January and I've never seen such a churning up of the soil. The garden works were endlessly held up but now they're finished it is a garden revolution, the great axis paths in the Orchard incorporating it into the geometry and perspective of the rest of the garden. Yesterday Julia collected the yew and the beech for the new hedges, yew up to the recumbent stag and beech from 'Covent Garden' to the Rose Garden, purple beech only in the former. The paths effectively divide the Orchard into five separate compartments with paths having blue arches straddling them embowered with roses.

Otherwise, I push on hard with *The Spirit of Britain*. I have reached the 1790s, gasping at the extraordinary excitement of an era when, for the first time, a British national culture of some kind was created. Asa Briggs was probably right when he said to me that often one is best writing on periods about which one knows little, because one comes to them with a fresh eye.

1998

10 FEBRUARY

A City dinner

I'd been booked by the past Master, John Missen, for this Barbers' Company dinner a year in advance so that there was no way out of it. But it marked the return of the great Holbein of *Henry VIII and the Barber Surgeons* from the National Gallery, where it had graced the *Ambassadors* exhibition. It was appropriate because thirty-seven years earlier that picture had prompted my first step into the limelight through my discovery of the original cartoon for it, now in the College of Surgeons. A dental surgeon had taken the X-rays and I did the rest, causing a great art sensation at the time. However, back to this evening. It was in its way a lustreless affair in a mean, modern 1960s hall with none of the rooms large enough: cramped, in fact. But there were some portraits to appeal and the people were sweet to me. In we went in procession, the usual old pile-up of City gents, creased and crumpled, wrapped in scarlet and fur and hung with chains and badges of office. The food was really awful, school dinner *par excellence*. Before the Master was laid a handsome silver mace, modern, like much of the silver to which I drew people's attention. That apparently gave pleasure. I then said how wonderful it would be to use it and why didn't they use this mace? So, much to my surprise, at the close the beadle leaned over and seized it and we all made our exit behind it. 'You've established a precedent,' I was told afterwards. Well, I hope I have.

18 FEBRUARY

Elgar's Third Symphony and William Hague

Elgar had said on his deathbed that no one should attempt to construct a symphony from his notes but the looming of the demise of the copyright led the family to allow Anthony Payne to do just that. John Birt asked us to the Sunday evening première at the Royal Festival Hall, along with a droll *ménage* of guests. Birt is like an intellectual Billy Bunter, rotund, with round eyes behind seemingly round glasses perched on a rubicund round face. He's a benign host but no good at introductions, so many of the guests, like Jack Straw, we never met. I suppose that the great thing was to meet William Hague, the Conservative's wonder boy now in his late thirties. How did he strike me? Conventionally dressed and of medium height, his is not a commanding presence. He is totally devoid of charm or small talk (in the case of the latter, what politician has any?) although he smiles a lot, for what that's worth. But there was no eagerness to meet everyone, only the usual beeline for whoever might jerk him up a little higher. But he is clever, that did shine through, and the dome of his head is like a luminous mobile mountain range. Among the rest who came our way were Michael Scholar of the Department of Trade and Industry, whose wife is a French scholar translating Rousseau's *Confessions* and seemingly never finishing it; Matthew Parris, as tiny and as dapper as I remember him; and James Naughtie, as bright and ebullient as ever. David Mellor, a poor forty-eight, had Penny Cobham in tow, an extraordinary beauty and the beast alliance. She, I thought, was good news, although I don't think that she enjoyed being a trustee of the V&A much; she was well dressed in a beautifully cut suit.

There must have been about twenty of us, occupying two rows

in the auditorium. It was an extraordinary occasion to hear music for the first time that had been written, or at least left in outline, in 1932. The finale, we were told, was pastiche and much had to be done to the first movement, but it was Elgar all right: solemn and grand, elegiac and poignant, lyrical and hauntingly sad. The *Daily Mail* asked me what I thought of it. I said that I was totally unqualified to pronounce but it had the 'blub' and 'this England' quality sure enough.

The Hagues left before the dinner, during which there was no conversation of any moment but much on everything from the euro to the fate of Peter Mandelson, who's charming, I gather, if encountered. But it was the reception of the symphony that was most to be remarked upon – the endless tides of applause, virtually the whole audience on its feet in utter rapture.

15 MARCH

Spring at Whitfield

Spring came remarkably early this year – in February in fact, which, after weeks of the deluge, was marked by warmth and sun on a such a scale that by early March we found the peach trees in blossom. So it was no surprise when we found a message on our telephone from George Clive at Whitfield saying 'The magnolias are at their prime.' George is a tree man and has a park to boot, for it is no use really having the one without the other. In social terms he's our nearest neighbour and he's seen our garden since it was a blank field. When we came here in 1973 I recall his mother, Lady Mary Clive, ringing and asking us to tea. She was there today, aged ninety, her brain as sharp as ever; as I'm one of the few knights around, I usually end up on her right. Things hadn't changed much since 1918, she mused.

The great change had come with the First World War but today's lunch party she viewed as something that could have taken place at any date since, although the dress might have been more formal.

There were twelve of us in all crammed around the table in the library. It is always roast beef and three veg followed by a killer of a cream-laden pudding and a Stilton cheese. The local ladies cook and *nouvelle cuisine* has never arrived. But somehow it doesn't matter, as it's all part of the 'Whitfield experience'. Mercifully the house has never been 'done over'. The front hall is a clutter of dog baskets, wellington boots and endless country coats piled up in heaps. There's no grand chandelier but a simple bulb in a lampshade centre ceiling. The family portraits, often the worse for wear, are a jumble on the walls. Beyond lies the staircase well but what's upstairs I know not, although Antonia Fraser, Mary's niece, tells me that the beds are narrow and the conditions Spartan. No matter, there's a handsome drawing room, which is quite an obstacle course, a late-Victorian clutter of innumerable chairs, sofas and little tables that everyone keeps falling over. The curtains are ancient and the wallpaper's blotchy and faded in parts, but somehow it all adds to the atmosphere and truth of the place.

It is difficult to believe that the house was abandoned in the Thirties because of the disappearance of staff or that the Victorian wing had been demolished. The effect is that it has always been like that, a gracious eighteenth-century house with symmetrical bow windows set high on a slope reflected in the lake, which George had created, before it. Really the garden's the thing, with some seventy varieties of magnolia – pink, white, magenta and every variable flush of one and the other. They are so superbly planted, some thrusting up to be reflected in the water, others set against huge tapestries of dark green yew.

On arrival we all fell out of our cars one by one and wandered, gaping and gasping with delight as the sun caught the water and the trees. Penny Graham, George's vivacious and delectable long-time girlfriend, was to leave sharply after lunch to visit a friend who was dying of cancer. I said, 'Live each day as your last.' She retorted, 'Live each day equally as your first.' And I felt the warmth of the sun on my face and looked and thought that this wouldn't have been a bad last day – friends, happiness, wandering through the explosion that is spring, wrapt in its beauty. The magic of the country house, park and garden never ceases to retain its hold as a perfection of life. How lucky we are that it still goes on in spite of New Labour.

16 MARCH

Prince Edward

Warren Davis, who is responsible for PR at the National Trust, had asked us to hear Prince Edward lecture on the fire and subsequent restoration of Windsor Castle. It took place in the Purcell Room of the Royal Festival Hall, which was packed; indeed, we were told that the demand had been so great that HRH was to do a repeat performance on the Wednesday. Middle England can't shed its cult of the Royal Family, even if he's only a minor prince who likes to be known as 'Mr Windsor'. With short-cut, fine and rapidly thinning hair, he was dressed as a male royal clone in safe tie and pinstripe suit, well cut but devoid of fashion. Working in the media, he had the advantage that the technical side, images and film clips, were good. Otherwise he's like a failed sixth-former, affable yes, but a dull performer with infantile jokes that fell flat. But what one can say? He lectured reasonably well for a prince. The trouble was that he didn't have anything to say that we didn't know already. What a shame that not one part of the 'new' areas at Windsor belonged to today, but the workmanship was dazzling in a post-modernist gothic way. Anything controversial he firmly avoided and there had, as we know, been much.

There was the usual somewhat anonymous dinner afterwards, an ocean of tables in the ill-named 'People's Palace' (pre-Blair!). We were put at a gardeners' table with John Sales, Mary Keen and John Simmons, so that was fine. Afterwards Lucy Lambton collared me about this government's relentless denigration of our past. She's doing a TV series so I gave her what I thought. As from September, I gathered, no history will probably be taught in schools to anyone under the age of twelve. I abhor the crudity of it all, like receiving the EU leaders in the Canary Wharf Tower (Thatcher's Eighties), set-dressed by Terence Conran with contemporary art and furnishings. (Terence modern? He's nearly seventy!) Then, recently, they had emptied Lancaster House of its historic pictures and put up new Brit Art for another meeting. And in the Dome our past has been expunged. Warren Davis said that at one point the National Trust was to be involved, but no, not now. He'd written a private letter to Mandelson about all this but expected nothing.

MID-APRIL

On the road

This has been a bleak, miserable April with horrendous rain and floods over Easter and now icy cold and sleet. So far this year has been a re-run of the *Diaries* for the paperback edition. So off I go to Islington, Bath, Shrewsbury, Bradford and Highgate, with more to come. Why on earth do I do it? Well, sometimes it can be very touching, like at the *Oldie* lunch at Simpsons yesterday, when people came up afterwards and thanked me for all I'd done. The lunch was chaotic, with half of the top table not turning up I fancy due to failure of admin. I sat on the right of Richard Ingrams, large and reticent, with Prunella Scales, thank heaven, on my right, her hair bright orange. I did a double-take, recognising her: 'I'm working it back,' she said. 'It had to go this colour for a part.' But she's a delight and a giver, recruiting me as a member of the CPRE, of which she's become President.

Thomas Pakenham turned up halfway through the lunch, looking more and more like his father, and spoke for too long on trees – although his book is a treat. A young journalist called Luke Harding read from his biography of Jonathan Aitken.

Bradford was in one of those out-of-town hotels, red brick and instant antiques. The Mayor and Mayoress came, benign, although the latter asked me: 'How did you get your knighthood? Did you inherit it?' I was landed with Janet Street-Porter, who can sometimes be as awful as she sounds. She had written a book on rambling but her speech was one long diatribe against bed and breakfast places and hotels. Not one redeeming feature was to be found in any of them.

Chichester was a treat. I lectured to the Friends of Pallant House. It was packed and there was an elegant party afterwards and an even more elegant dinner for twelve after that. Earlier we'd gone over to see Uppark, where there was no love lost between the family and the National Trust. Is there ever? I really don't know why they rebuilt it. It's not that interesting, even less so than I remember it. It was appalling to hear how the National Trust got all their contents out of the ground floor while the family stuff upstairs went up in flames.

The next morning we went to visit Patrick Garland and Alexandra Bastedo at their mini zoo. I hadn't realised the scale of it. The approach is dominated by a very large pond full every kind of duck you've ever seen and probably a few that you haven't, plus a horrendous and violent Norfolk turkey which beats up Alexandra. That's not the end of it, for you fall over animals everywhere, twenty something cats, swarms of poultry, enclosures crammed with rabbits and ferrets, Tibetan pigs and donkeys, all ailing or rescued. Alexandra is nothing if not dedicated and now appears in mud-stained country gear, gloves and untidy hair, a far cry from her Sixties blonde bombshell period.

But the greatest cause for concern was Patrick, one of Julia's oldest friends, my age but oh dear in such a state, with legs like matchsticks, in pain, unable to sleep at nights, his withered hands shaking as he handed me a cup of tea. The doctors don't know the cause. Has he been 'killed off' by the theatre? Chichester knocked him out twice. Thank God he's out of it, but he can't say 'No'. It's a ghastly drug and he doesn't need the money.

He made me think of John Bury, someone else 'killed off' by theatre, having lost all feeling in both his legs and feet; the last time that we saw him he slipped in and out of lucidity. All those years of grind, sitting in the dark and endless dramas in the end take a terrible toll. The body just turns round and gives out screaming signals and not to heed them is fatal.

19 APRIL

On I go. I've reached 1830 in *The Spirit of Britain*. Again it is very demanding indeed but endlessly fascinating. I had no idea that the period 1790 to 1830 was such an incredible period – but I do now.

30 APRIL

Hatchards Authors of the Year party

I travelled up to London yesterday in time for the Hatchards party for authors. Who were all these people? 'They're all twenty-five-year-old novelists', said A.N. Wilson. I've rather come to love him, standing as he was at the bottom of the staircase in his role as New Man, a baby sling around his neck with his daughter Georgiana within. His wife, Ruth Guilding, said, 'It's such a good name because it can later be used as it is or as Georgie or, if lesbian, George.' I said 'What about Little G?' which is what the great Duchess of Devonshire called her daughter of the same name.

A.N. Wilson looks like a cross between James Joyce and Lytton Strachey, a nineteenth-century face, quite small, with wire glasses. It is difficult not to be beguiled by him and I found myself effortlessly sliding into a conversation, cursing Holy Trinity, Brompton, and Alpha courses and then on to French Catholic modernist theologians disapproved of by the Pope. The benign James Naughtie crossed my path. 'How's your friend?' he asked and then I realised that he meant HRH Margaret. She's vanished and is now out of hospital. That I knew. Is it forty years of fags and whisky taking its toll? The next evening I was told that when she went into the hospital after the stroke an important doctor had travelled all the way up from the south-west to see her. He sat down by her bedside, at which point she turned to him and said, 'Have you never been told that no one sits in the presence of a member of the Royal Family?' 'In that case', he said, 'I'll withdraw', and he went. Who can blame him?

6 JUNE

A theatrical lunch party

Every year John Bury's wife, Liz, gives a luncheon party for seemingly fifty or more. For the last few years it has been very much a matter of 'will this be the last one?' This time John had been carried off to hospital a few weeks before with pneumonia but, as usual, he bounced back. He looked thinner as a result and was a bit logjammed as the buggy he uses to whizz around in – his latest toy – had packed up the day before. But he loves this annual *fête* and he looked on and chatted benignly to everyone.

Apart from a fleeting flurry of rain the day was a blessed one, sunny yet cool. Liz begins cooking a month before the event. Everything about it is beautiful. We were in a panic to arrive early enough to photograph the food, always an astounding tableau – three, in fact, stretching through the kitchen, dining room and conservatory. This is food as still life, like a series of Victorian colour plates from a cookbook by Mrs A.B. Marshall sprung to life. The *tour de force* is always the puddings, this year set around a flower-decked glass and silver épergne, the usual chocolate cabbage, a tart set overall with sugared rose petals, a vast jelly, two large summer puddings, two huge mousses encased in slices of a little Swiss roll arranged in a pattern, a pistachio cake and a pear and cream tart – to name but a few. Julia as usual snapped it all. I won't go on to describe the crab mousse encased in prawns and quails' eggs, the huge salmon with cucumber scales, the amazing pies, spinach tarts . . . Enough!

The house is Georgian, stone-built, set up on a hill at Minchinhampton just outside Stroud. At the back there's an awning with tables set up on a terrace, for the garden rises dramatically away from the house. Everyone and anyone are there, a *mélange* of play clothes by young and old, creators and craftsmen, all thrown pellmell together and left to introduce themselves to each other, but the link is always theatre.

There was much disillusion with New Labour and Chris Smith. Iain Mackintosh said 'Don't worry, he's going.' There's going to be a Cabinet reshuffle during Cup Final week and Harriet Harman is going to be pushed in. Peter Hall, all in funereal black, with Nicki and a five-year-old daughter, started screaming about them all. We agreed that what was under attack was excellence and anything that might be described as elite. One saw it everywhere. What other government has ever laid down guidelines like 'Don't go to the Royal Opera House or the Chelsea Flower Show'? Or, when the Queen gave her arts party at Windsor, Shirley Bassey was asked but not Janet Baker – let alone being landed with a Prime Minister who goes on chat shows like Des O'Connor and dumbs down with mother-in-law stories.

Peter had just been to a dinner at his old Cambridge college. Oxbridge is again on the New Labour blacklist. They're terrified. Peter said that he hoped that one of his daughters would be going there. 'Where's she at school?' 'Roedean', was the reply. 'Oh, that's unfortunate. We try not to take public school people.' The drift of our encounter was that elitism and quality were besieged as never before. Of course the arts at the cutting edge are always difficult; at their best they can be incomprehensible. But all of this is under attack, compounded by the dismantling of the country into its component parts, which again has cultural implications. On the whole England has sunk its identity to bring in Wales and Scotland. Now we shall have to rediscover Englishness and the identity we abandoned. What kind of society do we live in when someone from the Arts Council writes to Alan Ayckbourn as 'Dear Sir or Madam' and then asks him to list what it is that makes him fit to serve on it?

Iain Mackintosh told me that Starveling in *A Midsummer Night's Dream* at Regent's Park Theatre this year was modelled on me!

13 JULY

Highgrove revisited

I hadn't been back to Highgrove for five years and rather wondered how the topiary and hedges I had designed and cut were faring.

Andrew Lawson told me recently that they looked marvellous and that the garden had leapt ahead. When Stephen Lamport, the Prince of Wales's new secretary, rang me about the Diana Garden, I asked whether I could pop in and see how 'my' hedges had done. Then an invitation to Highgrove arrived from the Henry Doubleday Research Centre to a reception there, so it all came together. So off we sailed on a day of sunshine and showers, typical of this summer. Andrew was right: a lot had happened. The garden had matured, indeed in places had gone over the top. But the Bannermans I sense have been a force for good. The whole picture was much more coherent, instead of a series of separate incidents. I was impressed that all my hedge and topiary designs had worked. There had been such miles of it that I really sometimes wondered: but here were the swags, curlicues, windows and pompoms I'd designed. However, I suggested a few modifications to David Howard, the new head gardener.

There was a wonderful new fountain by William Pye and an entrancing Mediterranean garden around it contained within 'my' hedges. The Sundial Garden had acquired elegant new iron gates found by the Bannermans and the old larch-pole arch had gone. But the gates had been painted municipal black and needed to be another colour. The Bannermans' stumpwork area was quite extraordinary, with two wooden temples in the Repton manner and the tree stumps arranged hurly-burly and planted with ferns and hostas. The structures were all made of wood and fir cones and I wondered how long they would last. The Kitchen Garden was over the top and needed to be hatcheted back. But, yes, it was all terrific.

We ended up in the Prince's new Orchard Room, Arts and Crafts postmodern with an ethnic overlay, used for receptions. This particular reception was somewhat interminable, although HRH did his stuff in his beautifully cut, conventional grey suit and safe tie but sporting a knautia buttonhole. He's now very Hanoverian, all lower face, but he was very good at working his way round everybody. I can't do sycophancy any more so I didn't mince my words to Stephen Lamport on Aylard's regime and congratulated him on the change since. There's real ease-up. In the end I was wheeled up to HRH and I gave him the message: paint the gates blue in the Sundial Garden. I wonder whether he will.

16 JULY

The garden

It's been a tremendously wet summer, which has been terrific for growth. By now everything looks blowsy and needing to be cut back and all the architecture is fluffy at the edges, calling to be put in place again. We opened four times, tiring but well worth it. Julia really doesn't approve and disappears for the day; but what's the point of making this spectacular garden and not sharing it a little? It's always amazing how quickly startling innovations settle in. I've begun training the new hedge along Elizabeth Tudor Avenue and have pruned up the hollies to make them into standards modelled on those in the garden at Westbury-upon-Severn, where they arise out of the yew hedge. Andrew Lawson was astonished by the changes here and there must be more. I purchased two stone medieval kings in a Billingshurst sale, life-size, about 1800, part of the restoration of the Palace of Westminster at that date. I was offered so much for one of them that I then sold it. The other is to be placed in the Ashton Arbour at the close of the new long vista. Mary Keen and John Sales came round and John wrote afterwards that we had taken off where Lawrence Johnston left off. What a compliment! Still, there's a way to go and I feel that we must press on. Top of the list is to cut through the Rose Garden hedge opposite the new vista and to make steps down to the hoped-for rill on the other side. The Scandinavian

Grove has always been spaghetti junction and this will mean a good route out of the Rose Garden down to Muff's Monument and then Elizabeth Tudor. I still don't know how to create a route to the Serpentine! But then we had no idea that everything would escalate so much. But we must open the chequebook and press on this autumn.

8 AUGUST

A love child

Suddenly it is summer, soaring temperatures into the eighties with blue skies above. The result is to stay indoors and draw the blinds, rather strange really because it has been a gloomy, rain-sodden season so far. The garden looks quite incredible. My standard hollies along Elizabeth Tudor have reached four feet in two years! Our new gardener, Shaun, who can be scatty, is a whizz at hedge trimming and they've never looked better.

These are some of the deadest weeks of the year, enlivened only by Tony Snowdon's quite extraordinary production of a love-child by Melanie Cable-Alexander. It is known as the *Country Life* baby. It was the rather an amazing consequence of him editing the London edition. I feel really sorry for Lucy and her daughter Frances.

This month I led a tour of Dutch gardens and recorded this encounter.

16 SEPTEMBER

A gardening legend

British people are almost wholly ignorant of Mien Ruys. So was I until I noticed, in looking through pictures of late twentieth-century

Dutch gardens, how her name kept cropping up at virtually anything that caused me to yell 'Isn't that marvellous?' Then four years ago we visited her gardens and I began to understand why. She was ninety-two then and all one glimpsed was a black bundle in the distance as someone mumbled with awe, 'That's Mien Ruys.' The gardens were extraordinary, twenty-five or so of them laid out over a period of seventy years from 1925 onwards. They are unique in giving in one place the whole history of this country's gardens, from the tail end of the Arts and Crafts Jekyllesque style down to modern decking.

Ruys's gardens all have dates. These need to be referred to because only then can one grasp their full significance: the Reed Pond garden, 1960, with its innovatory plastic container; the Sunken Garden, 1960 again, with its totally original use of railway sleepers. Everywhere I wandered I was aware that in this series of small gardens one confronted a woman who had met the twentieth century full on, uncompromising, modern, with no looking back, no nostalgia, using today's materials, like concrete in every form down to recycled plastic in the Marsh Garden. Here were roof gardens for flat-dwellers, gardens for children, others for city-dwellers. This was gardening in post-war democratic Europe. The planting was always masterly and simple, employing masses of ground cover and simple herbaceous plants but always with a twist, like meandering blocks of asters beneath roses.

Suddenly one of our group rushed up to me and said 'It's Mien Ruys!' – and that she was looking for us. We gathered ourselves together in haste for this epiphany and rushed hither and thither to find her. There she was, now aged ninety-six, propelled in a bath chair, shrouded like a parcel, her feet in sensible shoes, her hat an old tea cosy. Her impact was electric, a presence was felt and everyone instinctively bowed to this figure. Julia said that we offered her homage, which I echoed. Her hands were puffed with thrombosis, her eyes rheumy and sunken in their sockets, her face weatherbeaten.

But the intelligence was there, and the dart of the eyes. 'I have been gardening for seventy years. Do you like my garden?' She lifted her bowed head. Indeed we did. A voice behind reminded her that she had met Gertrude Jekyll. 'Yes, I had tea with her. I am the last person still living who spoke to her.' 'At Munstead?' I asked. 'Yes, at Munstead.' One had encountered a legend, a link back to the gardening world of Lutyens and William Morris. Again and again she reminded us that what we looked at had taken seventy years. 'Young', I said, 'for a garden.' She smiled and understood. Little by little we made our adieus and the queen, as it were, resumed her progress.

This was a woman, tough, resilient, modest, exuding humanity, with a still compelling interest in the garden, what grows, what flowers, how is it looking, does it work, how can I make it better? Surely she will go down as one of the great figures in the story of the garden? I stood afterwards transfixed, stunned and silenced. So this is what it is to be like a true gardener.

19 OCTOBER

London days

London days are increasingly strange. There it is, all crammed in: a short TV interview on Malcolm Appleby the silversmith, a haircut, hosting a lunch for the RSPCA, the gym, a drink at Damien Hirst's Pharmacy and the Garrick Club, where I give John Hayes dinner. In between I sat huddled in the London flat writing the last chapter of *Spirit*. But, more to the point, what do I remember out of that kaleidoscope?

Clive, who cuts my hair and Princess Alexandra's, was terribly funny about her asking of her sister-in-law 'Has anyone seen the Cath-o-lick?' Peter Davies, Director General of the RSPCA, a fine man, traumatised me with the statistic that 70,000 cats and dogs have to be put down each year. And then there was the drink with Melanie Cable-Alexander in the Pharmacy in Notting Hill Gate. You have to look twice because both outside and in it is nothing but shelves of pills. And there was Melanie, tired, yes but somehow marvellous, her eyes lustrous and so adoring her child by Snowdon. 'Are you going to be a countess?' I asked. I already knew the reply. Of course she wasn't, but she adored him. I can understand that and all three, Tony, Lucy and Melanie, are trapped in a media mess. He sits alone in Launceston Place. Otherwise they move from one 'safe' house to another. All anyone can do is prop up but you can't climb in there. Who's going to be the winner? No one, really.

At the Garrick it was the usual *mélange* but I spotted Robert and Paddy Armstrong and afterwards went up and asked, 'Is the lady mentioned in the *Evening Standard* the next V&A chairperson?' Robert, honestly didn't know, and Paddy expatiated at length as to how demanding that job was, and unpaid. The V&A needs a new voice. Who knows but that this lady might be it?

I hailed a taxi in Trafalgar Square. The driver said, 'This is meant to be.' In front he had a copy of my *Story of Britain*. He'd swum the Channel twice but someone had converted him to education and he went for history. He held up another book that his course had prescribed. Couldn't cope with it. What I had written, he said, was so clear. I felt 'mission achieved' and signed his copy.

IO NOVEMBER

Spirit *finished*

On this day I finished *The Spirit of Britain* with the Anglo-Saxon chapter. It is the longest book I have ever written, yet pathetically short for such a vast subject. As usual, I felt 'Go, little book' – but it's not so little. All the same, I have written it with a sense of mission, like *Story*, and on the dedication page put the words 'Lest we forget'. English civilisation can't be thrown away for a sea of populism, which this government embraces so forcefully.

II NOVEMBER

The country house revisited

We came up to London for the Historic Houses Association's twenty-fifth-anniversary *fête* at the Tate Gallery. They were right to play it low-key. There's no crisis but the present government's attitude, emphasised by the quite appalling after-dinner speech by the Junior Arts Minister, is that they are irrelevant. The drift of that speech was its subtext, barely articulated, which was that in the past country houses were viewed as the summation of the English achievement – but that 'We don't think so any more'.

But there were two fine rooms filled with pictures from the great houses, well chosen but a *mélange*. The gathering was one's yesterdays: Graftons, Richmonds, Windsors, Rothschilds, Devonshires, on and on. I sat between Jane Compton and Patricia Rawlings, so I had an agreeable time, apart from the fact that I was wearing velvet and sitting roasted over a radiator vent. Patricia was screaming on about the chairmanship of the V&A. Alex Bernstein had wanted it. No way. Then her partner, Paul Zuckerman, wanted it. No way again. We all wondered who this Paula Ridley from Liverpool was who had got it. I wish her luck with a terrifying job.

9 DECEMBER

Rosemary Verey week and the Millennium beckons

This was 'Rosemary Verey is eighty' week. Although it doesn't happen until 21 December, no fewer than three parties are being given in her honour more or less now. Two are London-based, one at the Tate Gallery, given by its Chairman, David Verey, a distant relation, and the other by her friend Arthur Reynolds at the Garrick Club, courtesy of me.

The first was for *tous les grands* – or as *tous* as could be garnered – mainly those whose gardens had figured in Rosemary's television series, like the Carringtons, Cavendishes, Astors and Tollemaches. I was relieved that a message was read out from the Prince of Wales, which meant that the recent 'falling out' was somehow over. When and what that was about I know not. The Tate dinner was for fifty and was very well done. I was put on the right of the Chairman's wife, with the Astor lady, owner of Jekyll's Folly Farm, on my right. Afterwards we toured the Sargent exhibition, wonderful pictures ill-served by its hanging and installation.

The next night some twenty gathered at the Garrick for a much cosier and really far more enjoyable occasion, although Hardy Amies only gets more crabby as he gets even older. When he arrived I said to him that Rosemary was doing the *placement*. 'Never use that expression. It is what the French use for what they do with their money. The correct expression is *place à table*.' But I suppose at almost ninety you can get away with anything.

During the day I was just rushing all over the place but, which was a great treat, I bumped into Anita Brookner in the London Library. 'I only meet you on significant occasions,' I said. She asked me what I was writing and I said that I was about to embark on a biography. 'You're made for it,' she said. At this point Barbara Dorf pushed in, saying to Anita: 'Only David Walker could have put the shield of Achilles there' – a piece of weird overheard conversation worthy of one of Alan Bennett's *Talking Heads*.

I subsequently caught up with Anita walking up to Jermyn Street. She's a lugubrious, profound woman with huge eyes. 'Shall we walk together a little?' I asked. We did. I railed about the government, about the relentless populism and dumbing-down that seems to engulf everything like some irreversible tide. Soon we were both lamenting the abandonment of what we had always thought as sacred: excellence, quality and aspiration upwards.

That feeling was reinforced when I went to a meeting with Jocelyn Burton, the silversmith. Kept going by cigarettes and champagne, she has a wonderful sense of possibility and style, her mind and imagination reeling hither and thither. The meeting was about a bid to make medals for the Millennium, me as the iconographer, Jocelyn as the designer and maker, and the backer a jovial, astute man called John Wallace from a firm called Langfords. Once again we heard about the faceless ones of the Dome, of their rejection of our history and our great cultural achievements. Christ was on no account to enter into it, they kept on saying to him. It's about the last thousand years. But here, yet again, is the subtext of populism, dumbing-down and political correctness in action.

Never mind, we heaved to and put together a package of four medals, all with the same obverse (equality for all!) but with different reverses. For the many, some treatment of the ghastly Dome logo was unavoidable. For the few, my idea was dates that referred to events in British history of which we could be proud, like the abolition of slavery. For the obverse I suggested the night sky as we crossed into the year 2000, with, for the lucky few, the stars set with real jewels.

1998

13 DECEMBER

The Verey finale

On Sunday 13th we battled our way across country to RFC Rendcomb, which turned out to be a small private airfield with a clubhouse that had a tent tacked onto it for Rosemary's final *fête*. Everyone was standing outside in the cold and we wondered why. I couldn't work it out so, wanting to put down our coats and gifts, I pushed in as Rosemary passed me; on turning, much to my astonishment, I found myself face to face with the Prince of Wales. 'Hello, Roy', was the greeting. Apparently he had just flown in and deserves top marks for coming to this affectionate if desultory gathering of many of the same people for the third time, this time minus the Verey clan. I had another go at HRH about painting those gloomy gates in his Rose Garden. 'I know', he said, 'you want me to paint them blue.' I replied, 'I had to have a go at you', at which point he crumpled up with a guffaw. Somehow he's become more relaxed. Maybe being minus Diana and chucking a lot of the protocol has 'released' him.

He went before lunch, which turned out to be somewhat interminable. I was put at the head table with Jennifer Bute opposite me, complaining about the new generation of Butes letting the ancestral home go to pot and much else. On my other side was Sarah Faringdon telling me of Charlie's new life as a lord-in-waiting, trailing around during the German President's state visit. Windsor Castle had been *en fête*, there was the usual City dinner and the return match at the embassy, where Princess Margaret inconsiderately kept everyone up for ever while she kept swigging The Famous Grouse. One on from me was Hardy Amies, complaining about everybody and everything. If I live to that age, pray God that I never go that way.

NEW YEAR'S EVE

Farewell 1998. Rather a good year, although it ended on a somewhat chilling note. I'd done a bit with a journalist for the *Daily Mail* to promote *Story*. The topic was 'Me and My Health'. Shortly afterwards my brother Derek said on the phone, 'It's funny you didn't mention that you had Hodgkin's Disease.' I said that I had no idea that I had had it. He replied, 'The whole road thought you were a goner.' Suddenly, at sixty-three, I learn that what for decades I had accepted as a tubercular gland that had been removed from my neck when I was thirteen or fourteen was in fact cancer. One 'gland' was taken out surgically and the other by what I was told was radiotherapy. Thereafter followed decades of annual check-ups, looking for lumps that mercifully never recurred. Suddenly I felt the chill hand of mortality. I had never known any of that. I wish in a way that he had never told me. I recall the panic over my heart when I was young, when they thought that I had a hole in it and wouldn't live another year. That proved to be all wrong. But here I am, still grateful for each day.

1999

INTO THE NEW YEAR

The opening months of the year are always gloomy and inward-looking. It seems these days to be heads-down and get on with the next book, in this case *The Artist and the Garden* and the associated lectures at Yale. This book is a very different project from its predecessor, the mammoth 700-page *Spirit of Britain*, being instead close focus. It will inevitably be driven by its pictorial content so I shall miss the vistas across time that framed the three previous projects. But I do realise that in these quiet months I must press on and get as much done before everything as it were starts up.

Meanwhile, outside the rain has fallen in deluges through most of January, bringing all new garden work to a halt and reducing whole areas to a sea of mud along with rivers of water. But the workmen started again last week and suddenly the area around The Folly has been landscaped. The gravel path is there, so is the paving around the oak tree together with the linking flight of steps. We've planted a low tapestry hedge of golden privet, field maple and beech and in-filled behind with golden fastigiate yew, golden and spotted aucuba, species and other roses and lilac, not to forget more of Julia's beloved malus. We await the arrival of the blue *treillage* arches, a tunnel of them sweeping down to The Folly with medlars trained over them.

We really must do the wills again this year in a way that they provide for the preservation of the garden, but how? Some people are violently against the National Trust but Julia and I see it as having the back-up of a powerful organisation. The idea is to ask George Clive as our appointee to see through our intent, although health-wise I sometimes wonder whether we won't outlive him. But we want to continue to develop the garden.

Now *Spirit* is done I wonder how it will be received. Who knows? It's a 'Done our Best' book but the closing chapters did leave me terribly depressed as to what could happen and I find myself agreeing more and more with A.N. Wilson and Roger Scruton in seeing the deliberate destruction of a once proud high culture in the interests of crude populism. Also, it was only as work on the book drew to its close that I had that overwhelming sense of being at the end of something, the final phase of two thousand years of a civilisation rooted in the classical and Christian traditions, and that the framework of the former had gone before my lifetime and the latter during it. It was difficult not to feel an aching sadness and sense of loss. But on the positive side, work on that book left me ashamed of my own ignorance and what I hadn't read – so it's back to schooldays and I'm reading the *Aeneid* in translation, the whole of it instead of Book VI, which is all I did at school!

22 MARCH

Montacute

We travelled down to Montacute on the Sunday evening, a picture-book 'This England' little town. We had been booked into the King's

Arms by the National Portrait Gallery but, on arrival, were told that there was no food except from the local pub, The Phelips Arms. So off we went there for a truck driver's supper and met up with John and Ann Tusa, he being an assiduous National Portrait Gallery Trustee. This was all in aid of the new hang of early portraits in the Long Gallery, the NPG's first outpost and a 'child' bequeathed when I left in 1973.

The day of the opening was fine and we filled in time by going to East Lambrook, Margery Fish's garden. It was closed but mercifully I was recognised and we were let in. It has survived changes of ownership remarkably well and holds up to being a garden with a message, for I've never seen ground-cover planting more brilliantly done, with a hundred varieties of hardy geranium for a start. We must have bought fifteen that we hadn't got. Mrs Fish in her photos looked tough and Ann Tusa joked that she'd probably poisoned her husband with weedkiller.

Then back we went for the opening, which was very National Trust, with solid, well-heeled art and heritage aspiring Middle England present in force. It was all so safe and really a bit dull: everything seemed Armani beige. How I cursed Michael Jaffé for forcing the sale of the five great wooden chandeliers that John Fowler had designed. The gallery cried out for them, for anything really that would break the never-ending vista. But everyone was sweet and very appreciative and I did my inevitable 'down-memory-lane' speech. And that was it. But I'd have loved it to have been just a little more exciting. It's strange to think that the suggestion that we should do this kind of thing at my interview for the NPG in 1967 nearly cost me the job.

Lord Irvine's Party

It was a great surprise to be asked to a party given by Derry Irvine, the Lord Chancellor, staged at the Garrick Club in the interests of whipping up signatures for Andrew Patrick's candidature for the club. Well, perhaps he'd never read my send-ups of him in the *Daily Mail* . . . It was irresistible to go and, surprisingly, it turned out to be quite a small gathering that included Christopher Lloyd, Alastair Service, Bevis Hillier, John Underwood, Bill Drummond, John Baskett, Patrick Procktor . . .

I said to Bevis how much I looked forward to the second volume of his life of John Betjeman. He seemed quite thrown by that and obviously thought that I'd still be upset by his attack on me in the *Sunday Times* in 1980, as I'd recorded in my *Diaries*. 'I don't grind axes,' I said. It is, after all, some twenty years on . . . What a waste in some sense Bevis has been, which is a great shame. He played the wag for too long, made the mistake of going to the USA and somehow never quite regained his earlier ground when he returned. Patrick Proctor is now permanently sozzled, I fear, swaying from side to side, his speech slightly slurred and permanently aggressive.

At long last the Lord Chancellor arrived, not personable at all but affable enough, with somewhat shambling gait and filthy black hair smarmed down onto his head. I'm surprised that he hasn't been given a New Labour make-over. 'I remember coming to have lunch with you at the V&A,' he said. Oh dear: I couldn't, so I said 'I hope that I was nice to you.' 'Well', he replied, 'I was nice to you.' So I left wondering what that meant.

25 MARCH

Catholic encounter

As I walked back to Morpeth Terrace past Westminster Cathedral, who should turn the corner but Colin Amery. I hadn't seen him for years. There he stood, clutching a large book bound in black with gilt decoration and a bundle of vellum papers tied with a ribbon. 'I'm about to be received into the Roman Church', was the somewhat surprising opening line. So I expressed my usual opinions about the present Archbishop of Canterbury and how clones of Holy Trinity Brompton were ruining my life and that I was kept going by the Abbey and All Saints, Margaret Street. 'I was confirmed there,' he said. I suppose that must have been in the days when he was one of the 'Young Fogeys' and they all went to St Cyprian's, Clarence Gate. 'Don't tell me', I said, 'Father Michael Seed.' 'Yes,' he replied; all I could think of saying to this most recent 'seedling' was 'Bless you' and wended on my way.

4 APRIL

Easter Day

Easter Day and war in the Balkans. It's unreal, the flowers and the eggs, and then those horrendous pictures of refugees as though out of one of Callot's engravings of the miseries of the Thirty Years War, bringing tales of savagery to match what one sees in those prints. All one's gut feelings are 'Keep out of the Balkans'. There's no EU there but the jostlings of Catholic, Orthodox and Muslim and the after-math of the Roman, Byzantine, Ottoman and Austro-Hungarian empires. And those loyalties, too, linked to age-old ethnic groupings that have never dissolved. Any commentator here who understands the history is appalled at our involvement. But then politicians now-adays know no history and the Americans can't understand Europe. And once we start intervening in the affairs of a sovereign state on humanitarian grounds, where does it end? NATO could end up bombing and sending troops everywhere.

Blair's plastic face stares out from the television screen, promising everything he won't ever be able to give those refugees. The cost of the war will be horrendous. And what are we going to do? Occupy a great section of an inaccessible countryside for decades? All of this makes the Easter message ring both hollow and real this year.

18 APRIL

George Clive

Jackie Thompson rang in the morning to tell us that George Clive had died the previous night. She was crying and tears were shed here too. He was our Herefordshire friend above every other for twenty years. The last few weeks have been awful, above all a ghastly strain on Penny Graham, who has had to cope with virtually everything. He hadn't looked well since Christmas and then he fell down and was carted off to Hereford General Hospital, where they siphoned off two litres of fluid from around the lung and where he contracted a virus that dogged all subsequent medical treatment. He came out of hospital but he was breathless and there was some surface coating to the lung. Into the Edward VII hospital in Westminster he went, and when he was discharged from there Penny got him into St Thomas's. By then he couldn't cross the room without oxygen. It is pointless writing all these details down but in the end his sister, Alice Boyd, was told that it was some form of terminal cancer. The slippage was so rapid that one almost expected that call; but when it did come it didn't lessen the sense of loss and grief.

George was a large, fair-haired, blue-eyed man with a stammer that only left him when he spoke on the telephone. He was a born countryman, all tweeds and corduroy worn out of shape, totally unconscious of his appearance. His father was killed in 1943, when he was a mere child. That threw him close to his sister, Alice. I have no idea what came through from the Clive genes but quite a lot came from the Pakenham side. From his mother, Lady Mary Clive, he inherited an informed but not academic intellectual bent. He was bookish, yes, but he was not interested in the performing arts. He loved his garden and had a phenomenal knowledge of trees and plants. He created the lakes and vistas from the house at Whitfield with a mock ruined castle and a 'ship' sailing in the water, a perspective that stretched beyond his own land across borrowed landscape.

Educated at Eton, he belonged to a club that included Grey Gowrie, John Wells and Tristram Powell. He was hugely hospitable and the house had that quintessential English mix in its best form of a core of educated family and its connexions, but then further laced by the likes of Iris Murdoch, John Bayley and John Betjeman. I understand that there had been a steady stream of women in his life. We entered it at the brief Selina Hastings phase. But for the last eighteen years it had been Penny Graham. She brought with her a gaiety and vivacity that he clearly appreciated and I really cannot make out why he never married her. But there is no way of prying into those innermost parts. Yet there was an element in George that would have found such an arrangement convenient, bed and board with none of the complications. She was, of course, Roman Catholic and one is aware that the Pakenham family and its conversion to Rome had been at times divisive. But, poor thing, she now emerges a loser.

George knew our garden from a field. The sassafras he gave us has always been called 'George's tree'. And so it always will be. Later he gave us a few cowslips and now they have seeded all over the garden. Indeed, Julia was just about to put a flower in an envelope to send to him when the sad news came.

For us his death closes a phase in our life here. In the country life is very much a circle of like-minded people who know that when they go to each other's houses they will meet the same sort. George was our linchpin and there was endless coming and going over the years. To me he typified the old English squirearchy at its best. He was a true man for his county, loved his countryside, his dog, the shoot, the garden, but he also enjoyed playing his role as Sheriff, wearing absurd hired robes. To go at fifty-eight is really cruel.

ST GEORGE'S DAY

Farewell to George

We got up in London early to drive down for George Clive's service of thanksgiving at Wormbridge church. It was raining when we got up, rained all day and was raining still when we went to bed. 'George, the bringer of rain', as he was known to us because every time he came to see the garden it poured, had lived up to his reputation. This was an occasion to remind anyone that the death of a shy, gentle, man who loved trees and the countryside was not in vain. So many people, so much affection, a kaleidoscope of county and country, the grand and the humble, the odd and the ordinary, family and friends bound together to celebrate the memory of one man. It was a rite of passage of a kind known only to the country and to England and I give thanks for it.

The service was at noon; we arrived at 10.45 a.m. to find cars already parking. It was clear that there was to be an enormous turn-out. There was a marquee in the churchyard to take the overflow, for the church itself was small. It was also somewhat nondescript. There never was much cash in Herefordshire and this was a simple building 'gone over' in the Victorian period. I caught hatchments propped up on the ceiling beams but my eye mainly fell on the area in which we had been placed, the chancel. And then only one side of that, for opposite me was an array of plaques and memorials to the

Clive family. A Victorian couple stared towards me. She, enveloped seemingly in veils, had died at forty, greatly beloved. There were other memorials to Clive men, including one who must have been George's uncle, killed in the Spanish Civil War. It reminded me of the tragedy of this family in the present century, for George's grandfather was killed in the Great War and his father at El Alamein. And now, with George's death, the male line ended and the estate passed to his nephew, Edward Lennox-Boyd.

The church was wonderfully decorated, much of it by Henrietta Dunne. There were lilies on the altar flanked by huge branches of trees, and the nave, when I glanced that way, seemed embowered in the fresh green leaves of spring. At the back the font, I gathered, was adorned with some of George's favourite plants. Every seat was labelled. We sat on chairs in front of the choir stalls and there were others added on either side of the central aisle.

People still can't catch on to the notion that this is not a memorial service but one of thanksgiving (Penny had been quite definite about that) but most turned up festooned in black, which George would have hated. We were placed with friends and county, the Cotterells, the Dunnes, Lady De L'Isle, the Hazlehursts, Foleys, et al., along with one of George's former girlfriends, who visibly wept. Beyond, in the front pew, the family gathered. Mary Clive heaved her way in on a stick, indomitable; not long after, Frank Longford arrived, a quite incredible ninety-five, having come down on the train with his daughter, Rachel Billington, who said he had taken over the whole carriage with his stories. Penny in a fur hat sat with her cousin Mary North; on the other side I glimpsed Thomas Pakenham and Tristram Powell.

The service comprised a few hymns, a reading from a psalm, another from Ezekiel about the cedar tree (very beautiful), one read badly by the Dean of Hereford from a book entitled *The Man Who Planted Trees* (touching), and then came Thomas Pakenham's address. He did it well, a fair balance between eulogy and truth. But he got the man and why we were all there. He made us laugh and smile, and all that was so very right. And then everyone was asked back to the big house afterwards.

It is always the same at these affairs, a terrible feeling of 'the end of something' engulfs me. As we walked up the stairs to the front door I was seized with the memory of how we had stood there on a warm summer night watching the great comet hurtle across the heavens. Opposite, George's lakes and fountains stretched into the distance. How often we had walked that ground to admire the waxen blossom of his magnolias or the rarities in his secret garden. And now an era had come to an end.

Inside there was an unbelievable fracas filled with so many people we knew. It was exhausting. Mary Clive, looking radiant, sat holding court on a sofa; Frank sat opposite her on another one, telling the lady cleric that, yes, he was pro women's ordination. There was Lindy Dufferin, announcing her intent of coming to see our hedges. So indeed she shall! Drusilla Beyfus questioned me as to why I wasn't writing in Tony Snowdon's exhibition catalogue. It was a scrum, but a happy one: rain outside, radiance within.

Well, that's the end of an era for us. But it's good that the estate goes to a young couple. Edward Lennox-Boyd is only thirty. He and his wife Tamsim are a delight and to see her hold a child in her arms gave the house a new life stretching well into the next century. Someone said to me that they hoped they wouldn't change this or that and how wonderful it was that it was a capsule from the early 1950s. 'No,' I said, 'they must change things. They must make their own life there and move the house on.'

Penny and Mary came to stay in The Folly. We were touched that Penny should ask us. George has left her Rabbit Cottage and I'm glad because we'd all miss her; I'm glad too that her role in his life was fully acknowledged, the widow Clive *manquée*. She was wonderfully bright and composed, only the odd flash tweaking her back. Cupid had hit at a Victorian ball at the Reform Club in 1981 and never left them thereafter. She had crossed a great bridge, which one of us will have to cross one day, so incredibly bravely, an example to cherish.

8 JUNE

Tangier

I've been doing a Swan Hellenic cruise, talking on gardens and calling at ports around the Iberian peninsula, Morocco and France. It's well organised and extremely agreeable; the people are Middle England for the most part, with the odd American. But the couple of hundred Britishers gathered here represent some kind of corporate voice. Many remember the war, most are sixty-plus and most, too, have been or still are in the professions. Their views are consistent (I have a rule to sit next to someone different at every meal): anti the Dome, anti the Balkan war, deeply worried about the consequences of devolution and the break-up of the British Isles, and some of them – but very few – anti-European. This is the year of England, I feel.

A week or so ago I was up in Scotland delivering the Caledonian Foundation's Biennial Lecture in the Humanities. I decided the topic last year: 'Goodbye Britain?' tracing the cultural consequences of 1603 and 1707, on both of which occasions there had been a deliberate attempt to create a single British culture, especially after 1707 with its tenet of 'unity in diversity'. Thus it has pertained down until today; but does 1999 mean that all of this will goes into reverse?

It is interesting to record the widespread unease engendered by this government, of the fear of Blair's apocalyptic streak. And yet people realise that in all but name it is a Tory government; but where oh where is the opposition? How amazing it is to see us taken back to the thirteenth century, seemingly with no one noticing. One sees the sweep of this century. It began with Ireland going, then saw the Empire transmute into the Commonwealth and now Scotland and Wales about to depart. Australia too is on the cards. We're shorn and diminished but no one seems to notice or grasp it.

30 JUNE

Gardeners' rally

The Clerk of the Gardeners' Company rang me up: 'Your name was suggested by the Prince of Wales's office.' So I thought that I'd go and it turned out to be an attractive occasion on a sunlit London day. The event was the award of a prize to the best young organic gardener, the winner surprisingly called Leigh Hunt. It took place on the premises of the Honourable Artillery Company in Armoury House, City Road. I'd never been there before. There was a handsome Georgian oak staircase and we were all huddled in what was their court room, with a pretty Strawberry Hill gothick 'throne' for the head person and a wonderful grisaille frieze of trophies of arms *à l'antique*.

Gardening always produces a happy atmosphere and everyone seemed so pleased to see me there. It was very touching. Mollie Salisbury appeared like an extra from a Merchant Ivory film in a *c.*1910 hobble skirt and an absurd little cap with a withered feather stuck in it. There were real hands-on gardeners there from Kew, Henry Doubleday [Research Association], Capel Manor and Wye College.

Prince Charles entered, slim and smiling, with a face that resembles more and more the later portraits of George II, the lines running from the corners of his nose and curving round either side of his lips. But he continues in this post-Diana phase to be as one reborn, easy and relaxed, working his way around everyone. Someone gave him a packet of 1695 sweet pea seeds, which he loved. He always calls me by my Christian name now and perhaps he seems easier because I can't subscribe to all the old sycophancy any more. He knew that I would go at him over the gates at Highgrove. 'I know that you want me to paint them blue.' 'Well, stick some gold on them.' 'I have.' 'Well stick on some more.'

He'd loved me swiping at hanging baskets on the *Today* programme ('John Wood didn't build Bath for hanging baskets') and I repeated my invitation to see The Laskett garden. 'When I'm next in Herefordshire,' he promised. I told him that there were 'bits' of Highgrove in it and that it would make him laugh. It's odd but he really is endearing. The presentation was of a stunning engraved bowl, including a silhouette of one of the hedges I'd designed. It was difficult not to smile at the sight of it.

30 JUNE

Evening

In the evening I went to the topping-out ceremony of the National Portrait Gallery extension. Up we ascended through the building site to its summit, roofed but without walls and therefore with clear vistas across London. I felt very proud of Charles Saumarez Smith and, thirty years on, of all that the Gallery had achieved.

It was a select if eccentric gathering. The gnome-like, grinning Culture Minister crouched in a hard hat, along with Henry Keswick and Charles, for a press photo; I posed with Julia Somerville, the TV presenter and partner of the architect Jeremy Dixon, as though she was my long-lost friend. The Heritage Fund representatives were in evidence, with the self-important David Wilson to the fore, still enmeshed in museums and writing the history of the British Museum, a most inappropriate commission. I gave silent thanks for the fact that I had brought the curtain firmly down on that phase of my life. Two pretty girls from the *Daily Express* asked me why I was there. I said that years ago, before they were born, I'd been Director and how glamorous I'd been in velvet and ruffles and how everyone from Noël Coward to David Hockney had flocked here. They listened as though to a fairy tale.

JULY

Summer reflection

Beatrix Miller, my sage, remarked: '1999 has been a good year for you.' She's usually right, and always when she gives advice pronounces with such perception. I think how extraordinary she is, how lucky I've been to have her as a friend and how much I shall miss her when the time comes, which I hope will be long delayed. I love the honesty and stoicism, the sense of understanding human nature and its weaknesses, and her ability to forgive.

But she had a point. I've worked like blazes. Next week the advance copies of *Spirit* arrive. Three out of six booksellers have chosen it as the book for the autumn. That's cheering but as always I'm nervous. I pray that it won't be junked. It was written from the heart and it seems more and more to be a book of the moment as we toss away a mighty past. More, it's about England and what she stands for. England has forgotten what she's about and it's sad. I write this on the day that the Queen opens the Scottish Parliament. In May I voyaged north and gave a state lecture in Edinburgh (repeated in St Andrews) entitled 'Goodbye Britain?' examining what happened culturally after 1603 and 1707 and what could happen now. On both the former occasions there had been a deliberate effort to create a single British culture, represented after 1707 in the 'unity in diversity' principle. Now all of this could go in reverse, focusing on what divides as against what unites us. I came back from Scotland and opened the Hay-on-Wye Literary Festival, doing *Story of Britain* again, hopefully for the last time. But somehow I took off about England and what it represented, of the wiping out of our past, of the cankered perfidy of political correctness so that our schoolchildren now learn of the Spanish Armada through the eyes of a Spanish sailor! But I'm glad that the *Sunday Times* recorded that I memorably said I'd never thought to see the country dragged back to the 1290s in eighteen months without anyone seeming to notice.

There was too much travel too close together this year: Tuscan Gardens, Scotland and Swan Hellenic around Spain. All hugely interesting and enjoyable and, as Julia says, 'Gather ye rosebuds . . .' Who knows whether one will be in demand later? But the people fascinate me and their observation of times and tides. *Minerva* was well laced with ex-headmasters and headmistresses. They were mainly from the grammar school sector, ordinary, self-made people. The view that came back again and again was of the collapse of education and how there had been two generations of poor teachers and that a tradition had snapped. Labour's proposed abolition of the remaining grammar schools would only polarise things even more, the intelligent classes sacrificing virtually everything to educate their young rather than see them dragged downwards.

I'm busy on *The Artist and the Garden*. It's a lovely subject but I'm not that happy trying to go backwards and write an academic book. I'm not helped by having a somewhat remote editor at the

Yale University Press. But the benign Brian Allen sees me through and Julia MacRae, bless her, is reading what I wrote out of pure friendship.

5 JULY

Fungus in the knot garden

Gardening is always the same. Everything goes along smoothly as long as you keep up with the traffic, weeding, feeding, clipping, mowing or whatever, and then suddenly, wham, something happens. About a fortnight ago a mysterious fungus hit the knot garden in front of the house. I showed it to Rosemary Verey, who said we should rip out the plants and burn them. I did. One was sent to Elizabeth Bainbridge, the box 'queen' of the UK. We spoke. 'Hit it hard,' she said. Apparently it has cropped up all over the place on the *suffructicosa* variety, as in our case. No one knows why. She sent our plant off to a laboratory and we await the result. Meanwhile, we were put on to a spray. Needless to say, it rained and rained, spreading the fungus and not allowing us to douse the knot. Eventually, last Friday, we did but it rained afterwards! I looked this morning and it's still spreading. We'll hit it again with spray on Thursday and then pray. I dread it spreading, as it could wipe out half the garden. One's left with a gnawing sense of anxiety. Mercifully there's no sign as yet of it having spread beyond the *suffructicosa* in the knot.

This is a blow in a summer when rain has been abundant and the growth extraordinary. Shaun has lifted the garden. We can't find a weed anywhere and everything is shooting. The holly standards along Elizabeth Tudor Avenue are well on the way. The new border along the Serpentine is burgeoning and it looks so beautiful that I want to extend it the whole length of the avenue. Dare we? We were listed in *New Eden* as among the ten most innovative gardens in the UK since 1945. We never set out to be innovative, just ourselves really. But it's difficult not to feel a certain satisfaction after twenty-eight years of toil.

25 AUGUST

Masone, near Parma

We have been coming here each August seemingly for years and here we are again. 'Here' is Franco Maria Ricci's summer house, a converted barn, a stone's throw from his crumbling ancestral home. At the moment a fence is going up around that, with notices to keep out. Scaffolding is in evidence and piles of tiles, for Franco is embarking on the dream for his dotage, to build a library within the shell of the old house and then knock the latter down to fall like a Piranesi ruin around it. This man is an original, for he showed me massive plans for the vast labyrinth he wants to build nearby, in the middle of which there will be a two-thousand-seat arena and a chapel for the Mass. 'Perhaps the Pope will dedicate it,' he says *en passant*. Also on the cards is a lavish hotel for rich Americans who bring their own servants! They will come to listen to lectures on Giulio Romano and Correggio and visit the sites. I listen sceptically. It is all very Italian and people come and go about it and there is much ruminating as to how to get all the necessary permissions.

But Franco has flair, energy, drive and imagination. I'm told that he never reads any of the articles in his magazine, *FMR*, and that once he just turned the pages of a particular issue, sighing 'Too blue'. That sums up the originality of a man who adores his native Parma along with Italy and the arts. He's a man of the Mediterranean, Catholic and baroque, loving images of almost any sort from eighteenth-century angels to Twenties fake jewellery. Restless by nature, he is forever launching first this project and then the next. His energy is boundless, always producing new ideas that make me despair of British publishing. He has done more for Elizabethan painting by publishing *William Larkin* with masses of colour plates than all my other books on the topic together.

Life here is of a polyglot community that comes and goes. Breakfast is never earlier than ten, lunch tends to materialise at about two and dinner about nine. Otherwise you are left to get on with it. So I read and I write and I go to bed early and sleep. Oh, how I sleep, ten hours at a stretch! On some afternoons we all pile into cars and there's an expedition. Today in the scorching heat we went to Carpi. None of us had ever been there before. What a discovery! The main piazza is magnificent, with arcades like Modena and Bologna and houses shades of ochre, cinnamon and puce. Franco never gives up. La Sagrada, is closed so onto the mobile he gets and it is opened for us, a tiny jewel, and we peer at the frescoes and Romanesque carving. Outside it is an early Renaissance gem in brick. To get into the *castello* he pursues the mayor but, no, there's no one in the town hall and he denounces the indolent bureaucrats. So we saunter across the main piazza, pile into the cars and hurtle off to San Francesco. That's closed too: *in restauro*. So we hit the *autostrada* for Parma and here we are again.

For almost half a century Italian life has beguiled me. I'm not sure that I'd want to live here but a short, sharp spell acts like a tonic. Somehow the Italians always come down to basics: art and life, looking at things and making time for friends and conversation. The heart of this house is upstairs, where a granite table about thirty feet long stretches along an area open to the air on both sides, bar the ancient brick columns supporting the roof. On the table there are always papers and books, and we gather around it to eat. Laura Casalis conjures up food as only the Italians know how, making use of whatever is to hand or purchased in the market at nearby Fontanellato. Pasta sauces are improvised and meals take on any shape as plates appear, perhaps with prosciutto, a frittata, lasagne, local cheeses – above all Parmesan – an *insalata, frutta*, all swilled down with water and the local Malvasia Spumante. I always try to imitate this way of entertaining when I get back to England but it's never quite the same. How could it be?

9 SEPTEMBER

Spirit of Britain *is launched*

The day of the publication of *Spirit*. There was a wonderful dinner yesterday evening in its honour at Sartoria in Savile Row. Whatever one's differences with Terence Conran, he knows about restaurants. There were fifteen of us, all involved in the book, and I was so touched by everyone's commitment and support of me as an author. There were speeches and a toast, to which I replied, thanking each in turn for what they had contributed. Very touching. Bouquets, of course, to Julia MacRae, who has been my writing muse since *Story* and I couldn't help saying that I'd never have become an FRSL except for her. I told Will Sulkin of Pimlico of my next project for them, *Colloquium* or (as I thought later) *Feasting*, a kind of social history of eating in Western Europe.

We haven't yet reached the end of the reception of *Spirit* by the critics, which has been very odd and mixed. 'Prepare yourself for the knives,' warned Beatrix Miller, and they came. But after I'd read them all I thought, well they would, wouldn't they and so what? But incredible raves from A.N. Wilson in *Country Life* and Richard Morrison in *The Times*, a double page, and very good, considered pieces elsewhere by Victoria Glendinning and Robert Hewison, all people I respect. But it's number three on the non-fiction bestseller list in London and those in the media who've read it love it. Natalie Wheen on Classic FM totally understood its role to open doors, to present the subject in a way for those who, from time to time, move sideways from fiction to biography and hence to narrative.

This was a day of reeling from place to place: the ebullient Sheridan Morley, Adam Boulton for Sky News, *GLR* with a benign young novelist called Sean Hughes and *In Tune* on Radio 3 with Sean Rafferty, not to mention book signings at Hatchards, Selfridges, Pan Books, Waterstones in the King's Road, et al. Liz Sich, who arranges it all, is a whizz. Suddenly the adrenalin runs and I'm fine, taking it all as it comes. But everyone seems to really love the book and its modest intent. And then there are the titbits of information as to where we've got now, Sheridan screaming that New Labour has closed more theatres in two years than Thatcher did in eighteen. Adam Boulton is a shrewd observer. I pick his brains: 'What's happening?' The answer is intriguing. The proletariat won't take paying for elitist arts any more, unlike in other countries in Western Europe where they will, and aspire. So this government wants to save its middle-class vote but the middle classes, who've had art on the cheap from 1945 to 1980, will now have to pay for it. I can see that perspective. For decades a vast swathe of taxpayers has subsidised the tastes of a minority with free museums and cheap theatre seats. What a fascinating scenario to watch.

16 SEPTEMBER

Windsor Castle

The day of the Prince of Wales's party to launch Royal Collection Publications Ltd, or whatever it's called. The invitation said that it was to be held in the State Apartments, which I hadn't yet seen in their new guise, so I accepted. The weather was quite extraordinary, one of those blissful early autumn days when the light catches parts of the landscape one has never seen before. And Windsor Castle looked heroic in silhouette, in spite of Slough and descending aeroplanes.

The party was in the Guard Room. Assembled there were all the old museum/arts mafia, in the main those who had done or were doing catalogues, a sprinkling of media like Min Hogg of *Interiors*, the surprising appearance of the Warburg Institute in the person of the nice Nicholas Mann, a few collectors (including one of miniatures, for Graham Reynolds's catalogue of the early ones was also being launched) and one or two others, among whom we figured, along with Antonia Fraser and Harold Pinter, Flora Fraser, Mary Anna Marten of Crichel and David Starkey, who has written such violent attacks on the Royal Family that I'm surprised he was asked. But then they all generally fall for it.

Harold was complaining like blazes about a critic who had killed off the play he'd directed from coming to London, and then screaming that the critic had then asked him to dinner during the Edinburgh Festival. He tore the letter up. Paul Greenhalgh, Head of Research at the V&A, a sweet man, told me of the insensitive behaviour of the Museum over Clive Wainwright's death. I was surprised he'd taken so long to find that out.

The Prince of Wales entered, flanked by members of the 'heavy gang', seemingly chosen because they were shorter than him. He did his bit well, as usual going round the room talking to a lot of boring people. Then he spoke, in the main touting for sponsorship for the other royal catalogues. And why not? That's where we are. We were wheeled up for a quick word and he said 'I've just written to you.' I said, yes, and that it was a delightful letter thanking me for *Spirit*, saying how it would come in use for Prince William and ending by telling me that outside at Highgrove they were clipping the ball finials I had designed. He reminded us that he wanted to come and see our garden next year.

Eventually the doors swung wide and we could see St George's Hall, which I must say was a huge improvement on the old one, stunningly lit with a wonderful sense of theatre. And the octagon at the end was a monument to the crafts revival in woodwork, an essay in late twentieth-century gothick. All of it was a triumph and well worth the drive.

21 SEPTEMBER

The future of the garden, Winchester and the V&A

The solicitor from Pennington's, Julian Chadwick, came yesterday, Monday, and the decision was made. The wills will stipulate that the estate should pass to the National Trust, with the intention of opening the garden, so today I wrote to Martin Drury. It's so important for everything to be tidied up and in order when the time comes. I couldn't bear to leave an untidy aftermath. It would be wonderful if people, decades after, get joy from this patch that we've lovingly created and tended.

On Wednesday I was on the road to Winchester with *Spirit* to perform in the new hall of Winchester College. The audience was a hundred and fifty or so, at any rate as many as turned up for Melvyn Bragg, whatever that may mean. I wondered how it would all go but it went just fine and I got prolonged applause. They wanted to hear about England and who we were and where we're going. Lots of books were sold. The next day, back in London, I took Paul Greenhalgh to lunch at the Garrick. He told me something that I never knew. In the early 1980s the V&A reached 1.8 million visitors a year. Now it is down to 800,000 and the National Portrait Gallery is about to overtake it. In one way this made me happy and in another desperately sad.

25 SEPTEMBER

Hardy Amies

Hardy Amies rang. He wanted to tell me how much he loved the book: 'Each time I got to the end of a chapter I had to read on.' I said that he couldn't pay me a better compliment. What a strange man he is. One minute he's an old bitch and then, quite suddenly, genuinely thoughtful and kind. It made me feel guilty at having been so down on him.

13 OCTOBER

The plinth in Trafalgar Square

I went to London for yet another 'performance' of *Spirit*: the V&A, Chester and Cheltenham, Tunbridge Wells, Canterbury, Guildford and Windsor – and a few others to come. But I came to London a day early because John Mortimer had asked me to give my views as to what should be placed on the empty plinth in Trafalgar Square. This arose because at the moment the first of a series of temporary sculptures is there, a standing *Ecce Homo*, which looks like the pro-verbial molehill atop a mountain. The *Daily Mail* had asked me to write what I thought of it, which is not much: the scale is wrong and it's totally unrelated to the heroic imperial theme of Trafalgar Square – and, frankly, the figure has a whiff of the sauna about it. We owe this aberration to John Mortimer and Prue Leith of all people! I like both of them but what they know about sculpture I know not; but then they're New Labour luvvies. Shortly afterwards, John Mortimer wrote to me asking whether I would give my views. I said that I only had one, that it should be an equestrian statue of the present Queen when the time came. In spite of that, I was prevailed upon to appear.

I arrived at the Department of Culture, Media and Sport to find Brian Sewell on the other side of the hall. He smiled and raised his arm in greeting. 'Not after what you've written about me,' I said and turned my back on him. His arm fell limp at his side. I've never done that kind of thing before and I felt very mixed about it afterwards. How far to turn the other cheek? I can take criticism but not personal attacks and abuse, and his review of the *Diaries* overstepped the mark. For years I'd always taken it on the chin but I'm not in public office any more. He'd just taken things too far.

Then I descended into a basement committee room. John Mortimer, ebullient and benign, rather Falstaff-like, clutched my hand and gesticulated around the table to the assembled committee – or, rather, what was left of it, for the Scottish Republican Neil MacGregor had gone, along with the obligatory ethnic quota. Those who remained were a weird bunch: Peter Clark, an historian; Ruth Rendell, who sat beady-eyed, tight-lipped and never said a word; a councillor from somewhere; and that permanent fixture Richard Cork, minus most of his hair.

Well, I gave them a good run for their money. Heaven alone knows why this committee was ever set up. The plinth has been empty for decades: why not just leave it? What a waste of time. In the long term, I was told, the square was to become an approach to the National Gallery (splendid) but there's no money to do it. There's no money either for the statue. I said that the square was about iconography not art, an imperial Valhalla. Oh dear – that aspect really worried them. Thought had been given to emptying the place of all its existing monuments. I more or less told them to their faces that they were wasting their time. How can someone of the intelligence of John Mortimer get caught up in something so ridiculous? No one knew what to do and no one had any money and it wasn't necessary to do anything anyway. In the evening I passed the vast Ferris wheel going up on the South Bank. Oddly enough it was rather stupendous, like a vast mobile spider's web, airy and, in its way, rather beautiful.

12 NOVEMBER

The fate of the garden

We're back from the USA, where my lectures on *The Artist and the Garden* were a huge success and we were royally treated, but life on the seventeenth floor of a modern hotel for a fortnight is a little tiring. Among the mound of letters to which we returned was one from Julian Chadwick. No, he didn't agree with the National Trust's suggestion of a Trust headed by Alice Boyd. The Trust would take all our money and then start interfering in everything. So where next? What is clear is that it is going to be a long legal haul to endow and give away The Laskett garden.

19 NOVEMBER

The fate of the V&A

I continue to watch the V&A from afar, as a benign and loving parent does a wayward child, eternally in hope. It was sad to hear in September that the attendance figures for the National Portrait Gallery had now passed those for the V&A. The 50% fall in visitors cannot be laid solely at the door of admission charges. When I last had lunch with Alan Borg, whom I like, I felt he hadn't a clue where to take the place. I haven't seen a good line written about it for so long and I find myself agreeing with 80% of what the notorious and unremitting Brian Sewell writes. How could they bring back from the USA the exhibition *A Grand Design*? Who would want to see a show about the V&A in the V&A? When Alan asked me to come to the opening and be presented to the Queen, I invented an excuse not to go. I couldn't bear it. The only decent exhibition I've seen there of late was on Grinling Gibbons – and that was done by an American. The flair seems to have gone. *Art Nouveau* comes next year but I'm sure that the moment has gone for that, however splendid it will be. As for doing an exhibition on Queen Victoria in 2001, I just groan at the notion. How could they after their disastrous one on the present Queen?

I hope I live long enough to see the V&A rise again. Some may think that it's nice for me to see the place slip ever downwards since I departed but it isn't. I left it in good shape, with a whole raft of radical foundation stones upon which quietly to build. In the main that has not happened. I feel desperately sorry for the staff. No wonder that so many of its future stars are leaving the ship.

23 NOVEMBER

The great box disaster

The box fungus that began in the knot garden in early summer then spread to the Yew Garden and, weirdly, across the whole garden, including the J and R Parterre. The leaves brown and fall off, the internal twigs blacken, and that's it. We sprayed it, but no avail; its spread was relentless. Our new friend John Glenn came south from Lincolnshire with his business partner, Mary Anderson. This was the day of decision. We had to be ruthless, so all the infested box has to be burnt. This means the end of the two parterres in the Yew Garden, nurtured over two decades, and the knot garden. I'll try surgery on the J and R Parterre but I'm not optimistic.

This is the worst disaster to hit the garden since the frosts of the early 1980s. I'll never use dwarf box again but some of the tougher varieties of *sempervirens* seem pretty resistant. One mustn't lament – you lose some, you win some. That is gardening. Somehow, by spring the Yew Garden must have a new parterre of a kind in place. John Glenn presented us with eight handsome golden yews to be trained as standards, a wonderful start. I've arranged for the un-infected box to be put in a nursery bed in the hope that it can be saved. This has been a bitter blow.

24 NOVEMBER

The Royal Opera House previewed

The invitation card said that this evening of ballet was for the world of the arts and the residents of Covent Garden. Ah, this is the People's Opera House of New Labour! The previous evening presented the same fare to an audience of builders and craftsmen, with the Chairman and Chief Executive behind the bar. Signs of the times!

This evening had its ups and downs, downs in the sense that the old House had gone. The auditorium glistened and glittered but only the built structure, for the motley crowd in the seats lacked any sense of occasion. It wasn't a gala and there wasn't a single elegant woman in sight. Was the new meritocracy in the Royal Box? All I spied was a woman with lank blonde hair wearing a long-sleeved metallic top to no effect, and that was it. Cherie Blair was supposed to be buried somewhere in the place.

Along our row was Dennis Marks, saying that his firm was editing a garden programme in which I seemed to pop up non-stop. I said, 'Don't tell me.' It was the one where I sat and spoke to camera for three hours for £100. Further along was John Drummond, who'd just finished his memoirs. Later we glimpsed a few others we knew, but not that many.

They had already cancelled the production of Ligeti's opera because the computers didn't work to move the scenery. So tonight it was just drapes framing an ill-balanced programme of bits and pieces, *pas de deux* by Ashton and MacMillan, a reminder of past glories. The rest was pretty dire: scraps, by among others, Twyla Tharp, William Tuckett and William Forsythe. The last-named's ballet to Schubert's music was truly awful, frantic, with no changes of pace. None of these new choreographers seemed capable of producing anything beyond dance 'bites'.

However, the great thrill was the interval, when we all flooded into the Floral Hall, which gives the Opera House a spectacular place of parade. It was taken to audience's heart at once, thronged and alive *ab initio*. After the interval there was a bad speech by the Chairman, Sir Colin Southgate, whose enunciation was poor, followed by a passable and funny one by Chris Smith, a pint-sized, harmless and benign Paddington Bear. There was the usual breast-beating about accessibility and the people. Overall it was a dull evening.

29 NOVEMBER

Celebrating Hugh and Reta Casson

St Paul's is not my favourite cathedral but we were placed in the second row at the front and hence in close proximity to the Choir and the Sanctuary with its baroque *baldacchino*. Lit up on what was a wet and miserable late November day, it looked splendid. This was a gathering of the old establishment mourning the passing of one of their key members, Hugh Casson, who epitomised that bridgehead between tradition and muted modernity. Ahead of us were those who represented the Queen (Sir Oliver Millar, looking much older), the Prince of Wales (Sir John Riddell, bolt upright) and Princess Alexandra. At the end of that row was Richard Gloucester and, next to him, Princess Margaret in a wheelchair. A day earlier she had had a fall at Kensington Palace so it was a great surprise to see her, now a tiny old lady, her feet bandaged and in comfy shoes. Why she hadn't draped herself in some decorative rug I don't know. Large spectacles dominated her features and a dumpy black hat had been planted on her head.

Many people there hadn't taken in the fact that Reta Casson had also died, so that it was a joint memorial service. There were three addresses – one too many – but Philip Dowson PRA did an excellent short one and John Julius Norwich caught the human side, the fun of the man, although I don't think he knew him that well. The hymns were the conventional ones and very boring but the event was wound up with the final duet from Monteverdi's *Incoronazione di Poppea*, which Hugh had designed for Glyndebourne. Very touching.

Afterwards there was the usual fracas of old blacks out of the back of the wardrobe jostling to get out. We were among the select few bussed to the Royal Academy for lunch. Our bus was like *Burke's Peerage* on wheels, with Hugh Grafton on one side and two duchesses – Grafton and Northumberland, the dowager, in front of us. But it was good to see so many friends after a long time: John Ward (rubicund and cheerful), John Sainsbury (who was giving dinner that evening to the architect Jeremy Dixon and his colleagues), the Lasduns, the Philip Powells, the Gibsons, etc. And then there was dear old Sidney Hutchison, the former Royal Academy Secretary from way back, blind and on two sticks. A sweet man but I looked at him and wondered what woes would come my way in my dotage. But I did feel acutely the passing of the old order and the relentless formation of a new one by New Labour. The removal of the hereditary aristocracy from the Lords sounded a tremendous finality.

26 DECEMBER

Goodbye 1999

It has been a good year for me, friends tell me, but I'm not sure why. No matter. There's that wonderful, welcome and deeply melancholic lull between Christmas Day and the early days of January. Everything for us is gloriously quiet, no faxes, no emails or telephones ringing. Before Christmas there was Julia's *Nutcracker*, a revival of a production over a decade old. Julia was not happy doing it at the time but, I must say, when the curtain went up I was so pleased that she did. Peter Wright had virtually re-choreographed it, a huge improvement. When it was launched he was doing two *Nutcrackers* simultaneously and the Opera House one suffered. Now, for the first time, the whole production flowed as a single storyline and the sets had been relit. What a transformation! It was as though one saw it for the first time. So I was pleased for her – and so very proud for her also.

This has been the year of New Labour, unremitting and relentless – not that one has any time for poor William Hague. But I thought the way in which the hereditary peers were ditched was graceless, Margaret Jay coming out of it as a hard and class-obsessed with no sense of history and no sense of graciousness. Some ninety are left as a rump until it's decided what they are going to do. It's like devolution. Rush it through without any thought as to the consequences. This is the year when anything English or to do with England has to be done down and denigrated, the crowning insult being the Welshman Norman Davies's new history of the island or 'islands', as he calls Britain, in which the Reformation, the defeat of the Spanish Armada and the failure of the Gunpowder Plot are deplored. How sad all this is and where will it lead? New Labour hates England.

The Queen pulled herself together – or her staff did – and gave the best Christmas broadcast for a decade. With a multiplicity of settings, St George's Chapel, Windsor Castle, South Africa and Scotland to name but four, she sprang far more to life and even attempted, at the close, to give a final, faltering smile. But she must have had her time cut out with 'President' Blair and his pregnant wife, whose Christmas card was positively regal, deploying the elegant interiors of 10 Downing Street just as Beaton used Buckingham Palace for the Royal Family in the Fifties.

I was rung up by *The Mail on Sunday* and the *Daily Mail* to go to the Dome and write a piece. I refused, as I wanted to keep my powder dry. Also, a snap piece would be silly because it calls for time to think it through in order to reach a balanced judgement. But perhaps the Dome represents where we've got to, everything reduced to a dumbed-down interactive entertainment.

DECEMBER

Martin Charteris

Along with Hugh Casson's demise, this was yet another gathering-in of the old establishment: cancer of the liver and a swift six weeks. What more can one expect at that age? Still a link has gone. Martin was always extremely kind to me as a young man, when I was somewhat in awe of anyone in the Royal Household. But he was perceptive, wise, funny and a master of the discreet indiscretion. He would always ask me what I thought of 'them' – being the Royal Family. And he would always listen; on the whole we would agree and chortle together. To me he was always the man who saw the shifting social scene of the Sixties, acutely realising that adjustments would have to be made. I think he perceived in me a bridgehead between the old and the new, and in that I think he was probably right. So many doors were opened during the late Sixties and early Seventies to bring in a new lot, so that one noticed post-Martin, how those doors were shut again and how the Crown became inward-looking, not to break out again until Bill Heseltine.

Martin had all the charm and *double entendre* of the courtier. Being older than the Queen, when the chips were down he could tell her a few home truths. None of his successors has had that advantage, which may account for the way things drifted towards a crisis that could have been averted if action had been taken earlier. He was endearing as a man, wholly without pretension, deeply protective of his employers, whatever their failings, which he was the first to acknowledge. None of his successors quite matched him; but then he held office during a kinder era, before the media had stripped off every last veil. I recall him telling me that he'd done endless television interviews on the Queen and the Queen Mother. They should be interesting, although I'm equally sure that he carried discretion with him to the grave.

2000

ENTER THE NEW CENTURY

In the end we sat down and watched the box as it covered our entry into the new millennium. As an experience it was a hopeless muddle as cameras whirled around the globe from Fiji to Copenhagen, the presenters always managing somehow to get the place wrong. What we did catch was the firework display in Paris, in which the Eiffel Tower was the structure for a pyrotechnic display of the utmost style and glamour, quite ravishing in fact. It made the fireworks on the Thames a shambles in comparison. We were promised a river of fire, which for some odd reason never happened, but the night sky was certainly lit up by glittering explosions from which descended shimmering dappled drops of fire.

But my real interest focused on what was going on in the Dome. This was a quite surreal event, a parade of the iconography of New Labour on a gigantic scale, marred for them I'm sure by the presence of two gigantic anomalies, the Queen and the Archbishop of Canterbury. Both are timeless icons of the country's Church and State and as such bore no apparent relation to what was a cross between an arena pop concert and Notting Hill Carnival. The Queen looked ill at ease and the poor Archbishop, the decline of the Church of England made flesh and dwelling among us, reduced to the indignity of leading the audience of ten thousand in the Lord's Prayer, which most didn't know, sandwiched between two pop singers. We missed the Queen being forced to join hands for *Auld Lang Syne* but it was in the papers next day. When the cameras caught Blair, he had that Messianic look which always worries me. But we didn't miss (which followed John Tavener's wonderful new millennium piece) the explosion on the catwalk of virtually naked dancers gyrating and prancing, their nudity barely concealed by strategically placed powder puffs. Together they formed a rude assault upon Middle England, which stared in silent disbelief at this aberration presented as the essence of the country they loved.

This was a spectacle that swept away all Life Guards, Beefeaters, Elgar, the Royal Marines, Shakespeare . . . etc., etc. There was nothing recognisably English in the event at all. This was a dumbed-down television spectacular, the world of pop stars and superficial glitz with the intellectual content of a cheap box of Christmas crackers. Apart from Tavener there was no moment of true reflection. This could have been an occasion that reformulated the nation's aspirations in visual and vocal form. Instead it was a monument to where we've got to, in which any sense of the past is wiped out, in which virtually everything is surrendered to the hedonism of the moment for a short-term gain, in which also the whole world is one of surfaces and spin and a manipulation to seduce the lowest common denominator. We have entered the age of the battery-hen voter – keep feeding them with pellets and they'll march to the slaughter in a haze of cheap glitter dust, oblivious of the direction in which they're heading.

28 JANUARY

Florence

This is the seventh of our annual visits to Florence, up until now always in February or early March but this year in January as we're off to Australia on 25 February. In future we shall stick to January as we were able to walk straight into the Uffizi, something I have never before experienced. But it has been a happy three days, lifting the spirits during a flat period of the year, flatter this time as I'm struggling in to a new book tracing the etiquette of eating in Western Europe. Beginning is always a nightmare and I keep wondering why I started on this subject in the first place as I alight upon the mound of literature. But it's a delightful and appealing one, if I can keep out of food supply and the kitchen. So we chug around bookshops purchasing and ordering a small mountain of academic tomes in the hope that, pulling it all together, I can write something readable for a wider public.

What is striking after so many decades of coming to Florence is how one's preoccupations have changed All those years back, in 1955 I came starry-eyed about the *quattrocento*, brainwashed by Berenson; now my pleasures are rather fixed and different. I stand in amazement at the Medici funerary chapel: not the Michelangelo tombs but the whole concept of the place, the staggering richness of the materials, the craftsmanship, the overwhelming arrogance of it. All those multicoloured marbles and stones in claret, coral, puce, ochre, crimson, white, aubergine, grey, black, mottled and marbled and flecked, the vast golden statues of the dukes. The thought of this arising in the 1590s must have astonished all of Europe. And then we always have to see the Gozzoli frescoes in the Palazzo Medici Riccardi. We had them to ourselves this year. We just stood and looked and looked as the faces stared back at us, as they'd stared back at so many for centuries. What a shame that there's no key to the portraits because the faces are so individual, good citizens of Florence and Medici hangers-on. There's all the glitter and pageantry of the foreground, with its bejewelled kings and liveried servants, but I love looking up into the landscape, seemingly as fresh as the day Gozzoli painted it, rich greens marking out valleys, hills and fields divided by road and water. And, in the chancel, there's the garden lattice entwined with roses, always something upon which to let the eye linger.

In the Uffizi I gravitate to Piero della Francesca's portraits of Federigo da Montefeltro and his wife, a bit like the Gozzolis really, with that backcloth of landscape in which my eyes love to wander. Then there's the huge Hugo van der Goes altarpiece. Julia just sits immovable in front of it. The vase and flowers in the foreground alone are worth a visit to Florence. No sign of the return of the Valois Tapestries to the great encircling corridor. I miss them dreadfully, remembering how I was Frances Yates's student when she was writing her book about them. But no matter: I love that corridor with its windows, its ceiling arabesques, antique sculpture and friezes of portraits, good, bad and indifferent, and the stunning vista across the city and down towards the Ponte Vecchio, one of the world's great views. Now when I come to Florence I don't *have* to see anything and I bless the release from that world of academic compulsion. I just want to visit old friends that lift the spirits and give me joy.

17 FEBRUARY

Queen Margrethe at the Guildhall

We'd never been to a Freedom of the City ceremony before. Why our names popped up I can't imagine, but in the end we decided to accept, little knowing how rare such events were. When I bumped into A.N. Wilson I remarked, 'We're looking at all New Labour wishes to sweep away.' And so we were: aldermen in scarlet robes trimmed with fur; the officers of the City in black embroidered with gold, bearing sword and mace; the Mayor in his robes and chain of office; and the state trumpeters in crimson thick laid with gold.

There is always that curiously awkward routine of being announced and then processing to a hand clap up to the Lord Mayor and Lady Mayoress on a dais. We seemed to get a nice round of applause! Then one joins the clappers and spends the time looking at others enduring the ordeal. The Queen of Denmark announced that she would be wearing a hat. Nothing would ever induce Julia to wear one – and the result with so many was ludicrous. It was a freezing February day and the hats were Ascot, quite inappropriate. Nonetheless, it's always interesting watching people parade by because it reveals what is actually worn, as against fashion: there is no doubt that the jacket and short skirt have become the silk dress of the era.

Queen Margrethe eventually arrived, a Valkyrie in height, her head topped by a creation the result, one speculated, of a cull of ravens in Denmark. But she's a winner: intelligent, taking a delight in everything and everybody, recalling how she got to know London with her mother as a child on top of a double-decker bus. All the speeches were good and she was presented with the inevitable scroll in the kind of box in which ashes are interred. And then on to luncheon, fanfares, food and more speeches. It all looked terrific and it's harmless, past and present mingling in a way that is the essence of England. It is striking how Queens Beatrix (of the Netherlands) and Margrethe seem to be monarchs so much more in tune with our age, whereas our own devoted Queen seems increasingly to be a relic from another era.

22 FEBRUARY

The new book

January and February are nose-down months. I always seem to start into a book at this period, which is quiet and ideal for a read-in. As usual, I've started a quarter or so in with the Middle Ages. I haven't read so much Italian and French for years: it came as a surprise to find out what a vast academic industry medieval food has become. The stream of weird conferences is quite amazing. But I am fascinated. Will Sulkin, I can see, wants me to go in a different direction from *Story* and *Spirit*, with survey books more in the manner of my Thames and Hudson books of the Seventies, with masses of footnotes. In this way he seems to have set me on a different cycle of work. On thinking about it, I concluded that I'd reached the end of one of Beatrix Miller's seven-year cycles and I was about to start another. Pimlico brought out *The Cult of Elizabeth* before Christmas, a modest reprint of 3,000 copies, and promptly sold 1,500 thanks to the Virgin Queen's epiphany in the form of Cate Blanchett and Judi Dench in *Elizabeth* and *Shakespeare in Love*.

Gordon and Marilyn Darling, the great patrons of the arts in Australia, had been the driving force behind the creation of the National Portrait Gallery of Australia. I was asked by them to deliver the first grand annual lecture.

MARCH

Australia

I don't know why such an experience didn't prompt me to write daily but it didn't, so I'm writing slightly in retrospect. The reason for the visit? Australia now has a National Portrait Gallery, which opened last year in the Old Parliament House in Canberra. Gordon and Marilyn Darling, the movers and shakers behind it, wanted a profile-raising Founders' Day Lecture on 4 March. Who was to give it? Well, someone called Anthony Adair suggested me. Marilyn Darling gets what she sets her mind on, so in the end I caved in but only if Julia came too and that the trip was in comfort. No grumbles there. It was. The subject? That was difficult and I suggested things like 'Is there such a thing as national identity in portraiture?' – but oh no. So I threw in a chunk of the garden picture book and came up with 'Greenfingers: The Portrait and the English Garden'. It was snapped up, so all I found myself doing was abridging and rearranging what I already had. That was a relief.

We were there nine days in all, three in Sydney, three in Canberra and three in Melbourne. We were rushed off our feet. I hadn't been exposed to so many new faces and so much media for years, the latter sometimes irritating as no one had the courtesy to ask whether I'd do it or not. But it turned out to be pretty harmless.

The weather was heat all the way, in the nineties. Of all the outposts of Britain I'd visited, this remains the most resolutely English, Melbourne above all. But I loved the country. It has energy and brio and the landscape we went through was undulating and beautiful. And Australian landscape painting came as a revelation of the kind you can only experience when picture and actuality are joint discoveries. Strangely, Aboriginal art struck a strong chord in a way I'd never expected. In the Botanic Gardens in Melbourne we were given a tour by a young man who was of Scottish-Aboriginal descent. We were slightly dreading this but it was in fact revelatory. One could understand his quest for that part of his heritage and he made us look at the layers beneath the gardens to see what they had been when an Aboriginal meeting place, yet he showed no resentment, saying rather that although it looks different now, it effectively fulfils the same function.

The Opera House in Sydney is a huge paradox. Never has such a hopeless and unsuitable building bestowed such instant global identity on a city. Julia was so glad that she had said 'No' to designing *Madame Butterfly* there all those years ago. It would have been a nightmare. We visited Edmund Capon at the Art Gallery and I had a twinge that perhaps he should have succeeded me at the V&A. But it's too late to rewrite the past. He's a huge success here and has done great things and, after twenty years, still manages to exude oomph. I couldn't help admiring that fact. But then he's a big fish in a relatively small pond.

All that exposure to museums and galleries made me glad that I was out of it. The National Gallery of Australia in Canberra was clearly a hotbed of discontent, with everyone at daggers drawn with the new Director, Brian Kennedy. All the seething chitter-chat and machination were barely concealed. I couldn't face being embroiled in all that again.

Still, I was royally received and so touched that so many knew the *Diaries*, my garden and other books. Twice people came up to me and said 'You're Roy Strong aren't you?' and thanked me for my books. If you accept this kind of invitation you must work your passage and Julia and I gave our all. The lecture in Canberra was a *succès fou*. It was odd lecturing in the Senate House, with a second audience looking at me on a television in the House of Representatives: a bit like giving a lecture in the Commons relayed to the Lords! But it was a sell-out, which is why that happened, and they could have sold more tickets. The new National Portrait Gallery of Australia staff I could see learnt a lot watching me rehearse everything for over two hours. That made for a flawless performance.

The new National Portrait Gallery sits awkwardly in the Old Parliament House [a brilliant new custom-built gallery has since arisen], a bit like our National Portrait Gallery having to make do with the Savoy (same period). The initial encounter with it left me slightly depressed, as the two warred, but then the first photographic exhibition was stunning, superbly chosen and mounted, original and academically sound. Nor did they lack imagination, for a portrait of Dame Elisabeth Murdoch had been commissioned from the Victorian Tapestry Workshop [now the Australian Tapestry Workshop] in Melbourne. There was an invigorating visit with its Director, the perky Sue Walker, a powerhouse of creative energy, which recalled to me the genuine pleasure that association with new creativity had brought me at the V&A.

I had to do a final 'state' performance at a profile-raising dinner in Melbourne, to which Dame Elisabeth came, as did the Governor of Victoria and his wife, moaning about the laundry they were going to be landed with when the Queen came! Poor things. They're going to be a republic but they have a respect for the Queen. Oddly, without prompting, they were overtly anti the Prince of Wales, who seems to have left an awful trail behind him. That final event took place where we stayed, at the Melbourne Club, a glorious late Victorian neoclassical Valhalla, which looked like one of our own Pall Mall clubs before they went up in the world in terms of décor in the 1980s.

The Darlings couldn't have been kinder. Life takes extraordinary turns. But they are a great couple and he's done so much for the arts in Australia. In fact he's virtually blind and tone deaf but you'd never know it. By the time we left we felt a real affection for both of them.

23 MARCH

Selling books

The day of the publication of *Garden Party*. That got off to a good start, with a favourable review in the *Sunday Telegraph* by Richard Mabey. At 10 a.m. I set off with the Frances Lincoln publicist Emma

O'Bryen and began a mini-round of a kind to which I was all too accustomed: the Pan Bookshop in the Fulham Road, Harrods and Hatchards. The odd man out was John Lewis, where there was a grand set-up of a desk, a chair and plenty of books, but all to no avail for I attracted just one solitary purchaser! But it was all well meant and we rounded off the morning with lunch at Fortnums, where Bryan Moyne's daughter Thomasin suddenly came up after thirty years and talked to me about my stay at Biddesden about 1968 as though it were yesterday.

It was a day of odd encounters, like the American who greeted me in Hatchards having heard me perform in Philadelphia decades ago, and then an elegant fifty-something who stopped me in the street and thanked me for writing a piece on the leader page of the *Mail on Sunday* about the pernicious spread of bad language in the media reducing everything to the sewer. He announced that he looked after Charlie Watts of the Rolling Stones.

That evening I did my stuff at Waterstones in Hampstead, with the usual format: a lectern, a stool, a glass of plonk and an audience of about thirty. They were mostly, but not all, elderly women. But they were warm and appreciative and I found that a mixture of reminiscence and reading worked well and made people smile and laugh. Any book I do with Julia is special and that feeling rubs off when I talk about it. I loved writing those garden pieces and find myself happy to be back writing about gardens again.

28 APRIL

Stratford, Shakespeare and Judi Dench

This has been the wettest April since 1961. The garden is awash, rivers trickling through it with young plants engulfed in water. But today the sun actually shone as we drove to Stratford-upon-Avon for the opening of the re-done-over Birthplace. Judi Dench and Michael Williams were to perform the honours, so that was a draw for us. There was coffee in the Shakespeare Centre as a kick-off, while the crowds outside were entertained with dances and songs by a group in Elizabethan costume, all a bit Merrie England. Judi appeared, pert, small, definite and beaming, in very pale beige, with Michael, beaming also but one could see that he'd been ill – and probably still was. Judi kept her eye on him the whole time. On seeing us, she broke rank for a hug and a kiss and I said to her 'I've come because of you, Shakespeare and Gloriana'. There's always something touching about Judi, one of the big hearts around today.

Stanley Wells, as Chairman of Birthplace Trustees (of which I'm a sleeping member), told us what to do so we all traipsed out into the garden at the back of the Birthplace, which had had a broad ribbon tied all the way round it like a bandbox. This was a charming idea, for the ribbon had been re-woven from one Garrick had commissioned for the 1767 Jubilee. The Birthplace was surrounded by a hugely expensive, ghastly 'Britain-in-Bloom'-type garden, full of every flower gaudily flaunting itself in overdrive. The contrast between this and the Elizabethan glover's relatively humble abode could not have been more striking. But never mind: the punters lap it all up, just as they do floral clocks and hanging baskets disfiguring everything. Two hussars suddenly sounded a fanfare and a little boy raised a flag he had designed, a prize he had won via the *Blue Peter* television programme, all very jolly and PC. Judi did her stuff and then Michael at the door of the house untied the ribbon with a phalanx of cameras whirring and bulbs flashing.

We then snaked our way through the house, now 'put back', if that is the word, to what it might have looked like in the 1560s. Frankly, what is one to do? We shall never know what it looked like but here they've researched and slaved like mad and put together what works as an attempt at the interior of an early Elizabethan craftsman's house. There was lots of reconstructed furniture and re-woven textiles and re-created painted wall hangings. At least it was a home and not a shrine. There was the glover's workshop, the kitchen and its stove, the living room with its bed, a dining area with table laid. It reminded me of Julia's famous set for *Brief Lives*, which must have been a source for this kind of thing as much as the discoveries of academe. It was good to see the timbers limewashed and not scraped back, as they invariably are in old houses. They needed the light and its reflection. There were too many artificial flickering candles, but without them the public wouldn't see anything. We all purred contentment: really it was a huge improvement, but for the municipal floral aberration outside that engulfed it.

That done, we all traipsed back to the Shakespeare Centre for lunch, distinguished for me by the waitress who emptied half a sauceboat of cream down my back! But we were bidden to the high table (not high) with Michael and Judi, Stanley Wells and Susan Hill, so that was jolly. Judi was just back from Barbados, chortling over her grandson, Sam, whom she adores, and Susan spent her time trying to persuade me to pen an essay on England for her to publish. Judi was very funny about playing Gloriana in *Shakespeare in Love*. The dress weighed a ton and it called for two people to lift her in and out of it. Going to the loo was inevitably hell.

And then, suddenly, there was Barbara Leigh Hunt! No Dickie [Pascoe], alas, but love was sent. Oh, how it took me back thirty years to *People Past and Present* at the NPG! I told Ba how wonderful she was as a *grande dame* but she feels a bit stuck with it – Lady Bracknell and Lady Catherine de Bourgh. Judi told me Ba had been asked to play Mrs Malaprop but domestically they couldn't work it. What a shame! She'd have been terrific and very funny.

As we left we were handed a box which, on opening later, contained a paperweight of Shakespeare blasted out of stone from the wall demolished in the Birthplace garden! Judi wanted a bit of the Garrick ribbon, so I told Roger Pringle, who was wearing a waist-coat of it. I hope she got it.

2 MAY

Book blues

I'm into writing the next book, *Feast*. Chapter three, the medieval one, has gone off to my new editor. I had no idea that there was such an academic industry on medieval food – but there is! God knows I couldn't believe what the internet uncovered. But it's a lovely subject and I can't write a third 'Rose of England' book. I still feel a bit bruised from the fate of *Spirit*, although 14,000 copies at £40 can't be that bad. It'll be relaunched this autumn with a new cover: I chose the Georgian 'Club of Artists' [Gawen Hamilton's *Conversation of Virtuosis . . . at the King's Arms*, 1735], hoping that the appearance of people might prove more attractive than the roof of Ripon Cathedral! But Yale's commitment all of a sudden to *The Artist and the Garden* has cheered me no end. I had a wonderful session with Sally Salvesen, the editor-designer, and at least visually it'll be a knock-out. Who knows about the text, but I tried hard to do all my homework.

12 MAY

Tate Modern and Brighton revisited

This has been the kind of week that I've not been used to these days. It began with the *Mail* wanting me to review Tate Modern. I didn't want to but eventually succumbed to money and a request for 2,000 words. So up I came to London. Tuesday was Tate Modern. I'm sure that the *Mail* would have liked me to have panned it but how could I? In terms of fund-raising and getting things done on time it was a singular achievement. No doubt half the exhibits will end up being in store in fifty years' time, if they haven't fallen to bits before then, and much of it is not to my taste. I had to do the piece in longhand and dictate it, and then it didn't appear until Friday and was cut by a third. But no matter: at least it gave the Gallery a fanfare in a newspaper that might have been expected to go the other way. The editor, I kept on being told, was very pleased with it.

Our Australian hosts, the Darlings, were over, so that was Wednesday: lunch at the Australian High Commissioner's and we gave them a dinner at the Garrick Club. On Thursday we should have gone to see the Queen open Tate Modern but we didn't. Julia went home and I went to work in the book stacks at the Warburg Institute and then to Oxford to lecture to the Oxford History of Art Society in the Picture Gallery at Christ Church, where the slides went awry, which brings me to Friday.

I'd agreed to 'do' the Brighton Literature Festival on *Garden Party* in the Music Room of the Pavilion and that event became the vehicle for a series of nostalgic reunions. Gerard Irvine, who married us, now lives with his sister in Montpelier Road. There's nothing quite like those Irvines, although I was sad to learn that Timothy, whom we met at St Andrews, had since died of cancer in a really nasty way. The house is a phantasmagoria of clutter, furniture, books and pictures everywhere, across, up and over which their Burmese cats scuttle. Neither of them are in a good state. Gerard is, mercifully, thinner, but he's had two strokes and one leg is arthritic. He can only move with a stick and go short distances. Rosemary is equally large and also immobile. But they gamely struggle on, aided by a young monk and a man in his fifties who looks after the elderly as his mission in life. After hugs of greeting I took in just how tottery Gerard was; as his hands now shook, he couldn't cope with the computer any more. But he was ebullient and all his marbles were there. We talked of mutual friends, like A.N. Wilson (who has recently entered my life), whom he loves. I said that I thought he had returned to the faith. Gerard said that he'd heard that A.N. went to Mass every day. I wonder. But the Irvines' existence is circumscribed by their physical incapacity so that they just sit embowered in that Ivy Compton Burnett setting, a clutter of potted plants, nineteenth-century *buhl*, polychrome baroque crucifixes, canvases by Matthew Smith, vases, bibelots of every description jammed and jumbled and cascading on and off everything. Nothing looks very clean and all the furniture is damaged or the covers torn or worn threadbare. The stroke has affected Gerard's voice in that for the first time I could hear clearly every word he said. He used to talk in a wild rush of crescendos. The Church of England left him depressed but not half so much as the Catholic Church in France, where communion wafers were sent through the post and given out by a devout Catholic lady in a place he visited. In England the middle ground had gone. In Brighton there was no longer any middle-of-the-road Church of England with Matins. It was either raving evangelical or tired Anglo-Catholic. Sad. But I took them out to a slap-up French lunch and we all roared with laughter. I went on my way still grateful for that September day when he united Julia and myself, and much else besides.

I walked by St Michael's, the church I used to attend and of which I am the appeal patron. I walked up the steps and found myself in the porch but the door was locked. To the right, three gothic arches were filled with clear glass, with kneelers placed in each so that you could pray looking into this extraordinary building. There, on the right, was a large crucifix festooned with a canopy, while not far away against a pillar there was a multicoloured Virgin with rather a nasty veil draped over her. Then I noticed people and the door was opened. I'd been recognised and felt somewhat penitent about having done so little for their appeal but promised to try to do more. I recalled how I went there and how Julia, very Low Church, really hated it and sat like a rock through processions while I perambulated.

On to Vine Place and another memory. No. 11 is as pretty as a picture, with a walled garden, a bower of clipped box and cascading blossom leading to a conservatory, and then the tiny house with its elegant drawing room filled with Art Deco of the kind that even I liked. I'd known John Morley for over thirty years, perhaps over forty, going back to the Hans Eworth Exhibition in 1965. I'd brought him into the V&A, although I don't think that that was a success. But now he has cancer and he let slip that the doctor had told him that he only had a year to live. Jackie, his wife, understandably looked drawn. The cancer was at the top of the spine and he couldn't stand any more without pain, so he lay on the floor with two pillows under his head. His face was also drawn and his hair thin, but he was as cheerful and bright as ever. We did our post-mortem on the V&A and I learned for the second time that Terence Hodgkinson had wanted that job and what a blow it was when I got it. *Veritas temporis filia.* Somehow such conversations lay to rest the past, one which now seems so very distant, but talking through helps the process of reconciliation to all that had happened. It was sad to see the brain still there, to know that a book was almost written but could not be finished because John couldn't sit up to do it. I sense that I had truly entered the era of farewells.

On I walked, down Dyke Road towards Wykeham Terrace. I turned through the large iron gates and stood in front of no. 8. There it still was, my first house, still pretty with its gothick windows and crenellated parapet. Almost thirty years had passed since I led Julia up the stairs to the four-poster bed I had promised her. I wondered who was there now and hoped that they were happy.

Through the layers of window glass I could see a clematis frothing on what must have been my old gothic pergola. Maybe I planted it: I can't remember any more. Today seemed all about going back, but somehow I didn't feel wounded or disturbed by any of it. It was all laying things to rest, coming to terms with what had happened and knowing that none of it could be re-lived.

In retrospect the evening was almost an anticlimax. The audience was a delight and I read bits from the book and was quizzed by Stephen Phillips. There were questions afterwards, which ranged over everything from box disease to the Dome. I spotted another memory, Barbara Morris, now in her eighties and wholly unchanged. I managed to salute her. She was always special. Then there was the book signing, during which someone said they wished I had been asked what I thought about the restored Pavilion garden. It was in fact a delight, making me remember that day's filming there when we mocked up the Regency gardens with delphinium spires tied to bamboo rods! But we had helped the cause.

Finally Sue Knight and Sue Ayton, my performing agents, turned up. Through I'd had enough by then, there was no escape. There followed an Italian meal, after which the train did not get into Victoria Station until well after midnight. Even then, a day that had been spent re-living the past did not let up for, as I left the station, I bumped into another member of the V&A staff. I got to bed at 1.10 a.m., having to rise at 6.30 a.m. to catch the train home. Too much.

16 MAY

Farewell to Martin Charteris

The day began with an appointment with the Dean of Westminster, Wesley Carr, a kindly man much scarred by the media over the sacking of Martin Neary, the organist. He asked me whether I would be High Bailiff of the Abbey, a great surprise. It's a kind of double act with Douglas Hurd, in the main for royal occasions, which are infrequent, welcoming and processing in robes. I was touched because I'd grown to love the place and I later learned that the idea didn't come from David Hutt but from the Dean himself. They wanted to get out of the old establishment and political rut and bring in someone from the arts. I think I'll enjoy it and I may be able to help during a period of shifting sands.

Afterwards I lunched with Charles Saumarez Smith, not pleased that his name had been trailed for the V&A directorship in the papers, but there was nothing to be done about it. He was sweet, showing me the new extension to the NPG. How wonderful to be able to sweep up the stairs and, instead of being faced with a blank wall, finding a beckoning arch with a clean, clear-cut minimalist gallery beyond, with a huge escalator bearing everyone to the Tudors. Although the portraits had been moved, they looked exactly the same, jewels amidst the gloom.

But I'm drifting. The real event that I had come up for was the Charteris thanksgiving. Even more than in the case of the Cassons this was a gathering of the doomed in our Blairite era. I found myself two along from the Brudenells, Marian somewhat florid in a vast black hat and, next to me, someone ex-Buckingham Palace whom I'd forgotten. On the other side were Richard and Rose Luce, always a delight. Glancing a head, I said to him 'Mollie Salisbury looks like a cross between Madame Arcati and Miss Havisham.' There she was, pallid and with a pile-up of false hair and a hat topped with osprey feathers, all of it, face as well as head, tied up in a veil. Next to her sat Clarissa Avon, another ancient battleaxe, again with a vast black hat. I couldn't help but recall what Arnold Goodman had said of her, which was printed the other day: if she had to choose between a cruise and signing his death warrant she'd opt for the latter, albeit the warrant would be signed shedding a tear. Everyone was there: Norman St John Stevas looking flaccid, Paul Kelvedon larger, Nicko Henderson still large of frame while Mary seemed now hardly taller than the pews. There was a massive and rare turn-out of royals: I noticed Princess Alexandra with Angus, Prince Michael of Kent and then Princess Margaret actually walking with a stick and looking not bad – and less like a bag lady – then the Queen and the Duke, unsinkable.

It was a good service, with Eric Anderson giving a brilliant and very funny address. 'A+', Martin would have said. The congregation rippled with laughter. I was surprised to find myself singing 'I vow to thee my country', remembering that that had been Diana's chosen hymn at that fatal wedding. Best of all, there was a fanfare for Martin, not a bit neo-Purcellian but slightly jazzy in idiom, which caught the unconventional nature of the man. He would have looked down and chuckled.

As usual it was a jam of old black clothes trying to get out so I slipped through a side door. But oh dear, once again, as with Hugh Casson's service, this was a gathering of a whole world that was to go, more so because Casson drew in a wider sphere and young people. Martin's was a very courtly and aristocratic crowd, with a notable absence of offbeat people, which was a shame because he always loved them.

12 JUNE

The last of Robert Runcie

We're moored at Casablanca, half-way through our Swan Hellenic cruise around the Iberian peninsula, where I give a series of talks entitled 'The Floating Gardens', along with three other lecturers doing their thing before a crowded ship of some 330 passengers. But it's comfortable, the service is immaculate and there are interesting places to visit and even more interesting people to talk to.

At this point up popped Robert Runcie. Popped is hardly the appropriate word, for he has cancer and, as his wife confided in me, probably only has weeks and not months ahead of him. With that scourge, energy levels ebb and flow but when they flowed his brain was as bright as ever. I couldn't think that he'd remember me but he said, 'You're the person that saved Lambeth Palace Chapel.' Not quite true, but I was involved in turning it back into the private chapel of the Archbishops of Canterbury instead of the Anglican imperial Valhalla into which it had been turned. We made up a table of seven, protectively gathered around him, and he revealed his knowledge of wine so we let him order it and I billed it to myself. I was appalled to learn how the Church of England treated its archbishops. After doing all that that post involved there was not even a house into which to retire and a pension of only £11,000 per annum. I couldn't believe that they didn't have a few rectories as 'tied cottages' for such people. Someone, however, helped with getting them a small house in St Albans. Now his wife was faced with having to install a second-hand stairlift, which was to cost £6,000. How could they afford it? Someone to whom she gave music lessons came and said in an embarrassed way that she knew someone who would pay for it, a jeweller in Bond Street who was Jewish. Is this a caring Church? I felt ashamed that this brave man, who had served both it and his country well, was not taken care of. But that evening his intellect sparkled and we all laughed a lot. The Runcies still go to Royal Lodge for what they called 'the geriatrics weekend', everyone on sticks or crutches, Lord Hailsham among them. Typically, the Queen Mother never quite forgets a friend.

Life goes in circles and one of our table was James Thomson, a surgeon who lived in Winchmore Hill, my point of departure. He told me that he had written to me years ago, when I had done 'Prayer for the Day' on Radio 4. He had been driving en route to carry out a very difficult operation. What I said had seen him through. I was touched. One never knows what seeds one sows in life.

2 JULY

I become High Bailiff and Searcher of the Sanctuary

We drove up to London for my installation as High Bailiff and Searcher of the Sanctuary. We arrived in the Jerusalem Chamber at Westminster Abbey and, after much ringing of the bell, the door was swung open by the Dean's Verger. Julia was taken to her place next to me in the Choir and I was taken into Jericho, a small chamber with a vast cupboard in which hung the robes. The benign Wesley Carr entered in diaconal scarlet. Other canons and officers came in pell-mell, some in full fig while others added bits and pieces from the cupboard. I went with Kenneth Snow, my deputy as Bailiff, to view the scene.

The Abbey seemed empty and I remarked that few would surely turn up for Evensong. Not true. There were ninety from an American college already seated in one of the transepts and the unoccupied seats in the Choir were filling up with a motley collection of young and old in summer clothes. Walking through the screen, I spotted my magic robe laid ready. It was of blue velvet with petersham and gold braid trimming, cut like the robe worn by Lord Burghley in old age. It looked rather long for me; later I learnt that it was fresh minted, as a contrast to Douglas Hurd's deep red. The sleeves had been cut so as to avoid them falling into the food at table!

Back to the robing room with much hustle and bustle, David Hutt arriving from Canterbury, where he had preached. He was obviously so pleased. What an extraordinary thing for me to end up as part of such a group! I was then taken to sit in one of the choir stalls. Soon music by Tallis was heard from afar, exerting its mystery, and gradually the procession made its way, headed by the Verger with his silver-tipped wand.

Evensong followed, sung as it only can be in a great church. I could have done without the treacly Fauré but the 'Magnificat' and 'Nunc Dimittis' by Kenneth Leighton compensated. Then came my moment. I descended and was escorted towards the Dean, standing in the middle of the nave with his canons massed behind him. All I saw was scarlet on scarlet and beyond that the shimmering gold of the Sanctuary, of which I was about to be made Searcher. The Dean spoke, reminding everyone that this was one of the great lay offices of the Abbey. I uttered only one line of commitment, after which the Dean took my hand to read the charge. I was then robed, which was rather an unnerving experience, with much ado by the Verger with the fasteners at the front. I then made my way to my stall on the south side and sat, the Dean taking my hand and continuing the charge, after which he smiled and, with a twinkle in his eye, whispered 'Congratulations', and it was over. Julia later said that she was nearly knocked flat by the smell of mothballs when I arrived.

The Dean's sermon followed, then a hymn and a blessing, and then I took part in the procession, remembering to keep dead centre, observe the pace, and to split and come together again around the nave altar. The nave, I noticed, was three quarters full.

Afterwards there was champagne and nibbles in the Dean's grand drawing room with its Canaletto of the Bath Knights in procession and the portrait of Gloriana stuck with pearls over the chimneypiece. Others arrived, a froth of canons' wives, the Master of the Choristers, the organist, the headmaster of Westminster School and so on. David and Julia took snaps, lining me up with the Dean beneath the portrait of Elizabeth I. The Dean made a short speech and I found myself giving an unexpected reply. I hope that I acquitted myself well. David then showed Julia around his marvellous house and we toured the garden, where his two cats, Adam and Florence, won Julia's heart.

I'm sure that there are all sorts of arcane things attached to this office. One, I learnt today, was that at the accession of a new monarch the Steward and Bailiff escort the Lord Mayor to Temple Bar for the proclamation. I'm not sure I'll still be Bailiff by the time this happens! The robe weighs a ton, but less than its fur-trimmed predecessor, banished in the interests of ecological correctness. It's good to open a new window in my life in my sixty-fifth year, one that I think I shall enjoy.

4 JULY

The V&A returns to haunt me

Last week I crossed a bridge. It was not one that I had wished to, indeed I prayed that I might not. But there comes a time in life to stand up and be counted. God knows, I have stood by wringing my hands for years in silence, for etiquette demands it and to make comment is not only bad manners but means climbing back into the past. In the end, however, the question becomes a moral one. Can I look myself in the face if I just stand back and see a great institution dismantled? I decided that I couldn't, hence my article in last Tuesday's *Evening Standard*.

The information I received last September about the huge drop in attendance figures in 1999 had triggered real unease in me. But the final straw was an article in the *Sunday Observer* reporting apparent attempts by some to try and force Alan Borg's premature retirement.

I drafted the article while on the Swan Hellenic cruise. It was very carefully worded as it had to be unanswerable. It owed much to Beatrix Miller, to whom I read it three times. As it turned out it was indeed unanswerable because its publication evoked no reply, no response. But it's not quite true that there was no comeback. There was. A letter arrived from Alan Borg.

I'd have given anything to have avoided getting entangled in all of this again. It upset me when I was introduced at Yale last year as 'the last great Director of the V&A'. Perhaps I was. Who knows? All I am aware of is that the headhunters are hawking the directorship around. The advert refers to knowledge of information technology and carrying out the will of the Trustees but it asks for no knowledge of any of the Museum's collections. Charles Saumarez Smith is interested but I've sent him warning flares. You can't win in that scenario. Max Hastings also warned him off. At the moment I hope he listens.

I was taken into the Queen Mother's circle as early as 1968. Later she took to Julia. The service at St Paul's Cathedral to mark her centenary was one of her last great public appearances.

11 JULY

The Queen Mother is 100 and Julia is 70

Although the service started at 11.30 a.m., we were bidden to be seated by 10.35 a.m. So on a grey, chilly and windy July day we took the tube to Blackfriars in full fig and made our way it seemed to me too early but in fact not so. We entered the cathedral just after 10 a.m. and found it already a third full. It looked stunning, the gilding sparkling under the battery of lights needed for television.

It is always amusing to watch the arrivals. We were half way down the south aisle and I found myself next to Christopher and Frances Lloyd of the Royal Collection. I glimpsed the Gibsons, he minus a morning suit, the Luces, Nicko and Mary Henderson, the Airlies, Northbournes, Thomas Camoys, John Cornforth . . . one could go on and on. Women on the whole wore short-skirted summer suits or old-fashioned silk dresses. There were a great number of hats in stiffened straw stuck full of flowers and bows. Down the aisle on the right processed the ecclesiastical procession in copes and mitres with silver wands of office and a crucifer, George Carey in his 'flames' cope with that mitre that makes him look as though is hair is on fire; Richard Chartres, the Bishop of London, with a majestic actor's presence, knowing how to walk holding a crozier.

Meanwhile, as it filled up the organ played, then suddenly the Band of the Coldstream Guards struck up a tide of romantic music in the north aisle (the second movement from *Theatre Music* by Philip Sparke), which seemed more suited to a Thirties musical conjuring up the Queen Mother in tiara and crinoline descending the stairs to an adoring chorus of young men in top hat and tails. That certainly hyped up the atmosphere, which crescendoed to the entry of the Royals. Some came in via the south door and we never saw them; these included Princess Margaret and the Queen Mother herself. Those less frail walked down the nave: a big turn out, with Princess Michael bearing away the bell for style, with a superb large hat. The Gloucesters shuffled by affably, with her in turquoise and her youngest daughter, Lady Rose, with a spray of osprey feathers tucked into her hair. The Kents followed, she looking drawn, in pale cream with a close hat of feathers.

The royal line-up included the estranged Tony and Lucy Snowdon seated side by side two rows back from Princess Margaret. No sign of Timothy Laurence or, as one would expect, of the Duke of York. But one saw a haphazard lot of descendants gathered together, all those Kent and Gloucester children, not to mention Peter Phillips, the rugger star, but minus his tongue-studded sister, Zara.

With them all in place, the Great West Door was closed and then everyone got into position for the arrival of the Queen, stately processions racing hither and thither, the Lord Mayor and his train, the Gentlemen at Arms in glittering brass breastplates, and scarlet and gold carrying halberds, the Yeomen of the Guard also with halberds. To and fro they went, the Gentlemen and the Yeomen lining up beneath the dome. Finally the Queen arrived, well dressed in blue, with the Duke as part of another vast procession.

When the royals were all were seated, off we went: hymns, readings, prayers, together with superb music and singing. Lots of the King James Bible, which the Queen Mother loves. It was touching that the Catholic Archbishop of Westminster, in electric pink, used this version. Carey gave an unexpectedly good address – not easy I thought, but it was paced, affectionate and had humour. It all went like clockwork and ended, as all these things do, with the National Anthem, which we all sang with fervour.

Then came the great moment. The Queen Mother in apricot pink, on the arm of the Prince of Wales, walked slowly down the nave aisle. She is now very tiny but she's all there, looking to her left and right at everyone, acknowledging the tide of bows and curtsies which greeted her. The Great West Door swung wide and out she went to greet the cheers. We shall not look upon her like again.

It was also Julia's seventieth birthday mucked up, but she took it all in good heart. I gave her a cashmere pashmina and we drove back to a meal of avocados, smoked salmon and champagne, all her favourites. Oh, how lucky I am! But as the years slip by one keeps thinking for how long? Pray God that it is for a few more years. All it does is to remind us to cherish each day spent together. God bless her and us.

20 JULY

Christopher Lloyd and Great Dixter

We went to have lunch with God, as Penelope Hobhouse calls him. God is Christopher Lloyd, the gardening guru of the age – or, rather, plantsman for I fear that his interests don't extend either to history or design much. The day was a glorious one in the only week of good weather this summer, blue sky and sun, in fact a harsh light for a garden in July which is always a bit over anyway. Christopher is now seventy-nine, rather short, plump and with a stoop. His hands seemed somewhat puffy but he's benign, bright and has a twinkle. He shuffles rather than walks and, like so many people as they get older, has a penchant for the bottle: the two of us, with Julia only imbibing a drop, demolished two bottles of wine at lunch.

Great Dixter is as Lutyens left it. The hand of Colefax and Fowler, let alone Hicks, has never reached this time warp. Its interior is exactly like those *Country Life* early issues, mullioned windows through which shafts of light beam down on empty spaces of stone, wood and plaster. There was little furniture, rather minimalist in fact. We didn't really see the house, for Christopher seems to have retreated into the servants' wing. Bar the odd stove, it remained unaltered: butler's sink, wooden racks, kitchen range, dresser, wooden tables, all exactly pre-1914 – kitchen, scullery, butler's pantry. I fancy that it was the servants' 'hall' in which we ate, a long, narrow room, in the middle of which there was a stunning new table with a set of chairs by Rupert Williamson, bang up to date and beautiful. All the food, bar the fish, had come from the kitchen garden: artichokes, peas, spinach and raspberries.

Where were the garden writers, we both mused? There were gardeners, yes, but they couldn't write. Anna Pavord, certainly, but who else? I think that, like Valerie Finnis, Christo likes sitting in the middle of the net he's woven over so many decades, an eminence to be deferred to in his world. We chortled over Simon Hornby, Martin Lane Fox and his brother Robin ('not a boy any more'). Christopher's deaf, with an apparatus, so one had to speak loudly and articulate well.

Afterwards we wandered through the garden. The Rose Garden has gone and is now filled with exotics. He's bored with colour gradation (who isn't?) and opts for contrasts, has reds and yellows together, banging away like blazes. Much is owed to the massive walls of yew that contain these floral fireworks; indeed, what I did learn was to follow him in getting rid of yet more grass and to plant in vast drifts instead. The work was less than all that mowing.

He'd commissioned a delightful pebble mosaic of his two dachshunds by Maggy Howarth and, yes, more grass had been got rid of. He loved opening to the public, perfectly happy to jostle through the visitors who peopled the garden. A Dutch lady recognised us so we posed for a photograph. Rather touching, that. But it was good to have come to this horticultural shrine while the genius of the place is still there. It won't be the same when he's gone but the sense of hurly-burly, untidiness, humanity and whimsicality will go. He presented us with a pot of *Inula magnifica*, so that'll be him in the garden.

18 TO 19 AUGUST

Somerset weekend

Julia had first encountered John Patten on the set of *The Charge of the Light Brigade*. He was an extra making some cash in his hols by acting. She'd thought it was odd to see someone reading a book as most of them were yob-extras without a mind. He re-entered our lives with his wife, Louise, at a dinner given by Fleur Cowles. Then he suddenly wrote to us about Maine Coon cats, as they were thinking of getting one. So they came with their only child, a tiny tot called Mary Claire, to meet Larkin and Souci. We had loved their visit and also to see the child and the coons together was enchanting. A friendship thus began and has gone on for some years now, in the main as an annual box and cox.

This year it was their turn. Suddon Grange looked even more settled and lush, Somerset stone, looking vaguely vernacular Jacobean with endless bits added. Simon and Diana Heffer and their two boys were also staying, and there was to be a grand dinner that evening, to which Leonora Grosvenor and Ivan Massow with his partner, Nils, were to come. Simon is about forty, large and rubicund and very, very bright, with a wide-ranging mind and capable of producing books on subjects as discrepant as Thomas Carlyle and Vaughan Williams. He is very right-wing, patriotic and anti the Euro and what was referred to as the weekly 'monsters', something or someone in the *Daily Mail*. Ivan Massow has made millions as a financial entrepreneur. Leonora, as beautiful as ever, with those lustrous eyes and flawless aristocratic complexion, was invited to balance the table. But Ivan's secretary had phoned and asked if he could bring Nils, who was a bright-eyed, rather short Scandinavian.

Ivan is the new chairman of the ICA. I was put next to him. 'Oh, you're where the lady should be', he said Having been told that he wanted to meet me to discuss the ICA, I opened by saying that its problem was that it was past its sell-by date, upstaged by Tate Modern and the Serpentine. We really didn't get anywhere other than he was convinced that new information technology would produce an art as endearing as Pop.

I kept off the fact that he'd recently crossed from the Conservatives to New Labour, although it later emerged that he was already beginning to regret it. But he'd moved into a period house in Frome because it gave him access to the hunt, which he loved more than anything.

We loved our stay, enjoyed viewing all the 'improvements', as Miss Austen would say, and laughed a lot. But my general reflection on this Conservative haven is that it's going to be a long haul back into power.

31 AUGUST

The Plymouths' Golden Wedding and John Osborne's widow

Here we are at the end of August, with another summer gone. The Last Night of the Proms always signals that autumn is here and 'back to school'. After two days of light and warmth we drove north to Ludlow in the pouring rain to the Plymouths' Golden Wedding celebration, a 'reception', it was called, running from 4 to 7 p.m. We hadn't known quite what to expect but it was an enchanting and very English occasion. A large marquee and a few ancillary tents dotted the lawns of Oakly, one of them at least a child compound. Within the large marquee was a warm domestic gathering, young and old, high and low, all thrown together pell-mell and dressed in every conceivable style from elegant to casual, but somehow it didn't matter. It was all organised by their children, who'd apparently done the same thing for both their Silver and Ruby anniversaries. There was very little speech-making beyond a younger son bashing a metal tray and proposing a toast. The Plymouths sat quietly together at a table, she still tall and beautiful and he benign, but both have an engaging lack of pretension.

The tent was full of our Ludlow 'set' There were Jonathan and Mary Heale, he still opining about the tea service he'd had to make for the Queen Mother's 100th, which had to have strings of pearls and tartan on it. I cannot think how he solved that one. I didn't recognise him at first in a suit (bought, he said, in a sale in Shrewsbury for £90) and a tie (craftwork, he explained). There was Prue Bellak coping with Julian Critchley dying in Ludlow. He's got a brain tumour and cancer and today, when she'd gone to see him, he'd been bad tempered. But she's astonishingly brave, propped up by two other widows, Mirabel Osler and Helen Osborne. Mirabel always appears in variations of that gypsy ethnic look, an ever-changing arrangement of earrings, scarves, necklaces and God knows what, so that at times one feels one could almost rattle her.

Seeing Helen reminded me of the Leo/Virgo lunch at Clun a week or so before, a kind of annual gathering of 'birthday boys and girls'. This year it was at Clun, thanks to Helen. I'd never been there before: it's an imposing Victorian pile set on a lofty eminence with what Julia called 'proper rooms', unlike our poky ones. There, too, it had rained but fortunately the dining room was capacious, its tables and chairs pure Sixties, a relic of the Penelope Gilliatt era. Everywhere I looked the house was stuffed with John Osborne, whom Helen clearly really adored: posters and designs for plays, cartoons, caricatures, photographs, all redolent of an era in British theatrical history – that of the Royal Court through the Sixties. Helen is short and animated with a deep smoker's voice, a quick wit sizing up people. She's known that world for decades and her reviews are always worth reading. I told her that I was reviewing the biography of Hugh Casson and wondered whether all his flirtatious relationships with other women ended there. No, they didn't, she said,

But to return to the Plymouth 'reception'. This was non-Blair England as I want it to remain, the great house, the rain, the medley of people, town and country, respectable and raffish. Hopefully things will continue in spite of it all.

11 SEPTEMBER

RIP Larkin

It began as a normal day, seeing Jules Prown off to the station after his stay with us. Larkin jumped off the beanbag by the Aga and walked away. No usual jump onto the cupboard in the scullery for the daily ritual of picking him up, hugging him and telling him that I loved him. He had not done that for a couple of days. He seemed thin and we noted his breathing earlier. Indeed, on 1 July Julia had taken him to the vet, who said that there was nothing wrong with him. Today he clearly wasn't right but nothing prepared us for what happened next. The vets here (bar the lady who saw him in July) are wonderful. Mr Mistlebrook examined him and then the terrible breathing started, with Larkin's mouth open. Could he take a blood sample and X-ray? Yes. Could he sedate him? Yes. We sat it seemed for an age in the waiting room, far longer than the fifteen minutes we were expecting. And then Mr Mistlebrook came through. Larkin was in a serious state. They had drained off two pints of liquid around his liver already and there was more, but Larkin had turned blue and nearly died. We were taken to see the X-rays, really awful: a genetically enlarged heart with huge areas of liquid. And then one of those awful halting conversations about what was to be done. There was no guarantee that he'd survive the draining of the rest of the fluid and even if he did, it would be daily tablets and there was no guarantee of how long – a month or two, a year? This was a terrible moment and Julia and I went outside and cried and walked and talked, grief-stricken. Larkin was inside, sedated and sleeping peacefully. It is awful to act as God taking life but I don't see that we had any alternative. We went back to see him for the last time – a thin little body stretched lengthwise with a tube inserted down his throat, his paws stretched forward. We both stroked him for the last time and bent and kissed that handsome creature and with cries of misery left the room.

Oh cat, I loved you! You were my cat! You were always difficult, sweet and loving, fierce and fractious. We had an awful time touching and combing you, for you didn't like it. You loved your walk on harness round and round the kitchen garden, poking your head up at me asking for a stroke or, better still, to be picked up and carried around so that you could have an aerial view. It's the physical presence that is so potent, more than the visual, the sweet face and sad eyes, the warmth of the fur –and now you've gone. No more walks, no more face at the window, no more leaping on the kitchen counter for your fish, no more so many silly things . . . Just remember that we loved you . . . that's all.

21 SEPTEMBER

Lettice

I said to the vet that I couldn't face taking Larkin's corpse back then. When it was delivered the next day it was stiff, for veterinary rules lay down that dead animals must be put in the freezer. Mercifully he was wrapped in a towel as we couldn't have borne to have looked on him like that. As it was we were crumpled with grief. A grave had been dug in the Orchard and we lowered him into it, the tears falling. We laid our hands on him and told him to rest, to sleep in peace, and how much we would always love him. Shaun, our gardener, who'd lost a cat to cancer only weeks before, filled in the grave. We asked him to place a large stone on the top. Later my wife gathered branches of rosemary for remembrance and laid them on the grave.

What is it about animals that breaks your heart? They are so close, so terribly close. You pick them up and stroke them. They sit and go to sleep on you. Your day is punctuated by a myriad tiny things that signal their presence. When one goes, all you're left with is the aching emptiness that any death in a family brings, for pets are in a way closer than most friends. After the event at the vet's you return home and all those silly things that were his are still there, his harness on the hall table, the nests he curled up in scattered around, his brush and comb. Just as with any other death in a family, it is the breaking of a pattern. Being rational cannot take the sense of mourning away but it can at least enable you to think your way through it. No such luck for Larkin's half-brother, Souci. They'd never been parted, from the moment they had arrived here as kittens. The vet said that he'd get used to the fact that Larkin had gone. The great shared event of the day was always the ritual fish-eating. This time only one saucer went down. Souci wouldn't eat.

There's no way of explaining to the remaining cat what had happened to his brother. [I discovered that I was wrong about this when I learnt that you must always show the corpse of the dead creature to the ones that remain. They understand about death.] We piled affection on the creature. Little by little he began to eat again but he had already changed. Suddenly he was head cat and looked older.

Larkin was no more on the Monday but by Wednesday evening Lettice had arrived. This, I think, was a brave decision and not an easy one. Over breakfast on the Wednesday the decision was taken. I undertook the search for another Maine Coon cat. After frantic telephone calls we found Lettice in Reddish. It's been the week of the petrol crisis but our local driver had a tank full of diesel and off we set. We returned with our precious, tiny bundle, a tortoiseshell lady, lively and affectionate. Soon all our energies were consumed in running the nursery and working out how to reconcile the older cat to the arrival of this upstart. We still are.

OCTOBER

The Dome and the great cultural dumb-down

I seem to have done nothing but talk on *Spirit* and *The Artist and the Garden*, at Ilkley of all places, the Globe Theatre, Ludlow and Westminster School. *Spirit* seems to be gaining a new life this year and I've changed my presentation of it when I speak publicly from one of woe and doom to one of much-needed celebration. Somehow what I have been saying about that book has always been affected by the current scene and this autumn it's nothing but John Drummond, John Tusa, V.S. Naipaul, Doris Lessing and George Walden all screaming on about the dumbing-down of our cultural life under this government. I did a couple of appearances along these lines and then felt ashamed at leaving everyone so depressed! I felt that what's needed – now that New Labour's so-called 'vision' is crumbling – is celebration.

In that context I went at last to the Dome. I felt that I had to as I'd pilloried it publicly so often. The Underground journey was wonderful with its new stations, and then there it was. I didn't feel any joy in approaching it. Indeed, stretching before me was a desolate expanse awaiting the queues that never formed to get in. It was a walk past shops selling really tacky souvenirs and then I was in. Inside were school parties and family groups who'd got their cheap tickets from Tesco or some such. The Dome itself is a spectacular space. It's what is in it that is so utterly awful. As an essay in design, it is just a series of 'experiences' plonked down, with no uniting principle. The effect was a hideosity of ugly, jangling shapes soaring up amidst a sea of empty tables and chairs in front of endless rows of purveyors of cheap food, from Macdonald's to Bakers Oven. It was admittedly late in the season and therefore faded, dirty and tired.

I went in to five or six of the pavilions. The Human Body was just unpleasant. I didn't warm to my face being brushed by dangling pubic hair. The Faith Zone was deserted. At its close there were rows of desks with pads of paper asking visitors to write a message or prayer to the future. It was totally vacant. The Work Zone had a 1940s char with a turban, apron and feather duster welcoming you into a corridor filled with artificial mice on treadmills in cages. The Learning Zone had a revolting school corridor with filthy lockers with a headmaster's door at its end. I rather lost track of it all. There was one beautiful room, pitch black with shimmering trees reflected in mirror glass. But that was it. The show in the middle was a monument to brilliant acrobatics but with a scenario that was PC gone mad, making abundant use of streamers (always, Julia says, an indication of desperation).

In the end I just sat down and munched a tuna baguette and drank a cup of Italian coffee and felt an emotion that I hadn't anticipated. Not anger, disgust, rage at the poverty of it all, but grief. Yes, grief. Was this what our country had come to? Was this the vision to which the young must aspire, our past glories either omitted or derided, if they were there at all? Thank heaven that this has been a flop, a gigantic one. What is so appalling is that no one takes the blame for it, no one apologises, no one resigns. Decency such as that in public life has long since vanished.

3 NOVEMBER

Croome Park

The day, unbelievably, was fine, bright blue sky and sun after the torrential rains and the worst flooding since 1947. It was an uneventful drive, except that the road to Worcester was closed due to flooding, but we passed over what looked like lakes with trees arising from them, quite incredible. The occasion was the tree-planting in memory of George Clive as part of the restoration of Capability Brown's first great landscape garden now being restored by the National Trust. Miraculously, no less than £30,000 had been donated, more than three times what they wanted, so there was enough to create a fund to invest and buy trees as the scheme progressed. George would have loved that.

As a day it couldn't be faulted. Oh dear, why do all those country gents in old age end up looking the same, with flat caps, tweed or check jackets and often leaning on picturesque walking sticks, their faces rubicund? But there they all were, a rather old-fashioned gathering for the urbanite age in which we live, made up of estate owners and country people and intellectuals, like me, trying to look like estate owners! We assembled for coffee in Capability's only gothic church, now deconsecrated but with the stunning seventeenth-century marble tombs of the Coventrys, including that of the famous Lord Keeper. It was very pretty but with plasterwork sadly decaying. The Clive family was there in force, headed by Alice and Simon Boyd, children and grandchildren, plus a vast horde of people we'd met around the dinner table at Whitfield. There were many reunions and much whispering as to how this or that person had changed so much. But the atmosphere was good.

Off we trundled on a tour in groups led by a National Trust officer, who in our case was no good at what he was doing, didn't speak loud enough and was not concise. Nonetheless, the great greenhouse was quite something to see, with its floral garlands in the pediment seemingly carved by an icer of cakes. On we went past that and down through a rusticated arch and out and up and over a bridge to an island with a little temple and on again, up and over yet another bridge to where the tree planting took place. There were the little trees, the holes, the heaps of earth with shining spades to hand. Martin Drury, Penny Graham, Alice Boyd and Teddy Clive all simultaneously planted a tree. And that was it.

Eventually we were bussed back to the Estate Office, where there was a shooting lunch laid out on trestle tables in a metal shed open on one side. But it all went with brio. I sat with a cousin of George's and his wife to one side, utterly alienated by Blair, feeling that their world and its values had either gone or were under siege, and Lindy Dufferin on the other, irrepressible, with her pixie face, bobbing curls topped this time by a mini flat cap. I told her that she'd become quite a good painter (which she has) and I promised to go and see her exhibition in London. I also told her that she was responsible for me proposing to Julia. She didn't know that. It was at a party given at Warwick House by the Rothermeres. I had told her about Julia and how I'd like to marry her: 'If you think you can do it, do it,' she had said, and made me promise to propose to her next day, which I did. She added, 'I'll ring you to see that you have.' She didn't, but it really didn't matter. Lindy goes on my list of remarkable women and painting has seen her through. She's kept at it, something to be admired in a person who could have frittered her life away with a round of parties and frivolity.

In 1980 I had been awarded this prize given annually by the Alfred Toepfer Stiftung FVS foundation of Hamburg to the person in the UK who had done the most for the arts. I was the only museum person ever to had received it.

6 NOVEMBER

The 70th Anniversary of the Shakespeare Prize

It took me almost six hours to get to London, thanks to damaged rails and the floods. I wish I hadn't bothered. The occasion was a dinner given by the Culture Secretary Chris Smith to mark the 70th Anniversary of the Shakespeare Prize of the Alfred Toepfer Stiftung FVS foundation of Hamburg. No partners or wives were allowed, so I imagined it was going to be a glittering occasion filled with all those who shone in the arts. How wrong I was!

This was New Labour with a vengeance. It was held at Lancaster House. No black tie, no style, no nothing. No one was introduced to anyone. No one was received. And instead of the world of the arts it was a sea of second-rate bureaucrats in bad dark suits. Julian Barnes, Colin Davis and I huddled together saying who are these people? It lacked any sense of celebration or warmth of reception. How could they? For the gathering was a monument to elitism. Others there I spotted included Doris Lessing, Howard Hodgkin, Peter Shaffer, Neville Marriner and Peter Hall. Chris Smith, when he spoke, merely read out a grim, dull series of paragraphs cobbled together for him by some junior. There was not one mention or salute to the laureates. It made me so ashamed because the German speeches by Toepfer's daughter-in-law and Professor Haas were so deeply informed and spoken from the heart. I made a point of going up and thanking them both, ashamed that they had been present at such an evening.

At dinner I had a senior civil servant on my left. He'd seemed quite thrown when I asked him whether he was a 'Labour luvvie'. As far as he was concerned the country was going to the dogs, the infrastructure was collapsing, the politicians were only living for the next round of applause and there was a total lack of a decent opposition. John Major, he said, would go down as the disaster of the century. A lot of it I agreed with but that evening he seemed to have no conversation except about himself. He left after dessert without saying farewell.

This was a boring evening, relieved only by meeting the prize-winners, who all screamed about it, a very nice professor of German at the University of Birmingham, and the wife of the German cultural attaché sitting on my right, who was a singer and very pretty and funny. It made me realise what bores such dinners were. But oh how sad. It should have been wonderful and it wasn't. Above all, it reminded me of events behind the Iron Curtain before it fell, dowdy party men in ill-fitting clothes holding a party in an *ancien régime* palace.

7 NOVEMBER

Snowdon

One thing is certain: Tony Snowdon does seem to like some-one in attendance. The excuse he gives is how his mother, Anne Rosse, treated him, putting him down in favour of her children by Michael, a peer of the realm. Some time in life you have to get over this. Some time also you have to get over having been a married-in royal. He still even now has a touch of that Princess Margaret switch-on switch-off grandeur and distance, which will suddenly erupt during a hands-down conversation. This evening he was older, his face lined, and over the waistline of his jeans a large paunch protruded. He also seems to have become a little deaf and is now very lame indeed. He was wearing a black tee shirt and a frayed blue denim jacket, conjuring up exactly every reason why young people wouldn't be seen dead in this any more. It's what old people who want to pass as still young, at least in thought, put on to be 'with it'. The result is the reverse. But all his intelligence and sharpness of eye and observation were intact.

This was supper in the kitchen with Melanie Cable-Alexander and Anne Wright of *Country Life*. Melanie's affair with Snowdon was still ongoing, the resulting child, Jasper, a product of a London issue of that magazine three years ago. Lucy Snowdon was always sweet, suffering and silent but Melanie, in sharp contrast, has a sparkling brio and a get-on-with-it attitude. But she is not pushy in the least or calculating. She has rather a long oval face, straight brown hair and large, striking eyes; she was born to see the funny side of life. She seems to provide a life for him, as she did this evening, getting the picnic food and responding to his every 'Fetch this, fetch that'. But they were very hands on and 'darling'. Maybe she'll end up a countess, even if only for the sake of the child.

We were all called upon to admire his latest work. First came a set of contacts of the mid-thirties whizz-kid who had revamped Gucci. I can't remember his name but camp they certainly were, and clever, attired in black with his shirt unbuttoned lower than it should be, sitting on a black leather chair, back to back with another, empty one. Clever. And then there was a series of him reclining, as a kind of male odalisque. But as the evening hotted up, we were suddenly bidden to secrecy. Down Melanie trotted to the basement and up she came with an envelope of pictures. Guess who? Camilla Parker-Bowles. The best was a series in a plain white blouse and no jewels, just a happy middle-aged woman with not too much evidence of the make-over. We were sworn to secrecy. I marked up the two best with 'R'. Like everything else, they'll get out sooner or later.

Here I record what was to become a format in which I was to take part on numerous occasions: the great memorial service as is always brilliantly staged at Westminster Abbey.

8 NOVEMBER

Robert Runcie remembered

I'm struggling this week with some virus but the show must go on. The show in question this time was the Service of Thanksgiving for

Robert Runcie at the Abbey, the first occasion on which I wore my 'magic robe', as I call it. The weather was cold and drear but what a turn-out! Numberless applicants for tickets never got in, a great index of the affection for the man. It was miserable weather but by the time I arrived at the West Door the nave was already largely full. Waving a yellow card marked 'Procession' and annotated with the injunction to appear robed at the West Door by 11.30 a.m., I made my way to the robing room just before the Jerusalem Chamber. There lay the garment on a chair and there was Maureen assuring me that I'd have a ruff to put on next time! The Precentor took me through my paces right up into the Sacrarium, where two chairs were sited to the north, a little back from those assigned to the Dean and his colleagues. Then down to the West Door again, where they all were, including Douglas Hurd in crimson and the Dean and canons in new copes with old orphreys mounted onto them in that non-liturgical colour, blue.

The whole world and his wife whirled by, all in blacks, from William Hague to Matthew Parris, from Margaret Thatcher to Raine Spencer. Then came a flurry of those representing the royals and from then on we were in line, with me at the end with the Dean Emeritus, Michael Mayne, on my left (he now lives in Salisbury and honestly looked far fitter than when I interviewed him for a programme in the *Pillars of Society* series). I rather lost track of who was representing whom but along came sweet Leonora Grosvenor, affable Peter Carrington (who said that his head by Marcelle Quinton made him look like Robin Day) and Angus Ogilvy, agonisingly thin. Of the royals, Princess Margaret failed to turn up and was represented by a portly personage. For some reason Margaret Jay came along the line. I said to Douglas, 'Just as well the *Mail* didn't print what I wrote about her last week.' Edward Kent sailed down the line, followed by the Gloucesters and finally by the Prince of

Wales, who thanked me for my book and asked, 'This is a new role for you?'

The Dean took them to their seats in the Choir and then we were off, with instructions to follow the Dean. This will become an experience that I shall take for granted but, for the first time, it was rather unnerving being watched by a thousand pairs of eyes. Mercifully I lifted my robe before I fell on the steps leading to the Sacrarium. Up a step opposite sat George Carey, like an overblown schoolboy with a young robed flunkey in attendance. It is such a shame, for Carey exudes neither sanctity nor authority, nor, for that matter, intelligence. But it's a benign face. Directly opposite us sat the two bishops who were to say the bidding prayers, Mark Santer, Bishop of Birmingham and Jim Thompson, Bishop of Bath and Wells, looking so different from what his radio voice evoked. And then came the Abbey's Precentor et al.

Everything was a blaze of light, adding a shimmer to the occasion, which went like clockwork: prayers, hymns, readings, one by Runcie's daughter, then a second by the Dean of Canterbury of a passage from Runcie's enthronement sermon, and finally another by a Runcie son from the *bons mots* of Sydney Smith, which evoked laughter. A splendid address by Richard Chartres, the Bishop of London, I think pinpointing Runcie well as epitomising a change of style within the Anglican primacy as we moved out of an era of empire into one of Commonwealth and far beyond. Perceptive. There was wonderful music, including the Creed from the Russian orthodox liturgy. The Dean gave his blessing from the High Altar and we beat retreat in procession, remembering to stop in order to let all the royals out.

It was all a bit of a muddle at the West Door, as those things are in their dissolution. Rosalind Runcie, who had sweetly earlier proffered me her cheek to kiss, appeared with her son and daughter to receive. The royals queued up to say what they could of the right thing and

I made my way back to the robing room, where I helped Douglas Hurd with the hook-and-eye fasteners with which we were both trapped. All of this took place amidst a flurry of bishops bustling past from the Jerusalem Chamber, each carrying a little suitcase containing their garb. There were an awful lot of them: where I stood earlier on I'd seen the Cardinal and the Chief Rabbi steam past.

Off I went to buy a sandwich and pass the rest of the day in the real world: the London Library, to see Lindy Dufferin's pictures (she is rather good, with a real feeling for the Irish countryside, although she should avoid painting cows) and finally to a dinner given by Diane Lever in her new Eaton Square flat. She is always a delight but as we weren't bidden to arrive before 8.30 p.m., we knew that this was the late-late-show. More delights came in the form of the Northbournes and Valerie Solti, dinner for twenty-four at three tables in honour of the French ambassador, a rather charmless man. Everyone there was down on the government and groaning at the cronyism and lack of honour, at the consequences of what they were doing and of the hidden agenda to come.

10 NOVEMBER

Southwold

We were picked up to go to Southwold for me to perform on *Spirit* for the last time. A drear day and a dreadful journey, which took five hours: a crash on the A14 meant that we took forty minutes to go four miles. We therefore arrived at The Swan somewhat bad tempered but Kay Dunbar and Stephen Bristow, who run these literary festivals, are warm and unassuming people so we soon picked up. We began with drinks, at which I met Juliet Barker, author of the acclaimed Wordsworth biography, who turned out to be the same person who had written about the medieval English tournament. She was a contained, fresh-faced, highly intelligent and modest woman in her forties. I'm afraid that I lectured her as to how she needed to write and review and not only always plough on with the next book. This is an age, I said, when the intellectual elite needed to stand up and be counted.

The drinks phase lasted forever because Clarissa Dickson Wright was upstairs watching the box. She didn't appear until we were seated at table and so I greeted her saying 'We were just about to send out a search party'. Apparently she was sitting upstairs waiting for the sycophantic phone calls. No marks for manners scored there. Clarissa is an ex-alcoholic mountain of quivering flab containing a mind of a sort, together with a firm belief in her own self-importance. In repose her collapsed face was actually sad and care-worn, so one has to see through the bossy, loud-mouthed surface. She went on as though her series on the box was of national importance. It isn't. Sad really.

In the morning my event took place in St Edmund's Hall, jammed, with all two hundred and twenty seats sold. Once again I had a huge reception when I talked about English civilisation and how, in spite of what's going on now, it must be transmitted not, I'm afraid, by schools any more, but within families. Oh, how they long for a public voice on England! It was so moving. Afterwards I signed forty-two copies of *Spirit*, leaving eight unsold, together with a shoal of my other books.

Earlier we had walked through the grey and gale-stricken town. This is a little bit of England as I understand it, small domestic houses in a medley of styles, unpretentious and pretty, fishmongers and greengrocers, an outsize village, the sea front with its parade of beach huts in bright colours and the great church.

14 NOVEMBER

General Synod

To the Abbey yet again, this time beneath clear blue skies, for the inauguration of General Synod. On entering through the West Door the processions were already reeling around, carrying the labels of the various dioceses. The usual line-up at the West Door, this time with, to my left, the preacher, the Principal of Wycliffe Hall and the Archbishops of Canterbury and York in full fig, the former with his usual flames of fire cope and mitre. Opposite stood their crucifers. George Carey had obviously been wondering about my presence, having sat staring at me across the Sacrarium last week. This time I thought him a friendly soul, much better on individual encounter than how he so often comes across.

After much coming and going, the Queen arrived in a hideous bright emerald green coat and a hat shaped like a ziggurat. Down the line she went, extending a gloved hand but not saying a word until she came to the preacher, when she paused and said: 'Oh, so you're the preacher', with some emphasis. She is now a cross between Queen Mary, with the same grim countenance when in repose, and Queen Victoria in terms of height. If you catch her eyes they're sharp but with a twinkle, so that's still there.

It was the same drill. Douglas Hurd and I trundled behind the royal suite consisting of a plain-clothes officer in a suit, an RAF officer and an identikit lady-in-waiting in short skirt, large hat and mandatory diamond brooch. We arranged ourselves *en tableau*, with the Queen seated opposite on a stylish chair and *prie-dieu*. Sometimes she was attentive and sometimes she fiddled with her fingers.

This was Communion. A large table covered in enough chalices and patens for a Roman orgy stood at the bottom of the steps to the Sacrarium. Two rather mean chairs were arranged side by side, from which the two archbishops could preside and consecrate. The new service was used for the first time, not that much different from Series 2, but I fear not Douglas Hurd's cup of tea, as President of The Prayer Book Society a lost cause. The sermon was good, if hardly electric, and sent out all the right signals, particularly in respect of the sea of management-speak and bureaucracy afflicting the ever-shrinking Church.

The occasion had nothing like the hieratic splendour and humour of the Runcie thanksgiving. But then it was the dear old Church of England and I did rather warm to it, just seeing all sorts and conditions of people coming forward to receive Communion. It'll take a lot for all that to vanish. And I couldn't help but be moved to receive my own Communion from both Archbishops, reflecting on their line of descent back to Augustine and Paulinus. Oh dear, why can't the Church of England get its act together? I've clung to it so long, often in exasperation, but I owe both it and its priests so very much.

30 NOVEMBER

Oscar Wilde is a hundred

I went to the eight o'clock Communion at the Abbey, as I tend to do these days. It makes up for the well-intentioned vacuity of country parish services, and in a funny way being a lay member of the College makes me feel part of some kind of religious community. As I left I found Wesley Carr standing there, beaming, with two people. One, I twigged at once, was Angus Ogilvy, the other a woman sunk into a fur hat, whom I suddenly realised was Princess Alexandra. 'Oh', I said, 'I didn't recognise you in a fur hat.' 'That's useful to know,' came the reply. She said that she hadn't been to a service at the Abbey since her wedding and it was for that reason Wesley had arranged for them to come. I wonder, when it came to the hand-clasping, whether she was recognised? Probably not. You can't help loving her, a quiet, old-fashioned, hard-working princess who just keeps going. Would that they were all like that!

Today I lectured for two and half hours at the English Gardening School, which was a killer, after which Mary Strathmore drifted up, reminding me that we'd once sat next to each other in the garden at Clarence House. I might have guessed that the Queen Mother was up and dressed and had been downstairs (she'd recently fallen and broken her collarbone). One can't help but admire her but one has to say that her next great service to the monarchy would be to provide us with a state funeral, clearing the decks for the Golden Jubilee in 2002.

I returned to the Abbey in the evening for the Oscar Wilde Centenary tribute. I attended Evensong in my 'magic robe', feeling like Lord Burghley. Shedding that, I made my way to Poet's Corner, where a great number of chairs – far too many, in fact – had been set out for the event. No gathering of the world of letters and theatre here that I could register. Instead rather a shambling, shabby, huddled lot, among whom I glimpsed Anthony King. Tom Wright gave the event an ecclesiastical wrapping. The rest consisted of Simon Callow reading from *De Profundis* and a little from *An Ideal Husband*, and three singers doing Bunthorne bits from *Patience*. Simon performed well, with his actor's stance and articulation, but he vanished early, I presume to get ready for Dickens, in which guise he is now appearing under the direction of Patrick Garland, to whom I sent our love.

The eulogy was by John Mortimer, who really is now very very tottery and I thought a little senile. He's a great, if perverse man with his rotund, almost grotesque face, sensuous lips which seem ever open, and numerous chins. But the eyes are kindly and bright and he really exudes warmth. But oh those legs and feet! He's propped up by a stick and by his young wife but he finds it difficult to stand and walk. The eulogy, what I could hear of it, wasn't the greatest but it was heartfelt and elegant.

What was more interesting was the finale, in which Wilde's grandson Merlin Holland suddenly appeared and laid a sheaf of lilies in memory of his grandfather. He'd had quite a day, which began in Paris at the Père Lachaise cemetery followed by a requiem mass. One could see his grandfather in him, a soft, somewhat podgy figure with elements of Oscar's heavy-lidded, somewhat luscious features and an abundance of fine wavy light brown hair. That was interesting to observe. I think that the Abbey feared the occasion would be hijacked by the gay lobby. Instead it was the usual gathering of earnest, dishevelled English intellectuals.

9 DECEMBER

Floods

This has been the wettest autumn in the country's recorded history. The floods seen on television are bewildering but I thought that The Laskett, being on a slope, would be well clear of any such disaster. I was wrong. Being in London on Tuesday, I was rung to discover that we had succumbed. Julia had returned to the house in the afternoon to open the back door and find six inches of water coursing through the house. The downpour had been so severe that the field behind could not take any more and so disgorged its surplus waters through us: first the stable block and then on through the scullery and kitchen. Shaun, our gardener, was summoned and Dot, our daily, and her husband came to the rescue; any further spread of the water was then averted with bundles of newspapers.

Julia rang the fire station and an inspector was sent to establish whether or not we qualified for aid. Four well-meaning chaps arrived, minus even a stirrup pump. However, our Hereford firm of electricians came to the rescue with heaters, dehumidifiers and machines to drain water. Julia was very upset about the ruination of so much. When I got back it was a shambles, with floor coverings up and damp rugs and mats suspended everywhere. It will take months to dry out and put in order.

FAREWELL 2000

Friends tell me that I've had a good year. I think I have, but melancholy always sets in between Christmas and New Year's Day, clouded by too many memories of failures and friends gone. The New Year's Honours List was dull but I sent any letters that had to be written. Sad that Martin Drury wasn't knighted (as his predecessors were) but given a CBE. Christopher White got a knighthood: as an amiable, scholarly man it was difficult to work out how he fitted in with Blairite Britain with its dismissal of such things. So did Christopher Frayling. I did so much to launch him on his career but as soon as I resigned the V&A I felt I was on the whole dropped.

But here we are, happy together; even little Lettice has enchanted Souci and the two moggies bed down together. Outside the garden has grown hugely and the shock of destroying all that box has begun to recede in the mind. I began to clip the heathers in the parterres and the knot garden and felt glad that we had struck out in a new planting direction. There's really so much to be grateful for. I work hard but devoid of the appalling strain of old. I read of people who run museums now coping with ethnic and disabled quotas, accessibility and inclusiveness. Have we gone mad? Worst of all, I see a government that has set out deliberately to destroy the fabric of the society I have known and loved: the monarchy, the Church, the law, the forces – the sense of moral framework and public service, the reverence for tradition and continuity. The trouble is, once torn apart you can't easily put it all back. It is so sad, so deeply depressing. How utterly awful that everyone just accepts that there will be a second term of New Labour. There's a hidden agenda there which has been kept for their return. I dread it.

2001

The year as always enters somewhat dully, not helped by a winter of horrendous wet and now bitter cold and frost. Poor garden, with so many rosemaries and euonymus killed off with cold and turf churned to mud. The box disease reached the Rose Garden, a tragedy. Out it all had to come and, as usual, John Glenn came to the rescue with a promised gift of golden yew, which will arrive on 8 March. Only then shall I be able to bear to look on that garden again.

Julia agreed to the hedge up the drive being rooted out, a great transformation. The clipped thuya 'soldiers' already there were replanted as pairs of sentinels up the drive and a space cleared in the shrubbery near the front gate in which to build a garage. But the most exciting thing was to see the Howdah Court opened up and the view to the house. I had no idea that the old hedge was ten to twelve feet wide in parts. On the site of it we planted two mature beech plus yew bastions in the making and two silver hollies 'Elegantissima' sent by the holly lady, Louise Bendall, as a comfort on hearing of the fate of the Rose Garden box. Aren't gardeners nice?

We had our annual visit to Florence in January but this time with only one grey day without rain. That was a little disappointing but we had seven days in Madeira with the Garden History Society and that gave us blue sky, sun, flowers and agreeable company,

But it's a lacklustre time of year and now there's the gloom of foot-and-mouth disease spreading like the plague. It hasn't yet reached Herefordshire but no doubt it will. This time one's heart goes out to the farmers.

There's new Director of the V&A. I don't know him. Mark Jones is his name, from the National Museums of Scotland. From the moment that he was appointed the knife has been stuck in by his future staff. *Plus ça change* . . .

And then there's the curious case of my article on the arts in the New Year's issue of *Country Life*. It was, I admit, quite sharp, but it elicited no reaction until about ten days ago, when Frank Johnson of the *Telegraph* took hold of my passing reference to the Director of the National Gallery being ticked off for the exhibition *Seeing Salvation* as it was not politically correct. That I had from clerical circles last year and I did add 'I was told'. Johnson expanded it into a paragraph describing how MacGregor had been lashed into by Chris Smith! God knows where he got that from. Invented, probably.

What is so fascinating about this New Labour lot is that they can't seem to take criticism of any kind. 'Never complain, never explain' is definitely not part of their creed. Ainsworth asked a written question in the House which was denied by Smith, who also wrote to both the *Telegraph* and *Country Life*. He also wrote a letter to me, which I ignored. We live in the age of the Thought Police.

Then followed a letter from Alan Howarth, the Arts Minister, which began like a schoolmaster saying that I'd already been taken to task by MacGregor (I hadn't) and by Smith, and that now it was his turn! What I wrote about his speech to the Historic Houses Association was true. I was there and recall my rage. Julia, who has total recall, remembers him insulting the HHA to its face at what was its anniversary.

Now what is so very interesting is that they should have been led to write those letters. It was an indication that I had in fact targeted correctly in a piece which began with the words of Adam Boulton of Sky News to me: 'They are not interested in the arts but they want to control them.' Everything that we've seen confirms this, plus the relentless driving downwards of virtually everything. It is so sad to read of a proposal to do away with all teaching of any literature, including Shakespeare, before the twentieth century. But it's an index of where we are.

That control freakery was also revealed in their abortive Culture and Recreation Bill, which attempted to control the chairmen and the composition of trustee boards and violate their independence. I wrote to *The Times* on that one. After fifteen years of silence the time has come to speak up as a free spirit. Few are.

Meanwhile I plug on with *Feast*, having reached 1789, although I stopped to write a short book on garden design for Frances Lincoln, which I will finish next week. I sometimes wish that I didn't always have to work so hard . . .

27 FEBRUARY

Frances Lincoln

Felicity Bryan rang me with the news that Frances Lincoln had died yesterday of viral pneumonia at the age of fifty-five. It was a terrible shock. I am still finishing my first book for her and now she's gone. It is really sad, tragic for her family and for her firm. She was in her way an original, an ungainly figure with no dress sense, hair all over the place and large black glasses. It was difficult to reconcile this shy, awkward figure with the stream of publications that exhibited genuine flair and taste and a keen sense of style. She was underneath it all a gentle person with a formidable intellect. Delegation was never part of her scheme of things and I really wonder whether it didn't all wear her down. But now having just got to know her, she's gone. Fate plays strange, unexpected cards. One minute someone's there, the next they're not.

3 MARCH

Foot-and-mouth strikes

Gloom has descended. Foot-and-mouth arrived first at Llancloudy and then nearer, at Llangarron. I hear that it is rampant around Hay, the little town virtually deserted as farmers batten down the hatches. As I went for my pre-lunch jog to Hoarwithy I noticed that the farm nursery school was closed and then, further on, the stables were closed with bales of straw across the road. The Council has forbidden anyone to cross farmland, with £3,000 fines, but someone along the lane continues to exercise her dog in the neighbouring field. The weather is beastly cold and there is a threatening stillness. This is the first time I have felt a real sense of grief for the farmers. For thirty years they seem to have been monuments to greed and the ruin and rape of the landscape. Now they have been struck from without. From the local shop I heard that it's thought to have reached Orcop, three miles away. I hope it doesn't get any nearer.

12 MARCH

Commonwealth Observance

There we were again, Douglas Hurd and me, standing in line near the Great West Door of the Abbey. No copes for the clergy as this was an 'observance' and not a service. One minute I was next to an avuncular rabbi, the next to a minister of the Church of Scotland in London and he had Monsignor George Stack next to him. This is the annual jamboree to reaffirm the Commonwealth, the event which caused such angst to a previous Dean stuck with a curious hybrid of readings from various holy writings read by everyone from Buddhists to Muslims. This year's *fête* was dedicated to 'a new generation' epitomised by five luckless eight- to ten-year-olds who sat behind the Dean and ventured forth to ask banal questions like: 'Can we truly hope for peace within and between nations?', the replies to which came from a variety of clerics and gurus. The London Adventist Church, all Seventh-Day Adventists, livened things up with an evangelical number but they were capped by a group of Zulus singing and dancing their way around the Abbey. They really used the space and, at the very end, returned to burst out of the West Door to give the public something to think about.

The Queen appeared in a green version of the pillbox style she seems to have adopted for hats. Her hair was softer, protruding underneath, but in profile and repose she looked rather disapproving of everything and everybody. But she certainly does her stuff working along the lines. The Duke is a pretty sprightly seventy-nine but quite small now. I'd never met Blair and his wife before. Down the line they went like an untidy whirlwind, with no real sense of focusing on the people they were meeting. From afar he can look quite youthful but closer his features are puffing up and his hair thinning. She was wearing a plum-claret trouser suit, no hat and, I assume, dyed hair. She is as plain as her photographs would lead one to believe. All one sensed was that they clearly didn't want to be there but had to be. Neither of them knows how to move or comport themselves with any dignity. They are just terribly suburban. But then so was John Major – and most of them these days.

The Abbey was jammed with the invited and lots of children and there were some perfectly awful flower arrangements by NAFAS [National Association of Flower Arrangement Societies], with vases stuffed with eruptions of yellow and red composed of plants that ought to be outlawed. I kept on thinking that few people, apart from those invited, must have even been aware that it was Commonwealth Day. It had the macabre background of butchered farmers in Zimbabwe, where even the whites in the judiciary feel under threat. No wonder that we prayed for those thinking of a way forward for the Commonwealth.

22 MARCH

The World of Books at Buckingham Palace

The day of the Queen and the World of Books and the Palace party, to which we were both invited, along with the other five hundred and ninety-eight guests. This was a large gathering of the chattering classes doing what they do – chatter – sprawling through an ocean of gilt. I never caught sight of the Duke of Edinburgh but I spotted the rear of Her Majesty in a claret-coloured dress, with her tidy hair, being gracious. Edward Kent swooped on us, grateful, I felt, to find someone he knew, and the large features of the Duke of York were sighted. What a world it was! We were all handed a booklet listing off those present, which was, I must say, a help, not that one found most of them. The most startling apparition was Frances Partridge in a wheelchair, over a hundred, transparent but with beady eyes. The most surprising encounter was with Jilly Cooper, who suddenly sprang up from a chair and kissed me on both cheeks in gratitude for the *Diaries*! And the most disastrous was with Grahame Greene, who introduced me to Margaret Drabble; she reluctantly extended a hand and vanished. Only afterwards I remembered that I had panned *The Peppered Moth*. Flora Fraser told me that Mark Jones, the new Director of the V&A, is her former brother-in-law, that his real name is Powell-Jones and that he had dropped the Powell and hyphen when he stood as a Labour candidate. That explains a lot!

Sheridan Morley was very funny about what happened after I had had to leave the Foyles Literary lunch for Edward Montagu and Gyles Brandreth a fortnight ago. George Melly stood up and said something like 'You and I, Edward, were the prettiest things you'd ever seen on the streets when we were young. We could have had anyone darling . . . soldiers, sailors, police . . .'. The old ladies who come to these affairs sank low in their seats and poor Edward lit up, bright red.

But to return to the Palace, which I must say looked less of a mess than when I last went there. And, as this kind of affair goes, it was done perfectly well. It was good that they didn't ask the culture politicos, although the inevitable Lord Bragg was there with his immaculately coiffured hair. Graham Greene was groaning about DCMS's interference with the national collections and Simon Jenkins was as usual benignly condescending. The Pakenham clan was there in force, Elizabeth Longford somewhere but not seen, Antonia Fraser and, as I've already mentioned, Flora. William Rees-Mogg entered with Roy Jenkins. William said we had a hope that the next parliament would produce a crop of young Tory lions who would put the party back together again.

There were some six hundred of us all told. In the old days one would never have left before the royals but that rule seems to have gone and we weren't among the first to sidle off in search of a decent dinner.

24 MARCH

Footnote

I learnt from Sophie Blain that what I wrote about the National Gallery's *Seeing Salvation* exhibition was right. DCMS had tried to stop it.

12 APRIL

The Maundy

The day of the Royal Maundy at Westminster Abbey. I agreed with Douglas Hurd that we had no idea it was going to be so grand. Much to my surprise, on arrival we were presented with four Maundy coins in a little envelope labelled 'Fee': the fee, I suppose, for being in attendance. The Maundy only comes to the Abbey once in a decade these days. In the case of the clergy, out came their coronation copes, blue and silver with royal heraldic figures stitched on to them in Festival of Britain style. I arrived at 10.10 a.m. and the place was already jammed, the organ booming and a flurry of robed officials everywhere. Once robed and ruffed, I made my way to the Chapel of St George to the right of the West Door. Gathered there was an assortment of clerics, including one from Westminster Cathedral and what I took to be a Greek Orthodox bishop. On a table sat two vast chargers piled high with the Maundy gifts in little leather bags. Outside there was a barrage of photographers and inside a range of TV cameras whirring away. The stops had certainly been pulled out for this one. Suddenly the choirboys from the Chapel Royal at St James's appeared in scarlet braided with gold, the dress eighteenth-century, with knee breeches. Then the Yeomen of the Guard were marshalled to line the nave aisle. This was a Household event so the Bishop of Wakefield appeared in a golden mitre as Lord High Almoner, beneath his cope a linen towel tied around him, as it must have been in the Middle Ages. Nosegays of herbs and flowers were held by him and the Dean. It is difficult to capture the sense of flurry and spectacle, of carefully timed movement, processions ebbing and flowing and an astonishing richness of dress.

Then the Queen and the Duke of Edinburgh arrived, she in jovial mood in apricot, more relaxed than when I had seen her on previous Abbey occasions, surprising in view of what has recently been written of her daughter-in-law Sophie Wessex, which had resulted in a media field day and caused the Labour pro-republicans to creep out of the woodwork.

Suddenly the state trumpeters appeared above the choir screen. A dazzling fanfare sounded, the first hymn was sung and the procession moved. Douglas got off the mark this time and I followed. What was astonishing was to be able to see the Yeomen of the Guard that followed us bearing the Maundy chargers aloft above their hats. It was early Tudor England relived. Everything went like clockwork, the music magnificent and embraced Byrd and Purcell and, never to be forgotten, Handel's great coronation anthem for 1727, *Zadok the Priest*. As the Queen finally returned and ascended into the Sacrarium the choir burst forth: 'God save the king! Long live the king! May the king live for ever'. It brought tears to my eyes. The ancient prayers made me realise that these must have been used for centuries. Gloriana herself must have heard them. Finally, the National Anthem was sung with fervour by the whole congregation, accompanied by fanfares from the state trumpeters. Once again we moved off and it was over. I'll never see it again but I'm glad that I have. A reminder of history, of the past and yet embedded in it a lesson in humility for all to learn.

There was a gathering afterwards in the Jerusalem Chamber. One never knows what to say to the Queen, so I said, 'Thank you so much for the World of Books party. One saw everyone there one couldn't get on the telephone', to which the Queen, funny as always, remarked, 'I haven't a clue who was there as I forgot to put my specs on.'

WINTER

This has been an endless and drear winter. Fifty-nine inches of rain have fallen on the garden. It is sodden. The skies are overcast and it is so cold. It has been like this for so long, now into its seventh month, dull and depressing and not helped by the awfulness of foot-and-mouth, which encircles us.

Brian Goodwin, who farms the land at the back of us but who also owns a farm up at Orcop, rang back one evening last week. He apologised for not returning my call sooner but he had been calfing. The calf, he said, would be shot that week, only days old. It was just awful hearing this. I felt so helpless. Yes, he said, he would hand the keys over and his life's work would be shot. He said that he could have taken that, but he couldn't bear the thought of the corpses there for days before they were buried or burnt. This is a devastating time to be in the country.

On Saturday 14 April I returned from my jog along Laskett Lane and passed cars and men putting on plastic overalls. It was just where the sheep were in the field. That afternoon, unaffected though they were, they were shot. Two cows in the field opposite us were shot.

Brian Goodwin later covered the corpses with sheets of black plastic. They are still there today, Wednesday. Somehow we now feel caught up in this, hit by the tragedy and misery. It has left me depressed, a feeling of deadness and a horror at the utter wastefulness of it all.

Outside the spring has come so late. It is now the end of the second half of April and freezing cold, the sun a rare phenomenon. But the flowers are beautiful and the builders are busy. A new garage has gone up at the bottom of the drive and the gothic iron screen-work, sides of an old bridge, are being put in place to hold in the Howdah Court. Gravel has gone down from Muff's Monument to Elizabeth Tudor Avenue and paving is to be laid at the top of the new crinkle-crankle borders . . . That will take the garden to virtual completion in terms of layout [it didn't].

4 JUNE

Rosemary Verey

Rosemary Verey died last Thursday in Cheltenham General Hospital. She had gone in with a perforated intestine leading to pneumonia and the signs were ominous. She had in fact never been the same since a fall two or so years ago.

'You love pompoms, cut it into pompoms': thus Rosemary encountering the straight top of one of our hedges. We always used to enjoy walking around each other's gardens, making this or that suggestion. She, in fact, wrote the first article ever penned on The Laskett garden. Half-way round she paused and said, 'It's just like the Victoria and Albert Museum, all corridors with things at the end!'

So many people owe so much to her encouragement. Penelope Hobhouse, the garden writer and designer, and Andrew Lawson, the garden photographer, are two names that spring to mind, and to that list I add myself. When, in 1985, I was asked to write my first book on garden design, realising my lack of any formal horticultural training, I rang Rosemary and asked her what I should do. 'Write it,' she said; 'If you get stuck I'll help you.' Well, I didn't, but that is a cameo of her at her best. Later she brought me in to design and supervise the cutting of the hedges and topiary for the Prince of Wales, to whom she was devoted, at Highgrove.

At one point it seemed that a cloud might cross our friendship. At Gianni Versace's suggestion I was asked to design an Italian garden for Sir Elton John. Alas, the only site possible for this involved a bulldozer through one designed by Rosemary. I felt deeply embarrassed. However, not only did she forward me all her plans, but cheered me on my way. That revealed a true largeness of spirit.

I only began to know Rosemary well after her husband died, by which time she had already set in motion that romantic revival of the Jekyllesque Arts and Crafts garden style which was to be such a benchmark of Eighties garden making: firm, clipped evergreen structure of yew and box, the use of natural materials, wood, stone, gravel and brick, and embroidered on to it all a rich herbaceous planting. It was a style that was unashamedly backward looking, not only to Edwardian England but to the Elizabethan age. Gardening was always an expression of Rosemary's deep patriotism as much as of her design and planting talents. What she created could never be anything other than English.

Her significance lay in reinterpreting earlier, grander traditions scaled down to the smaller garden. In this she was aided by her love of writers like William Lawson, who described the productive and floriferous domains of the more modest gentry houses of Jacobean England. The knot and potager at Barnsley owed much to these historicist impulses. What made that garden so influential was the fact that everything in it was actually on a small scale, the laburnum

Historian of the nation: John Swannell's portrait of me on the cover of *The Bookseller* trailing *The Story of Britain*, April 1996

Right Presenting my history teacher with a copy of *Story* at the party in the National Portrait Gallery to launch the book, September 1996

Below With the elusive editor of *Vogue,* Beatrix Miller, on the same occasion, September 1996

Left Antonia Fraser and Harold Pinter came to stay with us for the Hay Festival, May 1997

Below With Mirabel Osler and Rosemary Verey at Felicity Bryan's tenth anniversary authors' party, July 1998

Opposite George Clive at Whitfield with one of his magnolias, March 1998

Opposite below With Peter and Sonya Wright admiring the view of The Laskett garden from the 'howdah', March 1998

Above Exploring Carpi with Franco Maria Ricci, August 1999

Left With my literary agent, Felicity Bryan, celebrating the publication of *The Spirit of Britain*, September 1999

Below At work in my writing room with Souci in his basket

Visiting the Victorian Tapestry Workshop in Melbourne, Australia to view its tapestry portrait of Dame Elisabeth Murdoch, March 2000

Garden talk during the 'Floating Gardens of the Atlantic' cruise, June 2000

I am installed as High Bailiff and Searcher of the Sanctuary, July 2000. I stand flanked to the right by the Dean, Wesley Carr, and to the left by the Sub-Dean, David Hutt

With Christopher Lloyd in the garden at Great Dixter, August 2000

With Gordon and Marilyn Darling, Australia, February 2003

Julia with her hellebores

tunnel, the knot, the pond and temple, the potager, all creations easily adapted for quite tiny spaces. Like most women designers, her strength lay in detail and incident and her weakness was a lack of monumentality and architectural coherence. Barnsley always remained a garden of separate parts rather than a coherent whole. But at its height, few could rival it for beauty, delight and welcome.

Her passing signals the end of a phase in garden design that was already waning. Her England was the now almost vanished one of the country house, the village and parish church, of which she was a churchwarden. In her silk dress, her string of pearls, her educated, well-articulated voice and graciousness of manner she approximated to every American's idea of the English gentlewoman, a fact that partly explains her enormous popularity in the USA. She takes her place firmly in a gallery of inspired horticultural amateurs, which includes Vita Sackville-West, Margery Fish and Beth Chatto, who have been driving forces in private garden-making through most of the twentieth century.

There was, however, a downside to Rosemary, which never came my way. She could be arrogant, abrasive and difficult. I never knew her before she was virtually sixty but she must in her day have been quite hot stuff. Certain houses in Gloucestershire, I was told, still would not receive her. She loved men and that was very evident. Her marriage must have been an odd one. She married in 1939 by convention but when David died she genuinely mourned his loss. I don't think that motherhood came naturally to her. There was more than a bit of 'the lady of manor' about her: I remember her once saying how she loved talking to the English because they were educated and genteel.

In her later years she would do anything to flee Barnsley and the situation was never satisfactory, since she vacated the main house. In the last few years even the garden began to slip. But I shall miss her. In a way a bit of England has gone.

6 JUNE

Rosemary Verey's funeral

We drove on a dry but lustreless day to Barnsley for Rosemary's funeral. We parked in the field near the house and made our way to the church half an hour before the service. It was already almost packed and we were shown to a couple of seats in the north aisle. The church was beautifully decorated with garden flowers in the colours she loved most, violet, lavender and shades of purple splashed with gold. The coffin sat in the chancel. At just before 12 noon the Prince of Wales arrived and took his place in the front pew,

This was a family service, the farewell of sons and daughters and grandchildren to their mother and grandmother and a farewell by the church to one who had been a churchwarden for thirty years. It was a touching sight to see Jane Wickham Musgrave carry both Rosemary's silver-topped wand of office and her own to the grave-side: simple, silly but very touching. The service was also simple and short. Old loved hymns like 'Praise my Soul'; readings by the family, including one from a children's version of *Pilgrim's Progress* by Veronica Bidwell; a direct touching address by Charles Verey, who said that as his mother lay dying she said 'I put my hand into God's hand'. What more need ever be said? At the close her sons and grandsons acted as pallbearers, something I had never seen done before but so incredibly moving.

We all followed the coffin out into that typical English church-yard and gathered round the grave for the committal. Each of the family threw a handful of soil onto the lowered coffin. And it was over. I said to the cleric as we left 'It was all as she would have wished it', to which he replied, 'Yes, if it hadn't been there would have been some knocking.'

The whole congregation was asked back to the house. There's always a certain poignancy about such occasions. Hardy Amies went almost at once. In church he was virtually bent double, propped up on sticks, hardly able to walk, clearly very upset at Rosemary's passing. I fear that his will not be long. But as we wandered through the garden it really was at its height: the panicles of brilliant yellow in the laburnum tunnel forming a waterfall canopy above the purple allium flower heads never looked better. But the knot garden needed replanting. We walked to the potager, which was magical, surely her most original and beautiful innovation. Virtually useless as a practical kitchen garden, as a work of art it cast its spell. I'm glad that there are so many plants from her in our own garden, above all the golden hollies in the Flower Garden, which stand as a testimony to our friendship.

It was a happy party with a dreamlike quality, all about a vision of England and Englishness which now seems under siege and about to slip away. But its centuries-old ritual still exerts its magic and power of consolation. As Charles Verey put it so well today, we see her off on a journey. I can't think of a better way of departing.

14 JUNE

The General Election

What happened? The boring election is over. I voted Lib Dem as I couldn't stand any of the others. It was inevitable that we'd be stuck with another five years of Blair. God knows where it will take us. I loathe their derision of the monarchy, Church, law, of any ancient established institution or tradition. They want to wipe out history. But I'll fight my tiny corner.

Last week I returned to the National Portrait Gallery and gave a lecture on my early days, the grey years 1959 to 1967 when I sat in the basement. It was the first time I had spoken at the Gallery for nearly thirty years. It was intensely emotional for me. I wrote, I think, one of the best pieces I've ever written, frank and direct. But I had no idea how much it would upset me. I virtually blubbed at the end. The applause went on and on and then someone who had been a young warder when I was there sprang up and spoke in tribute to me. He was a shy person. It was so touching that I could hardly bear it. When I got home I burst into tears. But it's over now and I get so much delight over all that Charles Saumarez Smith has achieved. It's a great gallery and I'm not sorry that he didn't get the V&A. It would have finished him. At the NPG everything went right as successors built on my foundations.

On Sunday we went up for the Garrick Club's Winnie the Pooh party in a series of marquees on the field of the Honourable Artillery Company. This was a free binge on the vast millions the Club had got by selling off A.A. Milne to Disney. Lots of friends were there: Hugh and Judy Johnson, Iain Mackintosh, John Wakeham . . . The dinner tables for a thousand were assigned alphabetically so I found myself sitting next to Sonia Melchett, who must be into her seventies. She told me that she never wanted to marry Hugh Fraser and how Hugh, believing that she would, had gone round to Campden Hill Square to find Harold Pinter glued to the television, watching cricket. 'You can have a divorce,' Hugh said. Harold was totally uninterested, waved a hand and said, 'Have a glass of champagne.' When Hugh got back to Sonia he asked her to marry him and she said 'No'. I never knew that Adam Boulton of Sky News was her son-in-law and she seemed very surprised that I had such an estimation of him. Later came the cabaret of Kit and The Widow, which sailed very near the wind, including a very sharp new satire song on demoted Robin Cook and his problems with the bottle. Whatever age we now live in, it is not one of reticence.

18 TO 21 JUNE

London

Four days in London is no longer my idea of paradise but it was full of bits and pieces that had to be done, with spaces in between. Tuesday was swallowed up with a meeting in the City with AXA Nordstern, filming about the Virgin Queen at the National Portrait Gallery, and dinner at the Garrick Club with John Hayes, who sweetly gave me a copy of his edition of Gainsborough's letters. Wednesday vanished with dealing with the plumber because the bathroom was leaking into the flat below; a meeting with Warren Davis of the National Trust over what could be done with the Garden History Society, which screams for a radical shake-up; lunch with Norman Tebbit; a meeting at the Abbey with Tony Platt and Barry Mazur about the adumbrated museum. Julia then came up and we went to the quite wonderful Vermeer exhibition at the National Gallery and dinner afterwards. Thursday was the gym, the London Library and a perfectly interminable National Trust Council meeting, the party to launch the re-jigged Royal Horticultural Society Hall in Vincent Square and then on to Campden Hill Square for the Marie Antoinette launch. In other words, this was just like old times. Too much so. We drove back, arriving home at midnight.

What on earth does one remember from all of that? Antonia's party, apart from the grandchildren, was a trip back to the world first created in the 1960s – Sonia Melchett, Drue Heinz, Lois Sieff, Tizzy Wells, Paul and Marigold Johnson et al., with Salman Rushdie and V.S. Naipaul glimpsed from afar. We were completely crammed, bumper to bumper. Gesturing towards a luckless string quartet, Antonia said 'They're not allowed to play anything after 1792'. It was so noisy that if they had struck up 'Land of Hope and Glory' no one would have noticed.

Prior to that it was Vincent Square, with Simon Hornby still bitterly complaining to me about what I'd written after that meeting he so disgracefully chaired about the removal of the Lindley Library from London. We won and the Library is still here. People loved my *Country Life* piece on the Chelsea Flower Show. Well, someone had to say it. And we met Simon's successor, the benign Richard Carew-Pole and his wife, who are coming on the tour of Italian gardens I'm doing in September. His style of presidency will be very different.

But I suppose that the event of the week was lunch with Norman Tebbit. He and I are the only two people in public life to emerge from Edmonton County Grammar School. Not that that was mentioned in the conversation, for, being the day of the State Opening of Parliament, with ghastly New Labour back as a dictatorship, we were into the political scene. As is so often the case, the reality of the man was very different from the perceived acerbic, hard-edged public profile bestowed on him. I really liked him. And we both chorused that who led the Conservative Party was almost an irrelevance. Until the Party had something intellectually to offer in the way of an alternative, it had no future. Whatever that was going to be would be a long haul. Both parties, after all, were composed of alliances of disparate groups that from time to time coalesced, with one group within each in the ascendant.

What concerned us both was the loss of any moral framework for society. Norman said that whenever a moral issue came up in the Lords the bishops never took a firm line. The failure of the Church of England to stand by a framework of right and wrong meant that that role had now fallen to the State and that that was not a good thing. Society needs bodies other than the State to provide a moral code and to be seen to articulate it, however unpopular. That's what put the Roman Catholics in a stronger position. One might not have agreed with Cardinal Winning's stance but at least it was clear and definite.

At the moment Norman is fishing around to establish some form of trust to do some Conservative thinking. He asked me if I'd contribute, if asked. I said that I would. In the meantime let us hope that the damage being done will not be too devastating.

31 JULY

The summer

Tomorrow will be my third day in London. It is stifling, just below 90 degrees, and I spend my time in the stacks of the Warburg Institute culling what I can on dining in Classical Antiquity. Julia is in and out of the Royal Opera House putting *Month in the Country* together for its revival first night. On Thursday we go to the country and stay put while I write chapter one of *Feast*.

It has been a hectic summer with too much time spent on sorting out the Garden History Society, time that I cannot afford. But I can't stand muddle and mess. I felt that I had to go to their annual conference in Norwich, but it was a casual affair with no proper timekeeping, no framework whatever as to what should happen. Slippage at its most extreme ran to as much as an hour and a half. The best thing was to see Lord Cholmondeley's new garden in honour of his grandmother, Sybil, at Houghton. But the event called for several speeches and when I got back there was yet another at Rosemary Verey's memorial at Cirencester. It was a huge turn-out in a large church but few went back to Barnsley afterwards. It was all well done but it did not have the overwhelming atmosphere of the funeral. Still, it was the end of a phase in my life and I shall miss her.

We went to Norway, to Tromsø, Bergen et al., on the *Queen*

Elizabeth II, with me lecturing. But it was cold and rainy. Then there were two dinners at the Abbey, one for Wesley Carr's sixtieth and the other called The Fish Dinner, when the Master of the Fishmongers Company presented the Dean with a salmon on a suitably bedizened silver charger. In fact this seemingly ancient ritual, a pretty harmless piece of invented pageantry, only went back to the 1960s! I sat next to Natalie, the Dean's wife, hoping that they would get a holiday – which meant, let us pray that the Queen Mother doesn't die in August. No chance of that happening, I thought, as the pictures of her at Walmer Castle and at a flower show at Sandringham demonstrated. Swathed in her usual props in pale lemon she seemed immortal.

Then there was the course at Hadspen, which I did for Penelope Hobhouse on 'The Garden as Theatre'. While there we got to know Nori and Sandra Pope better, he laid-back and plant knowledgeable. Wandering along his borders, I learnt much, including, at last, how to train roses like they do at Sissinghurst, in mounds. I need to get my hands on some green bamboo this autumn. I came back with four astrantia 'Hadspen Blood', a wonderful claret-flecked flower perfect to link in terms of point and counterpoint with our pink roses, *Alchemilla mollis* and brilliant new golden yew-containing hedges.

There was a very hot and sunny day spent with the Thames Landscape Strategy group. This was a real example of joined-up thinking and action, a kind of re-casting of that old chestnut, 'heritage', in twenty-first century terms, in which past and present, grand and vernacular fuse to everyone's benefit. It seemed to be the ideas of English Heritage's recent 'Power of Place' report in action. There was the chestnut avenue at Ham being restored, Marble Hill to be revealed from the river as well as work to other architectural monuments, and yet there was an equal concern with ordinary public spaces and walkways. Mavis Batey, in her usual affable, Mrs Tiggy-

Winkle guise, was there. It was true: the famous view from Richmond Hill was still a miracle, with the river winding its way through an Arcadian vision of foliage and splendid buildings, one or two of which were visible in the distance.

The Laskett garden has had its last opening. Every visitor loves the new crinkle-crankle flower borders and walk. Everything has grown like blazes and The Folly, once in its infancy, is now embowered in trees and shrubs. We gave a 'Cancer Fest' for friends born under that sign in the ascendant, which included Julia. Fifteen came, each bearing a dish, and we staged it on a chancy day in The Folly. But after lunch the sun decided to stay and we toured the garden, which was looking magical. The huge change of the gothic screening up the drive and the *treillage* opposite has moved the garden on again. I do wish Rosemary Verey had lived to see it. But in a funny way, I fancy that she has.

SEPTEMBER

We didn't go to stay with Franco and Laura this August. Our thirtieth wedding anniversary came and went on 10 September, and the day after was when the world suddenly seemed to change as we lurched into the reality of the twenty-first century. It has been a head-down period as I had to finish *Feast*, which I did, and there was, as a consequence, no time to write this patchy diary. Events and encounters have come and gone unrecorded. I'm conscious that I always need something to trigger me to write, coupled with corresponding space in which to do it. So much has slipped by due to the lack of the latter. Looking back, all I can see in my mind's eye is reading, writing, cooking, the garden, friends coming and going, the journey to East Anglia for the Garden History Society conference (chaos), to Italy for Specialtours (wonderful) and again to Italy with the Architectural Association (chaos again), but nothing that really radically stirred the pen. I suppose that the images which most stick in my mind are of Princess Margaret, a tragic wreck wheeled out of Clarence House on the Queen Mother's hundred-and-first birthday, and then those planes hitting the World Trade Centre. Like the rest of the globe, when the news reached us we just sat mesmerised at the television as the loop was played and replayed like some cruel aerial ballet for hours on end. As with the Kennedy assassination, everyone will remember where they were at the fatal moment. We were in the country, happy, tranquil, going about our business.

But 10 September was special. We hate parties [in retrospect not true in my case] and cherish our privacy. David Hutt wrote and said would we like a party in the Jerusalem Chamber at the Abbey. I told him that I knew him well enough to say that we'd hate it! But could we be remembered in the prayers at the Abbey on that day? And we were. *Laus Deo*. Can anyone ask more from life? Three decades of inseparable happiness. How much more of it is yet to come?

19 NOVEMBER

The V&A's British Galleries open at last

It was sacred flame time at the V&A. Flambeaux flanked the entrance as we made our way to the grand gala for the launch of the British Galleries. As we were asked in August, there was really no way of getting out of going – and as the saga of re-presenting these galleries goes back to 1979, I felt a moral duty to go. A week before the event a circular arrived with further details, with a separate line at the bottom which read 'It is expected that Cherie Booth, QC, will put in an appearance during the evening'. Mercifully, she never materialised.

The bonus was that the galleries were an absolute knock-out, splendid, glamorous, unashamed of richness and indeed flaunting it. The climate and light control made possible the integration of textiles, tapestries, dress, illuminations, watercolours and miniatures. The result was dazzling and not dumbed-down. It owed a great deal, I thought, to the V&A/Royal College of Art MA course in Design and the Decorative Arts, which moved scholarship on in the Museum from style and antiquarianism to the context of cultural history. So bravo! It left me feeling happy.

The event was well done. Mustard Catering, for a start – who else? But Paula Ridley in her feeble frock and Mark Jones in his faded dinner jacket didn't make up my idea of a reception line. I wasn't impressed by Paula Ridley's speech before the dinner (because all the MPs had to leave to go to the Commons to vote). It was good that Alan Borg got a huge round of applause and odd that the new Director said nothing. He doesn't seem to exist.

There was the usual gathering of moneybags: Jacob Rothschild, Leonard Wolfson, John Ritblat and doubtless many more of that ilk whom I didn't recognise. Apart from the ghastly garish green artificial palm trees beneath the dome, the flowers were superb, as were the décor, table decoration and dinner. Our table had Charles and Romilly Saumarez Smith, Ian Hay Davison and wife, John Style and wife, Amanda Vickery, Nina Campbell and Alan Howarth, whom I deliberately set out to look through.

No one looked really glamorous, which was sad, but that's we're in, the age of proletarianisation. Over who was going to be the next Director of the British Museum there was much talk. Charles was interviewed for it that morning, Neil MacGregor virtually denied to my face that he was in for it; the Chairman of the National Gallery later admitted that he was. Charles told me that the National Gallery Trustees had already set up a search committee for a new Director. *Plus ça change*. What a world! What a relief to be out of it!

28 NOVEMBER

'Lady Harding'

So Charles, 'Lady Harding', has died at the age of eighty-six. In the end I couldn't stand those lunches! But he was a wholly unmalicious man, egregious certainly, anxious to charm and please to an excessive degree, with a face like a dowager out of a play by Oscar Wilde, all pink and raddled, his eyelashes forever fluttering. He lived for those lunches he gave at his Cadogan Square flat, which ran on ambassadors' wives, widows of the *beau monde* and unattached men like Norman St John Stevas's partner Adrian. Those lunches belonged to a world that disappeared in the middle of the Seventies. Who in the Eighties could wipe out three hours in the middle of a working day? I'm afraid that in the midst of all the V&A crises I couldn't face them any more. The elegant tittle-tattle seemed ever more vacuous. Such gatherings epitomised the world of which I caught the tail end in lunches given by Cecil Beaton and Diana Cooper. Only the Queen Mother, at a hundred and one, is still, I suppose, giving them. But Charles was a well-meaning and generous host. He just loved gathering his little galaxy together, getting in the hired domestics and entertaining. It was all set-dressing: the food was pretty awful, the pudding always chocolate-chip ice cream tarted up in a fancy goblet. I don't think I've ever met anyone whose entire life was so entirely made up of fashionable attitudes and surfaces. He used to try and ask me to lunch after 1987 but no, I'm afraid I invented reasons not to accept. I felt a bit mean really but I no longer had the taste or the time for that world any more.

29 NOVEMBER

September the Eleventh remembered

Services nothing but services! Today it was the turn of Westminster Abbey, a final wind-up of September the Eleventh for the families of some eighty British who lost their lives in the collapse of the World Trade Center towers. The Dean had taken the decision to dress down, a wise one, so no ruff and robe for me or copes for the clergy, although the crucifer appeared in a remarkable 1920s dalmatic with astonishing embroideries of little children cavorting in a paradisal babyland. Wesley was recovering from an operation on his vocal chords so kept his voice for crucial passages in the service and let David Hutt do the rest.

Down the line came ex-President Bush, the United States ambassador and his wife, and the Prime Minister, looking surprisingly fresh, with Cherie, less frantic than on the previous occasion. George Carey was next to me. He is a large, second-rate man, well-meaning and stolid but with a ponderous voice that fails to touch the heart. He's benign but never radiates. He was more bent on having words with Douglas Hurd on the Hurd Report, telling him how he and the Mayor and Corporation of Canterbury were agitated at the prospect of losing their Archbishop. The Queen appeared in black with a broad-brimmed hat, looking less like Queen Mary this time; the Duke of Edinburgh, a lithe eighty, skipped past; and the Prince of Wales had both eyes, so I said that it was good to see that his eye had been treated, to which he chortled about the dangers of pruning. We all processed to the Sacrarium, the Chapter and Douglas and me on one side and the royal party on the other. Fortune Grafton was in waiting, looking like a grumpy headmistress, but suddenly beamed a smile at me across the Sanctuary.

It was quite a clever service and as far as I could observe meant much to those for whom it had been designed. The moment was telling when the Cardinal, the Free Church minister, the Rabbi, the Archbishop and a Muslim woman stood in a line at the top of the flight of steps to the Sacrarium and together pledged the commitment of the faith communities to justice and peace. Judi Dench, in black but with a trailing blue scarf, read two poems so well that, as one of the canons remarked to me after, 'You wouldn't have known that she was an actress.'

At the close the bereaved, clutching white roses, made their way, to the strains of a mournful melody by John Tavener, to the West Door, outside which they laid the flowers on the memorial to Innocent Victims – touching, as we saw in the papers the next day, for we were marooned forever in the Sacrarium. Afterwards there was coffee for a brief moment in the Deanery, memorable only for the sight of Cormac Murphy-O'Connor and George Carey lolling together on a sofa, looking like two clerics out of one of those cardinal pictures, all crumpled robes and smiles.

But, yes, as I gathered later from those who saw it on television, it was all incredibly moving, made so because those who had lost relatives had framed the service. It was what they wanted. For them it was the funeral they never had, for there were so few bodies. The image of the young widow clutching her baby in her arms bending to lay down her rose in farewell to her husband said everything.

NEW YEAR'S EVE

Usually Beatrix Miller tells me whether I've had a good or a bad year but she didn't this time. This was a year of marking time, consolidating and getting on with things. Working on the premise that my life goes in seven-year cycles, this is the end of the second such cycle since I left the V&A. Life just seems settled into a new pattern. Rosemary Verey I miss, a sad loss. But I finished *Feast* and I'm way into *The Laskett: The Story of a Garden*. The time is right to write that book and I shall enjoy doing it in 2002, a huge change from the ponderous apparatus of *Feast*, writing with joy from the heart.

2002

The Golden Jubilee phone-in

I had been asked to do a Radio 4 phone-in programme entitled *Taking Issue* and thought: why not? They'd rung through before Christmas and I'd suggested multiculturalism, but by January things had moved on, so I'd suggested the presidential airs of the Blairs. That too had become *passé*, as things move so fast, and I was asked to do the new Archbishop of Canterbury. I said that I couldn't do that, so I said why not the Queen's Golden Jubilee? There was much in the papers about apathy, so I wrote a rousing piece as an introduction, saying that £900 million had been frittered on the Dome and the government was doing nothing to thank Her Majesty. I drew attention to the fifty years and the monarch's epitome of duty and service. Both the producer and the presenter were highly educated and sharp people, so I felt no sense of a set-up. The calls piled in. On the air I went. I'd done my homework but I was stunned by the violent antipathy to the monarchy and the event. There was such hostility in the calls and in a manner that was quite frightening. It really made me wonder whether monarchy had any future at all. I held my corner, although I was against the ropes twice.

What I did learn, which was I think fair, was that this was not 1977, the year of the last Jubilee. Even those pro the monarchy said that. That did interest me. The Palace seemed to want a 1977 re-run. You can't. Things have moved on hugely. This is a different society calling for different things and I felt that a response was needed. Lifestyle and expectations have changed. To many who called in, the monarchy was an albatross, an anachronism which should be swept away. None of them had forgotten the death of Diana and the royals' reaction. I don't know how they'll pull themselves back from where they've got to. It left me profoundly depressed. But then it was a controversial programme and by its subject matter it was Madame Defarge time. As we left, David Jessel, the producer's twenty-something son, had sent him a text which read: 'Chop off all their heads'.

In the evening there was the usual Audit Dinner at Westminster Abbey, a much-diminished affair. The impact of 11 September on tourism had revealed the fragility of the Abbey's finances. It will have to find another, more permanent source of income away from its investment and entry fees. The Receiver General, David Burden, realises this and is proposing approaching a list of major companies, touching each for £50,000 per annum. We live in shifting times. Yesterday a letter arrived from Richard Luce wanting to meet over lunch. I shan't mince my words.

28 JANUARY

Neil MacGregor's dinner for Brian Sewell

Neil MacGregor gave a dinner for Brian Sewell at the National Gallery. We were rung and asked and, as I gathered that there were to be only eighteen of us and it was not a 'rent a crowd' job, I said 'yes'. It was a curious and happy gathering, including Max Hastings and his wife Penny, Wendy Baron and husband, Michael Leonard, Thelma Holt and Valerian and Annabel Freyberg. Later, I gathered that Brian was terribly anxious that we should come. He's such a complex man, who is afraid to show affection and must always go that inch too far. But he is brilliant: after dinner we toured the National Gallery and Brian talked stunningly about this or that picture. In his speech he recalled three missing people: Anthony Blunt, Johannes Wilde and Michael Kitson. They had taught him to look. They were, in fact, that heroic founding generation of the Courtauld Institute. A little later I had just caught the parallel group at the Warburg Institute. They had taught me to think and look in one way, Brian in another. I recall Frances Yates sighing over a typescript of a Courtauld article for the *Journal* and saying, 'I suppose we'll have to print it.' I remember also her realisation that I had an 'eye' and that made her nervous and suspicious of me, as though it was somehow corrupting.

Julia said that Neil spoke to her as though she was an old friend. In a funny kind of way he has become that, by osmosis. I was completely wrong about him: he has been the greatest Director of the National Gallery in the twentieth century. Slight, a trifle dapper but by no means camp, he looks extraordinarily young for his mid-fifties, with dark brown hair without a wisp of white. His eyes are set into his face, luminous and intelligent. I felt him to be a lonely man but one guided by integrity, a rare being in that all-too corrupting world.

The death of Princess Margaret

It is a curious fact that if she had died in the middle of the 1960s the response would have been akin to that on the death of Diana. As it was, she lived long enough for the bitter truth about her to become general knowledge, a monument to Michael Adeane's pronounce-ment: 'We can no longer protect them. They must stand or fall on their own merits.' In her case, as we passed into the Nineties, my own attitude to the Royal Family changed. I was brought up in the age of deference. It went and now a member of the Royal Family has to earn my respect and I can't indulge in sycophancy any more. When, in 1997, it came to my *Diaries* being published I remember sitting with Ion Trewin and the solicitor and the question: 'Do you care whether you see Princess Margaret again or not?' I said 'No'. A bridge had been crossed. The way she behaved by that date was so inconsiderate that I really couldn't stand any more of it. This was a princess from the era before 1789, who never seemed to think of any of the inconvenience she caused or that it was anything other than everyone's role to fulfil her slightest whim. All of this was so sad because, when young, she had been beautiful, vivacious and at times quick-witted. She was a woman with a sense of faith, too, and one who could, from time to time, actually be extremely kind. And, of course, she was a great parent. But the downside won and that's what the public in the end perceived. She was devoid of the common touch, attracting many to her circle who were sleazy glitterati and lived, it seemed, entirely for her own pleasure.

The end was so tragic, a half-paralysed, bloated figure in a wheelchair but, I suppose, fifty years of cigarettes and whisky had effectively destroyed the system, which just broke up. I respected the way she had written down the details of her funeral. On 19 April there is to be an Abbey memorial. She had asked for the whole of Fauré's *Requiem*, a massive demand in terms of singers and an orchestra. Opera, I know, for instance, wasn't her thing. A memorial evening by the Royal Ballet would surely have been more appropriate. But Fauré it is to be. The Queen won't enjoy sitting through that and I wonder whether the Queen Mother will make it. It's terrible to write this but there has been a need to 'clear the decks'. Will the Queen Mother last the Jubilee?

20 FEBRUARY

Lunch with the Lord Chamberlain

Richard Luce I always think of as an old friend, I suppose because he was the benign Arts Minister who ensured my exit from the V&A. Pink-faced and cheerful, he has a gentleness and charm of manner. And now he's Lord Chamberlain. So out of the blue came a letter asking me to lunch. I wasn't particularly surprised, as they must need allies in the Palace, and ideas and support from people who are publicly known to be monarchists and who know history and have a sharp notion as to where we are now. So in I went through the Privy Purse entrance, along the ocean of crimson carpet and gilt and up to his office. The walls of his secretary's office were lined with showcases stuffed with gifts from the Indian princes to Edward VII, a flashing phantasmagoria of gold and diamonds on scimitars, shields and anything else useless that you could imagine.

Lunch was *à deux* in his office, and once I got going he stood up and shut the door. In a way I'd been waiting for this moment. There was so much to be said, so much that had to be said to move things on and yet hold on to the historic essence. He agreed with me that this government wouldn't actually publicly denigrate the monarchy but they wouldn't help it either. I said that that meant the monarchy had to be ahead of government and public thought and perception. Also that any change should be piecemeal and evolutionary and not done in any public way.

My main mission was the reform of ceremonial. I told him that they ought to sit down and go through the lot – and ask what was it, when did it start, what did it represent and has it still relevance – bearing in mind not to destroy the greatest show on earth. Is it still necessary for ambassadors to arrive in horse-drawn carriages? Do we need the Garter procession every year? Shouldn't the State Opening of Parliament be revised – throw out the peers' wives, for a start? John Grigg had apparently suggested a different format, to be staged in Westminster Hall. There are things that should stay unchanged, like Trooping the Colour or the Ceremony of the Keys in the Tower or the Epiphany ceremonies in the Chapels Royal. Of course we must bear in mind that the Queen is moving towards eighty and her natural instincts are against change. But Richard at least didn't have to walk backwards in front of her. She'd gone along with that petition of his.

It was Prince Edward's constant exploitation of the Royal Family that had finally got the message through that things couldn't go on in this way. Richard seemed curiously ignorant of royal history. When I said that it still lived out an Edwardian pre-1914 sequence, he thought that Sandringham had been acquired in the 1920s, which I thought odd. I suggested that in the coming reign Charles should live in Clarence House and, following the example of the King of Spain, go to Buckingham Palace as the office and as a place for state events. He thought that the Princess Margaret obits weren't as bad as expected, although it meant that Kensington Palace was up for grabs. Basically it should be emptied, although the Kents and Gloucesters are still there.

'Everyone thinks that we're stuffy in here,' he said, 'But we're not.' Well, I'm not so sure, and I told him as I left not to go the way of some people one knew who get into the Household and end up as cloned caricature courtiers. And then he was worried about the young. I told him not to think about them but those in their thirties and forties. It's that lot who need wooing and who will take the monarchy through to the middle of the century. I also told him of the Palace's lack of style, so noticeable on my rare visits – awful flowers and lack of attention to visual detail.

'It was very hierarchical when I came here,' Richard said, 'But I go out and talk to the cleaners and the footmen.' Good grief, it makes me shudder to think that it's taken until 2002 for that to happen. But he's a good man, kindly, well meaning, not over-quick of intellect but sufficient – and the royals wouldn't like any explosion of brainpower in their vicinity. I left thinking 'Watch this space' and wondered whether this would be my last visit behind a closed door at the Palace. Yet it took me back to Patrick Plunket and Martin Charteris and those conversations *à deux* which always began with 'What do you think of them?'

18 MARCH

Commonwealth Observance

This has been a whirlwind of a few days. Up I went to Edinburgh to lecture to the Garden History Society in the Botanic Garden. All of that was enjoyable, with a wonderful and appreciative audience. Down to London on the Sunday to meet Julia in time to see the film *Gosford Park*, which had been hyped up for its country house 1930s accuracy and was in fact all wrong, besides being a monument to indulgent actors. On Monday David Cannadine lunched with me at the Garrick Club. Much talk of many things. Like me he had lunched with Richard Luce and in his case I thought had made the very pertinent observation that the weakness of the Golden Jubilee was that there was no storyline. There had been in 1887 and for the Diamond Jubilee in 1897, a triumphant century and an Empire. All that this reign had witnessed was decline and the dissolution of an Empire, let alone the sad state of the Royal Family.

In the afternoon I went to Commonwealth Observance in the Abbey. It was, of course, full, but when asked afterwards what I thought, I said that it's tired and old-fashioned. I could see from where I sat in the north aisle that the children were yawning. The Queen, today in electric red, passed by me afterwards and said, 'Bit of something for everybody.' I wonder. Its irrelevance was heightened by the Zimbabwe crisis and simultaneous elections there.

In the evening we had a reunion dinner with Paul and Ingrid Channon, he now Lord Kelvedon, at the Garrick. Ingrid is just seventy and seemed so much better and happier in her Kelvedon phase of life with her twelve grandchildren and bevy of Jack Russells. Paul had been ill. I could see that and was undergoing some form of treatment but I couldn't discover for what [it was premature Alzheimer's]. But he picked up through the evening. They had been at Princess Margaret's funeral, where one of the Royals had behaved badly, bowling up after and saying 'She always hated me . . .'. Geoffrey Stirling was at the next table and he said that the Jubilee website had had eight million hits, so I suppose on the day it'll be all right.

On Tuesday we went to the Beckford exhibition at Dulwich, which was a delight. Then on to the Royal Horticultural Society for the Spring Flower Show in Vincent Square, which was magic, and then to see the film *Iris*, which was both moving and disturbing. We went back to The Laskett on Wednesday, after which I finished writing the book on the garden. I began this only six months ago, but it has written itself. There's the endmatter, which is substantial, but the main narrative is done. It is so emotionally exhausting reliving one's own past. I read each chapter to Julia as I wrote it and blubbed as I read the final sentence of the epilogue.

On Friday we went to Oxford for the Literary Festival, where I was doing the book on garden ornament. I spoke at the Oxford Union to a good audience and we later dined with Felicity Bryan in her Kidlington house. Sue McGregor was one of the company, pushing her autobiography. All those years of getting up at 3.30 a.m. for the *Today* programme had taken their toll. In some lights she looked like a tired old lady and the headphones had eroded her hair. As a person she's a delight, but perhaps she has left it too late to make a second career. Media limelight quickly fades and public memory is more than short. She agreed that the BBC was dumbing down, abandoning any notion of its remit to educate and inform, hiving that off to the new BBC Four, which I confess we've started to watch in the face of a morass of soaps, police and hospital sagas, game shows and panel games on the rest. We have moved into the age where if you try to lift someone's mind you're accused of not being accessible or politically correct. God help us.

30 MARCH

The Fairy Queen departs

I was rung at 5.45 p.m. by the *Daily Mail*. The Queen Mother had died three hours before. Would I write a piece? I said 'Yes'. It doesn't come as a surprise. She had never left Royal Lodge since she went there from Sandringham for Princess Margaret's funeral. It was difficult to be upset because at a hundred and one it was to be expected and she had been weakening for some time. But it is the end of something. On the afternoon of Sunday 31st we were rung from

Buckingham Palace and asked to the funeral. Very touching, that. In media terms all hell broke loose and on Sunday I saw all the articles I'd written years ago about this or that aspect of her appear. Also those television obits of mine went out, but I never saw them.

The Queen Mother's funeral

8 APRIL

We watched the funeral procession on television. It was immaculately done, the streets jammed with onlookers, not only the old but a hugely varied crowd. What struck one most was that as the Queen left to return to Buckingham Palace the onlookers burst into applause. It was quite extraordinary and very moving. Later the lying in state went on through the night until 6 a.m., with queues right over Westminster Bridge and beyond. And again those who came were all sorts and conditions and ages. In spite of New Labour and the ghastly *Guardian*, who says that the Crown still hasn't the power to pull?

I came up on the Sunday evening in time for the funeral rehearsal at Westminster Abbey. No wonder British ceremonial is so good as it is immaculately rehearsed. The Abbey was awash with TV technicians, choirboys, gentlemen-at-arms, Yeomen of the Guard and the rest. A few were robed but most not. The Yeomen of the Guard wore their hats and held their halberds, which looked odd, and various other people came holding hats and batons. We went through the whole thing once and the procession in and out twice. The flowers were appropriately in sweet pea colours. I thought that the catafalque looked a little narrow. The great problem was how to rehearse it all without opening the Great West Door, so there was an almighty mess trying to get the start of the procession right, with young guardsmen carrying a coffin with lead weights in it, I guessed. Wesley Carr wore a Charles II cope and the rest their Edward VII ones, all very appropriate. Garter told me that he and Lord Lyon King of Arms from Scotland were being robed at the College. He'd altered the style proclaimed over the coffin, which had been drafted by Anthony Wagner, adding 'and Queen Mother' after 'Queen Dowager'. David Burden, the Receiver General, loves an event like this, for his military training goes into top gear. Everything is timed to the minute. Alastair Aird said 'Hello', looking weary but composed. From afar Richard Luce appeared thin, pale and exhausted. It was somehow odd going through the funeral minus the congregation and the key actors but it will provide a firm framework into which everyone who hasn't been rehearsed will fit.

Someone asked me whether I had been to Westminster Hall yet. I said that I was thinking of queuing and was promptly offered a ticket for direct entry on behalf of the Yeoman Usher. So over I went. It is always overpowering when you get away from *les grands* and come into contact with ordinary humanity moved. It was a huge mix of young and old, all sorts and conditions, silent, respectful, muttering, often not knowing quite how to react in the presence of something of this kind, the catafalque covered with purple velvet, her personal standard draped over the coffin, the wreath of white flowers from the Queen and the crown of a consort glittering on top. When I was there the guard was a Scots one, with feathers in their hats and leaning on staves. There was something dramatic about the experience, for the hall was darkened and carefully lit and yet the far doors were flung wide, welcoming in the spring sunshine and the roar of London. She would have liked that. I turned and looked back as I left and felt the tears come – they came even more as I walked past the Abbey and saw the bunches and wreaths of flowers being laid there. Some were florists' work but most were humble bunches with a touching message attached, many from children and families.

One, I thought, got it right when the tribute was to someone who was 'England'.

9 APRIL

This was an extraordinary event on a chill but sunlit day. We arrived by 9.30 a.m. and Julia got in on the dot of 9.45 a.m. and was seated in the second row lining the nave, close to the screen. She spotted Judy Hurd and so they sat together and watched 'the boys'. The Jerusalem Chamber was awash with the actors in the pageant. The Queen Mother's orders sat on purple cushions and it was a bit like inspecting the jewellery gallery at the V&A. Later, Garter was to recount that one of the bearers got shaky knees carrying some of them to the Dean, after which one of the canons laid them on the altar. He said that he had wanted to yell at the Dean 'Grab it fast, before he drops it!' Garter had been tied in to all his layers and I noticed his stockings, which were tights. For a time, he said, he went to Anello & Davide, suppliers to dancers, but they kept on laddering. So a General friend tipped him off about a lady's store which had non-laddering ones. So off he went to get some. The result, of course, was that he got some curious looks, especially when he said, 'This is where a General friend of mine gets his.'

It is difficult to describe the magnificence of the occasion, so perfectly executed. She would have loved every minute of it. Wesley wore one of the copes made for Charles II's coronation, the others copes made for Edward VII's in 1902. They made a fine show. The foreign royals were a noisy lot. They were put into St George's Chapel to the right of the Great West Door and the hubbub was like that at a cocktail party; so much was it at variance with the solemnity of a funeral that an official went in and told them to shut up. A pall of silence descended. When at last they moved, they formed a motley crew – Spain, Norway, the Netherlands, Sweden, Romania, the Hellenes, Belgium, Luxembourg et al. Queen Beatrix headed the clan, with a formidable hat like a drum and a coat which emphasised her square shoulders. Juan Carlos looked as though he had stepped out of a Goya, mottled complexion and all, his queen chattering and smiling this way and that, which was quite out of keeping with the occasion.

The fringe British royals formed another contingent, the Duke of Kent bulbous and red in the face in military uniform and clutching a baton, the Duchess looking deranged, very pale and moving as though under sedation. Princess Michael had her hair all over the place, the Prince bluff and browbeaten. Princess Alexandra was wraith-like, as though a puff of wind would flatten her. There was another group, this time of the female close-in royals, five of them: Sarah Chatto, Sophie Wessex, Serena Linley heavily pregnant and princesses Beatrice and Eugenie like kewpie dolls. Sarah Chatto was clearly devastated, her face contorted with grief. They faced the West Door and curtsied as the Queen arrived and then went on their way. The Queen whizzed down our line and she too went on her way with Richard Luce, clutching his white rod and looking less ill than yesterday, and Fortune Grafton bringing up the rear, her back now hunched so that from afar she rather resembled some sinister bird of prey,

Everything went like clockwork. From where we stood we could glimpse and hear the flurry of the bagpipes and see the shaggy head-gear of the pipers. And then the coffin heaved into sight with its glittering, ethereal crown and the Queen's white flowers. By then the choristers were in position and the Sentences began to be sung. This way round it was the usual case of follow the Dean. Behind us came the Queen's Almsmen, the insignia bearers, the pallbearers and then the coffin, after which followed the male members of the Royal Family on foot. Not that I was any part of that. The important thing is always to keep going and look straight ahead, vaguely aware of the Yeomen of the Guard, the gentlemen-at-arms, the royal choristers in scarlet braided with gold who lined the nave and choir, although I could take in that the stalls were filled with former prime ministers. On we went, Douglas Hurd and I, taking up our usual positions beyond the Dean and Canons but set back a few inches. Across from us were the two Archbishops in 'magpie' and a few steps down a row of the other readers, including the Moderator and the Cardinal. Garter and Lyon Kings of Arms took up their positions on either side of the entrance to the Sacrarium.

I looked across to the north transept, where sat the Queen and the Duke of Edinburgh with the Prince of Wales flanked by William and Harry, all in the front row. The Queen looked composed while the Duke indulged in his usual set of attitudes. The two princes looked thoughtful and the Prince of Wales looked as devastated as Sarah Chatto. Behind them sat the rest, row after row of them.

It was a traditional service well done. The poor Archbishop of Canterbury is never alpha-plus but what he said passed muster, although one did ache for a little magic, something transcendent. But then, poor man, he just hasn't got it. Opposite him was the Bishop of London, who didn't do anything but struck me as far too pleased with himself and aware of the figure he cut. Good for the Cardinal that he read from the Authorised Version, but the most touching reading was the one from Bunyan beginning 'I see myself now at the end of my journey . . .'. Wesley Carr's voice held out and he did everything very well in the face of all that episcopal competition.

Perhaps the most picturesque episode was the sounding of the Last Post and Reveille flanking Garter proclaiming the Queen Mother's styles and titles, language lifted from another age. There were comfortable hymns heartily sung and it was all wound up with the National Anthem. Then off we went again to the West Door, this time not following the Dean, where we watched the coffin and the Queen pass, bowing our heads as they went out into the spring sunshine.

It was over bar the *mêlée* that followed. There were so many faces and people that one knew, too many to do anything about. Leonora Grosvenor was complaining that she had been seated amidst her ex-husband's family. Norman St John Stevas, red-faced and coarse of feature, leant on a stick and hobbled, a purple scarf swagged around him. Rachel Billington wheeled me over to talk to her mother, quite a shock. Now in her nineties, Elizabeth Longford was in a wheelchair and not in a good way at all. Such a delightful woman; I shouted in her ear and made rapport. Bamber Gascoigne was behind, his opening remark to me: 'How did you get that job?'

Writing all this brings to mind a remark made by Bill Heseltine, an earlier secretary to the Queen, when he sat next to me. He was such a funny, fly man. I said, 'How's business?' to which came the reply: 'Well, what we really need is a good funeral.' He was right, but we did have to wait a long time for it; in a way it came just in time and to huge effect. For that we must be grateful, although there is still much to sort out.

Two royal deaths in quick succession are a rarity and both speak their own story about the persons deceased.

19 APRIL

Margaret Rose is laid to rest

This was a curious event, but apparently what she wanted. Princess Margaret's choice of Fauré's *Requiem* called for the combined choirs of Westminster Abbey, St George's Chapel, Windsor, and King's College, Cambridge, the orchestra of the Academy of St Martin in the Fields, as well as Felicity Lott and Bryn Terfel to sing solos.

These were ensconced in the choir, with the orchestra in the middle, so the usual procession had to go via the south aisle in and the north aisle out. One of the canons' secretaries had said to me the day before, 'There's a three-line whip on this one.' And, as I stood near the West Door, someone muttered that there had been fears of an empty house. But it wasn't. It was indeed full, but how could it avoid being other than an anticlimax so long after her funeral and after everything that had happened the previous week? It was a concert with readings, not many, but David Linley, who's now quite portly, read well – better than Felicity Kendal, whose presence I couldn't explain. There was no sermon or address. That was a lucky escape for someone. The Royal Family seemed enchanted with all of it, the Queen beaming. No sign of the Duchess of Kent, nor of Princess Michael, nor of Prince William, although the Prince of Wales had Harry, a tall, gangling youth with short, reddish hair who exuded trouble in the making. The Prince looked awful, each death seeming to bring his eyes closer together – so close that I began to wonder whether sooner or later he wouldn't become a Cyclops. George Harewood appeared in his Old Testament guise, a mass of grisly beard, with Patricia, who is now perfectly enormous, at the front. There was a sprinkling of minor foreign royals, like Luxembourg, but no major showing. Julia, who was well placed to the front of the north transept close to the politicians, said that Blair looked clapped out. Billy Tallon, looking dishevelled, rushed over to talk to her and she was able to say how much he had been in our thoughts.

This was a perfectly choreographed, unemotional ritual gone through like clockwork but lacking any spirit. How could it have been otherwise? There was one back-handed prayer, which included the line 'As memories fill our minds, forgive us things said or done which we regret . . .' I'm afraid that it made me think of those I'd said about her but, oh dear, she was such a capricious, arrogant and thoughtless woman. And yet she was a loyal, practising Christian with flashes of generosity along with wit. The common touch she had not. Tony Snowdon was some way back, on crutches; further back still sat Roddy Lewellyn, who perhaps had given her a little happiness. A lot of last week's cast reappeared, often in the same blacks. Fortune Grafton, once again like a bird of prey, followed the Queen. Afterwards we glimpsed the tough jawline of Camilla Parker Bowles beneath the obligatory bucket-shaped black hat as she climbed into a chauffeur-driven car. We didn't spot any of the ballet people. Perhaps they were there somewhere. A few children from the Royal Ballet School carrying the Princess's orders to the altar would have added a lightness of touch. But that was not to be.

As I said to the Receiver General, David Burden, 'You've had your dollop for this year.' The service closed in some disarray, the congregation heading for the West Door, cutting off the Archbishop, the Cardinal and other dignitaries, nor could the choir get by. There was no great gathering of the public outside, although sixty of them were let in to fill up vacant spaces because a train coming from the North had broken down. The British public makes up its own mind and passes judgement, and last week and this reveal that it is a considered one.

20 MAY

On London life

We came up on the Sunday for a dull Chelsea Flower Show. Through signing a deal with ITV, the Royal Horticultural Society seems to have lost most of its sponsors of the big show gardens, so no Yves Saint Laurent, no Cartier, no *Daily Telegraph* or *Evening Standard* for a start. So spectacle was sadly lacking. It was also the year of

Nature triumphing over Art, instead of the other way round, which is, after all, what gardening is all about. Still, a very pretty traditional garden by the National Gardens Scheme got the Gold. The Prince of Wales had the misfortune to have his garden sited next to one of the same type but better, staged by the Irish. He had, I was told, wandered into it thinking that it was his own and was thrilled – only to be told 'No', his was next door!

This was a muddled-up week, with Julia and I boxing and coxing. My job was to do a little publicity for *A Country Life*, out in paper-back. So it was a run of local interviews at the BBC and a round of bookshop signings, in one of which the book surprisingly turned up under History. I was persuaded to do a somewhat disastrous inter-view with the *Daily Telegraph*, which came out on the Friday and trivialised me and got me a ticking off from Beatrix Miller. So I felt humbled. It is always the same. Around every book there is tremen-dous pressure to give an interview. You cave in and later regret it. All of this is so difficult. If you make your living as a writer, you have to put your head above the parapet unless you are so successful and so well known that you don't need to. No such luck.

Tuesday also brought the opening of the new Queen's Gallery at Buckingham Palace, a triumph. Instead of trying to build some modernist art gallery, the premise was that this was a palace and we're exhibiting things made for palaces. So John Simpson built a bit more palace and everything looked wonderful in it. What riches, what splendour! And all we saw was the tip of a vast iceberg. The Prince of Wales was meant to appear but didn't. But the Wessexes materialised looking suburban, Princess Michael in a little box jacket with features stretched, David Linley boldly wearing a black tee-shirt Versace-style, and I glimpsed the Duke of Gloucester dive behind a screen.

This was one of a series of such viewings. There had been one on the Monday and who knows more, which explained why so many people we thought ought to be there were not; but it did make for pleasant viewing. Tony Thorncroft said he would see me at the Royal Academy's reception for the arts. I said, 'What reception?' – and if there was one, why should I be asked anyway? But I later read that there had been one, notable for Beryl Bainbridge thinking that she was talking to Vera Lynn when it was the Queen.

By then I'd gone back to The Laskett and Julia stayed up working on her *Bohème*. Her *Month in the Country* had been revived at the Royal Opera House on Monday and looked as stunning as ever. Sylvie Guillem is honestly better as Natalia Petrovna than Lynn Seymour, although she refuses to wear the period plaits and danced without tights. Deborah Macmillan and Julia screamed about the wilful behaviour of this dancer on the telephone later in the week. But it's wonderful when people still come up to Julia and thank her for her sets and costumes. They are after all 1976, a long time ago.

I came back to London on Friday and took Antonia Fraser to the Garrick. I don't think that we'd eaten *à deux* for years, so it was quite a reunion: I'd met her first in 1967. She was in her usual Jean Muir dress, a waistless, well-cut sack in blue, and moving in a way that sharply betrays that she has inherited her mother's arthritis. She can no longer hold back the effects of time in respect of her face but she's a marvel, a kind of immovable rock. I asked about Harold, who'd had cancer of the oesophagus. His operation was successful and he was at home, very weak and thin. I wouldn't recognise him, I was told. I sensed how tense it had been for her and how near she had been to losing him. So inevitably we talked a lot about wills. She's writing a short book on the Battle of the Boyne and so is learning Gaelic. We both talked of continuing to stretch the mind in old age. The *Telegraph* piece happened to be there. She ran her eye down it and said, 'But you're a serious person.'

On Saturday I went down to New Romney, a promise that I had made ages ago to speak at the AGM of the Romney Marsh Historic

Churches Trust. Needless to say, it turned out that there was work on the line so we were decanted at Maidstone East and trundled by coach half way round Kent. By the time I got there Julie Nightingale was ashen, thinking that she had no speaker. There was a rowdy fund-raising lunch in the village hall, where I was snatched away from Nigel Nicolson and 'eaten' by John Doyle, the President, a gregarious and tiresome eighty-plus. He, however, had founded the Trust and it was a huge success but he'd never learnt that cardinal rule about knowing when to go. Still, it was a happy meeting in a large, handsome church. The Brabournes appeared, she bent double and wavering between sitting upright and falling forward on to the church floor. But it all went well and I gave thanks for the virtues that made such an association and its work possible – those which the Queen embodies and which have surfaced in the year of her Golden Jubilee.

And I've decided that I can't go on with the presidency of the Garden History Society. I feel sad about this. It is the only time that I'd been persuaded to take something of this sort on, billed to me as a few epiphanies. It has, however, been two years of hell: rows, recriminations and battles. It's like being back at the V&A again. I don't want my energies in this phase of my life eroded in this way. What really makes me sad is that there's a young group in there who have a vision that I share. But life is finite and I can't spare what it would involve to fight all this out.

4 JUNE

Queen's Golden Jubilee

We experienced the Golden Jubilee celebrations at a remove, like so many millions, staring at the television screen for too much of the weekend. There was no reason why we should have been invited to anything, although we were to a garden party. I said to Julia that we ought to go, out of loyalty to the Crown. We arrived at 4.45 p.m. and left at 5.10 p.m. But it all seemed to work and we'd been there and done that. The Queen in pale green was smiling away, doing her stuff, with phalanxes either side. Not far away the Prince of Wales was doing his with a thinner gathering, while the Duke of Edinburgh we spotted virtually strolling on his own. It said it all, really. Patrick and Mary Cormack went to one to which Blair was also invited and were horrified to see him holding court on the Palace terrace. That, too, spoke volumes. But the Jubilee told me that the England I loved was still there in spite of him and that it had discovered (not before time) the ability to reinvent itself – hanging on to the past but embracing the present.

The Golden Jubilee seemed to round off what had begun with the Queen Mother's funeral, a rediscovery and rebirth of the Island and its patriotism, undimmed by the wiles of New Labour, but repositioned. By that I mean pageantry met pop in an alliance of past and present, which gives the Crown a formula to carry on through this century. The two are not opposed but complementary, conservation and innovation hand in hand. No one who saw the crowd stretch the length of the entire Mall singing 'Land of Hope and Glory' and 'God Save the Queen' will ever forget it. There's hope at last.

9 JUNE

A sermon

Sunday was the day of my sermon at Westminster Abbey. I was quite nervous about this, but David Hutt had persuaded me and so the die was cast. Sermons for the Sung Eucharist must last seven minutes and be about a thousand words. It was like writing a piece for page 8 of the *Daily Mail*, I wryly thought. Before the service I had tried the pulpit, which was cosy, but when I was delivering the sermon I was aware that much of the congregation was in the north transept, so I had to remember to look right. A.N. Wilson turned up and sat next to me, making me feel quite nervous, and then wrote such a funny piece in the *Evening Standard*, saying it was a masterpiece and that I should take Holy Orders and be the next Archbishop of Canterbury!

13 JUNE

Lunch with A.N. Wilson

No sooner had I got back home than it was up to London again for the Royal Over-Seas League on Wednesday, again a sell-out, and sixty-five books went. Thursday brought a mischievous lunch with A.N. Wilson, at which we both screamed with laughter, in the main this time about Fleur Cowles, who must have gone mad. I couldn't face going to her exhibition. This woman has an ego like no one else. It is so sad. She parades her exhibition with lines like 'under M. in my address book it reads Marilyn (Monroe), Marlene (Dietrich) and Mother (Teresa)'. I told A.N.W. that I'd always resisted going to her

Spanish house, the invitations to which run: 'I want you to fly to Madrid and then drive into the sunset . . .' 'Not if I can help it,' is my reaction. The house is not that comfortable and the fare frugal. It is partly a monastery, the major portion of which belongs to two bright young gay men who do have the staff and the swimming pool, and everything lacking with Fleur. Alexander Walker used to go and found it Spartan. But he got to know the neighbours and was invited by them to lunch and went. The other guests included the Spanish King and Queen. Fleur was mortified and told Alex that he would never be asked by her again.

Oddly enough, I had to write a piece about some really bad paintings for the *Daily Mail*. Henry Wrong rang me, chortling over what I had written but saying that he'd just seen worse: Fleur's exhibition.

14 JUNE

Falklands War anniversary

The real event of the week was a lunch on the *Queen Elizabeth* at Southampton to mark the twentieth anniversary of the Falklands War. This turned out to be an oddly touching occasion. I hadn't seen Lady Thatcher in the flesh for years. But there she was, immaculate in Tory blue, her hair thinner, now sandy coloured and backcombed in that late-Sixties style. No one expected her to utter, as she had been told not to undertake public speeches, having had a couple of strokes. She was given a picture and Carol Thatcher had written some words of thanks for her mother to deliver. But she tore these up and embarked on an oration whose subtext was 'Labour: ruination of the nation's defences'. But the rhythm and cadence of the great days were still there. She had banned the cameras but in the end they arrived and filmed the lot. One can't help having a respect for her. This was a conviction Prime Minister who believed every word she said, formidable, and a stunning contrast to the present incumbent, ever anxious to please and to say whatever the focus groups said that the public wanted to hear. The real star of the occasion was Simon Weston, who'd had his face burnt off on the campaign and put back. Honest, courageous and no frills, this is the kind of man whose values, heroism and sense of duty make me proud be British.

Everywhere we look there are flags bearing the cross of St George, flown in support of the English football team. Why has that become so important? It cannot all be explained by the football cult but it can be in the sense that this is one of the few channels allowed by which the English can express their identity without being accused under some New Labour PC watch.

10 AUGUST

Summer reflections

I have just finished reading Jan Morris's *Trieste and the Meaning of Nowhere*, an extraordinarily haunting and beautifully written book. At first it was irritating that there was no map, but by the end I realised that such a thing was superfluous, for Trieste was for her a mirror wherein to reflect her thoughts as she approached eighty. It was a rounded vision, a recollection and reconciliation of life, death and love, ups and downs, identity, both single and collective, and a passage of time seen in perspective, herself a figure in a European landscape that had shifted and changed through time and circumstance. It made me, sixty-seven in a fortnight's time, consider where one stood in what Beaton called 'the parting years'. In a way they are beautiful ones. What reason have I to complain? None. A second life has been made and when, for a brief period, I stepped a little back into the old one, finding myself on the Council of the National Trust, I realised how much I didn't want that any more. I have no longings to be a 'quangocrat'. I want to create and write. I want to live, in the main, in the country. I want to travel from time to time. I like performing publicly in small, appropriate doses and enjoy a late-found flair for tossing off an article for the leader page of the *Mail*. I want to talk to and see friends. I want people to come to the house, yes, but also in small doses. I enjoy going into my Writing Room at 9 a.m. and that unchanging day: work till 12 noon, jog, lunch, work again until 6.30 p.m., cook, bath, eat, look at the news, go to be bed by 10.30 p.m. I like, if the weather permits, to garden in the summer between 5.30 .and 6.30 p.m. and in the afternoons at the weekends. I like to keep abreast of current news and gossip but I don't want to be part of it. I don't want the London scene: that is, private views, dinners, the social whirl that I lived for so long. I don't want stress. I want tranquillity. I'm no longer after anything, and everything is over to a new generation. When that happens to be people I've encouraged or advanced, like Charles Saumarez Smith or Sandy Nairne, I feel a happy glow. But I would never publicly comment or criticise. Never, never go back.

This has been a drear summer, dull, overcast and wet, along with bitter winds. I wish I knew where the time had gone. Somehow it seemed dislocated by Shaun the gardener's wife leaving him and Dot's husband having black-outs. Strange how unsettling it is when the framework upon which you depend is upset. It disrupts everything. Advance copies of *Feast* are due in five days. And that has been another miserable drama, with a designer who seemed to do nothing and a publicist who did even less. But now I'm starting on a new book, on the Restoration of Charles II, really looking at how a monarchy is put back after two decades: what was restored and who remembered how things used to be done. I want to deliver the book in the spring of 2004. I wonder . . . [I never wrote it.]

Meanwhile we plod on. The imperial crown, suitably gold-leafed with 22-carat gold, went up on the pillar at the end of Elizabeth Tudor Avenue, matching the gilded antlers on the stag in the Orchard and Britannia's trident. No one can say that we haven't done the Queen proud. The pineapples on their plinths have migrated to the V&A Temple. Otherwise it's been an incredible year for growth, with new beds and borders jammed with plants. I used to apologise and say that ours was not a plant garden. I fear that it has become one, as I've never been so conscious of the swathes of flowers in the borders.

When Tessa Traeger and Patrick Kinmonth arrived to photograph us and the garden, they turned up at a bad time. Julia hates sitting for her photograph and wouldn't let Patrick 'arrange' her; however, the results were, I thought, good. He 'arranged' me and Tessa took a really good picture of me in profile, plus haunting ones of the garden. She's a pixie of a person but I have to admit a brilliant photographer.

I've been on the road for *A Country Life*: Hay, the Royal Over-Seas League, Dartington and now Edinburgh. And that's it. God knows if anyone's buying or reading it but it has evoked some touching letters. I feel that public gets confused over me: is this the same chap who wrote about Gloriana, about garden design and about British history? The list is disparate and I feel the disadvantage of being someone who can't easily be pigeonholed. But who cares? It's all too late now.

23 AUGUST

I am sixty-seven

I am sixty-seven and don't particularly feel it. The sun rises early over the Landmark Trust's Villa Saraceni, to which Francis and Christine Kyle have invited us. It is good to experience living in great architecture – Palladio – rather minimalist and post-modern really, harmonic and severe, with an overlay of a bit of splendour in the frescoed family state apartments. The stay is an agreeable mix of looking at things, *trattoria* lunches and dinners with the hurly-burly of doing it ourselves, which I never dislike. They were sweet and laid on a great surprise yesterday evening on my birthday, when they'd hired a cook to prepare dinner. Downstairs we went and Francis said, 'We've got a little surprise for you.' The door to the central *salone* was opened and there sat a string quartet of young German musical students who called themselves the Chagall Quartet (and why not, for heaven's sake?). They were absurdly young and fresh, twenty to twenty-four, all clad in black. Splendid Italianate upright baroque armchairs had been arranged in a semicircle; I was ushered to the central 'throne' and the quartet began to play Bach. It was curiously moving to hear music played in a *salone* by Palladio, the acoustics good, if a little hard. Dinner then followed. It was very charming and hugely generous. I'm sure that my seventieth will be nothing like as glamorous!

Well, what do I feel about it all? Not much. The latest book, *Feast*, arrived by courier and I felt well pleased with the design and production. I thought, hopefully, that it read fluently and well and was rather stunned by all that I'd ploughed through and then noticed that I might have muddled up two Cardinals d'Este in chapter four! But self-doubt always creeps in at this stage. The V&A now seems so very far off, although I still find people who keep on harking back to it. I can't somehow shrug it off. How grateful I am for all these years of new creativity; what a betrayal it would have been not to have made the leap. I try to keep a writing balance, working in different fields and, I suppose, keeping in mind saleability because, to be brutal, I depend on it for an income. I must at least double my so-called inflation-proof pension. But I've never ceased to enjoy researching and writing books. It's been part of my life since my twenties and, now that it occupies me the whole time, it becomes more and not less compulsive, driven on by the fact that one is not immortal and there's so much to learn and write about. How lucky I have been.

I write this in a villa that epitomises the ideals one cares about. It exudes harmony, order and precision in its proportions and elegance. It is an aesthetic experience to be here, reliving the Renaissance, for the villa had aspirations to culture. The faded frescoes suggest a military man come to rest and farm to make money in the countryside. The *stanza*, a double cube, has the history of Sophonisba as a frieze, a link with the humanist poet Trissino and the great production in the Teatro Olimpico in nearby Vicenza, with scenery by Palladio. Like all things Venetian, it combines splendour and restraint.

Oddly, I still live a school year at sixty-seven. There's the lull of August, the rest and taking stock, and then off we go again. It's Antonia's seventieth birthday next Tuesday and we'll be there. Extraordinary to think of all the decades I've known her.

27 AUGUST

Antonia Fraser is seventy

We'd had a letter from Harold. It was Antonia's seventieth birthday on 27 August and he was giving a dinner. Could we come? Of course we could! It was a fine August evening when we arrived at the Campden Hill house, with Huw and Vanessa Thomas bringing up the rear, both now with silvery white hair, most becoming them. And that, in some odd way, set the tone for the event, for there were so many people we hadn't seen for literally years, like Antonia's youngest son, Orlando, virtually a child when last seen at Eilean Aigas and now a tall and striking fair-haired man in his early twenties.

This dinner was special. A tent in the garden and six tables of eight, forty-eight guests in all, the majority family: Rebecca and her husband, Edward FitzGerald, Flora minus Peter Souros, Benjamin with his Mexican wife, then the brothers Paddy and Thomas Pakenham and cousins like Tristram Powell and the Phippses. On to that group were embroidered a few of us: Lois Sieff, Simone Warner, Vidia Naipaul, Ronnie Harwood . . . very few. I was placed to Antonia's left, a great honour, with Rebecca, pretty in black, to my left and Huw Thomas opposite. This was indeed a special evening and Harold was an attentive host and looked ten years younger, having got over cancer and become much thinner. Julia remarked that he looked better than she ever remembered.

There were speeches: a bad one from Ronnie Harwood, a riotous and ebullient performance by Edward FitzGerald, quite marvellous. Most touching of all was that by Harold. He described his illness and how often he thought that he was about to drown, would extend his hand up out of the water into which he had sunk, seeking help, to find it grasped firmly by a strong hand that could only be Antonia's. It was unaffected, honest, moving and sincere, and suddenly one realised that this was a great marriage. He then recited a little poem he'd once written, 'To A'. It was her, although he said that his mother-in-law had said to Antonia: 'Are you sure it's you?'

Antonia is extraordinary. She is like a rock, hugely considered and intelligent. She wore her hair up, which was fetching, and even at seventy her attraction is striking: I had said truthfully to her on arrival: 'Seventy years young'. Earlier that day they'd had a family picnic at Hampton Court, with the children running around. It was a memorable occasion. Vidia Naipaul gave me half of his fish as they'd forgotten that I was vegetarian. Huw Thomas told me how good *Story* was, which was some compliment coming from a scholar of his distinction.

Meanwhile, Julia was next to Tristram Powell learning that Hilary Spurling was to write his father's biography and how it had been a toss-up between her and Selina Hastings.

14 AND 15 OCTOBER

London and Birmingham

I travelled to London on the evening of the opening of the Versace exhibition at the V&A feeling, I suppose, wounded and hurt. Gianni Versace had come to the Museum through me and we remained friends ever after. But I was to be airbrushed out of it. Although that fact was known and that I'd written a book on his theatre designs and contributed to two other books of his, no reference was to be made to me. When an invitation came it did not even include Julia. I declined. Perhaps it is as well that I remember him as he was – smiling, expansive, inquisitive, gentle, affectionate – and I don't want to open wounds by journeying back. But the Museum's treatment of me was so deliberate and so calculated that it will be difficult ever to blot it from my mind.

Last week was Birmingham week, a really awful two days of good works which made me wonder why I did it. On Wednesday there was a fund-raising lunch for the Birmingham Royal Ballet at the Botanic Gardens. The intention was good, the food and wine execrable and the company the rich who could afford to come to midweek lunches. The woman who organised it seemed not to have organised such a thing before. I did my stuff like blazes and that went well. But she'd never thought through the implications of asking someone to come and do all this. No thought had been given as to what was to happen to us. We were stuck in the twenty-third floor of a tower-block hotel, from which Birmingham looked like a city in the Midwest. Foolishly, we had tried to walk to the theatre but came up against the freeways and retreated back and got a taxi.

The ballet, Bintley's *Far from the Madding Crowd*, was a lack-lustre B-movie job with music that all sounded the same, much like the identikit characters on stage. The choreography was limp sub-Ashton. The next day was passed seeing Birmingham. It was freezing cold and half the City Art Gallery, once great, was shut as the roof leaked. In the evening I did my stuff for the Birmingham Society of Artists at a meal to woo sponsors. They were sweet and well meaning. It was Penny Cobham who had landed me for that. God knows why I agreed, but she has guts and lives off being a quango queen, albeit one whose original features must still exist beneath the external plasterwork. She's still on the V&A Board and it amused me to outrage her. Julia had a good time with David Mellor, whose hair is his only asset and needs restyling on from a couple of decades ago. But he's knowledgeable and bright and a sad monument to the loss of someone we need.

OCTOBER

Feast: A History of Grand Eating *is launched*

Books don't only have to be written but they have to be sold, so off I go again doing a week of trolling round the bookshops, signing like blazes anything in sight that I'd written, on the principle that a signed book is a sold one, and doing a string of radio interviews, both national and local. The only one that wasn't a straightforward interview was *The Verb* on Radio 3, a gathering around a cellophane-wrapped plate of rather poor sandwiches which passed for a feast as we made dinner-table conversation. But it was bright and amusing, with a presenter who said that he'd never been to nor given a dinner party. I had a lovely time sending him up on that one. There was a beguiling American poet, Mark Doty, and an equally beguiling storyteller from Norfolk, Hugh Lupton. The real name there, however, was Margaret Drabble, hugely intelligent, if humourless and dour, and looking for all the world like I remember my aunts looking when they had jelled into that 1930s suburbia look. She'd suffered, and still does (although you'd never know it), from stammering. She's no sparkling star but I warmed to her inch by inch as the programme progressed. She'd clearly made up her mind about me again and was discomfited to have to revise her opinion, or so I felt.

Wednesday, however, was the great day. After a breakfast viewing of the Pompadour exhibition at the National Gallery (they killed her off), it was to the Abbey for the sixtieth anniversary of El Alamein. It was packed and with a roll-call of royals: the Duke of Edinburgh, the Princess Royal, Princess Alexandra, the Duke of Kent and the Gloucesters. It went off like clockwork but lacked something at the end.

In the evening there was an amazing launch dinner for *Feast* at

Syon House for those who had worked on the book and a journalist from *The Times*. It was dinner as it would have been served about 1750, correct in every detail, an event we owed to a stirling young man called Marc Meltonville, who headed the seven footmen in powdered wigs and full-skirted coats who pandered to our every need. Every single dish was cooked as at that period and the food presented as such: two courses and then we stood for dessert to be laid, so it was something like thirty different dishes in all. Oddly, it was visually not very exciting; but what was delightful was the intensity of taste, and the fact that one ate all these dishes like *mezze* in a Lebanese restaurant, a spoonful of this and a spoonful of that, all on the same plate. The evening ended with the lads tossing off their wigs and joining us. This was a PR event with something in it for everyone: Syon House; the food group called Historia; Cape, who published the book; and *The Times*, in the form of Richard Morrison. We were warned that what is weird is to have so many servants but we got over that quite quickly and conversation reeled across the table. David Hutt appeared in his Abbey scarlet with a *c.*1910 robe over it, which put us all in the shade. We had a crisis as one guest dropped out at the last moment, but we got Henrietta Green of the Food and Wine Lovers Society to step in. Looking like a *madame* by Toulouse-Lautrec, her forthright conversation set the tone and we never looked back.

It was such a crammed week. I started on coronations in the Abbey Archives, lunched with Arabella Pike of HarperCollins (who outbid Random House for *Coronation*), gave lunch to the evanescent Simon Thurley (who has decided that we're stuck with New Labour and therefore it is better to oppose inside the system than without it), went to John Birt's launch party at the Travellers where I saw Beryl Bainbridge, Roger Graef, Simon Jenkins (rather grand, as always) and David Mellor, and then on to the Wallace Collection for another bash, this time of the art mafia. All I did was rush and

rush. It was a week well spent but left me tired. I couldn't go back
to the old life.

24 NOVEMBER

Great Britons

This was a fiasco. I travelled up from the country to be part of the
audience (although Alison Weir and I were led to believe otherwise) in the BBC competition to find the ten 'Greatest Britons' by
popular choice. The ten made up a somewhat bizarre assembly, con-
firming one's views as to the decline of education and the absence
of any kind of powers of judgement by the populace. Churchill,
Elizabeth I and Newton appeared, unbelievably, alongside Princess
Diana and John Lennon. This was a madhouse of an occasion held
in an arena studio in White City, with all the usual paraphernalia
attending TV game shows. The presenter was the made-over Anne
Robinson, while the large-limbed Peter Snow cavorted before an
assembly of celebs and a screen describing the rise and fall in the
voting as though it were odds at the Derby. Indeed, this was the
world of *Hello* magazine projected backwards: any pretence that
the proponents of these heroes or heroines really knew anything
about them had been wholly abandoned, as inaccuracies whirled
around like confetti.

I can't recall who they all were now. There was a dull professor
advocating Old Noll; a baby-faced, fair-haired, Oxford TV don;
Tristram Hunt, who was way out of his depth backing Newton; bat-
eared but beguiling Andrew Marr plugging Darwin; Mo Mowlam, a
mound in pink with a blonde wig like tendrils of seaweed, Churchill;
suave Michael Portillo, his hair smoothed to perfection, Gloriana;
and the egregious and acerbic A.A. Gill, grinning like a death's head,

Shakespeare. I can't recall the rest. These sat on a circular rostrum facing each other as the tests of greatness were gone through and argued and as the audience yelled support and waved banners for their particular candidate.

The whole event was an index of the world into which we have moved, where Everyman's opinion has as much validity as someone who has spent a lifetime mastering the subject. It was in character, therefore, that the pert, blonde tabloid editor Rosie Boycott talked about Princess Diana as though she were Mother Teresa, Florence Nightingale and Naomi Campbell rolled into one. The only defence of all this ridiculous exercise was that it made those who looked at it at least realise that the nation had a history and that it was studded with remarkable human beings who had changed things forever. The same argument could be made for Simon Schama and David Starkey's TV histories. At least they epitomise the failure of New Labour's attempt to wipe out the nation's past.

It was a relief that Churchill won, meaning that even now the population had grasped that his victory was not only a military but also an ideological one. But Brunel as number two and Diana as number three made me cringe. As the ticker-tape and glitter dust fell from the ceiling and the winning proponents stood by their choices, wax figures imported from Madame Tussaud's, I groaned. Is this the survival and transmission of a proud history or is its proletarianisation? I wonder. I did my bit for Gloriana, yelling out that but for her and her reign none of the others would ever have existed. At least she rose from number eight to number seven, but what a waste of time!

DECEMBER

Death of a schoolteacher

Alasdair Hawkyard had always promised me that he would signal if anything 'happened' to Joan Henderson. I'd rung her the previous Friday. There was something about that conversation which worried me. It wasn't somehow right. The next week Alasdair rang me and said that she had fallen over and been carted off to St Mary's, Paddington. 'What's the exact situation?' I asked. 'No, I don't think she'll come out.' She wouldn't eat and already her system was breaking up. Her legs had started to bleed through the swelling and her heart was clearly failing.

I got there off the train on Monday. I knew that I had to go but that didn't make it any easier. I argued my way to her bedside. No, I wasn't family but, yes, I'd known her since I was twelve. She'd taught me as a child. I was gestured towards the sad spectacle. Alasdair, when he had gone, hadn't been able to leave in under three hours as she clutched his hand. She had now gone far beyond being capable of even that. There seemed little left beneath the bedclothes. She had tubes stuck into her and a mask over her mouth. But in spite of that, she looked much the same as I always remembered her.

What can you do but talk, and I found myself on a stream of memory and chatter, about the garden, the cats, the house, the weather – and then – I could see that she knew it was me. Her eyes rolled and her head lifted itself and I found myself recalling the old days, how last weekend I'd taken from the shelf *The English Icon*, which I'd dedicated to her. How she introduced me to the Elizabethan age, given me books by A.L. Rowse and C.V. Wedgwood to read, how I'd show her my costume drawings, how much I owed to her, to those years and that giving by a schoolteacher to a lower middle-class boy from nowhere at a grammar school on the fastnesses of the Great Cambridge Road, but stage-struck and mad about the Virgin Queen and her many dresses and portraits. I couldn't sustain this for more than fifteen minutes or so, I think. There was nothing I could do. No way that I could help. I could only offer her my love and thanks and say goodbye before my voice completely cracked up.

Away from it all, I did crack up. It was my childhood gone. I prayed that she would fade quickly and that prayer was answered. Thanks be to God. I saw her at about one o'clock on the Monday afternoon and she peacefully passed away at about four o'clock the following morning. It was as though she'd hung on, hoping that I'd come, and when I had it was somehow all right to let go. She was eighty-seven, so one mustn't mourn but give thanks that the end was quick and unprolonged.

To one's schoolteacher one is always a child. I don't think that she had ever grasped how much I had changed. She was such a prop to me when, shy, awkward, immature, I went up to the university. Always a letter would come. I was so grateful for that, amidst the isolation. And yet the relationship worked on certain principles, with parameters that were not to be crossed. Her letters, always after marriage, began 'Dear Roy and Julia', because I'm sure she believed that a married man should not be receiving letters from an unmarried woman. They always ended 'Yours sincerely', to the very end. Hers to me were an endless round based on the Institute of Historical Research, seminars and lectures, and her visits to Kew Gardens. I'm told that the interior of her house had to be seen to be believed. Her mother had brought her up to be a 'lady', so she couldn't cook or do anything domestic. The few who penetrated beyond the front door said that it was utter chaos. And yet she always appeared clad in a silk dress or suit, with her hair neat and with no trace of the mess from which she had emerged. A curious vocal mannerism was that she ended every other sentence with the word 'altogether'.

When I was in the sixth form she used to rush up to the Institute of Historical Research every Monday for Sir John Neale's seminar. That intrigued me and I was eventually to go to it myself, although I didn't warm to the old rogue. Joan was doing a thesis on the 1587 parliament. I can't think that she ever finished it. Her kindness to us was memorable. I once caught her out of the corner of my eye giving money to a working-class lad from Edmonton. That was a heroic period in the aftermath of the post-war Education Act, when teachers had a vision and a social conscience to help those forward who had never before had a chance. But she would tell me about exhibitions I ought to see and lend me the catalogue. At that age those small things are so important, glimpses into worlds unknown to one's family, the worlds of art and history to which I was so strongly drawn.

But her vision was also circumscribed. She had to shut out things. I recall that when my father died I wrote her a long letter on that fatal relationship, knowing that she had met my parents once and would therefore be the one person who would have understood the trauma of it all. But her letter back never referred to what I'd written. The door was shut. On my mother's death I wrote a similar missive but this time it was not sent.

She inspired great loyalty in a group of younger friends who looked after her, fetched and carried her and included her in many an event. She was stoic. She never grumbled or moaned, she was always interested in what everyone was doing. That was a rare and extraordinary quality, which endeared her to all those younger friends. My debt to her remains incalculable. Unlike Frances Yates, she had no will to intellectually dominate and hold you in subservience. In that sense, in the line of intellectual women who have littered my life, my relationship with Joan Henderson was one of the easiest.

2003

My lecture tour in 2000 was such a success that I was asked back to a country with which I had fallen in love.

13 FEBRUARY

Lunch with Dame Elisabeth Murdoch, Cruden Farm near Melbourne

We were invited to visit Rupert Murdoch's mother, the remarkable Dame Elisabeth Murdoch. She opened the door herself, an extraordinary ninety-four-year-old woman. She was so eager to see us, smiling, arms outstretched in greeting, eyes sparkling. I presented her with *A Country Life* and *Garden Party*. She knew what I'd written garden-wise back to front. 'Did Julia get what you'd promised her for her seventieth?' Alas, no, she didn't. It was a rill. But I was amazed at her retention of everything and the thrill of getting a second copy of *Garden Party* so that she could pass on the first to her gardener, Michael. Almost at once it was 'Let's tour the garden'. The buggy was drawn up at the front door. 'Only room for four,' she said. Dame Elisabeth took the wheel with Julia at her side. Marilyn Darling and I clambered on the back and off we whirled.

Dame Elisabeth in her mid-nineties was quite a phenomenon. In an odd kind of way she reminded me of the Queen Mother. She was a delight and interested in everything, wanted all the gossip about mutual gardening friends and acquaintances like Christopher Lloyd, Mollie Salisbury, Valerie Finnis and Anne Scott-James. She was dressed in the inevitable blue silk dress with diamond and pearl earrings, her face wreathed in smiles. The Darlings said they'd never seen her on such a high but, after all, it was one of those dreamlike meetings of gardeners.

The garden itself is a landscape one with a few formal touches. It gently cascades away from the house, which is embraced by richly planted beds and evergreens. The house itself, picturesque and asymmetrical, is a cottage that grew, painted white. The flower beds serpentine away from it and open vistas to what is a small park with specimen trees and a small meandering lake with two islands. Soft 1980s colours predominate: white, lavender, violet, blue and purple, but very little yellow. There is a potager with box hedges, including a pink-crimson dahlia named in her honour, and standard honeysuckles in the manner of Cranbourne Manor, which she admired. It is a very 1980s English-style garden, cottage into country house but with no real 'rooms' in the Hidcote or Sissinghurst sense. The atmosphere distils the graciousness and charm of the woman, one who was also alive to what is going on today. There is an absence of sculpture or built architecture, apart from a perfectly placed bronze of dolphins on a piece of rock.

The interior of the house is domestic, not grand or intimidating, with a nostalgic clutter in a setting that evokes a yeoman or lesser gentry house with rambling panelled rooms hung with fine paintings by the likes of E. Phillips-Fox, Augustus John, E. Bunny and Stanley Spencer. The drawing room is Edwardian Georgian, painted in light colours and with a bouquet of Marianne North botanical paintings. The dining room is dark-panelled and filled with two refectory tables. A friendly housekeeper cooked and helped Dame Elisabeth serve the food for what was an unpretentious lunch, with a bouquet of roses from the garden mingled with honeysuckle 'Graham Thomas' in the centre of the table.

The other guest was Sue Walker, who runs the quite marvellous Victorian Tapestry Workshop. This is one of Australia's great achievements: and we'd only just seen the stupendous tapestry designed by Arthur Boyd for the New Parliament Building. Sue was happy as she had commissions to keep the Workshop going for the next eighteen months. But I was struck by Dame Elisabeth's intense interest in her and her enormous curiosity about everything. To me she was the epitome of old age at its serene best: she was lucky to have the genes but lucky also to have that insatiable curiosity, enthusiasm and sense of delight. As with the Queen Mother, every day at ninety-four was still an adventure.

14 MARCH

Commonwealth Day

This is the end of a rare, hectic London week that began on Monday with Commonwealth Observance at the Abbey. This was quite the best I'd attended so far, although disaster struck at the end, for the exiting procession couldn't proceed through the nave as the final happening, whatever it was, was still going on. The result was that the procession ended up in a heap in the north aisle. It was chaos and I only just stepped back in time as the Queen, in purple and wearing a good diamond spray brooch, sauntered by. We never quite recovered from that and when we could eventually move off again Douglas

Hurd and I had become detached from the Dean. Our motto was 'Always follow the Dean' and we'd lost him; I then grabbed Douglas and moved up behind the Dean, who had now attached himself to the Queen. Little did we know that we'd pushed ourselves in front of the Prince of Wales. I don't think anyone noticed!

Hardy Amies we'd known for decades, he usually feeling the cloth of my suit and muttering 'nice bit of stuff'. He again epitomised the end of an era. He still believed that there was such a thing as a lady.

15 MARCH

Farewell to Hardy Amies

We drove down to Hardy's funeral on a bright spring day. Langford is one of those dream Cotswold villages where no peasants exist, everyone has a large bank balance and lives in a rose-embowered stone house or cottage. As we drew near it was clear that there was to be a large turn-out, about two hundred I would guess, with a coach bringing fifty or so down from the 'shop'. We made our way to the Old School House, pretty as a picture with box-edged beds filled with white hyacinths and the honeysuckle entwined over the front wall about to spring into blossom in response to the warm sunshine.

We got in through the back door to find the house full of desultory groups of the 'shop' and carers. We introduced ourselves to each other. It was an easy-to-run, unpretentious house, a large drawing room with a tapestry swagged along one wall, lined with bookcases, a sprinkling of blue and white china, needlepoint chairs (his work), a portrait of the Winter Queen – rather a bad version with the shaving-brush white plume in her hair – a bashed painting of a Jacobean lady and prints of various Stuarts. Either side of the chimneypiece there were double doors, one set leading to a commodious kitchen and the other to the dining room. Outside there was the garden, not at all large, consisting in the main of Cotswold stone paths and walls, a summerhouse and beds filled with roses. I was always puzzled by Hardy's reputation as a gardener. Upstairs there were two guest rooms, one of which was Ken Fleetwood's. Hardy's bedroom was hung with prints, good, bad and indifferent, of the Stuarts.

David Freeman had organised everything perfectly. The coffin was draped with a carpet that Hardy had embroidered with all his favourite flowers. On the top was his KCVO pinned to a cushion, together with swathes of the flowers that he loved. Inside the coffin there was a sprig of rosemary from his own garden; at the last minute a sprig was plucked from his sister's garden to add to it. I brought up the rear of the procession to the church, which was very near. It was crammed inside, while outside was a sprinkling of press photographers.

The coffin sat on trestles before the chancel arch with two clergy on one side and the singers on the other. It was a simple sequence of sung pieces and communal hymns, readings and prayers. Ian Garlant read the piece that Hardy had written for *Interiors* when he was ninety-two, which spoke of his love of the village: charming. I ascended the pulpit and gave my address and made them laugh, for he was a wonder and a wicked old thing. He ended up, however, a country gent in mock Jacobean and made his exit via the parish church.

Afterwards we gathered at The Barn [another part of Hardy's domain, away from the house] for a glass of wine and nibbles. Those there included villagers, those who looked after him, a phalanx from the 'shop' and local friends like the Faringdons and Hornbys. Apart from the odd bequest to the National Trust and others, he left the lot to David Freeman. I am so glad. David did everything for him during the final years.

It did strike me how little, apart from the building, Hardy had of any value. It was strange that he purchased reproductions of prints of the Stuarts when he could so easily have acquired originals. There was not a single decent picture in the house, not one, nothing in the least personal suggesting an accumulation through the decades. That I thought odd.

2 JUNE

The fiftieth anniversary of the Coronation

We travelled to London yesterday so that I could go to the rehearsal of the service at Westminster Abbey to mark the fiftieth anniversary of the Coronation. The Abbey looked stunning, with blue and yellow flowers and altar frontal and batteries of television lights. Like all rehearsals, it was a somewhat desultory affair with the incongruity of the Yeomen of the Guard with their hats on and no costume, clasping halberds bagged at the top, and the state trumpeters in mufti, their trumpet banners covered for protection. Wesley Carr rallied the troops and we went through our paces as it was quite complex.

Came the day and I arrived in good time to put on my new red and black, as worn by the rest of College, amidst the usual hustle and bustle of everyone vesting. At a given signal, off we went to stand *en tableau*, facing the West Door. Wesley and David Hutt, their 1953 copes fluttering, went down to the gates to welcome the Queen, who stepped out in pale yellow with a better hat than of late. The state trumpeters gave a stirring fanfare from the choir screen, after which we corporately greeted her. Then we all turned and a vast procession was formed, which, I gather, looked quite something.

Douglas Hurd and I went to our usual perches to the north of the High Altar, facing the two archbishops along with a phalanx of assorted clergy – canons, the Cardinal, the Free Church Moderator, the Bishop of London and others. As usual, at a diagonal, we could glance down to the royal party forming two rows in the south transept. The Queen with Prince Charles to her left, then Prince William and the Duke of York; on her right sat Prince Philip and, in the row behind, the rest. Prince William could become the new David Beckham, a real pin-up, fresh and sweet-natured and shy. Princess Michael, her husband in Russia, wore a ridiculously over-large hat; the Edward Kents together, she looking quite weird, her face ashen; the Princess Royal and her husband together; Princess Alexandra and Angus, he still looking emaciated; and then the Harewoods, he like a bearded Moses and she in a hat with a flower garland.

There were many of the loyal and aged tucked here and there. Julia spoke to Gay Charteris and opposite she saw poor Hugh Grafton minus both legs. I glimpsed Anne Glenconner. Julia found herself next to an eighty-seven-year-old canon from Australia who had been a minor canon at the Abbey in 1953. As far as one could ever make a service of this kind work, it worked. I thought it lacked some kind of movement or action, such as the crown being placed on the altar. But the theme of everyone sharing the Queen's ideals of dedication as epitomised in 1953 was about as good as you could get. Everyone read well and it went off like clockwork, with lots of trumpeting in the hymns and good singing.

After the blessing and the National Anthem, which we all sang with fervour, off we went again, this time out through the West Door. As the Queen appeared we all applauded, at which she lit up and smiled. What she was thinking about I know not. All the royals went down the line of choirboys, making chirpy remarks, and that was it. Douglas and I were at the back but we could study their faces: impassive, inquiring, ageing, ashen, lifted, wrinkled, sunburnt – each told a story.

Later that day I walked back from the London Library. As I passed the Palace a flotilla of taxis came out of it festooned with yellow and blue balloons and Union Jacks and the cross of St George. They were stuffed with children who'd been to the Palace party. Clever old Palace.

I agreed to take a group to look at some famous German gardens, which proved to be the preface to tragedy.

30 JUNE

A difficult year

We are in Weimar on a hot day and I am conscious that most of this year so far has passed without record. The urge to write ebbs and flows and usually calls for events to animate the pen. Often, however, those that do leave me so tired afterwards that I have no energy to record them. So how has 2003 been? The great success was the February trip to Australia, organised by Marilyn Darling and sponsored by the Circle of Friends. I worked ferociously hard: Brisbane, Canberra, Melbourne, Adelaide and Sydney. At each one a mega event in a gallery: a lecture and a drinks party, the audiences anything from three to six or even seven hundred. A lot of give-out, but I loved it all. I find that Australia lifts me with its freshness and enthusiasm. So that was wonderful.

I then entered the dark night of the book on The Laskett garden. The designer turned out to be a depressive who failed to turn up at the crucial meeting with the layouts of the book and locked himself in his office. Then followed five weeks of nervous tension and hell for me. I don't recall ever having gone through such a drama. The book meant so much to me. Had he done any work? What had he done with the material? This utterly exhausted me and the whole team around it. He wouldn't communicate by letter, phone, fax or email. Even when a delegation went round to him he wouldn't open the door.

The result of all of this was that a kind of eczema exploded all over me and I had a second hernia. It emotionally exhausted me with worry. Eventually the designer released what he had, revealing that the work had not been done and what he had done was all over the place. The luckless in-house designer was faced with re-laying out the entire book in four days. The publication date had to be moved forward a month. Everything has been affected. This is my worst publishing experience so far.

So it's been a very bad year on that front. It also meant that all my planning went awry and I had to cope with the book as the designer disgorged it, when I was committed to other things: an article on Beaton, a script for a poetry reading centring on Elizabeth I and heaven alone knows what else. What can be said about shunting a small group around this part of Germany is that I've had nine to ten hours' sleep every night and it has taken my mind away from the ghastly mess I've been through.

I'm within reach of 1533 in the Coronation book and there's a nice new job of being editor of a kings and queens series for the Folio Society. But I want to get on with the main book and I want the hernia operation out of the way. I see the specialist on 24 July and I've booked in to have the op on 28 July. That means being careful afterwards at The Laskett. *Feast* was nominated as one of three candidates for the food book of the year by the Guild of Food Writers but I didn't get it. I've kept trundling around lecturing: Scottish National Portrait Gallery, Waddesdon, the Purcell Room for the National Trust, etc. And a lot of radio and television snippets on Painshill, David Bailey, Queen Victoria, my candidate for the best novel, castle, garden, etc. Paul Brason's portrait of me hugging Lettice went into the Royal Society of Portrait Painters exhibition and Tessa Traeger's photograph of me *en profile* into the *Gardener's Labyrinth* exhibition at the National Portrait Gallery. There are too many portraits of me around, I feel. And I gave a lecture on regional portraiture to the Victoria County History historians, which is going to be printed. The lecture on the portraits of the second Earl of Essex went to the *British Art Journal*, together with the one which began its life at the National Portrait Gallery as 'National Portrait Gallery: No Lavatories' now re-titled 'National Portrait Gallery: The Missing Years'. Robin Simon, the editor, was thrilled to get them, especially the latter. It is good to get all of this stuff in print rather than not.

So now it's all calm before the publication of *The Laskett* on 1 October. It is to be serialised in *The Times* Saturday colour supplement for three weeks in September. I don't know how that book will be greeted but I felt compelled to write it.

21 JULY

Sickness and exhaustion

This continues to be a bad year. On Monday 30 June we got onto the plane at Frankfurt and didn't move for two hours, trapped into our economy seats. We were then told that the plane was no good and were taken off and eventually put on to another one. This was a journey from hell. By the time we got home that night we were done in. The next day Julia became breathless. I didn't like it at all so I persuaded her that she ought to see the doctor. Her appointment was fixed for 3.50 p.m. At 3.30 p.m. she said that she wasn't capable of driving there so we arranged for the doctor to come here. Dr England arrived just after 6 p.m. By then Julia was in pain under her left breast. The doctor didn't know what it was but thought that she ought to be in hospital. No bed could be found and the conclusion was that it could ride until the next day. Dr England's last words were: 'If she collapses in the night ring 999.'

By Wednesday Julia was really bad. I rang the surgery and asked that the doctor come to her. She came. An ambulance was urgent but took two hours to arrive. It was so awful. Thank God that we got Julia in to hospital in time. Every terrible thought tumbled through my mind. Next day I learnt what it was: DVT (deep vein thrombosis) thanks to the airline. A triple thrombosis is on her lung. If it had reached the heart she would have been dead. As a consequence she was in Hereford County Hospital in Accident and Emergency with an oxygen mask for the next five days. She had had a miracle escape. The shock and emotional toll all this has taken of me I cannot describe. This is not our year.

She came home the following Thursday, weak and on warfarin. I've cancelled everything and the intention is to stay put, be quiet and consolidate. I'm still troubled with eczema and there's the hernia operation to come. Julia has come back with a hospital virus, which now I've got. The message all this sends me is that the body is giving signals to slacken pace or else. So I'm never again going to take a group abroad. At sixty-seven it's a killer. Also, when it comes to book promotion, that must be controlled. The eczema began on my leg last autumn, when I was pushing *Feast* like blazes. All round it must be a more sedate pace of life.

On the up side, the builders are here and we're paving and transforming the Rose Garden with sandstone and gravel. The golden yew, sadly a mistake, is to go, making way for larger beds, low yew hedging and some larger roses. Having created the Rose Garden, my thoughts run to the porch of the house, with a plan to demolish it next year and erect a larger one, with a new front door flanked by a pair of free-standing classical columns made of reconstituted stone. Earlier this year I commissioned Reg Boulton to carve an inscription to go above the front door: 'PAX INTRANTIBUS' (Peace be to whoever enters this house). I saw it in Edinburgh when I was there for the literary festival. It is such a wonderful thought to express. He has now arrived with the plaque, which is beautiful. The top of the drive is being gravelled too.

8 SEPTEMBER

Stressed out

No diary written and it is hardly surprising. Here I am, sitting in the Nuffield Hospital awaiting my hernia operation. Julia is over the way in the Hereford County for the fourth time. This has been a quite DREADFUL four months. She has been in hospital four times. The first time she came home with a virus, which she gave to me, so the hernia operation was cancelled until today. She then got more thromboses, so went back in again. Then her legs became swollen. The local surgery said that it was phlebitis. It wasn't. Back in again. It was cellulitis. So out again. And then something else set in, which worried me to death. She hardly ate and her legs were in agony. She took ages to stagger downstairs and spent most of the day flat on her back. A blood sample was taken and last Friday she was taken back in again. They don't know what it is, probably some kind of blood poisoning and very likely another hospital virus. Poor love, she's so stoic and positive but all of this has eroded us. I'm terribly stressed out. The eczema on my legs is a horror of redness, flaking skin and scabs. It is difficult not to feel the tension of it all as we enter the third month of catastrophes. There must be a light at the end of the tunnel and so many people have been so kind. Friendship is a wonderful thing and I thank God for it. Antonia Fraser tells me to read the Book of Job but to skip the too gloomy bits!

Meanwhile, *The Laskett: The Story of a Garden* has arrived. It looks beautiful and I'm so glad to have written it, a kind of testament to a life. The result of all this is that I can't do cerebral work. I potter in the garden and go to bed at 9.30 p.m. and get nine hours' rest. I haven't felt like this since the worst V&A days. It'll pass.

3 SEPTEMBER

The garden

This is the year of the Rose Garden revolution. We had been planning to do this on and off for years. Julia drew up the scheme, a mixture of sandstone and Victorian industrial brick with the gaps in the paving in-filled with gravel, as we'd seen in the Botanic Gardens in Singapore. Geoff and Gerry Davies did a splendid job, a real architectural garden with all the geometry correct. These are spandrel beds, not to go round but to be looked at from one side only. John Glenn has produced a gift of 'Faulkener' box and I've splashed out and bought eight large box cones, which I will clip into obelisks to act as sentinels. Some twenty tons of new topsoil is needed and I've ordered more roses to top up the existing ones. The theme is pink with *Alchemilla mollis* and astrantia 'Hadspen Blood', as before. But there are to be large roses at the back, six to nine feet high and with hips to provide autumn interest.

Into that has fitted, as though it was meant to be, an exact copy of the Lutyens bench at Hestercombe. This is the almost overwhelming gift of an American, Wally Marx, who was 'converted' to gardening by a lecture I gave in Minneapolis. He petitioned to come and see the garden and he came and lunched and was a delight and is now an email friend. I feel almost embarrassed by his generosity; the plan is to add some kind of inscription to record the gift.

6 SEPTEMBER

Alone

So much of what has happened during the last two months has left me eroded and meditative. It was so awful that I nearly lost Julia. And then, during those days alone in the house, becoming conscious that it could, one day, be that way round. That would be something huge to come to terms with but God, I know, will give me that strength. I don't know how people manage without a faith, I really don't. Always it is something to sustain, to rest on in a strange way, to feel held by. Moments of recollection, prayer, giving thanks and petitioning for strength – remembrance of others – all gather the mind and its thoughts powerfully.

SENTENCE OF DEATH

I have just looked at my last entry. My fears have turned to reality. Last Thursday, 10 September, I was asked to come late to the hospital so that I could see Dr Williams. Julia was in bed in a room of her own. She looked so beautiful. Dr Williams came in and sat on the bed facing me and told me that she had cancer of the pancreas and liver and that it was terminal. It seems so cold to write this and I was stunned. Julia said, 'I'm going to fight it all the way', and she is strong, but this is a battle that can only be lost. She looked at me and said, 'How shall we handle it?' I said, 'Be open and honest about it.' The only way is head-on. I recall how a friend had once asked me 'What happens if she goes first?' – a comment that threw me but produced the immediate response 'God is gracious'. When the doctor left, I threw my arms around her and held her and told her how much I loved her and how I would to the end of time. But I was composed. She will need all the support that I can give her. I only cried when I got to the waiting taxi, where our village driver, the gentle giant Mick Davies, was waiting for me. He's a lesson for anyone about humanity.

Sarah Greenall brought Julia home on Friday. Julia loves her and the decision was reached that she should be a trustee. Gil and Sarah have been true friends, younger ones, which is what I will need in the aftermath. Everything whirs around in my mind so much that I don't know where to start. All the ringing up of everyone was a mighty operation. The hospital left us both with no direction as to what should be done. This particular form of cancer is quick. Anyone that I've asked says two to three months. Two have already gone. I don't think that she will last more than six weeks, but who knows? I pray to God that it is quick.

We agreed on openness, on dying at home in this beloved house and garden amidst the cats and the cornucopia of memory. We agreed no palliatives, no being seduced on the cancer ladder. The pain must be alleviated and she must be as comfortable as possible and she must die in her own bed, as she said, able to reach out with one hand to me and with the other to God.

This is a house of faith. The only thing I regret not happening in hospital, because the timing was all wrong, was that the chaplain was to have brought her the Sacrament. But I rang Kay Garlick and arranged for it to be brought weekly. On Sunday I placed two chairs for us, facing the garden, and on the table two candlesticks and a scattering of Palm Sunday crosses. I waited for Kay at the bottom of the drive, for it was Christ entering this house. The light was golden and surreal. I said to Kay, 'I welcome Christ' and he must enter beneath the inscription 'PAX INTRANTIBUS'. This was a powerful experience. The pyx box was placed amidst the wreath of crosses and she sat facing us. I'm glad for Julia's sake that it was the old words and for the first time ever she spoke the responses. After communing I took her hand and she extended hers to Kay. Julia hated the touching part of the new service, so this was very significant. With emotion I extended my hand to Kay and, with the three of us thus linked, we said 'Peace be with you'.

Julia is so amazing, so strong, so definite. There is so much to do and I want everything sorted while she is still *compos mentis*. We discussed the funeral, where her ashes were to go, the memorial service. 'No, I don't want "Nimrod"', and 'I don't want "The Lord is my Shepherd"', and 'I want the coffin in the church and not carried in to a dirge'. I got virtually everything arranged, down to a drawing of quinces to be on the cover of the service sheet for her memorial service – or rather, 'A Service of Thanksgiving for the Life and Work of Julia Trevelyan Oman'.

I owe a huge debt to David Freeman, who looked after Hardy Amies. I remember him saying ages ago, 'I'm an expert on carers'. Through him we got on to Miriam Warner, who arrived on Sunday. She's a star and told us everything that had to be done and organised.

Monday was a blitz day and I felt proud of myself. I arranged for Dr Davies to come during the day and not after six; he came about noon, and he and only he will deal with Julia. At four Miriam returned with Carol, a nurse, and much else was put in place. Julia liked Carol, which was crucial. At five the district nurse, Helen Marshall, came and more things were put in order. So now I await oxygen tanks, supplementary foods and visits from the hospice and the therapist.

I opened a little book in which to write everything down. I waved it at Julia while she was in bed and she said, 'It's the only way you'll get through this. It's a production.' I said to her that I thought that I ought to learn to drive again. She said, 'I've thought of that. You've got to have a Ford Fiesta with automatic gear change.'

Everyone is so grateful for our honesty, for facing this. I have never felt so sustained by prayer before. I know that I am held up by the thoughts and prayers of so many. Two candles burn in Westminster Abbey, where we are prayed for. It is a terrific experience to go through, one for which I need spiritual, intellectual, emotional and physical strength. And I have to think beyond it. I was told Valerie Grove's piece on me appeared in *The Times*. In a way this is like the last act in a play.

Julia was fine yesterday but there was a downturn on Sunday. She is in pain but doesn't want to start on painkillers until she can't bear it. I can see her physically change as she doesn't eat and from time to time there is a flicker of that otherworldly look. She eats little except soup, porridge, fruit purée and bland foods. I now cook and eat on my own, as I must not let my strength slide. I've lost half a stone already and that is not helpful.

The grieving process has started and I let my emotions fully flow away from her. That's not to say that there aren't emotional moments, but crying in front of her is no help. Her thoughts and worries will be about me. So I go into the garden or go for a walk each day and give way to grief and tears.

16 SEPTEMBER

A quiet day, Julia much revived. No mortuary for her but her coffin, when it leaves this house, is to be placed in the orchard with her head towards the stag, covered with a tarpaulin until it goes to the church. There will be no florist's flowers. Instead, she asked for them to be arranged by Carol Wells and Shaun to be like a Harvest Festival with medlars, quinces, apples and berries. Outside, the weather is a glorious Indian summer, far too hot, and the garden is a ruin through drought. Shaun asked me when she would come into the garden again. I said perhaps never. He said, 'I will get my video and bring it to her.' Neither of us wants the news, radio, television, newspapers – just the beauty of silence and each other. But all through the day the phone rings and there is so much for me to do on my own.

There is an equanimity and a peace and a pace to the situation today, after the shocks and dramas and organisation. The unknown quantity is how long. I pray for it to be short so that our minds are focused and each moment a marvel. If it goes on for months, I don't know how we will all sustain it. Life has to go on. I did buy a car today, a Ford Fusion, and also arranged my first driving lesson. That will give me something to focus on and conquer. But I can't work. How can I? Breakfast is late and then we sit together in the gothick sitting room. That is tranquil and precious time. And then from eleven on I must phone a litany of people. Today Julia began to phone herself. I work and give myself proper food and do her meals too, which are different. I must keep going as I am the linchpin of all this, but it is tiring. Once a day I have to get out and walk along the lane. There was not as much crying and grief today, rather a feeling of peace and collectedness. And all the time the sensation of those out there holding you in strength through thought and prayer. Today we have settled into something.

17 SEPTEMBER

A calm seems to have descended, a pattern and a tranquillity. I got up early, put on an old coat over my dressing gown and walked round the garden. It was so beautiful, misty and romantic, with all the golds, pinks and reds of autumn. I remembered what Shaun had said about bringing the garden into the house with his video. And I thought 'Get out your secateurs and bring the garden in another way', so I took my trug and filled it with branches of crab apples, red oak leaves, medlars, quinces, gourds and apples. And I arranged them as a still-life surprise for Julia in the gothick sitting room. 'Like a Caravaggio,' she said. She was better today, the spirit and the intellect there but tired in between. Shaun came in and hugged her, a great but beautiful surprise. As usual, I cried in the garden.

A catalogue of a country house sale arrived today and in it there was an eighteenth-century urn on a pedestal with four blank oval plaques. That's our tomb. Reg Boulton will do the plaques: JTO and dates, RS and dates, R and J and true lovers' knots, gilded rosemary and the Oman arms. I wrote to Garter King of Arms of my intent to adopt them: I couldn't afford to when I was knighted. This was a good and tranquil day. And domestic help appeared: Dinah rampaged through the house removing the cat fur and did a wash. I hated the house slipping. Now it's on an up.

18 SEPTEMBER

Tranquil. Beautiful. A wonderful therapist, Elizabeth Upham, came: such a gentle person, so unintrusive. What could make Julia's life more normal? One was a V-shaped cushion for her back and a different kind of cushion for the seat, to avoid sores. An incredibly sensitive woman, Elizabeth's parting words were 'The top priority is to get her out into the garden' – and it can be done with buggies and ramps. Then followed a panic as Julia feared those awful will columns published in the papers so much that much of the morning went on legal financial transfers to avoid anything appearing, so preserving our privacy.

The phone rang on and off all day. So much to do. We both reached the same conclusion, that I couldn't go on as we were. Much would have to change after the event. I'm ageing and will need a different set-up and more help. The break with beloved Dot will have to be in the aftermath and not later. Oh, how difficult. Thank God for breezy Dinah in her shorts, cleaning and dusting. I need someone like her. I deal with so many phone calls that I'm exhausted. Julia's sheer practicality is amazing, but it always has been. What has to be done and when and where and how can we work it? Has any man ever had a more extraordinary wife? I ache with love for her. Every day is like a dream.

19 SEPTEMBER

Elizabeth came with a wheelchair and ramps. Julia was disinclined to go out. She will decide. An apparatus for lowering her in and out of the bath was put aside until it's needed. The cushions, however, were accepted and used. Shaun did a blitz on the conservatory and I did a blitz on the tangle of evergreen geraniums. On the whole it was a tranquil day. Mirabel Osler and Prue Bellak came for just the right length of time, Prue looking ill and Mirabel like an autumn leaf in russets and reds. Julia told me to go to the Orchard and cut off two branches that had beautiful fruit hanging (I chose the 'Red Streak' apple) and tie them up with sprays of rosemary, in remembrance. Who could not be touched? She rang a lot of people, including Peter Wright and her old Royal College of Art friend, Jill. She wants me to stave off the family making visits. She wants to see Sir John Tooley. She sleeps most of the day and is resolutely not taking painkillers. Dinah takes the edge off the domestic chaos but most of my day goes, when not with Julia, on housework and administration.

I walked down to Llanwarne and looked at the church [for the funeral]. It's not really beautiful but we've worshipped there for years. It holds two hundred. Probably we'll need a relay to the village hall, which looks a wreck. We'll see. I found the hymn that she wanted from the service for Oliver Messel and faxed it through to David Hutt along with the text of Marvell's 'The Garden'. And I wrote to Patrick Garland asking him to read it.

Julia went to bed as usual at nine. She doesn't read, listen to the radio or look at television. She's contained within her own thoughts. I also went to bed at nine, for I too am so tired.

20 SEPTEMBER

Another day comes and goes. In the morning Julia struggled to her workroom and lay down on the 'casting couch', as she calls it and we went through the Trevelyan, Oman and Chadwick affairs, files and papers on pictures and objects. This took a long time and we didn't lunch until two. Nurse Marshall came, helpful as usual. We continued to think through the aftermath. I would need a cook-housekeeper living where Dot does now. We decided that the best solution was to try to buy another property, this time a good priva-tised village council house near here, into which Dot would go for her lifetime in return for help here. The estate can afford it and it would be an investment.

This was a quiet day, just what we needed. Julia shows no desire to use the wheelchair and go out. She always decides what she will do. She declared open acceptance of God and his will and her direct and simple Christian faith. A number of calls came, even one from beloved James Fairfax in Australia. More flowers arrived, including the prettiest Victorian posy from the production team at the Royal Opera House. Wonderful letters and cards were delivered, all of which go into a basket. The hall is awash with flowers.

I walked the loop to Hoarwithy and went to see David Wells to ask him to look out for the house we now wanted.

24 SEPTEMBER

Four days on. It was London on the Monday, a long and tiring day, in and out of the Morpeth Terrace flat and then to Westminster Abbey and David Hutt and finally to the Garrick Club to collect the Martin Leman painting of Larkin. David, as usual, was wonderful, much weeping and emotion on both sides. He'll take the funeral with Kay Garlick, and Wesley Carr has expressed a desire to come and give the Blessing. I was deeply touched and Julia, when told, humbled. We would all wear our red and blacks as members of the Collegiate Church of St Peter. That would meet Julia's desire for 'joyful colours'. David will put the service together and the service sheet will be printed in the Abbey. All around as I walked through the cloister I felt the strength of this house of faith praying for us.

Dot came in early, on crutches, looking really awful and tragic. It made me realise that I couldn't go on like this. On Tuesday David Wells came up with a small flat for about £65,000 or so in Tump Lane, a comedown after the comforts of Little Laskett. But you can't get a house for under £150,000 and that's a lot to lash out for no real return and I don't want a more complex property to cope with. Today I go to see it. The employment solicitor at Penningtons said that I was being more than generous: she would live in it for nothing during her lifetime, in return perhaps for two mornings here. But I fear that she won't like working for whoever I get. Oh dear, so many bridges to cross and all at once. I dread telling Dot. She has to have three months' notice to move out of Little Laskett.

On Monday Julia had Sarah Greenall for the rest of the day. Julia is so private that it is wonderful to see this real friendship and love between the two. I am so very grateful for it. More and more letters and flowers arrived. The Macmillan nurse came, a large and bouncy blonde. She was very good, but we're going to need a lot more in place beyond her. Friends keep me going: I ring Julie Nightingale, Julia MacRae and Beatrix Miller all the time. Beatrix excels all.

There's so much to do. I'm on the go all day, doing Julia's work and a lot of Dot's and all the administration. I flop into bed when Julia goes at 9 to 9.30 p.m. and get up at 6.45 a.m.

Julia began taking painkillers on Monday, just a couple of paracetamol, but Dr Davies told her to up the dose on Tuesday to be any good. She is very strong, but the weight loss is very noticeable and I can see the change in her face. I've always loved her to bits. It is so awful when she says 'I'm so sorry to put you through all this'. What is marriage about? It is about precisely that, seeing someone through to the very end.

25 SEPTEMBER

Paul Brason, that lovable bear of a man, came. Julia wanted to be painted by him. She had never wanted this before. I thought that it was to be pendant to the one of me and Lettice, but no, she wanted it to be conceived as she is now, reclining amidst shawls, with baskets of fruits and leaves and her beloved cat Souci nestling at her feet. No luck with Souci, who whisked off! But Paul's a big human being, so lovable to her. I was terribly moved by this. What he paints will be my memory of our last days together. As he went I hugged him and heaved with grief.

These are strange days. At 2 p.m. I went off with Paul, my driving instructor, a delightful, gentle man. I was stunned as he made me get into my new car and I drove it. It was not as worrying as I thought and his decision was such a right one. I do love the car. I'm going to keep at it until I can cope. Julia will then be reassured that I'm not marooned . . .

John Tooley, a stunning seventy-nine-year-old came. In spite of the disasters of his love life, this man has such dignity, directness and integrity. Julia adores him and they talked theatre for a long time, Julia never tiring. She asked him to do both the funeral and the service of thanksgiving addresses and he was both honoured and touched.

This was a good day, ordered, constructive, full of love and affection along with decisions and reality. Julia quoted the great Visconti: 'Death is part of life.' How true that is.

30 SEPTEMBER

Sunday and Monday were peaceful days, at the end of both of which Julia lay in her bed and said 'Thank you God for a lovely day'. Kay Garlick came with Communion again, this time administered beneath the Francia *Madonna and Child*. Julia seems on an even keel suddenly, eating more, lively but still tired, her legs and her left arm very painful. One has entered a mysterious time warp, not really knowing which day it is. It's a golden autumn with a beautiful light, marred only by the knowledge that the garden is in chronic drought. Julia is still composed, her face shrinking and more lined, with that attribute of the seriously ill of being wholly collected within themselves in silence and wanting no radio, television or music. I read the post to her as we sit looking at each other. I also read *The Man Who Planted Trees* sent by Nick Dunne. So many wonderful letters have arrived, which are put in a basket to be answered sometime . . .

The cathedral organist rang and I've got him or his deputy to play *Enigma* pieces at the beginning [of the funeral] but minus 'Nimrod', the cliché, and the march from *Nutcracker* at the end, following 'Now thank we all our God'. Julia said that tea ought to be provided afterwards in the village hall, a very good idea. To do it here would mean selecting a group of people, never a good idea. So throw it open to everyone and have a pell-mell. We find it strange not to know how long we have. Sensing this, we look each other in the eye and feel bewildered.

This, I fear, is the turning point. This week has been so good and then, suddenly, Julia's nose began to bleed in the afternoon. Her mother had the same thing with her cancer. Julia's nosebleeds over the last five years fall into place as a repetition of her mother's, signals of the cancer that we didn't know was there. The locum came twice and was very understanding but baffled. He plugged the nostril, and now Julia's face has a bloody stopper and bandages to keep it in place. The bleeding went on slowly all through the night. She did not sleep. Dr Davies came about noon on Saturday. The scenario was one he had hoped wouldn't happen. It is the one he dreaded. The choice was what to do that was the least negative. So the best option was to stop the warfarin so that her blood would cease being thin; but that would increase the danger of further thromboses. I now know that we are on the last journey. God give me strength and also love enough to cope with and bear what is to come.

I got on the phone at once to arrange a carer and a Marie Curie nurse, as Julia cannot be left on her own. She is very pale and weak. This is the worst-case scenario and I feel helpless. I mustn't go out of the house until someone is in post: a massive nosebleed or a thrombosis could occur, and that would be it. And yet I feel held by the prayers of so many supporting me: please, please, may they enfold me even more tightly during the period to come. Outside it is a lyrical, golden autumn day – the leaves change colour, crumple and fall – appropriate for what is happening indoors today.

5 OCTOBER

A quiet day. She looks so pale, so ill. Dr Davies came and unstopped the nostril. It didn't bleed. *Laus Deo*. But she looked so frail. I feel tremulous about this week. Kay Garlick came with Communion at 5 p.m. Beautiful. I am so grateful for that. I wish that I could get a focus on all of this but I can't. I'm suspended in time. But it goes on and on; when will it end and how? Everyone, though, is marvellous. This is something to sing about in old England, all those doctors, nurses and carers who give everything. It is so very moving. Day in and day out they do this work – unsung, uncelebrated – but Christ would be proud of them, if no one else.

7 OCTOBER

I've wasted so much time trying to get the various agencies to work in tandem, the District Nurse, the Marie Curie Nurses and Miriam Warner's Miracle Workers. All I want is someone in the house through the night. It will give me a sense of help and security. If Julia had a thrombosis I couldn't cope. The weather is windy and leaves are falling. My driving lesson is my only escape. It is so important to get out of the confines of the house, even for a brief period of time, for air, for the realisation of a whole world outside the closed drama within.

9 OCTOBER

Today she took a very sharp downturn. She is very weak. This has been a really terrible day. Julia will never go downstairs again. She will never get to the loo across the dressing room. She attempted to do it on her own and virtually collapsed. It upset her greatly. The decision was taken to have all-day care. So Dinah extends her hours and Dot comes in to give her a break. The bridge has been crossed, but with no real guidance from anyone. She is so pathetic. I hate to see her like this. Asleep she looks pale and beautiful but she needs oxygen a lot, being quickly reduced to breathlessness. I walked and cried and prayed that God would take her in his mercy. But we have both been strong, strong in the faith. So much love, so many prayers and thoughts from so many. Please God, may this end.

9 INTO 10 OCTOBER

The slide continues. She won't take painkillers: they make her sick. Her left leg is swollen with a huge thrombosis. I held her hand and had my last real conversation with her, a mutual declaration of love forever. She was worried about who would look after me. I told her not to worry. I'd be OK. And I said that there's a time to let go and that letting go was an act of love on both sides. I came downstairs and howled with grief.

12 OCTOBER

So much has happened. How can I begin and what do I write? Friday was a strange day. She was so weak. I caught glimpses of her in agonies as she was lifted on and off the commode. Julia was always dignified, always private. There were the District Nurse and her student, the doctors and carers. Sarah Greenall came to see her for ten minutes and stayed the day. Thank God she did. At midday Dr Garlick came and put Julia on a drip. Thank God again. She could no longer articulate but she could hear. So from time to time I went to the bedroom, sat and held her hand and talked. There was that terrible breathing of the dying. The last time I went in was sometime after three o'clock. I took her hand and told her I would love her forever. Those were the last words she heard. Not long after,

Dinah called me. Julia was dead, mouth open and eyes staring. I threw my arms around Dinah and praised God, who had answered my prayer. I am so glad that He took her into His arms. I rang David Hutt and he said, 'I know. I know exactly when she died.' I can't explain the sense of relief, grief and joy. The day seemed to last forever. The undertaker came. No, it wasn't a good idea for the body to go into the Orchard as it would decompose. It left the house for their chapel and will return on Thursday.

I couldn't sleep in that bedroom and so they all heaved to and dismantled the room and set it up for one. So far I've found no difficulty with Julia's death, only a sense calm, of beauty, of gathering in, of strength and loving and grieving. I've had no difficulty in sleeping. Everything was said, everything was done. It has been an overwhelmingly rich experience and I thank God for it.

Then there was the ring-round. Dinah came on Saturday and we spent the day dismantling a phase of existence. I started to rearrange the house. It's still full of her – how could it be otherwise? But the atmosphere is different. It went on through Sunday, when I was on my own. The body had gone but the spirit is still here. Everyone worried about me being on my own. Sunday was, in fact, a relief, no doctors, nurses, therapists, carers. It was lovely to be alone with the cats. I read them as knowing what had happened. They're near me, not mopey but making a new life.

What can I say about all of this? This was one of the great experiences of my life, so moving, so beautiful. I keep on thanking God for it. Everything was faced up to and said.

16 OCTOBER

The days go by like a dream. Outside it is an autumn of translucent splendour, reds, russets, golds, such beauty. I've lost track of time.

Each day brings a hundred letters of condolence. Where do I start? David Hutt arrived yesterday. In the morning we drove to Llanwarne church, which Carol Wells had filled with autumn beauty, soft and caressing. I drove for the first time, so I was well pleased. We came back here and then at noon the hearse came. There is a gulf between reading about or arranging a ritual and actually taking part. Dot, Mick and Shaun gathered in the Orchard. David in cassock and stole went before the coffin, reading psalms. I followed, weeping, all the way along Elizabeth Tudor Avenue and back up to the Orchard. The coffin was laid on trestles in a golden light, with Dot, Mick and Shaun around. I asked Shaun to pluck me a branch of rosemary. He gave it to me and I stood clutching it. David said prayers and with a branch of yew sprinkled holy water on the coffin. I lit a candle and laid the rosemary on the coffin. I was convulsed with grief.

What is so striking is the contrast between these moments which are so transfixing and then the sudden reversion to ordinariness, getting lunch, driving to Ross to shop, cooking the dinner.

17 OCTOBER

The funeral

The day of the funeral. I got up early as a requiem was to be said in the large drawing room. The altar was the Oman Louis XV commode, above which hung the Oman Francis *Madonna and Child*, on which I had placed the Oman Hester Bateman candlesticks. David covered its surface with a fine white starched linen cloth. As I entered, he was already composed and wrapped in prayer. It is difficult to describe the torrent of emotion, anguish, tears and thankfulness I went through. I choked reading the passage I'd chosen from the First Epistle General of Peter about resurrection, joy and suffering. But this gave a firm foundation for the day ahead, over which God had waved a wand, for it was of an autumnal beauty that was paradisal.

So much coming and going, and then at 12.30 p.m. the various readers and party arrived: the Marychurches had brought Patricia Routledge, Patrick Garland came on his own, Gil, Sarah and Edward Greenall, Lawrence and Elizabeth Banks. I'd also asked Julia's brother Charles. There were drinks and snacks and sandwiches. And then David made us rehearse our readings and took us step by step through the service. The result was therefore seamless.

At 1.45 p.m. they all left for the church. The coffin had gone in the morning. David and I followed and entered via the vestry. I couldn't face going through the congregation and then took my place in the choir stalls, where those who were to take part sat facing each other. I couldn't look round but sat, eyes cast down, praying that I would do her justice. The church I could see was full and had a golden atmosphere.

The organ was creaky but that added, I think, a rustic charm and the cathedral organist did his best. Elgar's *Enigma* was played, with no 'Nimrod', as Julia wanted. That ended, the clergy entered and we all stood. Kay Garlick was a star, welcoming everybody and telling them that this service had been put together by Julia and Roy. The first hymn followed: 'We plough the fields and scatter'. And then came my reading, the opening of *The Laskett* book about the elopement, honeysuckle and Dooks's rosemary. I was given strength, went into the pulpit, looked at the congregation direct, smiled and tried to gather everyone in my arms and read without faltering. Patrick Garland followed with Marvell's 'The Garden'. Then the hymn, 'Angel voices . . .', with its line about design, craftsmen's art, music and pleasure. Julia remembered it from Oliver Messel's memorial. Then Sarah read from St John's Gospel, with Mary at the sepulchre and Christ mistaken for the gardener. John Tooley followed with the address, fluent and moving, etching in the genius of the woman.

The organ played from *Eugene Onegin* while we reflected. There was another reading by Lawrence Banks from Revelation 21, like the first one, from the King James Bible. And then came the prayers by Kay, leading to Patricia Routledge reading Christina Rossetti's 'When I am gone . . .' Then came David doing the Commendation over the coffin, which lay covered in a velvet patchwork curtain that Julia had made and on which lay a huge sheaf of rosemary tied with blue and yellow ribbon. David went to one side of the coffin, I went to the other and took the sheaf of rosemary in my arms and clasped it to myself, shattered with grief. The pall was folded and the bearers lifted the coffin. All of this was done as the opening verse of 'Now thank we all our God' (the dedication of *The Laskett* book) was sung. David walked ahead, then the coffin and then me clasping the rosemary. Slowly we walked down the aisle and out of the church into the gold of autumn. And then came the journey to the crematorium. All of that seemed almost irrelevant, everything having been said and done. We were in and out with a couple of prayers in five minutes. I laid the rosemary on the coffin, and that was that.

2 NOVEMBER

All Souls' Day

I caught the morning service, which was for the bereaved as it was All Souls' Day. Inevitably I wept. What have the last few weeks been like? I have felt strong, strong in the faith, strong in the prayers and thoughts of others, strong in Julia's memory. Life has to go on. There are about six hundred letters of condolence to cope with, everyone from a roll call of the mighty like the Prince of Wales to 'a London family' wishing to express its gratitude for all that Julia created. It is no help to anyone falling apart, although Beatrix Miller keeps on telling me that at some stage I'll keel over. But I haven't. Julia wouldn't want that at all. I can drive perfectly well and try to do it every day. Friends are kind with invitations out but, at the heart of it all, I have to make a new life. I've rearranged most of the house. It is less cluttered, fuller of air and light, more masculine in character, but she remains everywhere. I've begun to get on with the book, but much time has gone on arranging the service of thanksgiving at St Paul's, Covent Garden, which is to be on 22 January.

I am not alone in this house. I really love being here. It holds me. I'm doing so much at once rather than holding back, so the builders have returned, working on altering the garage and doing work in the house. This is a new phase of life which calls for remembering and embracing the old but taking its riches into a different future.

I'm busy looking for some kind of housekeeper/factotum. The accountant says that I can afford one. It is important to get the structure of the new life in place and to be positive. But every day I wake up and stare at Julia's face smiling at me from its silver frame by my bedside. In a funny way that encounter is a wonderful start to the day, giving me the strength of love I need to go on.

16 DECEMBER

Life goes on

Whatever the British Museum has been noted for, taste and style have never been part of its tradition. It has always been a heavy, lumpen place. So the new Enlightenment Galleries came as something of a surprise. Wyatt's rooms are handsome, now transformed into rooms of parade, having artefacts in the cases that once held books, evoking the world of the eighteenth-century encyclopaedia.

Bravo Neil MacGregor, who is a saint to have taken on this albatross of a museum. The occasion was its two hundred and fiftieth
anniversary and I took Coral Samuel, so I knew that I'd have a good
evening, even if only at dinner *à deux* at the Garrick afterwards.

As it wasn't black tie, the occasion lacked glamour, rather a sea of grey
jostling and a mighty mafia of the museum and art-minded money
world. There was a special fanfare, which practically knocked us over,
after which Neil, looking twenty-five and not two hundred and fifty,
spoke well. Then came the Prime Minster. What is it about this man
that is so charismatically ghastly? It was a really terrible speech to such
company, revealing no knowledge or appreciation of what is one of
the world's greatest institutions – its collections, its learning, its global
activities should have been saluted and paid tribute to. But oh no. All
we heard about was *la famille Blair* trotting to the National Gallery
and Neil taking them around and how he made even their children
interested in the pictures. This is the British Museum, an institution
created in the aftermath of 1707, an early *British* institution!

There they all were: John Julius Norwich, larger than ever, with
Mollie; David Starkey, now a fat little tub, sadly changed; Loyd
Grossman, the benign Roy Clare and Neil Chalmers; tall, inscru-
table Mark Jones; Patricia Rawlings and Paul Zuckerman; Brian
Allen, Bamber Gascoigne, Helen Hamlyn, Diane Lever . . .

I've thrown myself into social life. Last week was one long *fête*:
dinner at the French Embassy for the Northbournes on Monday
(the cream of the Seventies and Eighties resurrected: Frank and
Kitty Giles, Kenneth Rose, the Quintains, Diane Lever, Marie Lou
de Zulueta, Patricia Rawlings . . . it was like the world of the *Diaries*
come back); Tuesday the Goldsmiths Company – I took Andrew
Wilson and we sat on the top table; Wednesday Beatrix Miller at the
San Lorenzo but she was ill so I went on my own and Mara wept
all over me; Thursday the Oldfields asked me to a vast *fête* at the
Natural History Museum . . .

18 DECEMBER

New directions in the garden

For the history of the garden this entry may be significant. Shaun asked me to walk around it with him. I had already begun to notice things last weekend. My activity had been centred on the house, clearing up and rearranging it, but I was suddenly conscious that the garden called, like everything else, for major decisions. The vast leylandii hedge along the lime walk has the beetle disease. It will have to go, at a price – £5,000! What the effect of the removal of this will be, I know not. I had thought of taking it out before but I knew that Julia would never countenance it. Now there is no choice. It has to go. I can't think how we'll re-landscape the area until it's down.

But to return to my walk with Shaun: Julia had massively over-planted. Any malus variety that she hadn't got had to be acquired; any free tree had to be found a home. The result in places has been trees struggling to live. In the Orchard, canker is rife. So our stroll was like an executioner passing sentence. Shaun had already put a bamboo next to the condemned. When they've gone, what is there will actually flourish and grow. In a way I recalled what David Walker said about my rearrangement of the interior. He said that I'd given it clarity. I'm giving the same to the garden, but I don't want to lose Julia: I want to treasure and enhance her areas, but the garden is nothing but about change. Some things, like the pine trees from Susannah Walton's La Mortola, I will regret; they shouldn't have been planted where they were and to move them now, when they're so large, is death. I don't think that I had any alternative but to be definite and move on. The garden is thirty years old and some things are past it – conifers, for one, are not immortal.

And then there were all the minor things, like the golden privet obelisks in the Birthday Garden. No good and to be moved and replaced with golden yew. The rosemaries at the bottom of the Beaton Steps are a burgeoning tangle that will have to go. Again we decided to use John Glenn's golden yew as sentinels, now a *Leitmotif* through the garden. How pleased he'll be!

It was torture to study just how dense the planting had become in places. Some trees looked in agonies. So 2004 will start a new phase in the garden's history.

30 DECEMBER

Farewell 2003

I don't want another year like this one. I'm haunted by mortality and partings. I pray for five friends who have cancer. When will it end? Still, I made a brave Christmas by giving a great time to two old friends who are widows. It was so good to have been on the giving and not the receiving end. And I went to London and loved Holy Innocents at the Abbey and came back and then over to Madresfield for lunch (Rosalind Morrison is a true friend) and finally up to the Cormacks tomorrow for dinner on New Year's Eve. They are good people.

And yet I give thanks for this year, for the unforgettable experience of being given strength through the prayer and love of so many people. I don't think that I fear death any more, for I see Julia there, waiting for me. Who could ask for more?

EPILOGUE

22 JANUARY 2004

Julia's Service of Thanksgiving

The day of Julia's Service. To the Abbey for the eight o'clock Mass, David Hutt celebrating and Julia remembered. I got to St Paul's, Covent Garden about 9.45 a.m. The flowers were fine: huge branches of pussy willow, rosemary, tiny buttercups yellow narcissi and apples, all in terracotta pots or baskets. David Hutt arrived and we went through everything. As I tried the pulpit, a figure appeared and stretched up his hand with a tiny posy of winter garden flowers and a little card attached: 'To a very special Lady . . .' It was the Queen Mother's Page. I was so touched.

Last week there was the crisis of Robert Tear being ill but the Royal Opera House sprang to and produced John Mark Ainsley, a quite wonderful singer. He sang Lensky's aria in Russian from the gallery at the back. I had to go to the Garrick to arrange the seating for the lunch and then dash back. It was a grey, lustreless, wet day. Reporters from *The Times* and *Telegraph* appeared, along with a photographer. I retreated to Mark Oakley's office, where we all

447

assembled in a rather pell-mell, muddled way. Antonia Fraser was in brilliant cerise, rather wonderful but quite thrown when I told her that Mary Henderson was dying. Alan Bennett arrived, looking like a 1950s provincial university student with a wonderful head of still-brown hair; Patrick Garland was in a corduroy suit, Patricia Routledge in blue beneath swathes of black capes, and John Tooley besuited as usual. David Hutt, Mark Oakley and the Dean of Westminster put on the works, all in copes.

You could watch the church fill up on the television monitor. There came the moment when the decision was taken to fill the choir stalls and later they carried in the churchyard benches. I reckon that there was some four hundred and fifty there, jammed. It was a huge turn-out.

Off we went on the dot and, because everything had been talked through in terms of movement and pauses, the result was flawless. The flow of it was perfect, and so also was the service sheet, sepia on ivory, with Julia's drawings of Souci, baskets of apples, cats, the garden and wellington boots. There was also the contrast of poetry, prose, communal and solo singing and varieties of voice from Patrick's slightly Gielgudian to Allan's North Country. It was touching, laying that great sheaf of rosemary on the altar at the opening. It brought this house and garden right into the rain-sodden Metropolis. So there it was – the welcome, 'We plough the fields and scatter', the laying of the sheaf on the altar by me and my reading of the opening passage of The Laskett garden book. Then came Patrick reading Andrew Marvell, Lensky's aria, John Tooley's address (a trifle too long, but fine), a hymn, Alan reading Patrick's account of Julia's set for Brief Lives, music from Onegin again (the organist adequate, but at sea from time to time), Antonia the Gospel with Christ the Gardener, David with the prayers, Patricia reading 'Remember me . . .' Then the hymn 'Now thank we all our God . . .' and finally the Dean's blessing. And then it was over.

ILLUSTRATIONS

Publicity shot for the first National Trust Lecture
Launch of the Canary Wharf Development
Picnic at Powis Castle
Jean Muir
Weekend party at Royal Lodge
Statues of the Four Seasons at Highgrove
Turfing the Jubilee Garden at The Laskett
Pleaching limes at The Laskett
Scything at Kensington Palace
Breakfast at Versace's Villa Fontanelle
Lunch party at Whitfield
Coffee in Bordeaux
At La Mortella with Susana Walton
Hugh Honour and John Fleming

The Bookseller front cover (John Swannell)
Presenting a copy of *The Story of Britain* to Joan Henderson
Beatrix Miller
Antonia Fraser and Harold Pinter
Mirabel Osler and Rosemary Verey

449

George Clive
Peter and Sonya Wright at The Laskett
Franco Maria Ricci
Felicity Bryan
At work in the writing room
The Victorian Tapestry Workshop, Melbourne
Garden talk during the 'Floating Gardens of the Atlantic' cruise
Installed as High Bailiff and Searcher of the Sanctuary
Christopher Lloyd
Gordon and Marilyn Darling
Julia in The Laskett Garden

CAST OF CHARACTERS

Sir Harold Acton
(1904–1994) Author, aesthete, gossip and owner of the villa
La Pietra, near Florence.

Anthony Adair
Patron of the arts in Australia, founding board member of the
National Portrait Gallery, Canberra.

John Mark Ainsley
Leading British tenor.

Sir Alastair Aird
(1931–2009) Queen Elizabeth the Queen Mother's Private Secretary
in the last decade of her life, having served in her Household since
1964.

David Ogilvy, 13th Earl of Airlie
See under Ogilvy

Virginia Ogilvy, Countess of Airlie
See under Ogilvy

Jonathan Aitken
Disgraced former Conservative MP.

Princess Alexandra of Kent, The Hon. Lady Ogilvy
See under Ogilvy

Dr Brian Allen
Art historian, former Director of Studies at the Paul Mellon Centre for British Art; Chairman of the Hazlitt Group and Trustee of the National Portrait Gallery.

Colin Amery
Writer and architectural consultant, adviser to the Prince of Wales.

Antonio d'Amico
Model, fashion designer and partner of Gianni Versace.

Sir Hardy Amies
(1909–2003) Fashion designer and dressmaker to the Queen.

Henry Paget, 7th Marquess of Anglesey
See under Paget

Shirley Paget, Dowager Marchioness of Anglesey
See under Paget

Noel Annan, Baron Annan
(1916–2000) Former Provost of University College, London and Vice-Chancellor of the University of London; Chairman of

Committee on the Future of Broadcasting and of the Trustees
of the National Gallery; Trustee of the British Museum.

Lady Elizabeth Anson
Cousin and party planner, including to the Queen.

Leonora Anson, Countess of Lichfield
Born Leonora Grosvenor, daughter of the 5th Duke of
Westminster; former wife of Patrick, 5th Earl of Lichfield.

Patrick Anson, 5th Earl of Lichfield
(1939–2005) Society photographer.

Major Sir Ralph Anstruther, Bt
(1921–2002) Scottish Army officer and courtier, latterly Treasurer
Emeritus to Queen Elizabeth the Queen Mother.

Malcolm Appleby
English engraver and silversmith.

Patricia Armstrong, Baroness Armstrong of Ilminster
Second wife of Lord Armstrong.

Robert Armstrong, Baron Armstrong of Ilminster
Former Cabinet Secretary, Chairman of the Trustees of the
V&A 1988–98.

Antony Armstrong-Jones, 1st Earl of Snowdon
Photographer, married 1st Princess Margaret (1960), 2nd
Lucy Lindsay-Hogg (1978).

David and Serena Armstrong-Jones, Viscount and Viscountess Linley
Son and daughter-in-law of Princess Margaret and Lord Snowdon.

Lucy Armstrong-Jones, Lady Snowdon
Second wife of Antony Armstrong-Jones, Lord Snowdon.

Sir Frederick Ashton
(1904–1988) Ballet dancer and principal choreographer to the Royal Ballet.

Clive Aslet
Writer, countryside campaigner and editor-at-large of *Country Life* magazine.

Naomi Aslet
Publisher, wife of Clive Aslet.

Irene Astor, Baroness Astor of Hever
(1919–2001) Philanthropist; widow of Lord Astor, former proprietor of *The Times*; active member of the Commonwealth Press Union.

Rosie Atkins
Horticulturalist, writer and former Curator of the Chelsea Physic Garden.

Richard Avedon
(1923–2004) American fashion and portrait photographer.

Sir Alan Ayckbourn
English playwright and theatre director.

Commander Richard Aylard
Retired Royal Navy officer, former Private Secretary to the Prince of Wales; now a Director of Thames Water.

Sue Ayton
TV agent, co-founder of Knight Ayton Management.

Elizabeth Bainbridge
Horticulturalist.

Dame Janet Baker
Great English mezzo-soprano.

Lawrence and Elizabeth Banks
Owners of Hergest Croft Gardens, Herefordshire; Elizabeth was appointed President of the Royal Horticultural Society in 2011.

Julian and Isabel Bannerman
Garden designers.

Richard Barber
Historian, founder of The Boydell Press and former managing director of Boydell & Brewer Ltd.

Juliet Barker
English historian and writer.

Nora, Lady Barlow
(1885–1989) Granddaughter of Charles Darwin after whom the Aquilegia (columbine) plant 'Nora Barlow' is named.

David Barrie
British diplomat, art collector and Director of the Art Fund
(formerly the National Art Collections Fund) until 2009.

John Baskett
London art dealer, former art advisor to Paul Mellon.

Alexandra Bastedo
(1946–2014) British actress, wife of Patrick Garland (q.v.).

Mavis Batey
(1921–2013) Bletchley Park code-breaker, garden historian
and author.

John Bayley
(1925–2015) Literary critic, Warton Professor of English at
the University of Oxford, husband of Iris Murdoch.

Stephen Bayley
Author and design critic.

Sir Cecil Beaton
(1904–1980) Photographer, stage and costume designer.

Mona, Countess Beauchamp
See under Lygon

Maurice Béjart
(1927–2007) French-born dancer, choreographer and opera
director.

Sir Geoffrey de Bellaigue
(1931–2013) Leading authority on the decorative arts, former Surveyor of the Queen's Works of Art and Director of the Royal Collection 1972–96.

Prue Bellak
Long-term partner of Julian Critchley (q.v.).

Nene Bellotti
Friend of Gianni Versace.

Alan Bennett
Leading British author, playwright and actor.

Gerald Benney
(1930–2008) Influential goldsmith and silversmith.

Paul Benney
British artist; son of Gerald Benney.

Jane Beresford
Former BBC producer.

Richard Beresford
Art expert, former partner of Neil MacGregor (q.v.).

Aline, Lady Berlin
(1915–2014) French-born wife of Sir Isaiah Berlin.

Sir Isaiah Berlin
(1909–1997) Philosopher, historian, essayist, diplomat, academic and man of influence, knighted in 1957.

Alexander Bernstein, Baron Bernstein of Craigweil
(1936–2010) Former Chairman of Granada empire and supporter of the arts.

Vanessa Bernstein
First wife of Lord Bernstein.

Drusilla Beyfus
Journalist and broadcaster, widow of theatre critic Milton Shulman, mother of writer Nicola Shulman and British *Vogue* editor Alexandra Shulman.

Lady Rachel Billington
Author, daughter of the Earl and Countess of Longford (q.v.) and cousin of George Clive (q.v.).

Mark Birley
(1930–2007) Entrepreneur, owner of high-class nightclubs and founder of Annabel's.

John Birt, Baron Birt
Former Director-General of the BBC.

Richard Bisgrove
Horticulturalist, garden historian and writer.

Cherie Blair (*née* Booth)
Barrister, wife of Tony Blair.

Tony Blair
UK Prime Minister 1997–2007.

Robert Blake, Baron Blake of Braydeston
(1916–2003) Writer and historian.

Marcia, Viscountess Blakenham
Potter and philanthropist; wife of Michael Hare, 2nd Viscount
Blakenham.

Emily Blatch, Baroness Blatch of Hinchingbrooke
(1937–2005) British Conservative minister, ennobled by Margaret
Thatcher.

Anthony Blunt
(1907–1983) Art historian, former Surveyor of the Queen's Pictures
and Soviet spy.

Countess Dominique de Borchgrave
(1941–2010) Philanthropist, interior designer and widow of Patrick
Pakenham (son of Lord Longford, q.v.).

Alan Borg
Director of the Victoria and Albert Museum 1995–2001.

Michael Borrie
(1934–2015) Former Head of the British Library Department
of Manuscripts.

Virginia Bottomley, Baroness Bottomley of Nettlestone
Former Conservative Cabinet Minister, Secretary of State for
National Heritage 1995–97.

Adam Boulton
Former political editor of Sky News.

Reg Boulton
Herefordshire artist and engraver.

Patrick Bowe
Garden historian and writer.

Sir Alan Bowness
Director of the Tate Gallery 1980–88.

Alice, Lady Boyd
See under Lennox-Boyd

Melvyn Bragg, Baron Bragg of Wigton
Author and broadcaster.

George Breeze
Former Director of Cheltenham Art Gallery and Museum.

Asa Briggs, Baron Briggs of Lewes
(1921–2016) Social historian and pioneer of adult education.

Susan, Lady Briggs
Widow of Lord Briggs.

Sir Nigel Broackes
(1934–1999) Member of the V&A Advisory Council 1980–83;
founder, Chairman and subsequently President of Trafalgar
House.

Nathalie Brooke
Russian émigré widow of Humphrey Brooke, Secretary of the
Royal Academy of Arts.

Anita Brookner
(1928–2016) Novelist and art historian.

Richard Broyd
Founder of Historic House Hotels, major National Trust
benefactor.

Edmund and Marian Brudenell
(1928–2016; 1934–2013) Owners and restorers of Deene Park,
Northamptonshire.

Felicity Bryan
Literary agent.

Sir Arthur Bryant
(1899–1985) Popular historian and journalist.

Julius Bryant
Keeper of Word & Image at the V&A; former curator at
English Heritage.

John Buchanan
(1953–2011) Director of the Fine Arts Museums of San Francisco
2006–11.

Lucy Buchanan
Museum fundraising veteran; widow of John Buchanan.

Martin Buckley
BBC producer, broadcaster and journalist; lecturer at Southampton
Solent University.

Esmond and Susie Bulmer
Conservative MP for Kidderminster 1974–83 and his wife, former owners of Poston estate, Herefordshire.

Judith Bumpus
(1939–2010), BBC radio producer specialising in the arts.

Jocelyn Burton
British silversmith and goldsmith.

John Bury
(1925–2000) Major theatre designer.

Jennifer Crichton-Stuart, Marchioness of Bute
See under Crichton-Stuart

Montserrat Caballé
Spanish operatic soprano.

Melanie Cable-Alexander
Journalist; former Features Editor of *Country Life* magazine.

James Callaghan, Baron Callaghan of Cardiff
(1912–2005) UK Prime Minister 1976–79.

Simon Callow
English actor, writer and theatre director.

Thomas Stonor, 7th Baron Camoys
See under Stonor

Professor Sir David Cannadine
Historian and author; Chairman of the Trustees of the National
Portrait Gallery 2005–12; married to Linda Colley (q.v.).

Sherban Cantacuzino
Architect and author; former Secretary to the Royal Fine Art
Commission.

Edmund Capon
Director of the Art Gallery of New South Wales 1978–2011.

Rt Revd and Rt Hon. George Carey, Lord Carey of Clifton
Archbishop of Canterbury 1991–2002.

Peter Carington, 6th Baron Carington of Upton
Distinguished Conservative politician; former Chairman
of Christie's.

Henry Herbert, 7th Earl of Carnarvon
See under Herbert

Very Revd Dr Wesley Carr
Dean of Westminster 1997–2008.

George Carter
Garden designer.

Laura Casalis
Italian author; wife of Franco Maria Ricci.

Sir Hugh Casson
(1910–1999) Muted Modernist architect, artist, writer and broadcaster; President of the Royal Academy of Arts 1976–84.

Margaret (Reta), Lady Casson
(1913–1999) Architect, designer and photographer; wife of Sir Hugh Casson.

Andrew Cavendish, 11th Duke of Devonshire, and Deborah Cavendish, Duchess of Devonshire
(1920–2004; 1920–2014) Custodians of Chatsworth House, Derbyshire.

Hugh Cavendish, Baron Cavendish of Furness, and Lady Grania Cavendish
Owners of the Holker Hall estate, Cumbria.

Camilla, Lady Cazelet
Wife of Sir Edward Cazelet.

Julian Chadwick
Solicitor, formerly of Penningtons; Chairman of Thomas Eggar.

Revd Professor Owen Chadwick
(1916–2015) Eminent theologian, university teacher and writer; former Chairman of the Trustees of the National Portrait Gallery.

William (Billy) Chappell
(1907–1994) British dancer, ballet designer and director.

Martin Charteris, Baron Charteris of Amisfield
(1913–1999) Secretary to the Queen 1952–77. Distinguished
courtier. Served the Queen first when she was Princess Elizabeth;
then Assistant Private Secretary 1952–72; Private Secretary
1972–77.

Rt Revd and Rt Hon. Richard Chartres
Bishop of London, 1995–2016.

Anthony Cheetham
Publisher; founder of several publishing companies, including
Century Hutchinson, Orion and Head of Zeus.

Sir Clifford Chetwood
(1928–2009) Former Chairman of George Wimpey Plc.

Patricia (Mary), Lady Christie
Wife of Sir George Christie, owner of Glyndebourne and son of
its founder, John Christie.

Eric Clapton
Prominent British rock and blues guitarist, singer and songwriter.

Peter Clarke
Ecclesiastical historian.

Sir Timothy Clifford
Director of the National Galleries of Scotland, 1984–2006.

George Clive
(1942–1999) Landowner and gardener, son of Lady Mary
(Pakenham) Clive.

Lady Mary Clive
(1907–2013) Journalist, author and centenarian; daughter
of Edward Pakenham, 6th Earl of Longford (q.v.).

Alec Cobbe
Designer, painter and art collector.

Penelope Lyttelton, Viscountess Cobham
See under Lyttelton

Sir Michael Codron
British theatre producer.

Jonathan Coe
English novelist and writer.

Valeria, Viscountess Coke
Former chatelaine of Holkham Hall, Norfolk; former wife of
Edward Douglas Coke, 7th Earl of Leicester of Holkham.

Linda Colley
Historian and author; married to Sir David Cannadine (q.v.).

Norman and Diana Colville
(1893–1974; 1924–2000) Owners and restorers of the Penheale
Estate, Cornwall.

Robin Compton
(1922–2009) Horticulturalist; presiding genius at Newby Hall,
North Yorkshire

Sir Terence Conran
Designer, writer, restaurateur and retailer; former Trustee of the V&A.

John Julius Cooper, 2nd Viscount Norwich
Historian and travel writer.

Richard Cork
Art critic, historian and broadcaster.

Patrick Cormack, Baron Cormack
Conservative peer, former MP for South Staffordshire.

John Cornforth
(1937–2004) Architectural historian; architectural editor of *Country Life* magazine.

Adrienne Corri
(1930–2016) Actress, who first appeared in Jean Renoir's film *The River*, based on a novel by Rumer Godden.

Sir John Cotterell, 6th Bt
Herefordshire landowner of the Garnons estate.

Howard Coutts
Ceramics expert and author; Keeper of Ceramics at the Bowes Museum, Co. Durham.

Fleur Cowles
(1908–2009) American journalist, socialiste and artist.

Jennifer Crichton-Stuart, Marchioness of Bute
Adventurer and fundraiser; widow of the 6th Marquess of Bute.

Sir Julian Critchley
(1930–2000) Former Conservative MP and bon viveur.

Susan Crosland
(1927–2011) American journalist and novelist; widow of Labour MP Anthony Crosland.

Hugh Trevor-Roper, Baron Dacre of Glanton
See under Trevor-Roper

Paul Dacre
Editor of the *Daily Mail.*

Stephen Daldry
Film and theatre director; Artistic Director of the Royal Court Theatre 1992–98.

Gordon and Marilyn Darling
Australian philanthropists and leading arts patrons; Gordon died in 2015.

Sir Francis Dashwood, 11th Bt
(1925–2000) Owner and restorer of West Wycombe Park, Buckinghamshire.

Marcella, Lady Dashwood
Italian film actress, widow of Sir Francis Dashwood.

Richard Davenport-Hines
British historian and literary biographer.

Norman Davies
British-Polish historian.

Major General Peter Davies
Retired British Army Officer and animal welfare campaigner;
Director General of the RSPCA 1992–2002.

Sir Colin Davis
(1927–2013) English conductor, President and longest-serving
principal conductor of the London Symphony Orchestra.

Warren Davis
Head of Communications at the National Trust until 2002.

Helen Dawson
See Helen Osborne

Ivan Day
Food historian.

Sir Robin Day
(1923–2000) British political commentator and broadcaster.

Philip Sidney, 2nd Viscount De L'Isle and Isobel, Lady De L'Isle
Owners of Penshurst Place, Kent.

Dame Judi Dench
Award-winning British actress.

Michael Dennis
Former Managing Director of Olympia & York.

Stephen Deuchar
Director of The Art Fund since 2010; former Exhibitions Director at the National Maritime Museum, Greenwich; Director of Tate Britain 1998–2009.

Dame Ninette de Valois (Madam)
(1898–2001) Ballerina, teacher, choreographer and director; founder of the company that became The Royal Ballet.

Andrew Cavendish, 11th Duke of Devonshire, and Deborah Cavendish, Duchess of Devonshire
See under Cavendish

Jean Diamond
Theatrical agent.

Clarissa Dickson Wright
(1947–2014) English celebrity chef and TV personality; former barrister.

Brian Dix
Garden archaeologist.

Barbara Dorf
Artist and art historian.

Simon Dorrell
Artist and garden designer; Art Editor of the gardening periodical *Hortus*.

Stephen Dorrell
Former Conservative MP; Secretary of State for National Heritage
1994–95.

Sir Anthony Dowell
British ballet dancer; former Artistic Director of the Royal Ballet.

Sir Philip Dowson
(1924–2014) Architect, President of the Royal Academy of Arts
1993–99.

Charles Garrett Ponsonby Moore, 11th Earl of Drogheda
See under Moore

Henry Dermot Ponsonby (Derry) Moore, 12th Earl of Drogheda
See under Moore

Sir John Drummond
(1934–2006) Arts administrator.

William (Bill) Drummond
London art dealer; former Controller of BBC Radio 3.

**Serena Belinda (Lindy) Hamilton-Temple-Blackwood,
Marchioness of Dufferin and Ava**
See under Hamilton-Temple-Blackwood

Sir Thomas and Henrietta, Lady Dunne
Owners of Gatley Park, Herefordshire; Sir Thomas retired as Lord
Lieutenant of Herefordshire in 2008.

David Eccles, 1st Viscount Eccles
(1904–1999) Conservative MP for Chippenham; Minister for the Arts 1970–73.

Susannah Edmunds
Former Head of Paintings Conservation at the V&A.

Max Wyndham, 2nd Baron Egremont
See under Wyndham

Dame Elizabeth Esteve-Coll
Director of the V&A 1988–95.

Peter Everett
Former BBC producer.

Charles Henderson, 3rd Baron Faringdon, and Sarah, Lady Faringdon
See under Henderson

Edward (Ted) Fawcett
(1920–2013) Garden conservation and history expert.

Ruth Roche, Baroness Fermoy
See under Roche

Valerie Finnis, Lady Scott
(1924–2006) Plantswoman and flower photographer, wife of Sir David Scott.

Margery Fish
(1892–1969) Gardener and garden writer, pioneer of ground-cover planting.

Miles Fitzalan-Howard, 17th Duke of Norfolk, and Anne Fitzalan-Howard, Duchess of Norfolk
(1915–2002; 1927–2013) Former Custodians of Arundel Castle, West Sussex.

John Fleming
(1919–2001) British art historian and writer; in partnership with Hugh Honour (q.v.).

Peter Florence
Director of the Hay Festival.

Christopher and Sarah Foley
Art dealers; Directors of Lane Fine Art, London.

Sir Brinsley Ford
(1908–1999) British art collector, connoisseur and patron; former Trustee of the National Gallery, Chairman of the National Art Collection Fund; married Joanna (*née* Vyvyan) in 1937.

John Forsyth
Journalist; former BBC producer and reporter.

William Forsythe
American choreographer.

John Fowler
(1906–1997) Seminal decorator and exponent of the 'country house' look.

Lady Antonia Fraser
Historian, novelist and biographer; daughter of the Earl and
Countess of Longford (q.v.).

Flora Fraser
Biographer, daughter of Lady Antonia Fraser.

Sir Christopher Frayling
Writer and educationalist; Rector of the Royal College
of Art 1996–2009; Chairman of the Arts Council
2005–2009.

Nicki Frei
Scriptwriter; married to Sir Peter Hall (q.v.).

David Furnish
Canadian film-maker; married to Elton John (q.v.).

Hélène and Patrice Fustier
Founders of the Journées des Plantes horticultural fair in the
grounds of their chateau at Courson.

Patrick Garland
(1935–2013) Actor, producer, director and writer; married to
Alexandra Bastedo (q.v.).

Rev. Prebendary Kay Garlick
Herefordshire priest; royal chaplain and Residentiary Canon
of Hereford Cathedral.

Bamber Gascoigne
British television presenter and author, married to ceramicist
Christina Gascoigne.

**Marjorie (Mollie) Gascoyne-Cecil, Dowager Marchioness
of Salisbury**
Noted garden designer; chatelaine of Cranborne Manor, Dorset,
and Hatfield House, Hertfordshire.

Robert Gascoyne-Cecil, 6th Marquess of Salisbury
(1916–2003) British landowner and Conservative politician.

Roy Gazzard
Architect and Arabist.

Christopher Gibbs
British antique dealer, collector and interior designer.

Patrick Gibson, Baron Gibson
(1916–2004) Former Chairman of the Arts Council, the National
Trust and the Pearson Group.

Sir John Gielgud
(1904–2000) English actor and theatre director.

Alan Giles
British businessman, until 2006 CEO of HMV Group.

Mary Giles
Indispensable member of the Department of Culture.

Sir Robin Gill
Long-standing player in the communications industry; founder of the Royal Anniversary Trust.

Sir Martin Gilliatt
(1913–1993) Private Secretary and Equerry to Queen Elizabeth the Queen Mother.

Penelope Gilliatt
(1932–1993) English novelist, screenwriter and film critic.

Allen Ginsberg
(1926–1997) American poet.

Jonathan Glancey
Journalist, architectural critic and writer.

Zorica, Lady Glen
(1913–2003) Art collector and philanthropist.

John Hope, 1st Baron Glendevon, and Elizabeth (Liza), Lady Glendevon
See under Hope

Victoria Glendinning
Biographer, critic, broadcaster and novelist.

John Glenn
Architectural and landscape consultant.

Gloucester, Richard, 2nd Duke of Gloucester
Youngest grandchild of George V and Queen Mary.

Arnold Goodman, Baron Goodman
(1915–1995) British lawyer, political advisor and negotiator.

Charles Gordon-Lennox, 10th Duke Richmond, and
Susan Gordon-Lennox, Duchess of Richmond
Former custodians of Goodwood House, West Sussex.

Alexander (Grey) Ruthven, 2nd Earl of Gowrie
See under Ruthven

Countess Adelheid (Neiti) von der Schulenburg, Lady Gowrie
See under von der Schulenburg

Fortune Smith, Duchess of Grafton
Wife to the 11th Duke and mistress of the Robes to the Queen.

Hugh FitzRoy, 11th Duke of Grafton
(1919–2011) Architectural conservationist.

Penny Graham
Painter; long-term companion of George Clive (q.v.).

Michael Green
Former BBC radio producer, Controller of Radio 4 and Chairman
of Carlton Communications.

Paul Greenhalgh
Director of the Sainsbury Centre for Visual Arts, University of East
Anglia, formerly Head of Research at the V&A.

George (Geordie) and Kathryn Greig
Former Literary Editor of the *Sunday Times*, now Editor of the
Mail on Sunday; his wife, Kathryn, is originally from Texas.

Sir Roger de Grey
(1918–1995) President of the Royal Academy of Arts 1984–93.

Grizelda Grimond
Daughter of Liberal politician Jo Grimond; secretary to Neil
MacGregor; one-time lover of film director Tony Richardson.

Leonora Grosvenor
See Leonora Anson, Countess of Lichfield

Ruth Guilding
Architectural historian; married to A.N. Wilson (q.v.).

Sylvie Guillem
French ballet dancer.

Bryan Guinness, 2nd Baron Moyne
(1905–1992) Lawyer, poet and novelist; former owner of Biddesden
House, Wiltshire.

Hon. Thomasin Guinness
Daughter of Bryan Guinness, 2nd Baron Moyne.

William Hague, Baron Hague of Richmond
Conservative politician, formerly MP for Richmond, Yorkshire.

Quintin Hogg, Baron Hailsham of St Marylebone
See under Hogg

Sir Peter Hall
Theatre and film director; founder of the Royal Shakespeare
Company and former Director of the National Theatre;
married to Nicki Frei (q.v.).

Ian Hamilton Finlay
(1925–2006) Scottish poet, writer, artist and gardener.

**Serena Belinda (Lindy) Hamilton-Temple-Blackwood,
Marchioness of Dufferin and Ava**
Artist, conservationist and businesswoman. Widow of the 9th
Marquess.

Luke Harding
British journalist, since 1996 a correspondent at the *Guardian*.

George Lascelles, 7th Earl of Harewood
See under Lascelles

Marion Stein, later Marion Lascelles, Countess of Harewood
See under Stein

Ian Hargreaves
Journalist, broadcaster, educator and political advisor.

Pamela, Lady Harlech
American socialite, former cooking editor of *Vogue*; widow of
David Ormsby-Gore, 5th Baron Harlech.

Harriet Harman
Labour politician, MP for Camberwell and Peckham.

Eileen Harris
American architectural historian and Robert Adam scholar;
married to John Harris.

John Harris
English historian of architecture and gardens, co-curator of the
Destruction of the Country House exhibition at the V&A; married
to Eileen Harris.

Rex Harrison
(1908–1990) English actor of stage and screen.

Wilhelmine (Billa) Harrod
(1911–2005) Writer and conservationist.

Nicky Haslam
English interior designer and socialite.

Selina Hastings
Journalist and biographer.

Alasdair Hawkyard
Historian and author.

John Hayes
(1929–2005) Director of the London Museum 1970–74 and of the
National Portrait Gallery 1974–94.

Jonathan Heale
British children's book illustrator and ceramic artist.

Sir Edward Heath
(1916–2005) UK Prime Minister 1970–74.

Diana Heffer
Journalist; married to Simon Heffer.

Simon Heffer
Journalist, author and political commentator; married to
Diana Heffer.

Drue Heinz
American patron of the literary arts; founder and publisher of
the *Paris Review*.

John Hemming
Explorer, conservationist and author; married to Sukie Hemming.

Sukie Hemming
Fundraiser, and writer; Director of Corporate Affairs at the
British Museum and Trustee of English Heritage; married to John
Hemming.

**Charles Henderson, 3rd Baron Faringdon, and Sarah, Lady
Faringdon**
Former owner of Buscot Park Oxfordshire, and owner of Barnsley
Park, Gloucestershire.

Charles Henderson
Former head of the Office of Arts and Libraries.

Joan Henderson
(1915–2002) History teacher at Edmonton County Grammar
School.

Mary, Lady Henderson
(1919–2004) Writer, linguist and hostess; wife of Sir Nicholas
Henderson.

Sir Nicholas (Nicko) Henderson
(1919–2009) Diplomat; former British Ambassador to France
and the USA.

Henry Herbert, 7th Earl of Carnarvon
(1924–2001) Soldier, aristocrat, manager of the Queen's racing
stables.

Hon. Sarah Hervey-Bathurst
Chatelaine and interior decorator.

Anne, Lady Heseltine
Supporter of the arts; former Trustee of the V&A and Imperial
War Museum; wife of Conservative peer Lord Heseltine.

Sir William (Bill) Heseltine
Private Secretary to the Queen 1986–90.

Robert Hewison
Cultural historian.

Susan Hill
Author and novelist.

Bevis Hillier
Art historian, journalist and biographer of Sir John Betjeman.

Penelope Hobhouse
Distinguished British garden writer and designer.

Howard Hodgkin
English painter, printmaker and collector.

Min Hogg
Founding Editor of *The World of Interiors*.

Quintin Hogg, Baron Hailsham of St Marylebone
(1907–2001) Conservative elder statesman; Britain's longest-serving
Lord Chancellor.

Robert Holden
(1956–2014) Art expert.

Merlin Holland
Writer and editor; only grandchild of Oscar Wilde.

Sir Ian Holm
English actor.

Stanley Honeyman
Consultant to Olympia & York and the Canary Wharf development.

Hugh Honour
(1927–2016) British art historian and writer; in partnership with
John Fleming (q.v.).

John Hope, 1st Baron Glendevon, and Elizabeth (Liza), Lady Glendevon
(1912–1996; 1915–1998) Scottish Conservative politician and his wife, only child of W. Somerset Maugham.

Jacqueline Hope-Wallace
Conservationist and companion of Dame Veronica Wedgwood (q.v.).

Sir Simon Hornby
(1934–2010) Former Chairman of WH Smith.

David Howard
Horticulturalist, former Head Gardener to the Prince of Wales at Highgrove.

Michael Howard, 21st Earl of Suffolk, and Linda, Lady Suffolk
Custodians of Charlton Park, Wiltshire.

Maggy Howarth
Designer of pebble mosaics.

Ted Hughes
(1930–1998) English poet, appointed Poet Laureate in 1984; married Carol Orchard in 1970.

John Humphrys
Veteran BBC broadcaster.

Gayle Hunnicutt
American-born actress, former wife of Simon Jenkins (q.v.)

Brian and Merle Huntley
Former Director of Kirstenbosch botanical garden, Cape Town.

Douglas Hurd, Baron Hurd of Westwell
Conservative politician, Foreign Secretary 1989–95.

'Duke' Hussey, Baron Hussey of North Bradley
(1923–2006) Former Chairman of the BBC.

Jeremy Hutchinson, Baron Hutchinson of Lullington, and June, Lady Hutchinson
Lawyer; oldest-living peer. Lady Hutchinson died in 2006.

Sidney Hutchison
(1912–2000) Art historian and administrator, former Secretary and Librarian of the Royal Academy of Arts.

Revd Canon David Hutt
Former Canon Steward and Sub-Dean of Westminster Abbey 1999–2005.

Richard Ingrams
Journalist, former editor of *Private Eye* and *The Oldie*.

Mary Innes-Ker, Duchess of Roxburghe
(1915–2014) Patron of the Royal Ballet; chatelaine of West Horsley Place, Surrey.

Derry Irvine, Baron Irvine of Lairg
Lawyer and judge, appointed Lord Chancellor by Tony Blair in 1997.

Revd Prebendary Gerard Irvine
(1920–2011) High Anglican vicar of St Matthew's Church, Westminster.

Sir Jeremy Isaacs
Television executive, former General Director of the Royal Opera House, Covent Garden.

Barney Ivanovic
Representative of Monaco in London.

Gervase Jackson-Stops
(1947–1995) Architectural historian.

David Jacques
Garden historian.

Michael Jaffé
(1923–1997) Art historian and museum curator, Director of the Fitzwilliam Museum, Cambridge 1973–90.

Christopher James, 5th Baron Northbourne
Farmer, businessman and cross-bench peer.

Marie Sygne James, Baroness Northbourne of Betteshanger
French-born wife of Lord Northbourne.

Margaret Jay, Baroness Jay of Paddington
Labour peer, former BBC television producer and presenter.

Stephen Jefferies
Ballet director and retired dancer.

Keith Jeffery
Former Adviser for External Affairs at the Arts Council.

Charles Jencks
US-born landscape architect and designer.

Maggie Keswick Jencks
(1941–1995) Writer, gardener and designer. Maggie's cancer care centres were founded in her memory. Wife of Charles Jencks.

Hugh Jenkins, Baron Jenkins of Putney
(1908–2004) Labour politician, Arts Minister 1974–76.

Dame Jennifer Jenkins, Lady Jenkins of Hillhead
Chairman of the National Trust 1986–90.

Sir Simon Jenkins
Journalist and author; former Chairman of the National Trust.

Elton John
Singer-songwriter; married to David Furnish (q.v.).

Jay Jolley
Retired dancer, Assistant Director of the Royal Ballet School.

Mary Keen
Lecturer, writer and garden designer.

Paul Channon, Baron Kelvedon
(1935–2007) Conservative politician, Transport Secretary 1987–89.

Sarah Kent
Art critic.

David Kenworthy, 11th Baron Strabolgi
(1914–2010) Labour peer.

Lloyd Tyrrell-Kenyon, 5th Baron Kenyon
(1917–1993) Trustee of the National Portrait Gallery 1953–88 and
Chairman of Trustees 1966–88.

Henry Keswick
Businessman, Managing Director of Jardine Matheson Holdings,
former Chairman of the National Portrait Gallery.

Patrick Kinmonth
Artist, opera director, set designer and curator.

James Kirkman
Art dealer.

Sue Knight
TV agent, co-founder of Knight Ayton Management.

Christian Lamb
Horticultural historian.

Constant Lambert
(1905–1951) British composer, conductor and critic.

Lady Lucinda Lambton, Lady Worsthorne
Architectural writer, broadcaster and photographer.

Sir Stephen Lamport
Receiver General of Westminster Abbey, formerly Private Secretary to the Prince of Wales.

Martin Lane Fox
(1938–2016) Landscape and garden designer, former Vice-Chairman of the Royal Horticultural Society.

Robin Lane Fox
Classicist, ancient historian and garden writer.

Brian Lang
Chief Executive of the British Library 1991–2000.

George Lascelles, 7th Earl of Harewood
(1923–2011) First cousin of the Queen; founder of *Opera* magazine; former President of the British Board of Film Classification and of English National Opera; married to Marion Stein (q.v.).

Sir Denys Lasdun
(1914–2001) British architect.

Doris Langley Moore
(1902–1989) Writer, fashion historian and authority on Byron. Founder of the Fashion Museum in Bath.

Andrew Lawson
Garden photographer.

Dominic Lawson
Journalist and broadcaster.

Tony Lee
BBC television producer and director.

James Lees-Milne
(1908–1997) Diarist, architectural historian and writer, and expert on country houses.

Sir Hugh Leggatt
(1925–2014) Art dealer and protector of the nation's cultural heritage.

Vivien Leigh
(1913–1967) Film actress, second wife of Sir Laurence Olivier.

Barbara Leigh-Hunt
British actress; widow of actor Richard Pasco.

Prue Leith
Cookery writer, restaurateur and broadcaster.

Alice, Lady Lennox-Boyd
Horticulturalist, former President of Cornwall Garden Society; wife of Simon Lennox-Boyd, 2nd Viscount Boyd of Merton (q.v.). Sister of George Clive (q.v.).

Edward Lennox-Boyd (Teddy Clive)
Nephew of George Clive (q.v.).

Sir Mark and Arabella, The Hon. Lady Lennox-Boyd
Former Conservative government minister and his wife, a well-known landscape designer, owners of Gresgarth Hall and Gardens, Lancashire.

Simon Lennox-Boyd, 2nd Viscount Boyd of Merton
Former Deputy Chairman of Arthur Guinness & Sons; owner
of Ince Castle, Cornwall.

Ray Leppard
British conductor and harpsichordist.

Rosa Maria Letts
Art historian, writer and curator.

Diane, Lady Lever
Widow of Lord (Harold) Lever.

Sir Michael Levey
(1927–2008) Art historian, Director of the National Gallery
1973–87.

**David and Serena Armstrong-Jones, Viscount and Viscountess
Linley**
See under Armstrong-Jones

Leonora Anson, Countess of Lichfield
See under Anson

Patrick Anson, 5th Earl of Lichfield
See under Anson

Sir Roderick (Roddy) Llewellyn, 5th Bt
Garden designer and writer.

Christopher Lloyd
Art historian, Surveyor of the Queen's Pictures 1988–2005.

Frank and Elizabeth Pakenham, Earl and Countess of Longford
See under Pakenham

Jules Lubbock
Architectural historian and writer.

Richard Luce, Baron Luce
Former Conservative Cabinet Minister, Minister for the Arts
1985–90.

Giuseppe Lund
Sculptor and designer of the Queen Elizabeth Gate, Hyde Park.

Mona Lygon, Countess Beauchamp
(1895–1989) Danish wife of William Lygon, 8th and last Earl
Beauchamp.

Penelope Lyttelton, Viscountess Cobham
Businesswoman, Chair of VisitEngland and partner of David
Mellor (q.v.).

Alastair McAlpine, Baron McAlpine of West Green
(1942–2014) Politician, businessman and author, supporter and
confidante of Margaret Thatcher.

Neil MacGregor
Art historian, Director of the National Gallery 1987–2002 and
of the British Museum 2002–15.

Iain Mackintosh
Theatre historian.

Elizabeth, Lady Maclean
Widow of the 11th Baron Maclean, Lord Chamberlain to the Queen.

Julia MacRae
Publisher; my editor for *The Story of Britain* and *The Spirit of Britain*.

Madam
See Dame Ninette de Valois

Sir Philip Magnus-Allcroft, 2nd Bt
(1906–1988) Historian, Justice of the Peace and Army Major, former Trustee of the National Portrait Gallery.

Robert Maguire
(1921–2005) American illustrator and artist.

Sir John Major
British Prime Minister 1990–97.

Annie Malcolm
Television producer.

Mary Malcolm
(1918–2010) Veteran BBC television announcer.

Nicholas Mann
Scholar and Director of the Warburg Institute 1990–2001.

Dame Alicia Markova
(1910–2004) English ballerina, choreographer, ballet director and teacher.

Dennis Marks
(1948–2015) Broadcaster, filmmaker and writer.

Richard Marks
Art historian, curator and writer.

Sir Neville Marriner
(1924–2016) English conductor and violinist.

Peter Marston
Designer and author.

Mary Anna Marten
(1929–2010) Former owner of Crichel House, Dorset; collector, traveller and supporter of the arts.

Ivan Massow
Entrepreneur, gay rights campaigner and media personality.

Syrie Maugham
(1879–1955) Leading British interior decorator, wife of Somerset Maugham.

Very Revd Michael Mayne
(1929–2006) Dean of Westminster 1986–96.

Jonathan Meades
Writer, journalist, essayist and film-maker.

David Mellor
Journalist, radio presenter and former Conservative politician.

Michael Milburn
Restaurateur.

Delia, Lady Millar
(1931–2004) Art historian, writer and wife of Sir Oliver Millar.

Sir Oliver Millar
(1923–2007), Surveyor of the Queen's Pictures 1972–88.

Beatrix Miller
(1923–2014) Legendary editor of *Vogue* 1964–84.

James Miller
Former Deputy Chairman of Sotheby's.

John Missen
(1936–2013) Former Master of The Worshipful Company
of Barbers.

Paul Mitchell
BBC producer and lifelong friend of Julia Trevelyan Oman.

David Mlinaric
Interior designer.

Renzo Mongiardino
(1916–1998) Italian architect and interior designer.

Edward Montagu, 3rd Baron Montagu of Beaulieu
(1947–2015) Founder of the National Motor Museum and former
Chairman of English Heritage.

Hugh Montgomery-Massingberd
(1946–2007) Journalist, author and editor.

Charles Garrett Ponsonby Moore, 11th Earl of Drogheda
(1910–1989) Chairman of the Royal Opera House, Covent Garden, 1958–74, and of the *Financial Times* 1971–75.

Henry Dermot Ponsonby (Derry) Moore, 12th Earl of Drogheda
Photographer.

Professor Joseph Mordaunt Crook
Architectural historian and writer.

John Morley
(1933–2001) Curator and writer; former Keeper of Furniture and Interior Design at the V&A.

Sheridan Morley
(1941–2007) Biographer, critic and broadcaster.

Barbara Morris
(1918–2009) Former Deputy Keeper of Ceramics and Glass at the V&A.

Brian Morris, Lord Morris of Castle Morris
(1930–2001) Professor of literature and Labour politician; former Trustee of the National Portrait Gallery.

Sir Charles Morrison
(1932–2005) Conservative MP for Devizes 1963–92; former husband of Rosalind, Lady Morrison (q.v.).

Richard Morrison
Cultural commentator and music critic of *The Times*.

Rosalind, Lady Morrison
Chatelaine of Madresfield Court, Worcestershire; former wife
of Sir Charles Morrison (q.v.).

John Mortimer
(1923–2009) Barrister, broadcaster, author and dramatist.

Bryan Guinness, 2nd Baron Moyne
See under Guinness

Jean Muir
(1928–1995) British fashion designer.

Dame Elisabeth Murdoch
(1909–2012) Australian philanthropist, mother of media tycoon
Rupert Murdoch.

Dame Iris Murdoch
(1919–1999) Distinguished novelist; wife of John Bayley (q.v.).

Cardinal Cormac Murphy-O'Connor
Archbishop of Westminster 2000–2009.

Jock Murray
(1908–1993) Publisher.

Anne Murrell
Conservator; widow of Jim Murrell.

Jim Murrell
(1934–1994) V&A conservator, artist and writer.

John Napper
(1916–2001) English painter.

James Naughtie
BBC radio presenter.

Carol Newman
Garden designer and historian.

Nigel Nicolson
(1917–2004) Publisher, co-founder of Weidenfeld & Nicolson; son of Vita Sackville-West, creator of the garden at Sissinghurst, and Sir Harold Nicolson.

Julie Nightingale
Member of the V&A staff and administrative head of the Friends of the V&A.

Miles Fitzalan-Howard, 17th Duke of Norfolk, and Anne Fitzalan-Howard, Duchess of Norfolk
See under Fitzalan-Howard

Christopher James, 5th Baron Northbourne
See under James

Marie Sygne James, Baroness Northbourne of Betteshanger
See under James

John Julius Norwich
See under Cooper

Diane, Lady Nutting
Chairman of the Georgian Group 1999–2014; chatelaine of
Chicheley Hall, Buckinghamshire.

Revd Mark Oakley
Canon Chancellor of St Paul's Cathedral; former Rector of St
Paul's Church, Covent Garden.

Princess Alexandra of Kent, The Hon. Lady Ogilvy
Wife of Sir Angus Ogilvy; first cousin of the Queen.

Sir Angus Ogilvy
(1928–2004) Businessman; husband of Princess Alexandra of Kent.

David Ogilvy, 13th Earl of Airlie
Scottish peer, Lord Chamberlain 1984–97.

James Ogilvy
Son of Sir Angus Ogilvy and Princess Alexandra of Kent.

June Ogilvy
(1938–2001) Former sister-in-law of Sir Angus Ogilvy.

Virginia Ogilvy, Countess of Airlie
Wife of the Earl of Airlie; Lady of the Bedchamber to the Queen
since 1973.

Laurence Olivier, Baron Olivier of Brighton
(1907–1989) Acclaimed British actor of stage and screen; married
to Vivien Leigh (q.v.) and subsequently Joan Plowright (q.v.).

Carola Oman, Lady Lenanton
(1897–1978) Historical novelist, biographer and children's writer;
daughter of Sir Charles Oman and aunt of Julia Trevelyan
Oman.

Sir Charles Oman
(1860–1946) Pioneering British military historian, Conservative
MP for Oxford University 1919–35 and grandfather of Julia
Trevelyan Oman.

Charles Chichele Oman
(1901–1982) Silver historian, writer and former Keeper of
Metalwork at the V&A, father of Julia Trevelyan Oman.

Julia Trevelyan Oman, Lady Strong
(1930–2003) Distinguished theatre, television, ballet and opera
designer; wife of Sir Roy Strong.

Bryan Organ
English painter, particularly of portraits.

Stephen Orgel
Historian, writer and Shakespeare scholar.

Richard Ormond
Former Assistant Keeper of the National Portrait Gallery; Director
of the National Maritime Museum, Greenwich, 1986–2000.

Helen Osborne (*née* Dawson)
(1939–2004) Journalist and writer; widow of John Osborne,
playwright (1929–1994).

Mirabel Osler
(1925–2016) Garden writer.

Russell Page
(1906–1985) Garden designer and landscape architect.

Henry Paget, 7th Marquess of Anglesey
(1922–2013) Soldier, military historian and conservationist,
Trustee of the National Portrait Gallery and National Heritage
Memorial Fund.

Shirley Paget, Dowager Marchioness of Anglesey
Writer, former Chairman of the Broadcasting Complaints
Commission and Vice-Chairman Museums and Galleries
Commission.

Elizabeth Pakenham, Countess of Longford
(1906–2002) Historian and author, widow of Lord Longford (q.v.),
mother of Lady Antonia Fraser (q.v.), Lady Rachel Billington (q.v.)
and Thomas Pakenham (q.v.).

Francis 'Frank' Pakenham, 7th Earl of Longford
(1905–2001) Labour politician, campaigner, publisher and writer;
uncle of George Clive (q.v.).

Thomas Pakenham, 8th Earl of Longford
Writer, historian and arborist.

Eduardo Paolozzi
(1924–2005) Sculptor, printmaker, film-maker and artist.

Matthew Parris
Journalist and former Conservative politician.

Andrew Patrick
Art collector; former Managing Director of the Fine Arts Society.

John Patten, Baron Patten
Former Conservative Cabinet Minister.

Anthony Payne
Composer, writer and broadcaster.

Professor Sir Alan Peacock
(1922–2014) Economist, writer and composer; Chairman of the
Committee on Financing the BBC (Peacock Committee)
1984–86.

Thomas Love Peacock
(1785–1866) Novelist, poet, close friend of Percy Bysshe Shelley.

César Pelli
Influential American-Argentine architect.

Sir Nicholas Penny
Art historian and writer; Director of the National Gallery 2008–14.

John Peter
Theatre critic.

Stephen Phillips
Writer and broadcaster.

Diana Phipps
Interior decorator and writer. Daughter of Countess Sternberg and friend of former Czech President Václav Havel; regained possession of one of her family's castles in Czechoslovakia.

Princess Luciana Pignatelli
(1935–2008) Italian socialite, model and jewellery designer.

Harold Pinter
(1930–2008) Playwright, screenwriter, director and actor; husband of Lady Antonia Fraser (q.v.).

Myfanwy Piper
(1911–1997) Art critic and opera librettist, wife of artist John Piper (1903–1992).

Joan Plowright, Baroness Olivier of Brighton
English stage actress, widow of Laurence Olivier (q.v.).

Patrick Plunket, 7th Baron Plunket
(1923–1975) Equerry to the Queen and, previously, to George VI, Deputy Master of the Royal Household 1954–75.

Robert Other Ivor Windsor-Clive, 3rd Earl of Plymouth,
and Caroline, Countess of Plymouth
See under Windsor-Clive

Sir John Pope-Hennessy
(1913–1994) Distinguished art historian; Director of the V&A 1967–73 and of the British Museum 1974–76.

Michael Portillo
Former Conservative Cabinet Minister.

Sir Philip Powell
(1921–2003) Architect.

Sharon Powell
Antique dealer, art consultant and architectural restoration project manager.

Tristram Powell
Son of Anthony Powell and Lady Violet Pakenham; television and film producer.

Princess Alexandra of Kent
See The Hon. Lady Ogilvy

Roger Pringle
Writer, publisher and poet; Director of the Shakespeare Birthplace Trust 1989–2007.

Patrick Proctor
(1936-2003) Prominent English artist.

John Profumo, 5th Baron Profumo of Sardinia
(1915–2006) Disgraced Conservative politician; social worker and fundraiser.

Valerie Profumo (*née* Hobson)
(1917–1998) British film actress, wife of John Profumo.

Jules Prown
American art historian and writer.

William Pye
British sculptor.

Antony Quinton, Baron Quinton of Holywell
(1925–2010) Academic philosopher, writer and broadcaster;
Chairman of the Board of the British Library 1985–90.

Marcelle, Lady Quinton
American artist, sculptor and writer; wife of Lord Quinton.

Sean Rafferty
Northern Irish broadcaster.

Patricia Rawlings, Baroness Rawlings of Burnham Westgate
Conservative peer and former MEP; owner, with Paul Zuckerman
(q.v.), of Burnham Westgate Hall, Norfolk.

Nancy Reagan
(1921–2016) First Lady of the USA 1981–89.

Peter Rees, Baron Rees of Goytre
(1926–2008) Conservative politician.

William Rees-Mogg, Baron Rees-Mogg
(1928–2012) Journalist and writer, former editor of *The Times*,
Chairman of the Arts Council and Vice-Chairman of the BBC.

Paul Reichmann
(1930–2013) Property developer, founder of Olympia & York and driving force behind the Canary Wharf development.

Ruth Rendell, Baroness Rendell of Babergh
(1930–2015) Crime writer.

Graham Reynolds
(1914–2013) Art historian, Keeper of Prints and Drawings at the V&A 1960–74.

Franco Maria Ricci
Italian art publisher.

Charles Gordon-Lennox, 10th Duke Richmond, and Susan Gordon-Lennox, Duchess of Richmond
See under Gordon-Lennox

Sir John Riddell, Bt
(1934–2010) Private Secretary to the Prince of Wales 1985–90.

Paula Ridley
Chairman of the V&A Trustees 1998–2007.

Dame Diana Rigg
English actress.

Angela Rippon
Television journalist, newsreader, writer and presenter.

Luke Rittner
Chief Executive of the Royal Academy of Dance; Secretary General
of the Arts Council 1983–90.

Andrew Roberts
Historian and journalist.

John Martin Robinson
Architectural historian and writer.

Ruth Roche, Baroness Fermoy
(1908–1993) Lady-in-Waiting and lifelong friend of Queen
Elizabeth the Queen Mother. Grandmother of Diana,
Princess of Wales. Widow of Edmund, 5th Baron Fermoy.

Malcolm Rogers
Art historian, curator and portraiture expert; Director of the
Museum of Fine Arts, Boston.

Graham Rose
(1928–1995) Gardener and gardening writer; *Sunday Times*
agricultural correspondent 1968–78.

Kenneth Rose
(1924–2014) Royal biographer and *Telegraph* diarist.

Father Kenneth Ross
(1908–1970) Vicar of All Saints, Margaret Street 1951–69.

Anne Parsons, Countess of Rosse
(1902–1991) Society hostess, mother of Antony Armstrong-Jones
(q.v.).

Sir Evelyn de Rothschild
Financier, resident of the Ascott estate, Buckinghamshire.

Jacob Rothschild, 4th Baron Rothschild
Investment banker.

Victoria Schott de Rothschild
Former wife of Sir Evelyn de Rothschild, divorced 2000.

Patricia Routledge
English actress.

A.L. Rowse
(1903–1997) Historian and writer, authority on Shakespeare and Elizabethan England.

Mary Innes-Ker, Duchess of Roxburghe
See under Innes-Ker

Robert Runcie, Baron Runcie
(1921–2000) Archbishop of Canterbury 1980–91.

Conrad Russell, 5th Earl Russell
(1937–2004) Historian and politician.

Anthony Russell-Roberts
Businessman and opera manager; nephew of Sir Frederick Ashton (q.v.).

CAST OF CHARACTERS

Alexander (Grey) Ruthven, 2nd Earl of Gowrie
Conservative politician, Arts Minister 1983–85; former Chairman of Sotheby's and of the Arts Council. Married to Countess Adelheid (Neiti) von der Schulenburg (q.v.).

Mien Ruys
(1904–1999) Eminent Dutch landscape and garden architect.

Anya Sainsbury, Lady Sainsbury of Preston Candover
Retired ballerina and patron of the arts; wife of Lord Sainsbury.

John Sainsbury, Baron Sainsbury of Preston Candover
President of Sainsbury's; businessman and politician.

Axel von Saldern
(1923–2012) Director of the Museum für Kunst und Gewerbe, Hamburg, 1971–88.

John Sales
Horticulturalist; former Chief Gardens Adviser to the National Trust.

Marjorie (Mollie) Gascoyne-Cecil, Dowager Marchioness of Salisbury
See under Gascoyne-Cecil

Robert Gascoyne-Cecil, 6th Marquess of Salisbury
See under Gascoyne-Cecil

Charles Saumarez Smith
Cultural historian and writer; Director of the National Portrait Gallery 1994–2002 and the National Gallery 2002–2007; Secretary of the Royal Academy of Arts.

Prunella Scales
British actress.

Sir Michael Scholar
Civil servant; President of St John's College, Oxford, 2001–12.

Countess Adelheid (Neiti) von der Schulenburg, Lady Gowrie
Wife of Lord Gowrie (q.v.).

Professor Clive Scott
Scholar of European literature at the University of East Anglia.

Anne Scott-James, Lady Lancaster
(1913–2009) Author, journalist, magazine editor and authority
on gardening. Wife of Sir Osbert Lancaster.

Roger Scruton
Philosopher.

Robin Scutt
Television producer.

Father Michael Seed
Influential Franciscan friar responsible for a number of prominent
Catholic conversions, including Tony Blair.

Sir Nicholas Serota
Director of Tate 1988–2016.

Alastair Service
Architectural historian and writer.

Brian Sewell
(1931–2016) Art critic.

Sir Peter Shaffer
(1926–2016) Playwright and screenwriter.

Shirley Sherwood
Writer and collector of botanical art.

David Shilling
Flamboyant designer and milliner.

Dame Antoinette Sibley
British prima ballerina.

Liz Sich
Former Managing Director of Colman Getty PR agency.

Sir Marcus Sieff, Baron Sieff of Brimpton
(1913–2001) Businessman; Chairman of Marks & Spencer 1972–82.

John Simmons
Horticulturalist; Curator of Kew Botanical Gardens 1972–95.

Valerie Singleton
Television and radio presenter.

Sir Reresby Sitwell, 7th Bt
(1927–2009) Patron of the arts and culture.

Sir Tim Smit
Dutch-born businessman, ecologist and horticulturalist, co-restorer of the Lost Gardens of Heligan and co-founder of the Eden Project, Cornwall.

Chris Smith, Baron Smith of Finsbury
Labour politician, Secretary of State for Culture, Media and Sport 1997–2001.

Sir John Smith
(1923–2007) Founder of The Landmark Trust with his wife, Christian, Lady Smith.

Antony Armstrong-Jones, 1st Earl of Snowdon
See under Armstrong-Jones

Lucy Armstrong-Jones, Lady Snowdon
See Lucy Armstrong-Jones

Nicholas Snowman
Arts administrator, Chairman of the South Bank Centre 1992–98.

Valerie Pitts, Lady Solti
Patron of music and culture; widow of conductor Sir Georg Solti.

Anna Somers Cocks
Editor of the *Art Newspaper* 1990–2004.

Tracy Somerset, Marchioness of Worcester
Former actress, environmentalist and former wife of the Marquess of Worcester.

Julia Somerville, Lady Dixon
Former television journalist and newsreader.

Stephen Somerville
London art dealer.

Michael Somes
(1917–1994) English ballet dancer.

Ron Soskolne
International developer; former Vice President of Olympia & York.

Sir Colin Southgate
Chairman of the Royal Opera House, Covent Garden 1998–2003.

Julian Spalding
Art critic, commentator, writer and former curator.

Raine, Countess Spencer
(1929–2016) Socialite stepmother of Diana, Princess of Wales.

Sylvester Stallone
American film actor and director.

Fortune Stanley
Cookery writer.

Edi Stark
Scottish journalist and broadcaster.

David Starkey
Historian and radio and television presenter.

Marion Stein, later Marion Lascelles, Countess of Harewood
(1926–2014) Concert pianist; co-founder of the Leeds International
Piano Competition; former wife of George Lascelles, 7th Earl of
Harewood (q.v.); subsequently married Liberal politician
Jeremy Thorpe.

Norman St John Stevas, Baron St John of Fawley
(1929–2012) Barrister and Conservative politician.

Sir Jocelyn Stevens
(1932–2014) Publisher and cultural administrator, Chairman
of English Heritage 1992–2000.

Dennis Stevenson, Baron Stevenson of Coddenham
Businessman, Chairman of Tate 1988–98.

Rory Stewart
Horticulturalist and writer.

Sir Angus Stirling
Director General of the National Trust 1983–95.

Revd Victor Stock
Rector of St Mary-le-Bow 1986–2002, later Dean of Guildford.

Thomas Stonor, 7th Baron Camoys
British peer and banker; first Roman Catholic Lord Chamberlain
since the Reformation.

David Kenworthy, 11th Baron Strabolgi
See under Kenworthy

David Strachan
Managing Director of Tern TV.

Janet Street-Porter
Journalist and broadcaster.

Michael Howard, 21st Earl of Suffolk, and Linda, Lady Suffolk
See under Howard

Will Sulkin
Publishing Director of The Bodley Head and Pimlico, retired 2012.

James Sutherland
(1923–2013) Distinguished civil engineer who served for many years on the Royal Fine Art Commission.

Dame Joan Sutherland
(1926–2010) Acclaimed operatic soprano.

Katherine Swift
Garden writer, designer of The Dower House Garden at Morville Hall, Bridgnorth.

William Tallon
(1935–2007) The Queen Mother's Page, known as 'Backstairs Billy'.

Judith Tankard
Architectural and garden historian.

Judy Taylor
Authority on Beatrix Potter.

Robert Tear
(1939–2011) Welsh tenor.

Norman Tebbit, Baron Tebbit of Chingford
(1925–2013) Conservative politician.

Quinlan Terry
British classical architect.

Margaret Thatcher, Baroness Thatcher of Kesteven
(1925–2013) British Prime Minister 1979–90.

Jim Thompson
(1936–2003) Bishop of Bath and Wells 1991–2001; regular contributor to 'Thought for the Day' on BBC Radio 4's *Today* programme.

Antony Thorncroft
Arts journalist.

Carla Thorneycroft, Baroness Thorneycroft
(1914–2007) Philanthropist, patroness of the arts and wife of Lord Thorneycroft.

Peter Thorneycroft, Baron Thorneycroft
(1909–1994) Veteran Conservative politician; Chairman of the Conservative party 1975–81.

Peter Thornton
(1925–2007) Writer and museum curator.

CAST OF CHARACTERS

Simon Thurley
Architectural historian and broadcaster; Chief Executive of English Heritage 2002–15.

Liz Tilberis
(1947–1999) Editor of British *Vogue* 1988–92 and of *Harper's Bazaar* 1992–99.

Alfred Toepfer
(1894–1993) German entrepreneur and philanthropist.

Timothy Tollemache, 5th Baron Tollemache, and Alexandra (Xa), Lady Tollemache
Custodians of Helmingham Hall, the family seat; Xa is a garden designer.

Sir Edward Tomkins
(1915–2007) Diplomat, British Ambassador to France 1972–75; former custodian of Winslow Hall, Buckinghamshire.

Steve Tomlin
Managing Director of Reclamation Services, architectural salvage, Painswick, until 2011.

Carl Toms
(1927–1999) Theatre, opera, ballet and film set and costume designer.

Sir John Tooley
Director General of the Royal Opera House, Covent Garden, 1970–88.

Joe Trapp
(1925–2005) Director of the Warburg Institute 1976–90.

David Treffry
(1926–2000) Colonial servant, financier and High Sheriff
of Cornwall.

Damaris Tremayne
(1918–2010) Descendant of the Tremaynes of Heligan.

Raleigh Trevelyan
(1923–2014) Publisher, author and historian.

Hugh Trevor-Roper, Baron Dacre of Glanton
(1914–2003) Scholar; Regius Professor of Modern History at the
University of Oxford.

Ion Trewin
(1943–2015) Editor, publisher and author; Managing Director of
Orion Publishing Group and Publishing Director of Weidenfeld
& Nicolson until 2006.

William Tuckett
Choreographer.

Ann, Lady Tusa
Historian, teacher and writer; wife of Sir John Tusa.

Sir John Tusa
Arts administrator and journalist; former Managing Director of
the BBC World Service.

Lucia van der Post
Writer, editor and style guru.

Paul Vaughan
(1925–2014) Journalist, broadcaster and presenter of BBC Radio 4's arts show *Kaleidoscope*.

Sir David Verey
Banker and philanthropist, Chairman of Tate 1998–2003.

Rosemary Verey
(1918–2001) Influential gardener and garden writer.

Gianni Versace
(1946–1997) Acclaimed Italian fashion designer, founder of the Versace empire.

Clive Wainwright
(1942–1999) Furniture historian, scholar, teacher and museum curator.

Sir Peter Wakefield
(1922–2010) Diplomat, collector and former Director of the National Art-Collections Fund.

George Walden
Diplomat, politician and journalist.

Peter Walker, Baron Walker of Worcester
(1932–2010) Conservative Cabinet Minister; Secretary of State for Wales 1987–90.

Sue Walker
Writer and educationalist; Director of the Victorian Tapestry
Workshop, Australia, 1976–2004.

Susana, Lady Walton
(1926–2010) Widow of composer Sir William Walton, guardian
of his legacy and creator of La Mortella garden in Ischia.

Gerald Ward
(1938–2008) Businessman, farmer and close friend of the Prince
of Wales.

John Ward
(1917–2007) English painter.

Sarah Ward
See Sarah Scrope

Giles Waterfield
(1949–2016) Art historian, curator and novelist.

Phillip Watson
American garden designer and horticulturalist.

Dame Cicely Veronica Wedgwood
(1910–1997) Eminent British historian.

Rt Revd Ambrose Weekes
(1919–2012) Former Archdeacon of the Royal Navy and Dean
of Gibraltar.

George Weidenfeld, Baron Weidenfeld of Chelsea
(1919–2016) Publisher and philanthropist, founder and Chairman
of Weidenfeld & Nicolson.

Arnold Weinstock, Baron Weinstock of Bowden
(1924–2002) Prominent industrialist.

Robert Welch
(1929–2000) Designer and silversmith.

John Campbell Wells
(1936–1998) Actor, writer and satirist.

Sir Stanley Wells
Shakespearian scholar, Chairman of The Shakespeare Birthplace
Trust 1991–2011.

Timothy West
Actor, husband of Prunella Scales (q.v.).

Louis and Gabrielle de Wet
Owners and restorers of Wenlock Abbey, Shropshire.

Patricia Wheatley
BBC television producer 1985–2005; Head of Broadcasting at the
British Museum.

David Wheeler
Horticulturalist and writer; founder and Editor of *Hortus*; creator
of Bryan's Ground, Presteigne, with Simon Dorrell (q.v.).

Natalie Wheen
BBC radio presenter.

Sir Christopher White
Art historian and writer; Director of the Ashmolean Museum, Oxford, 1985–97.

Roger White
Writer and lecturer.

William Whitelaw, 1st Viscount Whitelaw of Penrith
(1918–1999) Conservative Cabinet Minister, former Home Secretary and Leader of the House of Lords.

Sir William Whitfield
Architect.

Sir Andreas Whittam Smith
Financial journalist, founder of the *Independent* and its first Editor 1986–94.

Richard Wilding
Former head of the Office of Arts and Libraries.

George and Grizel Williams
Owners and restorers of 27 Broad Street, Ludlow.

Michael Williams
(1935–2001) Actor, husband of Judi Dench (q.v.).

Clough Williams-Ellis
(1883–1978) Architect and creator of Portmeirion village in Wales.

Rupert Williamson
English designer-craftsman of furniture.

A.N. Wilson
English writer and columnist; married to Ruth Guilding (q.v.).

Sir David Wilson
Art historian and archaeologist, Director of the British Museum 1977–92.

Penelope Wilton
English actress.

Other Robert Ivor Windsor-Clive, 3rd Earl of Plymouth, and Caroline, Countess of Plymouth
Custodians of the family estate at Oakly Park, Shropshire.

Nicole Wisniak
Founder and Editor of *Egoïste* magazine.

Leonard Wolfson, Baron Wolfson of Marylebone
(1927–2010) Businessman and philanthropist, Chairman of the Wolfson Foundation (of which his widow, Estelle, Lady Wolfson, is a Trustee).

Sir Hugh Wontner
(1908–1992) Hotelier and politician.

Peter Wood
(1925–2016) Stage director.

Tracy Somerset, Marchioness of Worcester
See under Somerset

Blair Worden
Historian and writer.

Sir Peregrine Worsthorne
Journalist, writer and broadcaster.

Anne Wright
(1949–2005) Chief sub-editor of *Country Life* magazine 1988–2005.

Sir David Wright
Former British diplomat.

Sir Peter Wright
Dancer and choreographer; married to Sonya, *née* Hana
(1927–2007).

Max Wyndham, 2nd Baron Egremont
British biographer and novelist.

Dame Frances Yates
(1899–1981) Historian, writer and scholar.

Alan Yentob
BBC TV executive and presenter.

Paul Zuckerman
Financier.

INDEX

'Sensitive and illuminating . . . Makes a powerful case . . . a daring attempt to explain the long-term origins of our present unrest' ━━━━━━━━━━━ *Spectator*

a[...] Pankaj Mishra comes to grips with the m[...]se dangerous times. This is the most astonishin[...] disturbing book I've read in years' ━━━━━ oe Sacco

'Richly learned and usefully subversive' John Gray, *Literary Review*

'Far from reassuring . . . a violent, bowel-churning kick in the guts . . . for Pankaj Mishra, the forces driving extremism and populist rage go right back to the roots of western modernity . . . Mishra shouldn't stop thinking' Christopher de Bellaigue, *Financial Times*

'This is a framework that pushes aside conventional, familiar divisions of left and right to focus on the profound sense of dislocation and alienation that spawned (and still spawns) movements ranging from fascism to anarchism to nihilism . . . a short book into which a lot of intellectual history has been packed' Laura Miller, *Slate*

'Stimulating . . . thought-provoking' Richard Evans, *Guardian*

'Mishra reads like a brilliant autodidact, putting to shame the many students who dutifully did the reading for their classes but missed the incandescent fire and penetrating insight in canonical texts . . . no one has discerned better than Mishra just how far we still are from the top' Samuel Moyn, *New Republic*

'Around the world, both East and West, the insurrectionary fury of militants, zealots and populists has overturned the post-Cold-War global consensus. Where does their rage come from, and where will it end? One of the sharpest cultural critics and political analysts releases his landmark "history of the present"' Boyd Tonkin, *Newsweek*

'Incisive and scary . . . a sharp study of how anger and violence have influenced modern societies . . . in this highly topical polemic, Pankaj Mishra describes a global pandemic of rage' Nick Fraser, *Guardian*

ABOUT THE AUTHOR

Pankaj Mishra is the author of *From the Ruins of Empire* and several other books. He is a columnist at *Bloomberg View* and the *New York Times Book Review*, and writes regularly for the *Guardian*, the *London Review of Books*, and *The New Yorker*. A fellow of the Royal Society of Literature, he lives in London.